M000036416

NAOMI OSAKA

NAOMI OSAKA

Her Journey to
Finding Her Power
and Her Voice

BEN ROTHENBERG

DUTTON

DUTTON

An imprint of Penguin Random House LLC
penguinrandomhouse.com

LIBRARY OF CONGRESS CATALOGING-IN-PUBLICATION DATA
Names: Rothenberg, Ben, author.
Title: Naomi Osaka : her journey to finding her power and her voice / Ben Rothenberg.
Description: New York, N.Y. : Dutton, [2024] | Includes bibliographical references and index.
Identifiers: LCCN 2023041150 (print) | LCCN 2023041151 (ebook) |
ISBN 9780593472439 (hardcover) | ISBN 9780593472446 (ebook)
Subjects: LCSH: Osaka, Naomi, 1997- | Women tennis players—United
States—Biography. | Women tennis players—Japan—Biography.
Classification: LCC GV994.O73 R68 2024 (print) | LCC GV994.O73 (ebook) |
DDC 796.342092 [B]—dc23/eng/20231023
LC record available at https://lccn.loc.gov/2023041150
LC ebook record available at https://lccn.loc.gov/2023041151

Printed in the United States of America
1st Printing

BOOK DESIGN BY KRISTIN DEL ROSARIO

To my dad,
whose love
and eagerness to travel long distances for sports
started this ball rolling
around the world

CONTENTS

NAOMI OSAKA

Like No One Ever Was

Naomi Osaka was ranked 127th in the world when I first met her. She was just eighteen years old, hadn't yet played a full season on the tour, and had never won any professional tournament. But despite that obscurity on paper, I was confident Naomi Osaka was someone readers should get to meet.

The 2016 Australian Open was my fifth time covering the tournament for *The New York Times,* and after years covering tennis I had honed my eye for what sorts of articles the paper wanted. Rather than rote match summaries, the best *Times* stories were of an interest to a broad audience across borders, using tennis and its players as a lens to explore broader societal and cultural themes and issues.

From what I had learned about her, Naomi Osaka seemed like a perfect fit. As a Japanese-Haitian-American, she spanned disparate cultures. She officially represented Japan, the country where she was born, but she didn't seem to fit into the traditionally narrow definitions of what it meant to be Japanese, both in her appearance and with her unreadiness to speak the national language, which caused her considerable stress when Japanese reporters in Melbourne had shown up in droves to ask her questions. In Japan, one of the world's most racially homogenous countries, multiethnic identities were viewed by many as though the hyphen acted as a minus sign: to be more than one thing was to be less than whole. *Hafu,* derived from the English "half," was what mixed-race Japanese were called.

Indeed, Naomi's appearance had often drawn confused reactions from those who hadn't thought a Japanese player could or should look like her. "Ever since I was little, as soon as I walk onto a tennis court, people stare at me and whisper: 'She's the Black Japanese girl,'" Naomi later said. "They don't know which box to put me in." And so as she played in the main draw of a tennis major for the first time in Melbourne, she was heartened to see Japanese fans in the stands supporting her as one of their own. "I always think that they're surprised that I'm Japanese," she said after winning her second-round match. "So the fact that there was Japanese flags and stuff, it was really touching."

Naomi had also drawn cheers from local fans, which made her think she might have a certain universal appeal, too. "Maybe it's because they can't really pinpoint what I am," she had said. "So it's like anybody can cheer for me." She certainly had given fans at the Australian Open lots to cheer about, blasting balls with scorching power to win five matches—three in qualifying, two in the main draw—to reach the third round. Parts of her game were still developing and unrefined, but all the raw ingredients were there for a star in the making.

After years of hearing players hide themselves behind clichés, I found Naomi's candor as striking as her power. As we sat across a table from each other for our interview in the tournament's players' lounge—a place where players, coaches, parents, agents, and other assorted hangers-on wait anxiously for matches and surreptitiously study their opposition—Naomi made it clear that she still wasn't comfortable being seen just yet, least of all by her idol, Serena Williams. When Naomi had spotted Serena earlier at the tournament, she told me she had tried her best to disappear. "I pretended that I didn't exist," she said. "I sat in the corner and pretended I was looking at my phone, because I was too shy."

Naomi had gotten a treasured selfie with Serena a few years earlier, which she told me had only made the situation worse now that they shared a locker room. "I feel like I can never recover from that," she said. "Because I feel like if you're introduced as a fan, they'll never look at you as an equal again."

But in a blend that fascinated me, Naomi's admitted self-consciousness was paired with immense self-confidence about what she could do on the court and what she could become. When I asked her about her hopes and dreams for her career, Naomi paused, then giggled. "'To be the very best, like no one ever was,'" she declared, then smiled proudly. When I didn't seem to get the joke, she apologized. "That's a Pokémon quote, I'm sorry," she said. "That's the Pokémon theme song. But yeah, to be the very best, and go as far as I can go."

· · · · · · · ·

It was big talk, but Naomi Osaka would make good on that Pokémon promise. Three years later, after winning the Australian Open on a court not far from where we had sat that day, she ascended to the World No. 1 ranking in singles, becoming the first Asian tennis player ever to reach that peak. She'd won the U.S. Open months earlier, too; she'd win both titles again a couple of years later to double her major singles titles count to four. With fascination in her spanning the major markets of the United States and Japan, Naomi Osaka would earn enough in endorsements to become the highest-paid female athlete in history by the time she was twenty-two, raking in a jaw-dropping $50 million per year. The Japanese Olympic Committee chose Naomi Osaka to light the cauldron in the climax of the 2020 Tokyo Olympics' opening ceremony, the first tennis player ever chosen for that honor.

But it was the second part of the Pokémon pledge where she made her biggest mark: Naomi Osaka would become the "very best *like no one ever was,*" evolving into something far bigger and more powerful than anyone could have foreseen. Naomi Osaka didn't just win; she redefined what a champion was supposed to be in a way that would resonate far beyond the confines of the tennis courts. In the sport her parents had chosen for her when she was still an infant, Naomi Osaka would create something new, entirely of her own. That same mix of self-assuredness and self-doubt that she had expressed to me in Melbourne would captivate the world, challenging core concepts of victory and defeat, of control and vulnerability. Naomi Osaka would become a worldwide superstar by facing down Serena

Williams, whom she had been too nervous to even look at years before, in the most tempestuous tennis match in history. Naomi Osaka would become a worldwide conversation, however, by admitting just how much she was struggling after she couldn't bring herself to face post-match press conferences.

Naomi Osaka became a generational touchstone for reasons that had increasingly little to do with her tennis results. Her name became a trampoline used to launch into discussions of race, gender, mental health, activism, multiculturalism, politics, business, and generational shifts. No public figure occupied these crossroads—generating traffic from the converging avenues of sports and culture—more than Naomi Osaka.

To be the very best, like no one ever was, Naomi Osaka would prevail amid deafening noise and eerie silence. She would embrace issues others dared not touch. She gained praise for her triumphs, but Naomi Osaka would earn even more accolades for sharing her tribulations on the world stage, finding her power and her voice, and forcing a shifting culture to reconsider what strength and weakness could and should mean, both in sports and the world beyond.

This is her story.

ONE

Paradise

In soft Spanish pinks and bright, buttery yellows, the banners and graphics emblazoned around the Indian Wells Tennis Garden proclaim each visitor's ascendance to a higher plane: "WELCOME TO TENNIS PARADISE."

Indian Wells, a small resort community in the California desert just southeast of Palm Springs, hosts the annual tennis tournament, which has grown into the world's largest outside the four Grand Slam events, luring in the world's best players for a two-week tournament with the paired promises of perfect weather and a prize money purse over $9 million.

Ever since Larry Ellison, the billionaire founder of the software company Oracle, bought the tournament in 2009, the most heavenly delights in "Tennis Paradise" haven't come cheap for attendees. The most expensive ticket packages inside the stadium can cost upwards of $13,000 per seat for the tournament. At the Nobu restaurant overlooking the court of Stadium 2, the lobster salad with grilled shiitake mushrooms goes for $65 and the grilled Japanese A5 Wagyu steak runs $38 per ounce, at a minimum of four ounces; either pairs nicely with the Rémy Martin Louis XIII Grande Champagne cognac for $350 a glass.

Hundreds of thousands drive over from Los Angeles or flock in on flights from colder parts of North America each March to pose around the grounds for carefully composed Instagram pictures in front of mountains and palm trees beneath the vivid, no-filter cerulean sky. For them, it's all a small price to pay to make other people jealous as they momentarily scroll past your life. Because at Indian Wells, where you're told every which way you turn that you're in paradise, your life is going to look just perfect from a distance.

. . . .

There is, it can be easy to forget, another class of attendees at Indian Wells who aren't there to eat, drink, and be seen: the people who are actually there for the tennis. In addition to its stadiums, Indian Wells has become a destination for ardent tennis fans hoping to see the sport's biggest stars up close and personal on the practice courts. With a grounds pass that can be bought for as little as $20, a fan with a plan can stake out a spot to see his or her favorite players warming up for their matches in a relaxed, intimate environment. For the most eager and outgoing, smart positioning near the exits of the courts can yield opportunities for autographs and selfies if the player is willing.

On Saturday, March 12, 2022, the twenty-four-year-old tennis player Naomi Osaka is scheduled to have her pre-match practice at 5:00 p.m. on Practice Court 1. Naomi is practicing late because she is on late: her second-round match against Russia's Veronika Kudermetova is scheduled to be the second match of the Saturday evening session, a slot that is a bit beyond prime time at Indian Wells but a showcase Sunday afternoon slot for the television audience in Japan.

There are a few hundred grandstand seats around Practice Court 1; in the minutes before she is scheduled to arrive, every seat is filled. Another row of people stands behind the back row on the side to peer over the seated spectators. Soon, a second row stands behind the first standing row. Soon again, a third row of people gathers to stand on tiptoes behind the first two rows and peers through whatever gaps there might be for a glimpse of the four-time major champion.

As the clock ticks past 5:00 p.m., Naomi's name and face appear on a courtside electronic display board, but Naomi herself is nowhere to be seen. "Is she coming?" asks one boy at 5:06 p.m. As the clock ticks past 5:10 p.m., kids holding the jumbo tennis balls used to collect autographs appear increasingly antsy. "Maybe she's waiting so there's a bigger reception for her when she comes," one man suggests. Around 5:20 p.m., those who had turned their backs to the court to look toward the players' patio spot Naomi emerging at last. But instead of turning left to Practice Court 1, she and her team walk straight across the field to empty Practice Court 7. Only a handful of the crowd at Practice Court 1 spot Naomi make her detour; they break off surreptitiously from the larger crowd so as not to cause a stampede that might cost them prime seating at the smaller, secluded court.

Naomi arrives with her team in tow: Wim Fissette, the forty-one-year-old Belgian who had been her coach for the last two and a half years, her strength and conditioning coach Yutaka Nakamura, her physiotherapist Natsuko "Nana" Mogi, and her young Belgian hitting partner, Seppe Cuypers. Naomi is dressed entirely in her favorite color, black. Above black leggings that end just below her knees, she wears a black T-shirt brightened only by the white logos of three of her primary sponsors: Nike, the software company Workday, and the skincare company Kinlò. She wears a black cap on her head that has her Nike-made "NO" monogram in white on the front, and the red-and-yellow logo of Mastercard, another major sponsor of hers, on the side.

As a handful of fans slide into the dozens of empty seats above and behind the court, Naomi begins a jogging warm-up, which both Nakamura and Mogi do alongside her, clapping and laughing. After stretching with a medicine ball, Naomi picks up her racquet and walks out onto the court, across the net from Cuypers. As the two begin by standing close to the net and hitting softly, Naomi holds the racquet only with her left hand, laughing and doing a pirouette between shots. The next day, a fan will upload a video of these moments with a soundtrack of bouncy Japanese pop music and the caption "The world's cutest girl who loves practice."

Slowly and subtly, Naomi and Cuypers, a twenty-three-year-old whose Association of Tennis Professionals (ATP) ranking peaked at 1,449th, have each backed away from the net while hitting and are standing on opposite baselines of the court, ramping up to whacking the ball back and forth at full strength. The pops from Naomi's crisp, clean contact with the ball against the center of her polyester racquet strings can be heard clearly despite the growing crowd, which has by now located her at Practice Court 7; her fans are resolutely respectful and even reverent, aware that they are watching a professional at work. But the work looks fun from the stands: even as she is crushing forehands, Naomi is still cracking smiles. When a ball skips off the net cord and over Cuypers's flailing racquet, she teasingly says, "Embarrassing, embarrassing!" When she nets a simple volley, she squeaks a quick "Sorry!" to Cuypers.

Naomi doesn't acknowledge the gathering crowd behind the court as she rallies with Cuypers, but when she switches sides of the court between drills a young fan says "Hi, Naomi!" as she nears. She looks up, smiles, and waves.

After a few minutes of serve practice, Fissette approaches Naomi and they begin to discuss specific patterns to employ against Kudermetova in the upcoming match. "First serves can go anywhere; second serves?" Naomi asks, and Fissette replies with a soft voice to lower the volume of the conversation below audience audibility. Fissette is collaborative in his conversations on court, listening rather than just lecturing. Naomi is deferential by nature, but Fissette doesn't exploit that to dominate their conversations, like many coaches would.

The practice wraps with Fissette softly floating several balls to Naomi for her to crush with full power, ending the brief session on an emphatic, confidence-building note. After Naomi finishes with the biggest bangs, like a fireworks display might, the hundreds watching cheer softly but warmly. After just twenty minutes on court, Naomi and her team are done and begin to pack up their bags. Naomi's older sister, Mari, walks on court as the team is wrapping up, and Naomi playfully pokes at her with a water bottle, which Mari bats away.

Mari Osaka used to play tennis, too, but not anymore. Now it's just Naomi.

As Naomi's team leaves the court and turns to walk back toward the locker room, Naomi drops her bag and jogs in the opposite direction, toward a cluster of fans who have amassed behind a rope cordoning off the walkway on the far corner of the court, so she can sign autographs and pose for selfies for everyone waiting there. When she finishes with that group, instead of walking the straight line back to the locker room, Naomi runs to the far corner of the field between the practice courts and locker room, to start at the far end of the line and work her way down the dozens of fans waiting for her along the fence. Naomi smiles with her lips closed and holds up two fingers—a typical Japanese pose—for each photo. Several times, when a less tech-savvy older fan struggles with the camera app on their phone, Naomi will take the phone from them, tap the necessary buttons, and frame and snap the selfie herself before handing the phone back to them. Judging by their reactions, having their phones handled momentarily by a star was not an intrusion but a thrill.

As Naomi works her way down the line, satisfied fans peel off the fence and giddily compare their selfies with one another. "No pushing!" a security guard shouts as Naomi reaches the end of the fence.

. . . .

Unlike athletes in other sports who can meticulously plan their schedule each day of a competition, tennis players often have to deal with uncertain start times because of the variable lengths of preceding matches, sitting and stewing as they wait their turn to play. In this Saturday evening session, the first match goes the distance; Stefanos Tsitsipas needs more than two and a half hours to complete a win over Jack Sock in a third-set tiebreak. By the time Tsitsipas has finished his on-court interview and left the court, Naomi has been waiting for nearly an hour, most of it alone with her thoughts in the locker room. A tournament manager then tells her that it is time for her match. She is driven in a golf cart from the locker room to the court entrance.

With her white Beats by Dre headphones stretched over her black Nike visor and covering her ears, Naomi walks onto the Stadium 1 court.

"Ladies and gentlemen, she's our 2018 champion!" tournament emcee Andrew Krasny announces through the speakers on all sides. "Please welcome: Naomi Osaka!"

. . . .

In fact, before her 2018 title at Indian Wells, the lucrative tournament that had earned the unofficial title of the "Fifth Slam," Naomi Osaka had never won an official professional tournament anywhere, even at the lowest levels of the sport. To earn the trophy and the $1,340,860 in prize money at the lucrative tournament, Naomi had to win seven matches—the same number it takes to win a Grand Slam title. Just twenty years old and ranked 44th in the world, Naomi ran a gauntlet that included some of the sport's biggest names: five-time major champion Maria Sharapova in the first round, former No. 2 Agnieszka Radwańska in the second round, former No. 1 Karolína Plíšková in the quarterfinals, and then No. 1 Simona Halep in the semifinals. After beating all four of those established stars in straight sets, Naomi finished with another straight-set win over fellow twenty-year-old rising star Daria Kasatkina in the final.

But more than Naomi's awe-striking power and poise in her 6–3, 6–2 win over Kasatkina, the lasting memory from Naomi's first final was how unprepared she seemed for the trophy ceremony that followed, where she had to address the audience in the stadium and watching on television in a customary champion's acceptance speech. Naomi fidgeted with her jacket collar and hesitated about whether or not she should touch the microphone.

"Um, hello?" Naomi said with a giggle. "Um. Hi, I'm Nao— Oh, okay, never mind." As she neared the close of her remarks, which never got more fluent, Naomi declared herself a failure: "This is probably going to be, like, the worst acceptance speech of all time."

But though she had sputtered and swerved and stalled throughout—or, perhaps, *because* she had—the crowd was thoroughly charmed by Naomi. Even billionaire tournament owner Ellison, stiff-faced in the front row, had cracked a smile by the end of Naomi's speech. She had been awkward, yes, but in a way that was seen as eminently relatable and unpretentious, particularly by those close to her Gen Z age.

That day at Indian Wells made clear to a broader public three things about Naomi that close observers of hers had known for years:

Naomi Osaka was one of the best tennis players in the world.

Naomi Osaka was different.

Naomi Osaka was cool.

On a stage that primarily showcased polished and prepackaged athletes, Naomi was a winner who offered something different, something authentic. From the stands and in front of televisions around the world, new legions of fans—and sponsors—were taking notice, and they would continue to take more notice throughout the year.

"This place definitely holds a lot of really good memories for me, and it definitely did propel my confidence," Naomi said in her pretournament press conference at Indian Wells in 2022.

Naomi immediately followed up her win at Indian Wells in 2018 by beating Serena Williams in their first match in Miami days later. Six months after that, Naomi again beat Serena, this time in the final of the U.S. Open for her first major title. By March 2022, Naomi's major title haul was four, the most held by any active player on the women's tour not named Williams. She had a diverse and growing portfolio of off-court holdings as well, including an equity stake in the burgeoning cryptocurrency website FTX. Within months, Naomi started her own sports management and media production companies. With over $50 million a year in endorsements, Naomi seems well on her way to her goal of becoming the first billionaire female athlete.

· · · · · · ·

Over those four years, the highs had been exceptionally high for Naomi Osaka. But her ranking had fallen considerably by this Saturday night. Remarkably, considering the four major titles to her name were more than those of any other player in the draw, Naomi had arrived at Indian Wells with a ranking of 78th, so diminished that she only squeaked into the draw just days before the tournament began once several higher-ranked players had withdrawn from the field.

It was more than just being able to get into tournaments: Naomi admitted at Indian Wells that she often wrapped up her self-worth with her ranking. "For me, that was everything," Naomi said at Indian Wells. "And I can't be bold enough to say I've completely changed that mindset. . . . Like, if I'm valuable to someone's life, I feel like they treat me better or something like that, you know?" she said.

On this evening in 2022, few are doubting Naomi's continued physical ability to play world-class tennis. What is less certain, however, is her mental readiness. Naomi had pulled out of the French Open the year before for mental health reasons, saying she had "suffered long bouts of depression" since her first major win. When she returned to the tour months later in Cincinnati, and to the press conference format that had been a particular source of anxiety for her, she left the podium in tears. Weeks later, after she lost in the third round of the U.S. Open as defending champion, she again teared up at the podium. "I honestly don't know when I'm going to play my next tennis match," she said, her voice quavering. "I think I'm going to take a break from playing for a while." Her hiatus ultimately lasted just about three months. But choosing to step away, she said when she returned, gave her a sense of control she hadn't felt before. "Just saying out loud that 'I'll take a break and I'll come back when I am truly in love with the sport and I know what I want to do here,' it gave me time to reset myself," she said.

These moments of public vulnerability—a radical departure from the tough exterior world champion athletes normally display in front of cameras and competitors—changed perceptions of Naomi both within and beyond the sport. As she returned to Indian Wells, she noticed fans connecting and interacting with her in a "more personal" way than before. "Usually when I walk around, there's people that are like 'Win the tournament!' Or, 'I have tickets to the finals, see you there!' That kind of thing," she said. "And actually, everyone was just saying, like, 'I hope you have fun.' So I know that's not the biggest difference, but it really meant a lot to me."

. . . .

Most star players at Indian Wells had received a bye in the first round, which gave them a free pass into the second round. Naomi was well below that Top 32 threshold and thus needed to play a first-round match: she drew a tough one: 38th-ranked Sloane Stephens, the talented but streaky American who had won the U.S. Open in 2017, one year before Naomi's first win there. In blustery conditions with wind gusts upward of 40 miles per hour, Naomi toughed out a 3–6, 6–1, 6–2 victory.

After the win over Stephens, Naomi's coach Wim Fissette had expressed his relief and confidence in a conversation with Naomi's longtime agent, Stuart Duguid. "I remember saying, 'Stuart, I really feel like, after that match, I really feel like the troubles are over,'" Fissette later recalled to me. "'Like, we're in a good state. It's going to be a great year this year.'" Fissette then laughed wryly and shook his head. "And then, yeah, the next day, it was a different story, right?"

Naomi's second round opponent on this following day is Veronika Kudermetova of Russia. She is twenty-four years old, like Naomi, but she has not reached Naomi's heights: she's ranked 24th, a career-best for her. In what is Osaka's seventh and Kudermetova's fourteenth match of the year, Naomi wins the coin toss and chooses to serve first. When the match begins just after 9:00 p.m., the 16,100-seat stadium is about half full. Many are sticking around to see some of Naomi; others are perhaps waiting to sober up a bit before driving back to their hotels after a long day spent between the Corona tent and the Moët & Chandon tent.

On the first point of the match, Kudermetova pounces on Naomi's second serve and rips a clean backhand return winner, initiating her strategy of immediate attack. "Naomi likes to be aggressive, to be dominant," Kudermetova's coach Sergey Demekhin told me, explaining their plan for unnerving her. "And when you put her in a position that she's on defense, it's not common for her. She's not feeling comfortable." A second return winner by Kudermetova puts her up 0–40, and another confident backhand winner clinches the opening game.

The two players switch sides, with Kudermetova leading 1–0, and stand on the opposite baselines to begin the second game. "Veronika Kudermetova to serve," chair umpire Paula Vieira Souza intones into her microphone. But before Vieira Souza can finish the sentence, another woman's voice from behind her cuts through the thin desert air.

"Naomi, you suck!"

The woman's voice had come from somewhere in the northeast corner of the stadium, in the upper part of the lower bowl, perhaps in one of the suites. Immediately, disapproving murmurs circulate through the crowd. "Kick her out!" another woman shouts. "Yes!" a second agrees. "Kick her out!" a third echoes.

"Thank you, please," Vieira Souza says from the umpire's chair, wanting to settle the unrest. Kudermetova is about to serve when Naomi adds her voice to the mix, initially apologetically.

"Sorry," Naomi begins. "Actually, can you, though? Can you, though?"

The crowd begins to cheer as Naomi, fidgeting with her visor, walks up to Vieira Souza's chair. "Kick her out!" several fans shout anew, glad that Naomi stepping up should get the interjector ejected.

"Sorry, I didn't hear you," Vieira Souza says once Naomi reaches her.

"Can you kick that person out?" Naomi repeats.

"The person?" Vieira Souza asks.

"Yeah," Naomi replies.

"I don't know," Vieira Souza hems as the cheers of the crowd continue. "I can ask. If the security doesn't know who it is, I don't know who it was. But I can ask them to keep an eye on it."

Naomi nods once to show she understood and begins to walk away, but then stops, unsatisfied. "Okay, but like, what if someone was to point in her general direction?" Naomi queries Vieira Souza. "I'm just asking," she adds preemptively, holding her palms up in a gesture of helplessness.

"Yeah, we will try to ask the security for some help, and then let's see what we can do," Vieira Souza says.

Naomi turns and jogs back to the baseline to resume play. Her wavy blond hair bounces as she springs back and forth on the court, seemingly trying to elevate her mood from the ground up. She takes shadow swings of her forehand and then her backhand, trying to switch back into tennis mode.

Kudermetova double-faults the first point upon resumption, and soon Naomi holds two break points at 15–40, giving her a chance to level the match. But Kudermetova steadies, reeling off four straight points to hold for 2–0 in the first set. Kudermetova growls a quick "C'mon!" to punctuate the game.

The ball kids roll the balls from Kudermetova's end of the court down to Naomi's, and bounce two toward her so she can begin serving in the third game. Soon Naomi draws her left hand, which is already holding two tennis balls, up to her eyes, so it can also hold back tears. Naomi then pulls the brim of her black Nike visor down over her eyes. With fans and cameras encircling her at 360 degrees in the stadium, and a close-up of her face projected on the large video screens around the stadium, there isn't anywhere to hide, but Naomi is trying as best she can. With her other arm, Naomi uses the black Nike sweatband on her right wrist to wipe the tears from her right eye, then her left, then her right again. Naomi walks back to the baseline. She's on the clock and could receive a penalty if she waits any longer to resume play.

As the crowd sees her struggling, the cheers grow louder. "We love you, Naomi!" they shout as Naomi continues wiping away tears. Naomi takes several gulpy inhales, then a couple of cool exhales, and she serves to resume play. It's a long rally: ten shots, and Naomi has an opening for an inside-out forehand winner—a signature shot—to finish it off. She takes two small steps, positions herself in the center of the court, and swings—but she misses her target badly, sending the ball well wide beyond the right sideline.

"C'mon," Kudermetova growls again.

Naomi turns her back to the court again and exhales coolly once more, forming a small circle with her mouth almost as if she's whistling. She then double-faults.

Kudermetova misses a return on the next point into the net and the crowd cheers loudly, far more than they normally would after a simple error. The thousands in attendance are trying to will Naomi back into a match she seems to have already lost in the opening minutes.

But across the net, Kudermetova does not relent. Tennis players are trained to sense weakness and attack it: like an MMA fighter, a tennis player will keep pummeling an opponent when they're down. But in tennis, there's no winning by knockout, and there's also no waiting out the clock, either; you have to keep swinging to win; relent even a little bit, and you risk letting an opponent back into the match. After an exchange of backhands, Kudermetova breaks Naomi again for a 3–0 lead and the match has its first changeover stoppage.

The stadium deejay puts on a remix of Rod Stewart's "Da Ya Think I'm Sexy?" as Naomi slowly walks back toward her chair with her head down. She gets a step past the net, then turns around and suddenly looks up at Vieira Souza in the umpire's chair, struck with an idea.

"Can I have your microphone?" Naomi asks Vieira Souza.

Vieira Souza doesn't understand the request, and so Naomi repeats herself, pointing up at the umpire's chair. "Can I borrow your microphone?"

"I have to ask the supervisor if that's okay," Vieira Souza says, shaking her head slightly to show disapproval of this idea, even as her words are conciliatory. "I'm going to ask them. What do you want to say?"

"I just want to say something—I'm not going to curse, like, I don't curse—it's just on my heart," Naomi says, tapping her chest as her voice quavers slightly. Speaking her feelings publicly, either at a press conference or on social media, has often brought Naomi clarity and peace of mind, but she's never tried to do it in the middle of a match before.

"Okay," Vieira Souza says. Naomi then sits down and Vieira Souza gets on her walkie-talkie, waving over her supervisor. "Uhhh, Clare? Do you mind to come here, please?"

Clare Wood, the Women's Tennis Association (WTA) supervisor on duty this night, walks across from her seat in the corner of the court to the umpire, a ribbon of Ukrainian flag colors pinned to her credential to show support for the country, which Russia had invaded weeks earlier. After

Vieira Souza explains the situation, Wood approaches Naomi and asks her what she'd like to say.

"Yeah, I just wanted to say, like . . . ," Naomi says before pausing for several seconds, revealing that she hadn't yet figured out what to say. "'I appreciate everybody wanting to be loud, but there's, like, a difference . . .'" she suggests, trailing off.

"Right now, it's probably not appropriate," Wood replies, shaking her head. "But keep calm and stay on the tennis. Is it distracting you?"

"I mean, it's hard for me to play," Naomi tells her. "It's in my head."

As Naomi blots her eyes with a towel, Wood tells her that if the person makes any more noise, they will be found. Naomi isn't satisfied but rises to resume the match, again pulling her visor low over her eyes. The delay has taken nearly four minutes, far longer than the ninety seconds allotted for changeovers.

The crowd roars for Naomi as she retakes the court. Shouts of "We love you, Naomi!" ring out once more, several in children's voices. There's another close game, but Kudermetova wins it, and then wins the next, pulling ahead 5–0. "It's hard watching her from up here," Lindsay Davenport says of Naomi on Tennis Channel. "Something obviously triggered her early on in this match. And, you know, you just want to send someone out there to give her a hug, to be able to let someone from her team talk to her. Unfortunately, that's not this sport. And an individual sport, you can't take that time-out. You can't make that substitution. The heart breaks for her."

Kudermetova, unrelenting, takes the first set 6–0, and Wood again returns to Naomi's chair. There's no progress to report back, but Wood tries to assuage her, albeit with an official detachment. "Yeah, but why do they get to yell at me?" Naomi asks Wood on this visit. "That's all I think about . . . I just wanted to say something."

According to its own regulations, the tournament could have found and ejected the heckler: "We reserve the right to refuse admission and service to anyone and to relocate, remove and/or evict anyone not cooperating with Event staff or not complying with the rules and regulations of the [Indian Wells Tennis Garden] or otherwise engaging in illegal, disruptive, or dangerous behavior," reads the small print when a ticket is bought. But there was no success—and perhaps not much effort—in identifying the woman, or in convincing Naomi that they were doing all they could.

．．．．．．．

Daria Saville, a gregarious Australian veteran who had won her second-round match on Saturday afternoon, told me she came back to the locker room to find Naomi already looking downtrodden before her match against Kudermetova had begun. As she saw Naomi struggling on court later that night, Saville felt helpless.

"Then I watched it on TV and I was like, 'Well, shit, like anything could have tipped her over at this point,'" Saville said. "So it's really sad. And there's nothing, really, you can do . . . I was like, Oh my God, I wish I could just, like, give her a hug." Saville has been friendly with Naomi, she said, but didn't feel like it was her place to approach her with concern in the moments before a match. "You give them space; they still have their team," Saville said of her approach to peers in the locker room. "Like it's definitely not my place to be like, 'Are you okay?' Because maybe she was okay; I don't know. Maybe just me saying 'Are you okay?' could have tipped her over the edge."

．．．．．．．

Naomi wins the first game of the second set to get on the board in the match. The second set proceeds without incident, and more competitively, but Kudermetova breaks in the seventh game of the set to take a 4–3 lead. Kudermetova closes out the win, 6–0, 6–4. On her way up to the net, Naomi bows her head quickly to Kudermetova—a subtle but distinctly Japanese gesture she's done throughout her career—and then the two clasp hands.

Naomi again approaches the chair umpire and then talks to Wood. "Can I say something *now*?" she asks again. This time, the request is granted. Andrew Krasny, the tournament emcee, first interviews the winner, Kudermetova, as is standard practice.

"First of all I want to say it was really tough match for me," Kudermetova says. "I play against Naomi: she's the great player, she's the good fighter. And I'm really happy about my performance today, I was so focused, and I'm so happy to be here and play in front of you guys. Thank you."

"We wish you the best of luck," Krasny says. "Through to the third round, Veronika Kudermetova."

Naomi, who has been sitting with a towel draped over her torso, rises out of her seat. "Ladies and gentlemen, uh, Miss Osaka is a former champion at our tournament," Krasny tells the audience, "and she's requested to come up to the microphone and say a few words."

The crowd cheers heartily for Naomi once again, as they had throughout the night, adding supportive whoops and whistles as she approaches the microphone carrying her racquet bag. Naomi smiles widely but keeps her lips together, forming more of a grimace.

Naomi has said that when she gets nervous, her voice gets higher and squeakier. "Hi!" she begins, several octaves above her normal pitch. "Uhh. I just wanted to say thank you?"

More cheering, more shouts of *"We love you, Naomi!"* from the crowd.

Naomi wipes a tear again, then giggles wistfully. "Uh, yeah, I feel like I've cried enough on camera, but . . . I just wanted to say, uh . . ."

"Don't worry about those dumb people!" a woman shouts from the crowd, drawing more cheers. Kudermetova, who has stayed on court to watch this scene, also claps softly.

"Um, to be honest, I've gotten heckled before, like it didn't really bother me," Naomi continues. "But um. It's like, heckled *here*. Like, I've watched a video of Venus and Serena getting heckled here, and if you've never watched it you should watch it. And I don't know why, but it went into my head and it got replayed a lot. I'm trying not to cry, but . . ."

"You got this!"

"Uhh, I just wanted to say thank you, and congratulations," Naomi concludes, raising her arm toward Kudermetova. "Yeah, just thank you."

As Naomi picks up her bag and turns toward the exit, Krasny quickly interjects, trying both to comfort the distraught star and salvage this suddenly dark moment for his tournament. "Naomi, I think I have to tell you that on behalf of everybody here, that out of about 10,000 people, one person's voice can't weigh out 9,999 others," Krasny says. And we love you here, okay? Ladies and gentlemen, Naomi Osaka."

"That's right! You are loved!"

Naomi wipes more tears and tries to smile as Krasny speaks but keeps moving toward the locker room and is soon off the court.

"I love her—she's so sensitive," a Black woman who was standing in the lower bowl cheering for Naomi says to me. "He said the right thing, the interviewer. But that's what happens so often: we do so well but we focus on the one negative thing and let it get in our spirit. And words hurt. You can't take them back."

Those three small words—"Naomi, you suck"—had pierced Naomi's armor that night. And her own words on the court, referencing the tournament's darkest moment, had suddenly torn open a twenty-one-year-old scar that Tennis Paradise had worked for decades to plaster over.

· · · · · · · ·

Serena Williams, a nineteen-year-old in a bright pink dress and braided blond pigtails, should have been the local favorite at the Southern California tournament during the 2001 Indian Wells final. Serena, famously, had grown up only about a hundred miles to the west in Compton. But on this sunny Saturday afternoon, the overwhelming majority of the crowd of 15,940 would be against her.

Serena had been scheduled to face her sister Venus in a blockbuster all-Williams Thursday night semifinal, only for the match to be called off minutes before it was set to begin, with Venus citing knee tendinitis as her reason for withdrawing. The late cancellation announcement of the marquee match enraged the expectant audience of thousands who were already settling into the stadium and reanimated rumors that results of matches between the sisters were predetermined by their father, Richard. Elena Dementieva, the player whom Venus had trounced in the quarterfinals, had been asked for a prediction for the all-Williams semifinal and said it would be up to their father. "I don't know what Richard thinks about it; I think he will decide who's going to win tomorrow," Dementieva said. Richard did little to quell the swirling rumors when he was asked about Venus's withdrawal by a Reuters reporter that day and claimed not to speak English in response.

Chanda Rubin, who had been the top Black player in the mid-nineties when the Williamses first began their takeover, told me that she saw the overwhelmingly White tennis establishment reluctant to embrace these "two athletes that the sport had never really seen" before. "It was always still, from my perspective, this undercurrent of, like, you *had* to accept them," Rubin told me. "You didn't want to really accept them; you had to accept them."

When Serena walked onto the court for the final—carrying the bouquet of flowers that women's finalists are often given at tournaments—the overwhelmingly White crowd at Indian Wells made clear that it was done begrudgingly accepting the Williamses, and began booing immediately. When the crowd spotted Richard and Venus on the long walk down the seating bowl aisle to their courtside seats, the boos renewed. When he reached his seat, Richard turned and put his fist in the air, a defiant Black Power salute that drew a few more boos. While the ESPN crew carefully avoided any such diagnosis, British broadcaster Simon Reed didn't hold back in his match commentary on Eurosport: "An American crowd booing an American family," Reed said somberly. "And you have to say that it does smack of a little bit of racism."

"I looked up and all I could see was a sea of rich people—mostly older, mostly White—standing and booing lustily, like some kind of genteel lynch mob," Serena later wrote. "I don't mean to use such inflammatory language to describe the scene, but that's really how it seemed from where I was down on the court. Like these people were gonna come looking for me after the match."

The crowd cheered raucously for Kim Clijsters, Serena's Belgian opponent, but Serena silenced them as she pulled away in the third set. She capped off the 4–6, 6–4, 6–2 by smacking a crosscourt forehand winner into the open court. Victorious, Serena walked to the corner of the court to greet her family; the jeers grew louder as father and daughter hugged each other. Both would later report having heard racial slurs.

The family drew a hard line in the sand around the desert tournament after that day. Serena did not return to Indian Wells the next year to defend her title. Neither did Venus. The two biggest stars in American tennis would stay away from the second-biggest American tennis tournament for fourteen years. When the WTA classified Indian Wells as a mandatory tournament during a tour reconfiguration in 2008, they added provisions that allowed the Williamses to continue skipping it.

Eight years into the boycott, Serena wrote that "because somewhere some little girl might be watching," she owed it to those who looked up to her to stand firmly on her convictions. "If I don't make my small stand on this, it will be harder for them to make their small stands when they come up."

· · · · · · · ·

As a tween, Naomi Osaka found an online video of Serena on court at Indian Wells in 2001. She was enthralled. The Williamses had been the blueprint her parents had followed since she was an infant, leading them to uproot the family from Japan to New York and then to Florida, devoting their daughters' childhoods to the relentless pursuit of tennis excellence. But when she watched her toughest moment, Naomi felt more inspired by Serena than ever before. "For me, that was 'How can a human be so strong?'" Naomi later told *The Undefeated*'s Soraya Nadia McDonald. "That's one of the reasons I love her so much." Naomi had crumbled in her own low-stakes youth tournaments when the parents or friends of her young opponents would taunt or tease her, she said, but in Serena's image on her screen she found a new strength she had never known was possible. As a sixteen-year-old, Naomi told Japanese reporter Aki Uchida in 2014 that watching Serena had taught her a lasting lesson: "Even in such adversity, you can win."

Serena had returned to Indian Wells in 2015 with much fanfare and celebration. Venus returned a year later. But on this night in 2022, after a year of her own public struggles, Naomi Osaka only related to Serena's pain.

* * * * * * *

The second-round match between Naomi and Kudermetova wasn't supposed to have been big news, regardless of who won or lost. Especially as it finished late on a Saturday night, few news outlets would have been planning to cover it. But once Naomi cried, and then rattled the skeleton in Tennis Paradise's closet, the match suddenly became one of the biggest news stories of the tennis season so far. No matter how far her ranking had fallen, Naomi Osaka remained tops in tennis when it came to generating headlines and discussion.

Within minutes of the match finishing, reporters from both the *Los Angeles Times* and *The New York Times* were writing articles. Because the sports desk had shut down for the night in New York, where it was nearing 2:00 a.m., the *New York Times* correspondent had scrambled to find an editor who was awake in an Asian bureau to handle the breaking news of the shaken superstar.

Per the tour's rules, Naomi was required to do a post-match press conference, but she had absconded into the night. "I did a dash," she would later tell me. Regardless, photos of Naomi's teary eyes were splashed across the tops of news and sports websites the next morning, often second only to coverage of Russia's nascent invasion of Ukraine. Eventual Indian Wells champions Taylor Fritz and Iga Świątek received a fraction of the media attention for winning the tournament that Naomi did after losing in the second round.

Sergey Demekhin, Kudermetova's coach, told me he watched Tennis Channel the morning after his player's big win. "I see some highlights, a few points, and an interview of Naomi and the commentators speaking about Naomi's situation . . . Nothing about that Veronika won the match, or some speech of hers," Demekhin said. "So this is how it works, but you get used to it."

Other star tennis players at Indian Wells who were asked about Naomi responded with a mix of sympathy and resignation. "The only thing that I wish her is [to] recover well from that, wish her all the very best," Rafael Nadal said. "But nothing is perfect in this life, no? We need to be ready for adversities."

While she had a degree of empathy from the locker rooms, those in tournament offices were dismayed by how the latest Naomi storm was clouding the blue-sky brand of Tennis Paradise. There was growing frustration that the outsized attention on her emotional well-being was darkening the mood of tennis tournaments with increasing frequency. Tommy Haas, the Indian Wells tournament director, told me that while he would "never condone" heckling of the sort Naomi received, he thought she could have handled it much better. "I get it that she was a little bit frustrated," Haas said. "At the same time, she's got to be professional enough to say, 'Look, you know, just because of one fan, I'm not going to let it get under my skin, I'm just going to try my best.'" Haas also was annoyed by Naomi lingering on court only to dredge up bad memories for his tournament. "She waited around long enough to make a statement that brought back memories to a place where she was two or three years old when it happened," Haas said. "It didn't really help anyone in the end of the day."

. . . .

As it had several times before, Naomi Osaka's tear-stained face became a cultural Rorschach test across mainstream media. Some, like *The Indianapolis Star*'s Gregg Doyel, celebrated Naomi for showing her vulnerability. "Naomi Osaka is standing at a microphone and trying not to cry, and I'm watching it happen on television and silently urging her to let it out," Doyel wrote. "It's OK, Naomi, really. Be who you are—hard but soft, athletically supernatural but ultimately so very human. Cry, Naomi."

Others, particularly conservative commentators, conversely, used Naomi's pain as ammunition in the culture wars. "A thousand cheers vs. one heckle. Fragile. Weak. Embarrassing," wrote Jason Whitlock. "The news here isn't that she was heckled. The news is we've produced a culture that celebrates weakness and victimhood." On his Web show *Fearless with Jason Whitlock,* Whitlock invited Republican congressional candidate Royce White to further tie Naomi to societal ills. "I think Osaka having this breakdown is maybe the single greatest indictment of the prevailing ideology of wokeism in today's culture," White declared.

The story was ubiquitous enough to make it into late night comedy material. In a sketch on *Late Night with Seth Meyers,* the comedian Amber Ruffin paired gushing support for Naomi—"Naomi, we are so proud of you and we love you and we're going to support you no matter what you do"— with cartoonish threats toward the unknown heckler: "I'm going to rip you up like a piece of paper. You want to yell 'Naomi, you suck?' Well, you know what sucks? Your chances of survival."

· · · · · · ·

Away from the noise across the internet and the airwaves, a quieter but more intense conversation was happening around Naomi herself inside the luxurious house the tournament had rented for her. "The next day we had a serious meeting, all of us together," her coach Wim Fissette later told me. "After the match, you're not going to push someone who's super disappointed and crying. But the next day, yeah, we had a big conversation: okay, this is what needs to happen right now."

Naomi had been the face of conversations about the importance of mental health—literally, on the cover of *Time* magazine with the headline "It's O.K. to Not Be O.K."—and had signed a deal to endorse Modern Health, a mental health services company. But those close to her knew there was a disconnect between her public presentation and private reality: she hadn't been getting any professional psychological help of her own. The topic was a delicate one—not least because Naomi was the employer with sole hiring and firing discretion of everyone on her team—but after her latest public struggle they were resolved to help her. Her agent Stuart Duguid had already begun researching therapists she might like.

Yutaka Nakamura was also there for the all-hands-on-deck meeting.

"I'm a strength and conditioning coach; Wim is a coach; she has a hitting partner and all that, but she needed somebody to talk to," Nakamura told me. "Naomi knows the team doesn't judge her, but she just needed to have somebody else that was not tennis-related, but more on a personal level. We talked about that, and she agreed with that."

Fissette told me he had previously suggested adding a mental coach to the team after her moments of public struggle, but this time Naomi was more ready to listen.

"I would say the reason why I waited so long is because I have a hard time talking to people, so it's a bit hard for me to, like, open up to someone—especially someone that I'm supposed to tell them, like, all of my worries," Naomi later explained. "Things that I wouldn't even tell, like, my sister or something. So it was just hard, learning how to trust someone."

Naomi's sister had, in fact, been the difference-maker in this all-hands meeting. "Mari also spoke up," Fissette recalled. "Like, 'Naomi, I'm your sister and it is time.'"

Naomi had a lingering desire to solve her issues on her own but later said Mari "seemed very concerned for me," which had caused her to take the group's pleas more seriously. Though the world was full of opinions on Naomi Osaka, Mari was the only one who had been with her from the beginning, ever since two parents who had found each other from a world apart looked at their daughters and saw a vision they risked everything to chase.

TWO

The Motherland

I n Japan, the Land of the Rising Sun, the morning light first touches Nemuro. A windswept fishing town of around twenty-seven thousand, Nemuro is on the eastern tip of the northern island of Hokkaido, one of the most remote parts of the densely populated country. Nemuro is on the edge of Japan, geographically, and on edge, geopolitically. Several smaller islands and islets northeast of the Nemuro Peninsula, the closest of which is only 1.6 miles (3.7 kilometers) away, are part of the Kuril Islands, the closest of which have been disputed between Japan and Russia since the Soviet Union's invasion and occupation of the archipelago in the closing weeks of World War II in August 1945. Japan still claims the islands and calls them its "Northern Territories" and includes them in the Nemuro Subprefecture, but they remain administered by Russia. Despite the many decades passing since the end of World War II, Russian patrol boats still cruise through the narrow Goyomaisuido Strait in a frequent show of force. The Osaka family, who lived on the islands and worked as fishermen, were forced from their land when the Russians arrived and have been unable to return since. Tetuso Osaka, who was born near the end of the war, has lived in Nemuro, staying as close as he can to the lost land. Though sporadic skirmishes between Russian patrols and Japanese fishermen flare up—which involve Tetsuo in his role as head of a local fishermen's collective—life in Nemuro offers serenity in seclusion.

Twenty-seven years after Japanese surrender ended World War II, Nemuro was briefly back on the world map. When Sapporo, the capital city of Hokkaido, became the first Winter Olympics host city outside Europe or the United States, the torch relays wended a scenic route around the island in early 1972. One flame was carried all the way out to isolated Nemuro, briefly but brilliantly bathing the remote town in the glow of the global gathering.

A spiritual spark from that flame seemed to ignite something in one of Nemuro's youngest residents: Tetsuo's infant daughter, Tamaki Osaka, was just one year old as the relay passed through her hometown, but the torchlight seemed to illuminate a path she would follow the rest of her life: out of Nemuro, across to the island's opposite coast, to Sapporo—a world city that opened the door toward a multicultural existence largely alien to her homogenous hometown—and toward the dedicated pursuit of an ambitious sporting dream. One day, Tamaki's daughter would carry that same torchlight herself.

· · · · · · ·

Tamaki's mother had finished at the top of her high school class, but a woman attending university was given little consideration in that era. She married her husband, Tetsuo, shortly after graduation, and never worked outside the home. "I don't know if it's because of her background, but she was the kind of person who always let her child do whatever she wanted," Tamaki wrote of her mother in her 2022 memoir *Through the Tunnel*. "I think she probably wanted her child to do whatever she couldn't do herself."

When Tamaki was fourteen, her mother encouraged her to take the entrance exam for a high school in Sapporo, the city of two million on the opposite side of Hokkaido. With an education at a Sapporo high school, her mother knew, Tamaki could get on the elite educational track toward a top university, which had been inaccessible to her. With her mother's blessing Tamaki took a train three hours west of Nemuro to Kushiro to take the entrance exam, which she passed. As Tamaki described in *Through the Tunnel*, the idea of sending a girl to a distant school was resisted by her father—"Why? Girls don't have to go to a school in Sapporo!"—but her mother's wishes won out.

In Sapporo, about seven hours from the eastern tip of Hokkaido where Nemuro sits, teenage Tamaki had a degree of independence from her family she had never before experienced. Her branching out reached another level when she changed the concentration of her coursework from piano to English in her second year in Sapporo. Tamaki had been interested in learning the language that could open doors to the world beyond her island nation from a young age: she had taken extracurricular classes in the language in Nemuro and sometimes spoke English with American missionaries in the town. "This English ability will greatly change my destiny," Tamaki wrote in *Through the Tunnel*. In the English program, she found like-minded classmates who shared her sense of adventure and spent more time exploring the city. When she returned home to Nemuro during school breaks, she felt herself growing apart from her family. "They are people who never left their hometown, who never ventured out into the unknown," Tamaki wrote. "Every time I returned to my parents' house from Sapporo, I felt a growing sense of incongruity within me."

After finishing high school and a two-year college, Tamaki got a job doing clerical work at a bank in Sapporo that provided fishery-related loans. After work one day, Tamaki went shopping with a friend. A foreign man working in a shop tried to speak English to Tamaki's friend, but the friend got nervous and ran to the bathroom. Tamaki, though, felt no such apprehension speaking English with strangers, so she asked Leonard Maxime François a question.

"Where are you from?"

· · · · · · ·

Tamaki was confused by Leonard's initial reply, thinking he had said "Aichi," Aichi being the Japanese prefecture about six hundred miles south; the actual answer was "Haichi," meaning Haiti, the small Caribbean nation half a world away. But though Haiti was his homeland, Leonard had moved to Brooklyn in his teens and became a naturalized American citizen; in her book, Tamaki introduces Leonard as "an American from the Republic of Haiti." Leonard, a straightlaced student who drove a taxi in New York, had traveled to Japan with a Japanese friend he had met on a night out in Manhattan. He liked Japan so much he decided to move there permanently, and even persuaded a couple of Haitian friends from Brooklyn to join him there, too. Once in Japan, Leonard became an unlikely celebrity: Takeshi Kitano, the famous Japanese comedian and game show host, had featured Leonard on a recurring basketball segment on one of his shows, where he dunked on overmatched locals. "He was an amazing athlete," Pedro Herivaux, one of the Haitian friends from Brooklyn who followed Leonard to Japan, told me, marveling at how Leonard "would jump out the roof" during their dunking contests. Herivaux laughed as he told me Leonard, athletic though he was, became "the Michael Jordan of Japan" through his celebrity on the show. "In America he would be nobody, but in Japan he's supposed to be *the* good basketball player," he said.

"Basketball Max-u," as he was called on the show, parlayed his fame into other appearances; Leonard and Herivaux even appeared together in a *Cool Runnings*–themed ad campaign for a Japanese ski resort. Women in Sapporo came to Leonard's shop, where he sold imported clothes from American streetwear brands like FUBU, just to see him.

Tamaki had wandered into the shop by accident, but Leonard was quickly eager to see more of her. He asked for her phone number, and because she didn't yet have a cell phone—and shared her Sapporo apartment with her parents, who had moved to the city—she gave him the phone number of the bank.

He called her there soon after, and they began dating in secret. In *Through the Tunnel*, Tamaki describes their courtship as fitting in a '90s rom-com, including scenes of Rollerblading along the banks of the Toyohira River in Sapporo. Leonard was five years older than Tamaki, and they had little in common, but they were deeply in love. Eventually, as her father began to nominate various qualified suitors for her to date and marry,

Tamaki decided she could no longer hide the truth and told him she already had a boyfriend. When she told her father his name, and her father realized his daughter was dating a dark-skinned foreigner, he was shocked and furious: "Blacks are only for watching on TV or in movies, not for dating," she said he told her.

Her father tried to shut down the relationship. Instead of being able to bike around Sapporo freely, Tamaki was driven straight to work and then picked up and driven straight home.

A year passed without Tamaki and Leonard seeing each other, until he called her one day in the summer of 1995. He had moved 650 miles away to Osaka in southwestern Japan, and he wanted her to come see him there. He bought her a plane ticket, and she packed a duffel bag and left for the airport, giving her parents no indication she was leaving Hokkaido.

Their romance continued in Osaka, and soon the couple was ready to wed. But in order to obtain the documents she needed for a marriage license, Tamaki had to return to Nemuro. Though she had tried to be stealthy, a friend in Nemuro had tipped off her parents, who had filed a missing person's report after her unexplained disappearance from Sapporo. Soon after Tamaki and Leonard married, police knocked on the door of the newly-wed couple's Osaka apartment, accompanied by her parents. Police interviewed Tamaki, who was pregnant with the couple's first child, suspecting she had been kidnapped; she assured them she was there of her own free will.

Tamaki stayed in Osaka, where she gave birth to her first daughter, Mari Osaka, on April 3, 1996. Their second daughter, Naomi Osaka, was born a year and a half later, on October 16, 1997. The parents from opposite sides of the globe both passed on their citizenships—the girls were born as dual citizens of Japan and the United States—but the couple chose to give their daughters Tamaki's last name for ease of living around Japan, where foreign names often caused consternation. Tamaki also wrote in *Through the Tunnel* that she had also wanted to pick first names that could be easily understood and pronounced by non-Japanese speakers. She wanted her girls to be ready for a bigger world than she had known.

. . . .

Leonard, known for his basketball prowess, enjoyed many sports and ran the Sapporo Marathon; he thought he could have been an elite athlete if he had been given the proper nurturing in his youth. Tamaki, too, had been athletically inclined, enjoying swimming and speed skating. One evening when Naomi was seven months old, her father turned on the television in their one-room apartment to watch sports, as he often did. The sport Leonard had tuned into on this night filled their small apartment room with the orange glow of clay a world away. It was the women's doubles final of the 1999 French Open, featuring four teenagers: Martina Hingis and Anna Kournikova versus Venus and Serena Williams. The match, which was overshadowed by the men's singles final won by Andre Agassi that same day, had been roiled by rain delays, full of stops and starts, blustery winds, and similarly strong shifts on the scoreboard. Venus, eighteen, and Serena, seventeen, had led by a set and 5–1 before letting their lead slip, and then found themselves down championship point with Kournikova serving at 5–4 in the third. But the sisters steeled themselves and Kournikova crumbled, double-faulting on break point. Four games later, they broke Kournikova again, finishing off a 6–3, 6–7(2), 8–6 win for their first major title together. They held their arms aloft, jumped, and embraced, then went to the stands to hug their mother. "It was all very dramatical," Venus recalled in a 2021 Instagram post.

A world away, two parents with two daughters of their own saw something beyond the drama. "Both he and I were astounded by the majestic performance of these Black women and sisters," Tamaki wrote in *Through the Tunnel*. "I thought I had found the future possibilities that I had been looking for . . . The ray of light that led to hope was the Williams sisters."

Richard Williams, coincidentally, had also been inspired to get his not-yet-born daughters into tennis by watching the French Open on TV; the $20,000 check that 1978 champion Virginia Ruzici had pocketed for her win convinced him there was big money to be made. But for Leonard and Tamaki the prize money that day in 1999—Venus and Serena each won roughly $100,000 for winning the doubles title—wasn't what had caught their attention. Instead, it was these young Black women themselves, in whom they could see their own daughters. "Living without any clear idea of the future, I wanted to instill a dream more than make money," Tamaki said in 2023. "The way [the Williams sisters] flew around the world and influenced society blew my mind."

· · · · · · · ·

Tennis coaches told Tamaki her toddler daughters were too young to begin lessons, so she first put them in gymnastics classes to help them work on their balance. Mari finally took to the tennis court at age three; Naomi, who stood by the fence and watched, has said her clearest memories of Japan are of watching Mari playing tennis. The girls were small enough that Tamaki pushed them in a stroller to the courts. They trained at Marine Tennis Park Kitamura in Osaka, a sprawling facility with twenty-five courts near a hospital and a small harbor. They also set up a makeshift net in their small apartment and threw balls for the girls to chase back and forth.

The dedication to tennis came during what Tamaki describes as "extreme poverty" as she and Leonard struggled to make ends meet in Osaka. Tamaki, who worked part-time in a call center for a mail-order catalog, had been cut off financially from her parents; Leonard imported American streetwear clothing and co-owned a Haitian-themed bar, Zoz's. There were fun times, including when the Haitian rap star Wyclef Jean popped into Zoz's, but neither operation was profitable. "Rather than being loved as a bird in a cage, it was more important to be able to live freely as a wild bird, even if it meant problems finding places to live and even food," Tamaki wrote. She scrimped and saved as she could, using methods like waiting until evening to buy tofu, when it was less fresh and the prices had dropped by 20 percent.

As they continued living in poverty, "seeing the Williams sisters took our minds off our struggles to make ends meet and started us dreaming a brighter future for our little girls," Tamaki said in 2022. Even though their daughters were still toddlers, their parents' dream became all-consuming, freighted with desperate stakes. "Tennis is the only way our family can succeed," Tamaki wrote in *Through the Tunnel*. The money they could save went to their dream: "My husband and I were maddened by tennis fever for our children," she wrote.

The fever led to restlessness. Mari and Naomi had gotten into a competitive kindergarten, and Tamaki had already bought the school uniforms, but the couple fretted over the lack of tennis opportunities in Osaka, where there were few youth tournaments. A message then came from Leonard's mother: his sister had moved out of the family's house in New York, and she wanted him to move back there to help her.

The family connection was a draw, but tennis was the bigger pull. At the time Leonard and Tamaki were getting their daughters into tennis around the turn of the twenty-first century, Japan had little success producing professional tennis stars: Japan had only ever produced one Top 10 singles player on the women's side, Kimiko Date; no Japanese man had even broken into the ATP Top 40.

If his daughters were going to be like the Williams sisters, Leonard knew, they'd have to go to their home country: America. "The blueprint was already there," Leonard later said. "I just had to follow it."

Leonard and Tamaki left Osaka in the spring of 2001 and moved their family to New York. Naomi, who was three years and five months old at the time of the move, wouldn't return to Japan for nearly a decade. Part of the appeal of America was the freedom Tamaki and Leonard would have to live and love as an interracial couple without the judgment they and their mixed-race children would face in Japan. Years later, Tamaki used the name "Liberty" on her social media channels, and celebrated the anniversary of *Loving v. Virginia*, the 1967 Supreme Court decision that nullified the enduring laws banning interracial marriage in sixteen states. "Was 'disgrace' to the family, had been in the desert&jungles for decades, I'm still surviving," Tamaki wrote. "#HappyLovingDay."

Over the next decade, Tetsuo and Tamaki slowly rebuilt their relationship. Mari and Naomi would sometimes have phone conversations with

Tetsuo, whom they called *Ojiichan*, Japanese for "Grandpa." Speaking to his granddaughters, Tamaki said, her father was warm, funny, and gentle; he would sometimes ship a box of Japanese snacks to America for the girls to enjoy. But when Tamaki got on the line with him, she said, his tone abruptly changed. "You're going to be homeless in America and die on the side of the road," she heard.

THREE

Where Dreams Are Made Of

Whereas the family had lived an isolated existence in Osaka, estranged from Tamaki's parents, they were surrounded by family in New York, as well as a wider Haitian-American community. Leonard and Tamaki still lacked money, but their network of support was immensely stronger. Leonard's family bought a new house in Elmont, a diverse suburb in Nassau County just east of Queens, as the new arrivals came from Japan; Leonard's parents, with whom they lived, spoke little English.

Mari and Naomi attended Alden Terrace Elementary two miles from their home. Though their new environment was considerably more diverse than the racially homogenous Japan they had left behind, other kids at the predominantly Black school sometimes bullied them for their different-looking eyes and hair, Mari told me. But both girls also made friends. Mari excelled in art, taking classes before and after school. When Mari was eight and Naomi was six, they were both commended in a local newspaper for participating in a local politician's "reading challenge" at the school.

Away from school hours, the focus was tennis. Leonard studied books and instructional videos on the sport just as Richard Williams had—and also read and watched Richard's interviews. "When driving through fog, the lights of the car in front of you are the only guideposts: just look at them and keep going," Tamaki wrote in *Through the Tunnel*. "That's how we've followed the Williams sisters. Without them, our family would have never made it in tennis." Leonard trained his daughters on run-down courts at public parks around Queens and Nassau County. For a more special setting, they occasionally traveled to train at the U.S. Tennis Association (USTA) National Tennis Center in Flushing Meadows, the site of the U.S. Open. Leonard trained his daughters before school, after school, and on Saturdays. "I just remember watching all the other kids take their summer vacations, and we had to be on the courts," Naomi said in 2022. "Which, I'm happy he made us do it now. But at the time, I was so jealous of everyone else."

Naomi hesitated when once asked if her parents had forced tennis upon her. "I think in the beginning, yes, for sure, but as I grew up, you know . . . I started thinking that those dreams, they're things that I really want to accomplish," she said. "So yeah, I think it was more like a push." Her sister was blunter: "It wasn't really our choice," Mari said.

Tamaki has said onlookers and park administrators repeatedly called police on the family to interrupt the long hours Leonard spent training his daughters on the courts. Once, a park security guard called police because Leonard did not have a coaching permit; they assumed Leonard must be a commercial coach because of the large quantity of balls he had on the court to train them. Tamaki later wrote that she thought there was a discriminatory element to these interferences. "Tennis is still a sport for the White community," she said. "There must be many people who feel uncomfortable watching Black people and Asians practicing tennis hard."

The family was not only practicing, they were competing. Naomi played her first official tournament when she was just six years old, in February 2004 in Port Washington. Her opponent was a seven-year-old, Katrine Steffensen. The result was inauspicious: Naomi lost 6–1, 6–0. Nearly two decades later, Steffensen told me she still remembered the match because of a desperate tactic Naomi employed to try to change the match in her favor: standing on the service line to return and trying to hit Steffensen's serve out of mid-air. The two young children weren't sure if that was allowed (it's not); Steffensen remembers her mom laughing on the sideline as she watched. "Once she started volleying my serve, I kind of knew that this must be her first match," Steffensen said of Naomi. "We were both still pretty tiny. But yeah, that was probably a funny moment. And, obviously, my claim to fame."

Six-year-old Naomi's first eight recorded matches were all straight-set losses; Mari, eighteen months older, won about half of her matches in those days. The lack of early results did not daunt the family, however. To support her family and their tennis ambitions, Tamaki worked long hours in an office in distant Manhattan. "I have so many memories of her waking up at four in the morning, catching the bus, catching the train," Naomi said in 2020.

Tamaki often found unusual ways to save money: once, when her daughters had asked to go ice skating at Rockefeller Center, she poured some oil on the floor of their home and told them to slide around on that instead. "Looking back, I don't know why we had to be so frugal with our money," she later said.

While Tamaki worked and commuted long hours, Leonard did not hold any full-time job. Instead, he spent his time on the court with his daughters, and off the court to make another vision come to life.

. . . .

Using his full name, Leonard Maxime François (or sometimes just Maxime François), Leonard cast, produced, filmed, directed, and edited three independent films. In a sharp contrast from the optimism behind his tennis ambitions, the stories Leonard told on-screen were unwaveringly dark. In three feature-length films in a mix of English and Haitian Creole, Leonard focused on self-destructive behavior and falls from grace, weaving tales of troubled marriages, adultery, misogyny, violence, legal jeopardy, and immigration issues. Bennchoumy Elien, a Haitian-American musician and actor, starred in all three films, each time playing a flawed protagonist who lost his battles with his demons. Elien, a handsome leading man, had two less experienced costars in his first feature-length effort with Leonard: Naomi and Mari.

Leonard had cast his daughters as Rachel (Naomi) and Alicia (Mari) in *Selfish Love,* the two children of the fraught marriage at the center of his first feature film. Leonard also kept the story close to home by shooting much of it inside his family's own house in Elmont, as well as at other locations around their neighborhood. Much of the cast was from his extended family and other neighbors, all of whom lacked experience in the film industry. Leonard enlisted Sulaah Bien-Aime, a Haitian-American writer whom he was introduced to by Elien, to create the screenplay based on his vision in just two weeks.

In a climactic scene where the girls see their father beating their mother—the *fourth* such on-screen beating in the film—Mari's character dials 911. Bien-Aime told me she asked Leonard during production how he felt about his daughters being in those violent scenes. "I didn't know to what extent he wanted them exposed to it, even though it was fake," Bien-Aime told me. "And he said, 'Well, I wanted to create a movie where if they're ever in a situation like that, they know what to do and they don't have to take it.'"

Production centered around the family home, which Bien-Aime said had as many as fifteen to twenty people there at a time. "We were shooting around the clock," she told me. "Wherever we could find a space in the house was where we would lie down and take a few z's, and then we would get right back up." Bien-Aime also filled various crew roles, such as applying the makeup for the bruises. "We were all very committed," she recalled.

No one involved in the small-scale production—all filmed on one camera—was paid for their work on Leonard's passion project. Bien-Aime said their work was a gift to Leonard, whom she, like many others, calls Max. "To have all these people rally for Max was something to behold," she said. "It's also his personality: he has that very quiet disposition, but you're aware that he's there. The intensity, you feel it, but then he's also very relaxed and laid back."

After weeks of intense work, filming was complete. "There was this sense of pride in his face, like, 'Yeah, this is me getting this done,'" Bien-Aime said. "He was just really proud of himself, you know? Because everybody has dreams. And when you have dreams, you often need a team to make that dream come true."

Leonard's filmmaking, which has been discussed little during Naomi's life in the spotlight, can seem incongruous with the rest of the family's story. "People sometimes send me clips of myself in the movie and it's so embarrassing," Naomi said in 2022. "But it was a really good time for me when I was younger."

Bien-Aime suggested that seeing her father realize his cinematic vision could have had a lasting positive effect on Naomi. "I think that once you're able to see your parent start something and finish it to the end, believe it or not, that memory, at the time that you need it, will propel you forward," she said. "It doesn't matter what field; it's just the idea of completion. Because many people want to start things, but they don't know how to complete it."

. . . .

Though the family was establishing roots, Leonard was dissatisfied with the progress they were making on their tennis in New York, where it was too cold to play for several months of the year. Indoor courts were scarcely available and prohibitively expensive, around $100 per hour. The tennis climate also lacked his ambitious ardor: rather than turning professional, the stated goal of most tennis parents was their child earning a collegiate athletic scholarship.

As he continued to follow the Williams blueprint, Leonard saw a clear next step: in November 2006, with another winter approaching, he abruptly announced the family was moving to Florida. Leonard followed through on his impulse with urgency: he packed their luggage, loaded it into their used Nissan Quest minivan, and ordered the girls, whom he had hastily withdrawn from their school, to get in and say goodbye to their mother. "I was really sad to leave," Naomi said years later, particularly regretting never getting to say goodbye to her best friend from school, Jasmine.

Though she had been on board with the earlier move from Japan to New York, Tamaki felt blindsided by Leonard's sudden upheaval. She was the family's sole breadwinner and liked the job she had in Manhattan; she didn't feel right leaving abruptly. When she hesitated, Leonard decided to take the girls without her. "Isn't this the same as kidnapping?" she wrote in *Through the Tunnel*.

Suddenly living alone with her in-laws, Tamaki began looking online for jobs she could take in Florida. As her Manhattan job asked her to stay for another month so they could find a qualified replacement—her job required someone bilingual in English and Japanese—Leonard grew impatient and began accusing her of infidelity and disloyalty. "'You must have a boyfriend after all; it's suspicious that you can't come right away—I wonder if you're plotting something,'" Tamaki recounted him saying in *Through the Tunnel*, adding that she could hear her daughters' voices—"Mom, Mom!" in the background of the calls.

Under pressure, and unable to bear the separation from her daughters, Tamaki ultimately left New York three weeks after her husband and daughters had, leaving her employer in the lurch and completing the family's relocation to the place where dreamers from around the world chased after fuzzy hopes of tennis fame and fortune.

Naomi has said she didn't question her father's decision to uproot their lives for tennis, either then or in the many years since. "It definitely seems like a really big gamble, because we could have gone to school like normal kids and stuff," Naomi said in 2019. "But for me . . . what he did shaped my mentality, made it the way it is, which is not to question things too much."

Chasing Sunshine

South Florida has become to tennis what Nashville is to country music: if you have a stringed instrument in your hand and a dream in your heart, it's the place to go to make that dream come true. By the 1970s, the bouncy, lemon-lime-colored orbs* had joined citrus fruit as a Florida cash crop. After the majors began awarding prize money and allowing professionals to compete in 1968, Florida's year-round warmth made it a hothouse for growing tennis talent. In 1978, a decade into the tennis "Open Era," a tennis coach named Nick Bollettieri opened his namesake tennis academy in Bradenton, Florida. With tennis courts and palm trees, the Bollettieri Academy looked like a tropical resort, but it was in fact a trade school, giving its young students the world's most immersive tennis education offered to make it in the increasingly lucrative world of professional tennis.

As Bollettieri churned out stars—Andre Agassi and Monica Seles were among his early breakouts—more academies began popping up around Florida. Bollettieri's remained the biggest, expanding to serve hundreds of tennis players (and eventually aspiring athletes from other sports after it was bought by the sports management conglomerate IMG). After her retirement, Chris Evert put her imprimatur on the Evert Tennis Academy in

---

* The International Tennis Federation began allowing yellow-green balls in 1972, as they were more visible on television broadcasts than the previously used white balls.

Boca Raton. The USTA got in on the action, too, opening its own training center in Boca Raton and later a massive complex in Orlando.

Nearly all top tennis players pass through at least one academy during their development. The Williams sisters were no exception to the gravitational pull of Florida, moving from Compton to Florida in 1991 and setting up camp at the Rick Macci Tennis Academy for four years, a move funded by Macci himself.*

Though Macci was often left out of the Williams mythology, those who studied their story closely learned of his role and their Florida chapter. "It always sounded better as 'From Compton to Centre Court,'" Macci told me. In droves, parents who looked at their kids and saw future tennis champions came to his academy. "You've got to understand: since 1995, it's been in the thousands, that 'I have the next Venus and Serena,'" Macci told me. "It's brutal, and it's just unfortunate." Macci said sometimes parents will bead their daughters' hair, like the Williamses had worn as children, in a sort of cosplay to show their similarities. "I've had people tell me their kid is going to be better than Serena—and they don't even play tennis!" Macci said. "I'm going, 'Well, let's at least start them hitting balls!' It's crazy."

What Macci doesn't dispute in this blueprint, however, is that Florida is the ultimate tennis mecca, for both climate and culture. "Weather: you can train every day, so that's number one," Macci said. "Number two, it's a melting pot of people from all over the world that relocate here. There's tournaments every weekend, from West Palm to Miami."

The weather is warm, but the competition is what burns. Neha Uberoi, a former WTA player who studied at Princeton and Columbia to become

---

* It wasn't until the 2021 movie *King Richard,* in which screenwriter Zach Baylin included Macci (played by the actor Jon Bernthal) and his academy as major elements, that Macci's contributions got more recognition. The revision was incredibly gratifying to him. "It was big-time," Macci said. "Because it's the truth." Macci completely redecorated his academy to celebrate the Hollywood vindication, hanging movie posters and images of himself and the Williams family at the premiere all around the grounds of the facility. "Be Alive," the Oscar-nominated Beyoncé song from the *King Richard* soundtrack, plays on loudspeakers around Macci's academy each evening like a sort of national anthem. Macci also increased his hourly rates for private coaching by several hundred dollars an hour after the movie's release.

a psychotherapist and social worker, described her "culture shock" when she moved from New Jersey to the "Florida jungle" of junior tennis savagery. "Every ball that's six inches in is out, and you don't know what to do," she said. "You get a very different education. It actually really serves you well in later years, post-tennis, where you can spot a liar and a cheater and you know how to handle it."

. . . .

The advent of online homeschooling led to the further explosion of tennis academies in Florida around the time of the Osakas' move. For the rest of their childhoods, Mari and Naomi did not attend a traditional school, a drastic drop-off for their social development compared with their previous years at school with friends and neighbors in New York. "I grew up very— I don't want to say 'sheltered,' but I knew five people in my whole life, you know what I mean?" Naomi later said. Naomi didn't have a cell phone until she turned eighteen, she explained, because "I was always with my father and I didn't have any friends."

The transition was difficult for both sisters. "I was upset about having to switch to homeschooling," Mari told me. "Lifestyle-wise it went from being surrounded by peers to only seeing three other people—my parents and my sister—for almost six, seven years. It was rare to have interaction with [other] people unless my dad took us to an academy for training. I was constantly complaining about not having friends and thought about running away a lot."

Interactions with the world beyond their household, for the most part, were limited to screens. Whereas Mari had enjoyed art classes at her New York elementary school, once she was homeschooled she switched to digital art forums like DeviantArt and Gaia Online. Naomi similarly found herself honing her personality and her sense of humor online. "I feel like I'm a child of the internet," Naomi told me in our first interview, when she was eighteen. "And so the internet has raised me, and its jokes might not be appropriate at certain times, so I keep them locked inside . . . If you go to the dark side of YouTube, yeah, you would find some of the jokes that I would tell."

· · · · · · ·

The name-brand Florida academies get the attention and the top crop of talent—and can also charge the highest tuition to families who may have more money than talent—but the surplus crop of kids and parents chasing tennis dreams has also birthed a sort of gleaner class of upstart coaches, who make their own smaller-scale livings coaching at public parks around South Florida, scooping up the kids whose parents can't pay the high fees charged by the big names.

Andrei Kozlov is one of these coaches. After growing dissatisfied with the low hourly wage he made working at the Macci Academy—where he was a sparring partner for players like Jennifer Capriati—Kozlov started his own academy once he got his green card, leasing public courts at C.B. Smith Park in Pembroke Pines. Kozlov, a junior champion in Russia in his youth, runs his drills with a distinctly Soviet intensity, keeping the kids jogging in place while standing in line during group drills, feeding them well-worn tennis balls. The spartan, militaristic milieu is matched by Kozlov's own vigor, working "362 days a year"—only taking a few days off each year around his wife's birthday.

When the Osakas moved to Pembroke Pines, the Kozlov Tennis Academy, four miles west of their apartment, was one of their first stops. "Naomi Osaka, she's coming from New York, she's coming to me," Kozlov recalled in his typically direct manner. "I remember she looked nothing special . . . In tennis, you never know."

Kozlov admired Leonard and his work ethic, but the respect wasn't enough: Leonard said he couldn't afford Kozlov's normal hourly rates, and as he ran his small business, Kozlov had no room for nonpaying customers. The Osakas only lasted a week at the Kozlov Tennis Academy before moving on. "And after she don't have money, she can't pay, she go to another place," Kozlov said of Naomi.

That basic business equation might seem self-evident: no money = no coaching. But as they roamed from park to park around South Florida, Leonard found some people that were willing to help them out for free—and also made promises to other people who thought they were getting something in return but never did.

· · · · · · ·

Much of the time, Leonard was training his daughters by himself at public parks around Broward County. Though they didn't continue with Andrei Kozlov's coaching, Leonard brought Mari and Naomi back to C.B. Smith Park frequently. Stefan Kozlov, Andrei's son who became an ATP player in his own right, said he had vivid memories of the Osaka family's van parked near the courts as they trained on and off the court. "I remember always seeing them running hills, religiously running hills," Stefan Kozlov told me. "At, like, seven, eight a.m., just running the hills nonstop, their dad pushing them."

Johnnise Renaud, who trained alongside the Osakas for years, said it was clearly "dad driving the boat at first" when it came to the family's tennis commitment, but in a way that ultimately became contagious for his daughters. "When you drop everything as a parent as far as your daily job or things you do for yourself and fully put it all into your child, your child is going to feel that," said Renaud.

The family roamed the South Florida suburbs in the area looking for courts they could play on for free or for cheap. Eliseo Serrano, a tennis director at Lakeshore Park in Miramar and later Brian Piccolo Sports Park in Cooper City, recalls Leonard and his daughters playing for three to four hours a day on his courts. "From Monday to Friday, they practiced a lot," Serrano told me, saying that weekends were designated for play in various local tournaments. The public hard courts were free, Serrano said, but a maintenance fee was required to play on the clay courts (a disparity that might have had a long-term impact on Naomi's tennis). Sometimes other coaches and families were there, Serrano said, but it was just the three of them 80 percent of the time, with Tamaki occasionally stopping by for a few minutes during breaks from work. Watching them at length, Serrano liked what he saw. "The father was nice, he was working so hard with them," Serrano said. "He just had so much patience, you know? He worked a lot but had a good sense of humor, never got angry . . . Some other parents don't treat their kids like that."

While the Osakas were on their own at times, they joined up with coaches and other players as well. Bill Adams had briefly worked with the Williams family while living in Delray Beach, which he figures might have been what attracted the Osakas to him. Adams, a Guyanese-American who was a pupil of Australian coaching legend Harry Hopman, had long worked with players from around the Caribbean and was more amenable than Kozlov to bending business practices to help out. "I don't run a non-profit program," Adams told the *South Florida Sun Sentinel* in 2019. "But sometimes you see someone, see their passion, and if you see they don't have money you find a way to make it work."

When it came to the Osakas, Adams told me, "obviously there wasn't much money." But he saw the passion he was looking for in Leonard, and so he struck a deal: if Leonard helped out with drills for other students on Adams's courts, his daughters could train there for free. "He would feed balls to some of the other courts I had, and that was the way we compensated for them not paying," Adams told me. "And I was very happy with it. I don't normally make those arrangements; I rarely ever do that. But, yeah, there was something that I liked about the family."

The Osakas were using the courts so much that Adams gave them their own key to unlock the gate and come and go as they wished. The next coaches the family worked with, however, wouldn't end on such trusting terms.

• • • • • • •

Christophe Jean, a Haitian tennis player, moved to South Florida in 2001 and soon began coaching, he told me at the Pompano Beach tennis courts where he said he trained the Osaka sisters five days a week for two years. "Five or six hours on the court, every day," he said. "You have to play hard in two years to go up and up and up. That was a lot of training; we spent a lot of time on the court. I'd push them really hard and they didn't have any problem with it."

Eddie Sposa, director of tennis for the Pompano Beach Tennis Center, gave the Osakas free time to work with Jean, one of his favorite employees: "Seven dollars and fifty cents an hour," Sposa told me of the usual rate for a court. "Add that up."

But unlike Adams, who was a well-established coach with a larger program, Jean said he couldn't afford the long hours on court with the Osakas without being paid at all. Nor, he concedes, could the family afford to pay him. "They didn't have money at that time," Jean told me. "I told the dad to give me even three hundred dollars a month so that I can buy the balls and gas." After paying for one month, Jean said, even that was too much. "He told me, 'Christophe, my wife, she's the only one that's working.' He didn't work at that time, for the tennis, so he didn't have money."

And unlike Kozlov, who automatically stopped working with the family when they couldn't pay, Jean wanted to make something work because of their shared Haitian roots and the potential he saw in the girls. "I don't like to say no to kids who have talent," he told me. "I know the kids can make it; I don't want to say no to the kids. And he's Haitian, too; for me that was good to do that for them . . . We have a connection. You see, when you meet a Haitian, you know them, even if you really don't."

Jean said he would teach lessons for other clients in the early morning and late afternoon in order to earn enough money to live on. "We Haitians, we can live any kind of way," he told me. "At that time I lived in a little apartment; I didn't have a lot of bills throughout that time, so I managed to make it. But that was all about them. I put all my time on them, because I knew they were going to be good."

Still, Jean, who said he normally charged $60 an hour for private lessons, wanted a degree of financial security. Months into their work together, a friend of Jean's wrote up a contract:

"Between Christophe Jean and Leonard Francois on behalf of Marie [sic] Osaka, Naomi Osaka (Tennis Players). It is agreed as follows: Both parties agree on a fixed fee of twenty percent (20%) on every tennis contract or monetary agreement on behalf of Marie [*sic*] Osaka and Naomi Osaka. The term of employment shall be indefinite."

The contract, dated March 21, 2012, and notarized, was signed by Jean and also by Leonard on behalf of his daughters. "He accepted everything," Jean told me. "The thing is, at that time, they didn't know Naomi was going to be that big. He wanted it so badly, even if I asked for 30 percent, they were going to give it."

But they gave nothing, Jean says. And soon, the Osakas were gone, on to the next coach.

· · · · · · ·

Patrick Tauma, a Frenchman with roots in Guadeloupe, began coaching the Osakas as he started up his own academy, bonded by their shared Francophone Caribbean roots. "I saw a connection right away," Tauma told me. "The father was so cool and everything." Tauma said he realized how little money the family had when, after promising Naomi to make her Nutella crepes after a strong result at a tournament, he visited their apartment. "I brought food and everything and I cooked for her," Tauma recalled. "When I came to their house, I figured out how low-income they were. Two-bedroom with no dining table."

Tauma, like Jean, understood the family had no money to pay him for his work, but wanted a degree of financial security. "They didn't have any money, no problem. I say, 'The only thing is, I want you guys to sign a contract,'" Tauma said. "Of course the father would say, 'Oh, but come on, you're part of the family. We'll never forget about you. Come on, we're not going to do like other people. We're not like that.' I said, 'Yeah, but you know what? I really need it.'"

Tauma said he sent a contract to Leonard "a couple weeks" after they started, but it remained unsigned. "After months, I said, 'Hey, did you read the contract?'" Tauma recalled. "He said, 'Yeah, but you know, my wife is in Japan, you know, so she has to come back. She's busy over there.' Okay. A month after that: 'Uh, did you read it? Did she come back?' 'Yeah. But, uh, my attorney has a trial and everything, he's busy.' There was always an excuse."

Leonard, who had continued his filmmaking in Florida and did some freelance videography work there, made promotional videos for Tauma and some of Tauma's other players as a way of showing appreciation. Tauma said he worked to introduce the family to sponsors and agents so they would have the money to pay him, but they demurred each time. After a year of working without pay, and incurring expenses like hitting partners and physiotherapists, Tauma said he reached a breaking point. "I say, 'Look, I don't have any contract or anything—I feel vulnerable, and I need it, you know?'" Tauma told me. He then thumped down his hand on the table as if to show me the thud of his heart when he heard Leonard's reply: "He said, 'Look, Patrick, we're not going to sign the contract.' And I feel like he knew it [always], that he's not going to."

. . . .

The Osakas then went to veteran coach Harold Solomon in Fort Lauderdale. Solomon, a 2004 inductee into the International Jewish Sports Hall of Fame, had a small but robust academy; unlike Jean and Tauma, Solomon started his relationship with the Osaka family with a clear-eyed understanding and acceptance that they wouldn't be paying him. "I had already done well in my tennis and in other things," Solomon said. "It wasn't a big deal for us to not get compensated. We had other kids that we had on scholarship that were here, too; they weren't the only ones that we did that with."

Solomon was quickly impressed by Naomi's serve and forehand. "The power was incredible and the ceiling was really high," he recalled. "If you have two great shots, that's usually enough in tennis. And she's big, obviously, and she hit the hell out of the ball. I mean, she hit the ball *really* hard. She was a raw talent. She wasn't moving great at the time, nor in the greatest shape. But she was still young."

Tom Downs, a veteran Australian coach who worked for Solomon, focused on teaching Naomi to use more strength from her legs in her groundstrokes to generate power. But for Downs, tactical adjustments were just as important: Naomi, who once referred to her early mentality as "the queen of grinding," needed to play assertive, attacking tennis, which he believed would best exhibit her physical gifts.

"She really has some firepower and some serious weapons—but she's not hitting the ball, you know?" Downs recalled. "She's just making balls. Once she overcame that and started to play the right brand of tennis for her, well, she took off. And that was the main thing: getting her to use the weapons to physically dominate people—that was the terminology we used."

Ultimately, the relationship between Solomon and Naomi ended not because of insufficient funds but because he felt shortchanged by her effort.

"I had an expectation of what their end of the bargain was going to be," Solomon told me. "I'm tough about that. I wanted her to know that if I'm going to come on the court with you and spend time and take time away from other people, that I expect you to do the work. One hundred percent, all the time. Do the work."

When Solomon found Naomi's effort level repeatedly wanting, he reached a breaking point. "I'm out there with her and Mari and we're practicing and she's putting in what I would call a subpar effort," he said. "And I gave her a couple of opportunities. I said, 'Look, pick it up or I'm just going to send you home.' She didn't pick it up, and I sent her home. I said, 'Just go. I'm not going to waste my time on the court with you.'"

And so Naomi walked off his court, never to return.

Leonard called Solomon that night and told him that his younger daughter wouldn't be coming back. "She thinks you disrespected her," Solomon recalled Leonard telling him. "And I said, 'Well, I really feel like she was disrespecting me, not working hard the way she should work on the court.'"

Downs chalked the moment up to a culture clash between the

hard-driving American coach and his more reserved Japanese pupil. "I wish it hadn't gotten that far," Downs lamented. "I wish they had been able to figure it out, and I wish Naomi had been able to come back, because I thought we did a good job as coaches and I thought she was making some good progress. But anyway, she obviously became great anyhow."

FIVE

Early Start

Not only did they start playing tennis at three years old, but the Osakas were also early birds when it came to playing their first official professional matches on the International Tennis Federation (ITF) Pro Circuit. According to the WTA rule book: "A player who has not yet reached the date of her 14th birthday may not participate in any Professional Tennis Tournament." Mari played her first in July 2010, three months after her fourteenth birthday. But there was another less-known clause to the age eligibility rule that Tamaki had found: "A player's age is determined by her age as of the date of the start of a Tournament's singles Main Draw." Because tournament main draws were going to start on Monday, October 17, 2011, Naomi would be eligible to play in the qualifying draws that started the day before her fourteenth birthday.

With Naomi restlessly eager to play as soon as she could, the next thing to do was to find a tournament where Naomi could play when she was thirteen years and three hundred sixty-four days old. The only stateside tournament that week was in Rock Hill, South Carolina, about a seven-hundred-mile drive north of the family's Florida home. But the South Carolina tournament was *too* accessible for the Osakas' purposes: enough more experienced American players were likely to enter such that there wouldn't be any open spots left for an unranked player like Naomi. They needed to find something a bit more out of the way. Instead of driving north, they'd be flying about 550 miles south.

• • • • • • •

Richard Russell was determined to put Jamaica on the tennis map. There were no Jamaicans among the more than twelve hundred women in the WTA rankings, and only a handful of players from other Caribbean nations, so Russell, a patriarchal figure in Jamaican tennis, spearheaded a series of sanctioned professional tournaments at the lowest level—a tier optimistically dubbed "Futures" events—in Montego Bay.

The prize money on offer at Futures tournaments is a pitiful pittance: players in the qualifying draw earn no prize money and have to pay a $40 entry fee; a first-round loss in the main draw earns you only $98. Even the champion only receives $1,568, which might just barely cover her flight and expenses for the week. The more valuable prize that Russell's tournament had on offer was ranking points, which lured lowly ranked and unranked upstarts from around the globe to Montego Bay in hopes of getting themselves onto the WTA ladder. "We were very popular with players looking for an opportunity to play a tournament that wasn't so strong, which gave them an opportunity to pick up some points," he told me. A player at a Futures tournament could earn one ranking point for winning a first-round match in the main draw and twelve ranking points for winning the whole tournament. It pales in comparison to the two thousand ranking points and millions of dollars awarded for winning a major title, but everyone has to start somewhere.

Naomi Osaka was unknown to the others in the field when she arrived with her sister and father to Montego Bay, but her visible youth soon raised eyebrows. "The day I signed in for the draw, it was raining, so we were all chatting," Naomi recalled years later in an interview with Japanese journalist Aki Uchida. As the players packed together under the shelter, someone asked Naomi how old she was. When she replied "thirteen," under the legal ITF age, it raised eyebrows. "People were wondering," she said.

Russell said he could "just vaguely remember" Naomi at his tournament. Her height and visible strength at a young age, he said, left an impression. "Because of her age and her appearance, you could tell she was a very promising youngster. She kind of stood out from the girls."

Naomi's first opponent in the qualifying draw was another unranked player who had taken a very different path to Montego Bay. Twenty-two-year-old Anamika Bhargava had played collegiate tennis at Pepperdine University in Malibu for four years and decided she wanted to give professional tennis a shot before she gave up the sport that had been the center of her world since she was a young child. "I started playing when I was five, like most pros start playing, and then basically that was life," Bhargava told me. "Every day it was just what you did." Bhargava had dedicated her life to tennis since a young age; getting into a university—she got a full ride to Pepperdine due to her talent in the sport—was always the primary goal. "There was not an option to not do college," she said.

Bhargava, who was born in New York and grew up near Memphis, had played a few professional events as an amateur before college, but Montego Bay was her first stop in her attempt to make a bona fide pro career for herself after college. "A lot of us newbies went to Jamaica; it was the first tournament for a lot of us," she recalled. When the draw came out, Bhargava saw who she would play in her first match and went to google her first opponent; there was almost nothing to be found online when she searched for "Naomi Osaka."

But once the two took the court together, it soon became clear who Naomi Osaka was. "I remember getting out there and she just hit the shit out of the ball," Bhargava said. "And I was like, 'Oh goodness.'" Bhargava was used to playing against more powerful players than herself; her game was built on hitting soft dinks, chips, and slices that could disrupt her opponent's rhythm—a style often described as "junkballing" with varying degrees of affection.

Bhargava remembers Naomi doing an intense warm-up with her father before the match, but the thirteen-year-old seemed unprepared and discomfited by the awkward shots coming back across the net. Naomi started to miss more and more, but the match remained tight and competitive throughout. "I remember it being pretty close and just being stressed out—like, you can't lose to a thirteen-year-old!" Bhargava said. "She just hit the crap out of the ball, but she made a lot of mistakes." In the end, in front of what she recalled as "a handful of people watching," Bhargava prevailed 6–3, 6–4, handing Naomi a loss in her long-awaited first professional match. Mari, who had also made the trip to Montego Bay, didn't fare much better, losing in her second qualifying match. The two sisters would leave Jamaica with no prize money and no ranking points for their efforts.

Despite her ties to the region—Montego Bay is only about 350 miles west of where her father grew up in Jacmel, Haiti—it was the last time Naomi would play a match in the Caribbean, due to the paucity of professional tournaments there. "I haven't been to Jamaica since then; I really want to," Naomi told *Teen Vogue* in a 2020 interview about various firsts in her life. "But yeah, I lost that match, so I didn't really have the greatest memories."

Bhargava carried the momentum from beating Naomi throughout the rest of that week in Montego Bay, winning five more matches before losing in the final. It was a strong beginning but also a peak: Bhargava would only make one more Futures final in her career. Her ranking topped out at 608th three years later. After years of "lower-level tournaments in those random-ass places just to get some points," Bhargava retired from the sport at age twenty-five, having earned $22,009 in prize money in her three years on tour. "It's hard to give up something that you've done every day," she said. "You don't know what the next step is."

After she hung up her racquet and got a job working for a human resources firm in San Francisco, Bhargava kept tabs on the player she had faced that day in Montego Bay. "I never thought, ever, that she would be No. 1 in the world, but here she is," Bhargava said. The seeds of success were already planted way back when, she thought: "It's down to her smacking the shit out of the ball, and her dad being strict and on top of it and making it happen." As Naomi's career soared elsewhere, those who had been around her in Montego Bay took pride in remembering being there for her professional origin story. "We were pleasantly surprised, and very, very happy that a player like her came to Jamaica early and then became a world-class player," Russell said. "We were very pleased."

SIX

Sister Act 2

Even for those who knew nothing about the Osaka sisters and their origin story, the template they were following was obvious to casual observers. "When me and my sister used to train at public courts and stuff,
random people would be like, 'Are you the next Venus and Serena?'" Naomi
recalled years later.

The Osaka sisters eagerly embraced their respective archetypes: Mari,
the older sister, rooted for Venus; Naomi, the younger sister, was a devoted
Serena fan. Differences between the families were apparent, but the two
pairs of sisters had one intrinsic thing in common: like Venus and Serena
before them, Mari and Naomi were going to get compared to each other a
whole lot.

. . . .

Venus and Serena are regarded as the two best players in twenty-first-
century women's tennis so far, but, to the surprise of many early observers,
not in that order. When Venus first gained national media attention in the
early 1990s, Serena was usually mentioned late in articles as an after-
thought, if at all. Even those who watched them up close were reliably more
impressed by Venus at an early age.

Rick Macci, who moved the family to Florida to train at his academy,
told me he was convinced, because of both her physicality and mentality,
that Venus was going to be the more successful Williams. "Venus—and I
tell people this all the time—I think she could have been the best of all

time," he said. "She had gifts from above that Serena didn't. The next female Michael Jordan: her jumping ability was amazing and her wingspan . . . I would have taken any bet Serena was not going to be better than Venus."

Though the attention Venus garnered was massively larger than anything the Osakas got as children, Mari similarly got far more attention and expectation than her younger sister. "When she was young, Naomi didn't seem to stand out as talented in tennis compared to her older sister," Tamaki wrote in *Through the Tunnel*.

Bill Adams, one of the first coaches the Osakas worked with in Florida, said Mari was the clear focus when the family first came to him. "It was all about Mari," he said. "Naomi was not even on the radar."

Johnnise Renaud, who often trained alongside the Osakas at Adams's courts, said that there was no doubt that Mari was "the forefront" and Naomi was "not the main focus," due in large part to her lackluster results at youth tournaments. "Naomi used to just be sitting on the sideline: she used to be getting out in the first round while me and Mari were going deeper into the tournaments," Renaud said.

Christophe Jean, who coached the Osakas for years, said that Mari's playing style appealed to him more when he worked with them. "She was my best player at that time," Jean said of Mari.

Being underestimated, Naomi has said, lit a fire in her. "When I was a kid, people didn't really think that I was going to be good, so I always felt like I had to prove people wrong," she said. "And I guess that just carried on into my adult life. I would say I definitely realized [that motivation] pretty young, and I wasn't sure if it was going to be a good thing or a bad thing."

* * * * * * *

There was another—perhaps superficial—reason why Naomi wasn't judged to be a top prospect as a child. "She was actually a bit out of shape; she was the chunky girl back then," Renaud said. "The baby weight, honestly, it was everybody's main concern."

Jean was more blunt in a 2019 interview with the *South Florida Sun*

Sentinel. "She was fat," Jean said of Naomi, pointing to a corner where Naomi often plopped down. "She'd sit right there, tired. The dad told me she ate a lot. I run a tough program. I had them do a lot of running, a lot of exercise."

Renaud said she saw an eventual transformation in Naomi. "As the time went on, she just lost the baby weight and just sprouted out," she said.

Beyond her physical appearance, Adams said he'd had foundational doubts about Naomi's interest in becoming a tennis player. "As a matter of fact, I saw her recently once and I said, 'Naomi, you know, at the beginning I thought you did not like tennis,'" Adams told me. "I'm a coach, you know? You can tell when a kid is on the court if they show that enthusiasm, that drive. No, no. I didn't see that."

· · · · · · ·

Though Venus was perhaps more physically gifted than Serena, their parents said Serena would ultimately grow up to be the better player because of her fire. "She's meaner," their mother, Oracene Price, said in 1999. "Venus is more controlled. Serena can be very calculating if you do anything to her. She won't forget it. She'll pop you."

That popping was sometimes literal. "You've got to understand, Serena is the most brutal competitor ever," Venus and Serena's early coach Rick Macci said. "I mean, she pushed people out of the way to get a drink. When we played tag in the sandpit the first time—we had forty kids in a sandpit—Serena went in there playing tag with a closed fist! I go, 'Hey, Meek, whoa, whoa, whoa! You gotta play with an open hand!'" As she matured, Macci said, Serena learned to refine that rage into the competitive fuel that rocket-powered her career.

None of Serena's wrath was aimed in Venus's direction, however, which fit with how the family wanted to be seen as an unbreakable unit. The story the family wanted to tell was the Williams Family vs. the World, not Venus vs. Serena. That choice was consistent with how Venus and Serena themselves had coexisted on the tour. Promoters hyped up the battles between the sisters as the ultimate showdown, but instead of their matches against each other having something extra, viewers usually found they had something less.

"It was hard for both of them," Macci told me. "If they played full tilt, it'd be the Greatest Show on Earth. But it wasn't because the intensity wasn't there. They weren't ripping the ball. They weren't going for the jugular. And when they played, the matches weren't that great because at the end of the day, they felt both of them won. And usually when you play, you hate to lose more than when you want to win, and you just never saw that when they played."

It was not seen on-screen, either. From Aeschylus to Shakespeare to *Succession*, sibling rivalries have reliably ratcheted up the stakes in many of the greatest real and fictional dramas of history. But when the Williams family produced their 2021 origin-story film, *King Richard*, they conspicuously omitted from the script any notion that Venus and Serena would ever have to battle against each other, denying each other trophies.

Even when they weren't across the net from each other, there was rarely (if ever) any playful sisterly friction at any point in Venus and Serena's public lives. They spoke of each other, as people and players, only with the utmost respect, reserve, and reverence.

For as closely as the Osaka family had worked to follow the Williams blueprint, this was not at all the case with Mari and Naomi. Naomi refused, as younger siblings often do, to cede any territory to Mari. In her book, Tamaki tells a story of the girls getting into a fistfight because Naomi thought Mari took more than her fair share of some smoked salmon. The household competitiveness is also on display in one home movie their mother filmed of her daughters hitting golf balls at a Florida driving range. "Can I play with your wood?" twelve-year-old Mari asks ten-year-old Naomi. "It will just take a second." Naomi shakes her head; she has no interest in sharing. Naomi hits her next shot, turns to her mother, and smiles. "Golf is fun!" Naomi says as she watches her ball. The camera then pans to her sister. "Let's see what Mari can do," Tamaki narrates. Mari, still visibly bothered, swings her club hard into the ground before it reaches the tee, knocking the ball forward by only a few yards. "I can't believe it," Tamaki whispers in unfiltered shock before stopping her recording to give a forlorn Mari some tips.

From the moment they first cracked onto the tour, Mari and Naomi traded barbs of varying degrees of playfulness. And like the Williamses, the younger Osaka was the "meaner" one. At her very first WTA tournament, Naomi was asked if she had a "rivalry" with her sister and responded witheringly. "It's not a rivalry, because I'm obviously better!" Naomi replied. "But she can try. I feel like she thinks she can get better, but I'm obviously going to win all the time, which is sad. But she keeps trying!"

Naomi hasn't shied away from claiming Serena's role as the "meaner" sister, which she said could be an advantage on court. "I felt like she was always a bit too nice," Naomi once said of Mari as a player. "Like, I'm the mean sister; she's the nice sister. There were always situations where I thought she was really nice . . . If an opponent cheats, she wouldn't cheat back, that sort of thing."

Naomi's willingness to play dirty extended to her sister, as she explained in 2016 when recapping a recent "roasting battle" the two sisters had over text. "Basically we were dissing each other, and so I just kept posting pictures of her," Naomi said. "Like, the most unflattering pictures ever. Then after a while she stopped responding. I think I hurt her feelings. But, yeah, we're still like best friends and whatever."

Mari seemed able to disregard Naomi's teasing without it wounding her. As Elena Bergeron of *The New York Times* wrote in 2020, Mari likened Naomi "to the character Stewie Griffin, from the animated TV show 'The Family Guy,' whose malevolent genius is subverted by the constraints of being a baby."

· · · · · · ·

Because Mari was older, she began every phase of her tennis journey first. With her parents largely flying blind as first-time coaches of a young tennis player, they learned by trial and error. By the time Naomi began competing in tournaments, she benefited from a more experienced and patient version of her parents than Mari had endured.

In *Through the Tunnel,* Tamaki wrote that Leonard struggled to accept Mari's losses when she first began to play tournaments, quoting him saying things like "Why did you make the same mistake over and over again? Good players make adjustments the second time. Why don't you attack your opponent's weak points?"

"No one loses because they want to lose," Tamaki wrote. "I stopped him because I thought of Mari's feelings, being rubbed with salt on her wounds by him continuing to preach to her when she was more shocked than anyone else, both in the car on the way home and after we got home."

Tamaki said Leonard was resistant to her protests but that eventually his methods softened, waiting to show videos of matches during practice sessions rather than tearing into his daughter fresh after a loss. By the time Naomi was playing, their methods had improved. "There have been many times when we tried it out with Mari and modified it with Naomi," Tamaki wrote. She feared, however, that the change may have come too late: "I have mixed feelings when I think that the criticism he gave back then still leaves a scar on Mari's heart."

As an adult, Naomi recognized that she had a different experience as the one who got to follow in her sibling's path. "I do think my parents were more relaxed on me than my sister," Naomi said in 2019. "I was sort of left to my own, in a way, so I could explore more than she could. My sister would definitely say I'm spoiled."

* * * * * * *

In their 2020 book *The Best: How Elite Athletes Are Made,* Tim Wigmore and Mark Williams collated several studies that showed the athletic advantages of being a younger sibling, including a 2010 study of seven hundred pairs of brothers who had played Major League Baseball. "Younger brothers were 2.5 times as likely as their older brothers to record superior career batting statistics," they wrote. "Overall, among hitters and pitchers, younger brothers played an average of 2.5 years longer than older brothers and in a total of 226 more games." The baseball study also showed that the younger brothers were bolder, more daring players, 10.6 times more likely to attempt to steal a base.

Many of the world's greatest athletes started as the second best in their family. Having an older brother to challenge himself against, Michael Jordan said, gave him the fire and ferocity that became his signature on the court. "I don't think, from a competitive standpoint, I would be here without the confrontations with my brother," Michael said on *The Last Dance*. "When you come to blows with someone you absolutely love, that's igniting every fire within you. I always felt like I was fighting Larry for my father's attention . . . When you're going through it, it's traumatic. Because I want that approval, I want that type of confidence. So my determination got even greater to be as good as—if not better than—my brother."

Naomi said many of the same things in a 2021 Nike video she filmed alongside Mari. "My sister has been a driving force for me," Naomi said. "The way my personality is, is probably a lot to do with her, because when I was little she would beat me every day."

"Yep!" Mari chimed in, stopping Naomi mid-sentence.

"You just had to say something," Naomi said, glaring with sisterly annoyance until Mari giggled.

"I feel like [losing to Mari] shaped my competitiveness a lot," Naomi continued. "It just made me really want to win all my matches. That is a job that an older sibling doesn't get enough credit for. So, definitely, I'm always really grateful for her, even though she's annoying most of the time."

After she reached the No. 1 ranking, Naomi credited Mari. "I don't think I would be in this position without her," Naomi said. "Growing up, we both pushed each other; she pushed me more than I pushed her, because I kept losing."

. . . .

Naomi lost a whole lot. TennisRecruiting.net has records of 268 matches Naomi played from age six to thirteen; the majority were losses: 121–147

(45.1 percent). Mari's record over a similar time frame was much better but not exceptional: 195–131 (59.8 percent).

Their head-to-head record against each other was far more lopsided: for most of their lives, Mari had beaten Naomi every time they played against each other in practice. The sisters also played two official youth matches against each other that were tracked by TennisRecruiting.net; Mari won the first 6–0, 6–0 and the second 6–3, 6–2. Two subsequent times they were slated to play each other in youth tournaments, Naomi was withdrawn before the match both times, citing illness. "In the win-loss record, she's up by like a million or something," Naomi once said.

But Naomi never let herself surrender completely. "I'm going to beat you tomorrow" became her daily mantra. Beating Mari, she said, was what kept her in the sport. "I don't remember liking to hit the ball," Naomi said. "The main thing was that I wanted to beat my sister."

The exact date when Naomi finally first won a set against Mari isn't clear; Naomi was either fifteen or sixteen years old. Nor is the score; Naomi has said it was 6–2 or 6–4 on different times retelling the story, which she has done often. But Naomi does remember it was on a green clay court, which gave her extra satisfaction because it was one of her least preferred surfaces.

Naomi was, by none of her own accounts, a gracious winner once she finally bested her sister. "Wiped that obnoxious grin off her face," Naomi told me in our first interview in 2016.

"I went home to my mom and I was bragging," Naomi told CNN in 2019.

"She gave me the excuse she was so tired from the other day; she didn't even do that much the other day!" Naomi said in 2022. "Honestly, that's my number one victory, like way before, like all the Grand Slams and stuff like that. For me, I'll count it as my best victory ever. And, I'm sorry, but she cried! Like what am I supposed to say? I told you I was going to beat you eventually!"

"I remember you made this face—the most annoying face in the world—that made me want to punch you," Mari told Naomi during a joint interview in 2020.

· · · · · · ·

When I asked Mari about the first time Naomi beat her in practice, which Naomi has repeatedly called an inflection point in her career, Mari understandably had less enthusiastic memories. "It was never really as intense as it could be because either she gave up when she was young or I gave up when we were older," Mari said.

The matches that stood out more to her, Mari said, were the two official professional matches she played against Naomi on the ITF Pro Circuit. The first was in the semifinal of a $10,000 tournament off Amelia Island, in the northeast corner of Florida in September 2012. The second was in the second round of a $25,000 tournament in Irapuato, a city in central Mexico, in March 2014. Mari said that the matches had come with instructions from their father. "The first time I won but my dad had told Naomi to let me win," Mari told me. "The second time he told me to let her win because he didn't want to see us fighting after the match. I still fought during, but I stopped myself most of the match. I'm not sure Naomi could have beaten me even if she wanted to in Amelia Island, but I knew that I could win in Irapuato."

Mari said she believed her father's pre-match instructions—the sort Richard Williams had been suspected of giving his own daughters on much bigger stages—were given to keep peace between the sisters. "We just usually fight in general 'cuz we're close sisters," Mari said. "My dad didn't want the road trip home to be constant arguing in the back seat, I think."

· · · · · · ·

Naomi also proved to be a winner when it came to the genetic lottery of their shared DNA. Just as Michael Jordan only reliably began to beat his brother once he grew significantly taller—Larry Jordan's hopes of being a top-level basketball player fell short when he only grew to be five foot eight, ten inches below his superstar brother's height—there was also a clear size disparity between the Osaka sisters as they reached their teens. Mari grew to be five foot five, six inches shorter than the five foot eleven Naomi reached. While Naomi's height and wingspan allowed her to more easily play a Williamsesque brand of serve-dominant power tennis, Mari's build limited her into being more of a scrappy, crafty counterpuncher.

Harold Solomon, who began coaching the Osakas after Naomi had already passed Mari in the rankings, said he had a blunt talk with Leonard about the diverging trajectories of his daughters. "She was getting a little bit better, but incrementally better compared to what was going to happen with Naomi," Solomon said of Mari. "I had a conversation with their dad about it. I said, 'Look, you have one that's going to be really good—and we'll find out how good she's really going to be, but she can be really good. And the other one works really hard and is really serious on the court, but she doesn't have the physical skills that the other one has. So there's going to be this huge discrepancy and Mari is going to have to deal with it.' And she did work hard, but clearly she didn't have the weapons. I mean, look at the size difference: you wouldn't even know they were sisters from the same family, the way that they're different in their builds."

Though Mari was still able to beat Naomi often when he watched them in 2014, Darren Cahill could see that Naomi was going to develop into the much better player with time once everything clicked into place. "You could see the upside potential, certainly, in Naomi's game: just slightly bigger, slightly faster, slightly more power," Cahill told me.

Mari's own game was more limited, but Cahill believed that the positive example she set on court helped mold Naomi into the champion she became. "We're all dealt the cards we're dealt with and we try to make the most of what we have," he said. "I couldn't fault Mari's work ethic, her endeavor, her attitude on the court, or the smile she brought to the court. She made it fun. I thought she was delightful, to be perfectly honest. And she might've been part of the reason why Naomi's been so good and been able to achieve what she's been able to achieve: because Mari's been the perfect foil for Naomi through the years, and the perfect friend."

Mari's struggles to break through, Cahill believes, may have helped to both ground and motivate Naomi, allowing her to "keep things in perspective and have an appreciation" for her own successes. "She's seen her older sister battle and do it the tough way and try to make a living out of the game, which is incredibly difficult," he said. "She's been able to come through and break through a little bit easier, but I think that's been able to keep her feet on the ground to a certain extent."

Naomi often acknowledges the many things Mari can do better than she can: She's a more skilled artist. She's a better dancer. She speaks more fluent Japanese. "For me, I've always felt like it's a bit weird, but I'm only good at one thing, and that's tennis," Naomi said in 2021, comparing herself to her sister. "I sort of chased this relentlessly."

SEVEN

The Dotted Line

The Osakas' dedication to the Williams' blueprint included copying Richard's unique decision to keep his daughters out of the elite eighteen-and-under ITF junior tournaments to keep them fresh for when they could make their debuts on the WTA Tour. Thanks to Venus's stellar success in twelve-and-under competitions around Southern California, the ensuing scramble to sign her, and Richard's reliably colorful interviews about their "Ghetto Cinderella" story, Venus's photo was on the front page of *The New York Times* when she was just ten years old. Speculation about what the Williamses could do—and when—swirled constantly through the early 1990s. "Ask people in the stands: fewer of them know the name of the number-five girl than know Venus Williams," Michael Mewshaw quoted an exasperated agent saying in his book *Ladies of the Court* about the 1991 tennis season, when Venus was only eleven.

Naomi has said playing against adults as a child paid dividends in her tennis. "I always thought it was really good that my dad had that mentality, because I feel like I got really strong in that aspect," she said. I was always playing against people that either hit harder or were just stronger in general."

But where the Williams' avoidance of the junior circuit increased the mystery and intrigue around them before their big-stage debuts, the Osakas taking of that path only ensured their obscurity. Neither daughter had anything close to Venus's undefeated record in youth tournaments as a calling card, and neither was lighting it up in the pros. Nor did Leonard or Tamaki have the bravado that Richard had used to hook agents and media. Outside of the circle of coaches they had worked with and the players they encountered at low-level tournaments, no one in tennis knew who they were.

Without affiliation with a major academy or national federation, the Osakas were unsupported and isolated. The cold emails Tamaki sent to potential agencies, sponsors, and equipment makers went unanswered. "I asked here and there, but the answer was 'No' or I was ignored," Tamaki wrote in *Through the Tunnel*. "I didn't get a single good answer."

Eventually, her persistence paid off. When Tamaki got rejected by the American division of the Japanese racquet maker Yonex, she mailed a handwritten letter directly to the president of Yonex's head office in Japan, Tsutomu "Ben" Yoneyama (son of Yonex founder Minoru Yoneyama).

Tamaki's letter become a part of Yonex lore. "Tamaki was desperate and she [conveyed] that spirit by writing that letter," Nori Shimojo, current president of Yonex USA, told me. "Ben Yoneyama started to think, in this era of email, phones, and stuff, she actually wrote a handwritten letter to me saying, 'Please support us.' And then it's a Japanese company, and they are Japanese, also."

Yoneyama contacted Hiroaki Ebihara, then head of the American division, ordering Yonex USA to help "the mother of a tennis player named Osaka-san." The deal did not provide direct financial compensation, but the free and discounted Yonex goods were a crucial lifeline. "It wasn't a big amount of support at the time, but thanks to the racquets and shoes and the many T-shirts, we managed to survive this period," Tamaki wrote.

To take the next step, Tamaki's younger daughter would have to show what she could do with those racquets.

• • • • • • •

One idle day in the spring of 2013, Daniel Balog, an intern at the McLean, Virginia, office of the global sports management company Octagon, was scrolling through the recent results of one of his agency's most promising clients, the Swiss wunderkind Belinda Bencic. As a sixteen-year-old competing in 18-and-under tournaments, Bencic dominated the world, reeling off a thirty-nine-match win streak that included the girls' singles titles at both the French Open and Wimbledon.

Bencic was also flying up the charts of the professional ranks in 2013, taking her ranking inside the Top 200. But amid the ascent, which included several wins against players ranked inside the Top 100, one curious loss stood out to Balog: an incongruous 6–3, 6–3 defeat in the first round of a small pro tournament in Alabama to a player ranked 1,024th.

This player was seven months younger than Bencic. But unlike Bencic, to Balog's perplexity, she had never played a single ITF junior match, nor had anything ever been written about her in any publication he could find. "I'm like, 'Okay, who is this girl who beats Belinda Bencic?'" Balog recalled asking himself after the internet could provide no satisfying answers. So he set about digging deeper, to see if he could find out anything about this mysterious Naomi Osaka.

* * * * * * *

The win over Bencic would become the fifteen-year-old Naomi's calling card, but her day at Alabama's Pelham Racquet Club hadn't begun auspiciously. Despite being scheduled for a late match, Naomi hadn't eaten anything since breakfast and found her stomach growling as her match approached. "I was just thinking to myself, 'Wow, I'm kind of hungry,'" Naomi recalled. "Should I be going into this match hungry?" She and her father decided that no, she should not, so Leonard ran to a store and bought her some diced pineapple.

While unsure if she should eat, Naomi was well aware of what her opponent brought to the table. "I remember, like, other players at the tournament talking about her," Naomi told me. "She had a lot of stuff going on that I couldn't even comprehend," Naomi said. At a young age, Bencic already had the trappings of success: she not only had a clothing sponsor outfitting her in the latest Adidas apparel; she had five additional sponsor patches sewn onto those Adidas outfits, giving her the look of a NASCAR driver. "I was like, 'Oh, that's kind of cool she has that already,'" Naomi recalled.

Ivan Bencic, Belinda's father and then coach, told me they didn't think about Naomi at all. "Because Belinda, 'til then, she has beaten all, all, all the girls her age—so we didn't care about Naomi Osaka," he said with a laugh.

Despite disparities in their outfits and pedigrees, Naomi showed that she was ready for the moment. Playing on a green clay court without any ball kids or line judges, Naomi belted the ball past Bencic at will. Naomi's power, particularly on her serve, was new to herself, too. "When I was fifteen, I suddenly discovered that I was able to hit my serve hard," Naomi said. "Yeah, there was a time in my life that I was just hitting everything as hard as I could."

Naomi's onslaught left a lasting impression on Bencic. "I actually do remember that match—Pelham, Alabama," Belinda Bencic said with a laugh nine years later. "I remember she was already hitting the ball very hard—I mean, harder than you were used to from other junior girls. But obviously she was different because she didn't take the junior road, so she was already used to playing against women, more than me."

Naomi's power, particularly on her serve, was new to herself, too.

Ivan Bencic watched as his daughter had no answer for Naomi's newfound serving prowess, the likes of which she'd never seen from an opponent her own age. "Belinda was better in the rallies, but Belinda couldn't break her—no chance," he said.

Naomi finished the 6–3, 6–3 victory with a final break, cracking a backhand return crosscourt that left the outstretched Bencic staggering to her left, barely able to get her racquet on the ball. "Yehhhssss," Naomi said with relief and satisfaction as she walked to the net for the handshake.

"And, since then, we have known Naomi Osaka," Ivan Bencic said with another laugh.

Naomi would lose her next match in Pelham to Monica Puig, but for reaching the second round she earned nine ranking points, more than she ever had at a tournament. With those points, Naomi leapt more than 200 spots up the rankings, breaking into the Top 1,000 and passing hundreds of older players—including, for the first time, Mari.

Presciently, Leonard had mounted a camera on the back fence to record his younger daughter's match against Bencic; footage of his daughter's most powerful shots and her moment of victory against Bencic became the centerpiece of a sizzle reel he compiled later that year. But even just the score line from the match, flickering on Balog's computer screen weeks later, was enough to get Naomi the attention of a major agency for the first time.

. . . .

Once he learned the Osaka family lived in Florida, Balog tracked down a phone number for Tamaki and gave her a call. A few weeks later, Balog flew down to Florida to watch the Osaka sisters practice. "I still remember those public courts; they had cracks in them," Balog said. "The first thing that I noticed about Naomi was just this raw power that she had. She could hit the ball so hard with such ease. And at the beginning I was still a rookie as an agent, but I was like, Wow, that's pretty impressive." Balog, who had played collegiate tennis at Georgia State University, was quick to commit.

After the family had the contract reviewed by a lawyer, they signed. The Osakas were thrilled to have someone from the tennis establishment believe in them, he said, and Balog was thrilled to have a name on his nascent roster. "It was the first client I signed for Octagon," Balog told me. "My first tennis client was Naomi."

. . . .

It had taken Balog an unusual effort to find Naomi in obscurity away from the well-worn track of the junior tennis circuit, where agents lay in wait for the best young prospects to shine. After the frenetic first week of a Grand Slam event, most agents and sponsors spend the second week of the tournament scouring the outer courts for the world's best teenagers, listening for the most impressive shots, and watching for the most appealing looks.

As Balog began working with the Osakas, joining the junior circuit remained an open question. "We were debating: Should we play juniors?" Balog recalled. "Because all the brands would be at the Slams, typically. We were weighing out the pros and cons. If we go juniors, it might not go so well, then it could maybe hurt the chances a little bit. I remember that was the thought process, and I was fine with it."

With Naomi steering clear of the traditional junior avenues where sponsors traditionally did their window-shopping, Balog worked to make Naomi an attraction as best he could. During the Orange Bowl, the prestigious annual junior tournament in Florida, he invited sponsors to come watch Naomi practice nearby. "Let's tell the brands that are going to be in Florida anyways to come down and see Naomi, right?" he told me. "Let's do a little showcase." Representatives from Adidas, Prince, and Wilson came to watch Naomi, and Balog said many were impressed, but none were ready to pull the trigger on a deal.

EIGHT

Making Moves

I n 2019, when she was ranked No. 1 in the world and had earned tens of millions in prize money and endorsements, Naomi Osaka explained that she didn't think she was much better at tennis than her peers, despite what the rankings might suggest. "There's a certain point where talent isn't useful anymore, and from there you've just got to want to win more than everyone else," she told *Allure*. "I think that's something I noticed from an early age, so that's what I've been fortunate with. I mean, the way that I grew up and the circumstances that sort of surrounded me kind of forced me to think that way.

"My parents weren't exactly the richest, so what am I going to do?" she continued. "I'm not really the smartest. I've been playing tennis my whole life, you know? So there's nothing [else] I can imagine myself doing. It's either I have to be the best or I'm going to be homeless."

In the summer of 2014, that prospect had seemed very real.

• • • • • • •

In the WTA rankings for the week of July 7, 2014, Naomi Osaka had No. 367 next to her name. Her older sister, Mari Osaka, had No. 560 next to hers.

On a different database that week, their parents had COWE-14-006889 next to theirs, their new case number in the Broward County Court system for the family's eviction from their home.

The new owners of the family's Pembroke Pines condominium had given the eviction order to Tamaki Osaka and Leonard François in June, permitting them a month to move out. "Tenants fail and refuse to surrender possession of the premises to Plaintiff(s)," read the complaint filed on July 8. Two days later, an employee of Gotcha Legal Services, Inc., attached a copy of the eviction order to the entrance of the Osakas' residence.

Within weeks, Tamaki and Leonard had settled with their landlords, agreeing to vacate the apartment "without paying any rent, provided Osaka complies with the terms as provided herein. Osaka shall fully and completely vacate the premises no later than 3:00 p.m. on August 18, 2014. Osaka shall remove all of their personal belongings and all trash, leaving the premises in 'broom swept' condition." If the family failed to comply, they would be charged retroactive rent of $1,200 a month.

The sisters' tennis results hadn't been paying the bills. After losing in the first round of a small tournament in El Paso where she had made the final a year before, Naomi's ranking fell outside the Top 400. Mari still hadn't ever broken into the Top 500. Both were looking at long slogs ahead in the lower levels of tennis, and breakthroughs weren't anywhere in sight. Even though they took cost-saving measures like driving to tournaments as distant as Texas and bringing an electric stove to cook food in their hotel rooms, their earnings weren't nearly enough to cover their expenses: Naomi had made just $6,290 through the first six months of 2014; Mari had managed just $2,160. Neither had any paying sponsors.

. . . .

Tamaki, who controlled scheduling decisions for her daughters and closely watching the entry lists for all possible tournaments, had signed Naomi up for the waiting list for the qualifying draw of the Citi Open in Washington, D.C., in late July 2014, a tournament on the lowest tier of the WTA Tour. If enough players pulled out, Tamaki was hoping, Naomi would be able to get a spot in the qualifying draw of a WTA event for just the third time (she had lost in the first round of qualifying in both of her previous WTA events, in Quebec City and Tokyo).

But suddenly, Naomi started soaring up the entry list for a larger tournament that Tamaki had signed her daughters up for as a long-shot backup—a "reach" application to a place known worldwide for its tough admission rates. The Bank of the West Classic, held on the campus of Stanford University in Palo Alto, California, had attracted many of the best players in the world year after year. Top-ranked Serena was in the field, as were eight more players in the Top 20. Venus would be playing there, too.

But after the initial entry list, in which the last player into the qualifying draw was 194th-ranked Sachia Vickery, players started dropping out of the Stanford field at a rapid pace. Tamaki had already booked hotel accommodations for her family in Washington, but as Naomi continued to climb closer to making the cut for Stanford, she decided to reroute Naomi to California. Tamaki booked flights and a hotel room with two beds for the father and daughters to share; 406th-ranked Naomi and 542nd-ranked Mari—who would also make it into the qualifying draw—would share a bed before playing the biggest tournament of their lives thus far, with their family's financial stakes at their most dire.

"I wonder what would have happened if she had participated in the Citi Open in Washington, DC, as originally planned," wrote Tamaki years later in her memoir of the crossroads that would forever change Naomi's career. "I don't know where that fork goes."

. . . .

In her first qualifying match in Stanford, Naomi faced Alla Kudryavtseva, a 130th-ranked player from Russia. The daughter of a world-champion Greco-Roman wrestler, Kudryavtseva was most famous for having upset Maria Sharapova in the second round of Wimbledon six years earlier. While Naomi had only once before beaten a player ranked as high as Kudryavtseva, she prevailed 6–4, 3–6, 6–1. Naomi was the only one of the family to make it past the first round: Mari had gotten a more favorable draw, against 370th-ranked Marina Shamayko, but lost in three sets.

Naomi carried the family's hopes into the second and final round of qualifying, where she faced 197th-ranked Petra Martić. After losing the first set in a tiebreak, Naomi rallied for a 6–7(4), 6–4, 6–1 victory, thus earning her first berth into a WTA main draw.

Martić, an athletic Croatian who had been ranked inside the Top 50 a couple of years earlier, told me she only learned Osaka's age after their match in Stanford had ended, which left her even more impressed by her sixteen-year-old opponent. "She played smart: she would attack; she would hold back," Martić told me. "I felt like she was pretty mature for being so young then." More than Naomi's tennis, Martić said, she was struck by her aura, focus, and composure that day in Stanford. "She had that presence already then," Martić said. "You could feel her energy right away. It's something you feel on the court; it's hard to put in words. I felt like she was out there to do her job; she didn't care that it was her first WTA. If any other girl shows up and plays her first event, you feel the nerves, you see she's a little bit overwhelmed or something. And she just looked as if she's done it many times before. So I thought, Okay, not everyone has that."

The next day, Naomi would have her first chance to show what she had against one of the game's best. And for the first time, the world would take notice.

· · · · · · · ·

Naomi Osaka landed into one of the toughest possible slots in the stacked Stanford main draw: she was pitted against 19th-ranked Samantha Stosur of Australia, who had stunningly routed Serena Williams in the final of the 2011 U.S. Open less than three years earlier.

A thirty-year-old veteran, Stosur had a powerful serve and heavy forehand that were well known. Stosur, conversely, knew absolutely nothing about Naomi, whom she had never laid eyes upon. Stosur told me she only had some vague archetypes from her years on tour in mind before their match. "There's always exceptions to the rule, but you know the Czechs are going to have great backhands and Aussies are going to have a good serve and Americans are going to have good forehands, typically," Stosur said. "So, you kind of go through that. I remember seeing the draw against a Japanese qualifier. I hadn't watched the qualie matches or anything, and obviously had no idea who she was.

"And I thought, Okay, Japanese: she's going to be small—the typical kind of player from Japan," Stosur said with a laugh. "And walking out to the match, I was like, 'Uhhhh, this is not what I was expecting.'"

Naomi, whose curly hair was wrapped in a tight bun, stood five foot eleven. She wore beaded bracelets on each wrist and pink nail polish that matched her pink shorts, pink visor, and the pink collar on her black T-shirt.

As soon as they walked on court and the warm-up began, Stosur found herself going toe-to-toe with a player who "served bombs," matching and beating her own considerable power.

The raw force coming from Naomi's racquet drew gasps. Early in the first set, Naomi cracked a first serve that registered at 120 miles per hour on the courtside display screen, putting her in the top echelon of powerful hitters in women's tennis. Later in the match, Naomi boldly ripped a second-serve ace past Stosur's outstretched forehand, clocked at 113 miles per hour.

Despite being fourteen years apart in age and 387 spots apart in the rankings, and despite the fact that Naomi had never before faced any player close to Stosur's caliber, the match was a nail-biter. "You try and work things out in the warm-up and all that, but even then, it's not like she gave a whole lot of rhythm," Stosur recalled. "She served big, always tried to hit aggressive shots and line up that forehand. You could tell she was a good player, just still pretty raw at that point."

Stosur pulled ahead first, taking the first set 6–4. The second set went into a tiebreak, and Stosur earned a match point up 7–6. But Naomi saved it, and then won the next two points to level the match and force a third set.

Simon Rea, who was at Stanford in his first tournament as Stosur's coach, said he was struggling to see how his player could take control of the unexpectedly tight match. "I just remember reflecting as the match played out that there were no easily observable weaknesses, no obvious holes," Rea told me of Naomi's game. "And in fact, there was a whole bunch of weaponry that was coming at you off both sides, and on the serve."

Sometimes it appeared as though the occasion might get to Naomi: wanting to block out the moment and the biggest crowd she had ever played in front of, she draped a towel over her head, even while walking to and from her chair during changeovers. Other times, Naomi seemed preternaturally ready for the moment. When Stosur stepped back to give herself more time and space to react to Naomi's booming serves, for example, Naomi savvily started hitting shorter-angled slice serves that curved and zipped away from her opponent.

"I kept thinking, Well, Sam's class will ultimately prevail," Rea said. "Sam has the track record here, and she'll find a way through this match. And, she didn't. Naomi was, as we've seen, fearless under pressure, and backed her weapons with positive intent throughout."

Stosur took a 5–3 lead in the third set, but Naomi reeled off four straight games to take the match in dramatic fashion, clinching a 4–6, 7–6(7), 7–5 win.

Stosur remembers dazedly walking to the running track near Stanford Stadium to process the stunning defeat in solitude. "I was pretty upset and feeling a bit demoralized about losing to this unknown player," Stosur told me. "I was really like, Wow, what's happening here? And then, obviously, history has kind of proven that it wasn't such a bad loss after all."

As Stosur struggled to comprehend what had happened, those who spotted the score of the untelevised match were taking note of a new name who had just posted one of the year's most stunning upsets.

"Who is Naomi Osaka?" tweeted the British tennis writer Hannah Wilks. "Should I know? Is this a thing?"

• • • • • • •

When WTA communications manager Kevin Fischer polled reporters onsite at the Stanford tournament to see if there was interest in having a postmatch press conference with Naomi Osaka, he asked the room, only half jokingly, "How's your Japanese?" It was a pragmatic query: most players representing Japan on tour speak little English, often leading to interviews that don't yield much insight and are uncomfortable for both player and interviewer alike.

Fischer couldn't go into the locker room to find players as his female colleagues did. Instead, he spotted Leonard and Mari, whom he had seen sitting courtside, and asked them if Naomi would be able to do an English-language press conference. When they answered in the affirmative, Fischer led Naomi into the pressroom. Instead of having separate areas for press conferences and the media workroom, as most tournaments do, the Stanford tournament used the same room for both functions. So if any reporter sitting in the rows of tables glanced up from their laptops toward the far end of the room, they would have seen a sixteen-year-old girl in a baggy white T-shirt sitting at the podium, ready to formally introduce herself to the world's media for the first time.

"Questions for Naomi?" Fischer asked the room.

"How does that win rank in your career?" asked Doug Robson of *USA Today*.

"Um, do I speak into this thing?" Naomi asked of the microphone.

"It's probably like the second-best win of my life, probably?" Naomi began. "First being when I first beat my sister. Because I was like, 'Yeaaaaah, in your face.'" Naomi paused, then added an "Okay, yeah," to show contentment with her first answer.

"So the family win is bigger than the, heh, tour-wide win?" Robson followed up, already audibly amused and disarmed by Naomi's unexpected sororal savagery.

"You know, it's like every day, I'm like, '*I beat you,*'" Naomi confirmed. "So, yeah."

After a few questions about the match and her powerful serve, Robson asked Naomi about her obvious American accent, saying she sounded "like you've been spending some time in the U.S." Naomi explained that she had moved to the United States when she was three and now lived in Fort Lauderdale, where she had been coached by Harold Solomon for "a couple months."

"Is there someone else that's been more involved in most of your career coming up?" Robson asked.

"Not really, no—my dad," Naomi replied.

Another reporter then asked Naomi about her apparent comfort in this new environment. "You don't seem too wowed by the occasion," he began. "Is that because there's a belief in you that you can win these kinds of matches?"

"Yeah," Naomi replied. "I don't think anyone goes into a match thinking they can't, they don't deserve to be here. And I feel like I do deserve to be here, so."

"And what is your goal in tennis?" asked Bill Simons of *Inside Tennis* magazine. "What do you hope to achieve?"

"The cliché answer: being No. 1 and winning as many Grand Slams as I can," Naomi replied, sounding almost bored with the idea.

"Do you think you can do it?" Simons asked.

"Yeah?!" Naomi replied with a sudden exaggerated indignation that drew laughs from the room. "I take offense to that question."

"How soon?" Simon parried back.

"Um, hmmmmm," Naomi hesitated. "I feel like I'm being put on the spot here. How soon? As soon as I can. Is that okay?"

"That's great," Simons replied with a smile.

Naomi then answered that her family had moved to the United States for tennis and that she was originally from Osaka.

"Is it just a coincidence that your name and your hometown are the same?" Simons asked.

"No, because everyone that was born in Osaka, their last name is Osaka," she deadpanned in reply, drawing some stifled laughter from a few reporters, while others nervously wondered if that could somehow be true. "No, I'm just joking. I'm sorry," Naomi said, breaking the tension and drawing louder, relieved laughter now that everyone was in on the joke. "Yeah, it's just a coincidence."

"Your first main draw win; do you think you can carry that momentum further on?" Robson asked.

"Yes," Naomi replied immediately. "Period mark," she added, drawing more astonished laughter from the room.

"Do you think you're better as a tennis player or as someone working a press conference?" Simons asked. "Because you're doing an awful good job."

"Oh, okay, thank you," Naomi said, audibly surprised. "I'm not really good at talking, so I was kind of nervous."

Press conferences rarely prompt reviews, but Naomi received raves, with the gathered press gushing about her on social media soon after she left the dais. "Quite cheeky and brimming with confidence," tweeted Robson. "Absolutely hysterical," tweeted Tennis Channel intern Matt Dowell. "Naomi Osaka just absolutely slayed her first ever press conference," tweeted Courtney Nguyen of *Sports Illustrated*. I was in Washington, covering the concurrent tournament there, when I received an email from Nguyen with an audio file of the press conference and the subject line "YOU GOTTA LISTEN."

· · · · · · ·

Near the end of her press conference, after she had made one more last dig at her sister—"I was obviously better than her"—Robson asked Naomi whom she had admired while she was growing up.

"Serena," Naomi immediately replied.

"Why?" Robson asked.

"Um, because she's everything?" Naomi answered. "I just like how she's down and then she can come back and win, and you'd never know. I saw her in the room and I was like, 'Oh my Gaahhhhd!'"

Naomi had first laid eyes upon Serena Williams at Stanford in the tournament players' lounge. "I stayed away," Naomi said, betraying her shyness for the first time.

"Were you scared?" Simons asked.

"No?" Naomi replied, unconvincingly.

In an interview the next day, Naomi told *Sports Illustrated* that she was nervous someone would tell Williams about her idol worship. "It'd be super creepy," Naomi said. "I don't know how I'd feel about playing a tournament with someone who was like 'Oh my God.'"

But later that day, the two would indeed meet. Fischer, the WTA communications manager who had seen Naomi light up the pressroom a day before, brought her to a meet-and-greet event for VIP ticket holders to be interviewed by the event's emcee, Andrew Krasny. Serena, as top seed and star attraction of the tournament, was attending the VIP event as well, and Fischer was determined to introduce her to Naomi.

"She had talked about how she had always wanted to meet Serena, but she was shy, at that time at least, so she was never going to initiate that, I didn't feel," Fischer told me. "Getting them together, looking back, was pretty timely on-the-spot thinking, but then it was just a moment in time that was fun to capture. Serena was in a good mood; she normally was at the Stanford tournament, because it was pretty laid back."

The two chatted briefly; Serena asked Naomi where she lived, and they joked that their shared South Florida turf was a "great neighborhood." The thirty-two-year-old and sixteen-year-old also posed for a selfie together, snapped by Serena.

"Naomi may have wanted to throw darts at me because it really wasn't the way she would go about it," Fischer said. But though she cringed through the awkwardness she felt, Naomi was ecstatic. When in 2022 the tournament reposted footage of the two taking the selfie, Naomi replied: "Hahah I remember thinking that was the best day of my life [crying emoji]."

· · · · · · ·

Naomi took the court again the next day for her second-round match. Her opponent was the woman ranked one spot above Stosur: 18th-ranked Andrea Petkovic of Germany. The second-round match was Naomi's first time in a televised match, broadcast both internationally and on the stateside Tennis Channel.

"A very intriguing match," Tennis Channel announcer Ted Robinson told viewers as he began the broadcast. "A veteran who is back with a resounding French Open semifinal this year, Andrea Petkovic. And she takes on someone that none of us have ever heard of before, Naomi Osaka."

Courtside reporter Rennae Stubbs interviewed both players before they walked on court. "Um, truthfully, I'm just thinking nobody really knows me so I don't have anything to lose," Naomi told Stubbs. "But at the same time I'm trying to decide whether I'm excited or nervous."

Asked about her opponent, Naomi told Stubbs that she had "watched everyone here play," including Petkovic, but Petkovic understandably couldn't say the same of Naomi. "Well, I'm quite aware that she's a very talented player—if you beat Sam Stosur in a first round here in basically your first WTA match, you have to be special," Petkovic said. "So I'm very ready. I normally stalk my opponents on YouTube the day before; there was not a lot to find about a sixteen-year-old. But as I said, I'm very aware of how talented she is, and I'm ready and I'm going to try my best."

Petkovic was ready for the challenge indeed: the match lacked suspense. Though Naomi went through several spates of losing bursts of points and games rapidly, Stubbs and color commentator Lindsay Davenport found reasons for excitement at their first glances of the sixteen-year-old.

"She has *huuuge* weapons," Stubbs gushed. "I mean, once she gets everything under control and controls the nerves and all the excitement, you can see that she definitely can, when she gets a little bit older and more experienced, have some big wins."

"It just takes time to develop as a player," Davenport agreed. "Especially when you do have those weapons: how to use them, when to pull the trigger, especially at the very highest level. But you're right, Rennae, just to see the speed on the serve and the forehand that she's not afraid to go after, those are both great attributes."

"I know someone has really big weapons when I sit here and in the middle of the point I go, 'Wuhhhh! Wow,'" Stubbs said from her courtside seat. "And that's her."

Stubbs grew more effusive midway through the second set, when Naomi, who trailed 6–2, 3–0, began swinging more freely and unloading on her forehand at maximum power. "Keep in mind, that was in slow motion," Stubbs reminded viewers as they showed a replay of Naomi's eighth forehand winner of the second set. "What I've seen today from Osaka, there's not many players in the world that hit the ball—when she's in her hitting position—as hard as she does," Stubbs added. "I know that's a big statement, but . . . if she continues to work hard, and work on the basics, this is somebody we're going to see around for a long time."

Petkovic completed a 6–2, 6–2 win, and reached across the net to rub Naomi's shoulder, offering words of encouragement to her sullen opponent. Naomi then went over to the edge of the court, where several fans were waiting for her. "You don't see this often when a player doesn't win, still hanging around to sign some autographs," Davenport said.

"They're playing the futures market, those fans, wouldn't you say?" Robinson added.

Though it had been a routine victory on the scoreboard, Petkovic was left agog by the power from her opponent, particularly one forehand winner she had blazed across the court at over 100 miles per hour, an unheard-of speed in women's tennis. "Did you see her forehand?" Petkovic asked reporters after the match. "I mean, what the hell?!"

Petkovic gushed further in her press conference. "She's so talented," Petkovic said. "The forehand is just off the chain, and her first serve also. I think she was serving at 120 miles per hour—and at age sixteen, too! I'm not even serving that hard now, and I'm twenty-six. But I remembered myself when I was sixteen: you have great shots, but you can lose your focus for a few games, and you make some wrong decisions because you just don't have that experience. I knew if I just played solid it would be tough for her. But I think we're going to be hearing a lot about her."

· · · · · · · ·

Naomi Osaka left Stanford with $10,000 in prize money for reaching the second round, which very nearly equaled the amount ($10,005) she had earned in the entire 2012 and 2013 seasons combined. In their time of need, the sudden windfall would stabilize her family and her tennis career. There would be no future pay disputes with coaches. Naomi also earned eighty crucial ranking points, which catapulted her ranking up the ladder from 406th to 272nd.

But perhaps more importantly, Naomi's unique personality had left a mark on the tennis press corps that would keep them hooked for years to come, and her win over Stosur had earned the recognition and respect of the sport's best. When Naomi surfaced onto the main tour level a couple of years later, the best were already on the lookout for her. "I was like, Well, *I* know who this chick is," Stosur told me with a laugh.

Serena Williams, who had gone on to win the title in Stanford that week, said she had watched Naomi's win over Stosur herself. "I saw that match," Williams said in 2016. "She's really young and really aggressive. She's a really good, talented player. Extremely young. Very dangerous."

· · · · · · ·

When Balog arranged his next sponsor showcase, there was considerably more interest. Balog told brands that Naomi would be showing her stuff during the U.S. Open at John McEnroe's academy on Randall's Island in New York City. Nike and Adidas, eager for a look at this teen who had knocked out Samantha Stosur, paid for the cost of the family's airfare and hotel in Manhattan. Balog arranged three days of auditions for the apparel companies: one for Nike, one for Adidas, and one for Asics. This time there were more bids. Adidas—whose German reps were especially friendly with the German Balog—bid the highest, offering Naomi a deal worth $50,000 to $70,000 per year. "For that time, the offer was pretty solid—it was a good offer, I think," Balog said. "And the other brands were just like, Okay, if you have that offer, just take it."

· · · · · · ·

Before signing Naomi to a multiyear contract, the next step for Adidas was to kick the tires at its Las Vegas training facility. Unique among apparel sponsors, Adidas ran its own player development program to help its sponsored players in those years, hiring blue-chip coaches to work on improving the odds that their clothes were seen winning as many matches as possible, the sort of collaborative coaching work usually left to national tennis federations.

Darren Cahill, an Australian coach well known to American tennis fans as ESPN's best male tennis analyst, was one of the Adidas program's star coaches. Cahill had coached both Andre Agassi and Lleyton Hewitt and would later coach Simona Halep to major titles. Cahill knew little of seventeen-year-old Naomi (or eighteen-year-old Mari, who joined her younger sister in Nevada) before she arrived, so he talked to Leonard to get some background on his daughters. One of the things Leonard had told Cahill before they arrived had staggered him. "He said to me, 'My youngest daughter can serve 120 miles an hour,'" Cahill recalled. "And I went, 'What?' And he said, 'Yeah, she can serve 120 miles an hour.' And I said, 'Oh my God.' He goes, 'Yeah, that's the positive, but the negative is that she serves at about 15 percent of first serves in.' I started laughing and I said, 'Really?' He goes, 'No, she just cannonballs it, every first serve.'" Naomi's serve became one of Cahill's focuses, helping her remove hitches from her service motion.

What Cahill found trickier from a coaching perspective, he said, was talking to Naomi, who was "really quietly spoken" and didn't always seem to be engaged in conversations. "You didn't quite know whether or not whatever you were saying to her was getting through," Cahill said. "You would say something to her, and you'd walk away going, 'I'm not overly sure that she's really listening to me. I'm not 100 percent sure it's getting in.' Yeah, and then two days later, she would go, 'Hey, listen, that thing you said to me on the court—I was thinking about that and I agree with some of it but I don't agree with all of it, and this is why.' So yeah, she's a very, very deep thinker. She takes a lot of stuff away, she processes it, tries to get to the bottom of what she believes is right and wrong, and then she'll come back and swing around, either to challenge you on it or agree with you on it, whatever it may be. So there's a lot going on in her head—you could tell that pretty early on."

Learning about Naomi's mindset, inspiration, and background was a major component of the Adidas assessment, and Cahill said most of the insights he got into the family came away from the court. "It was more about getting to know them as people and as kids and as parents," he said. "Understanding what they're going through, asking a lot of questions about their background and how they got into tennis and what their dreams and goals are, all that sort of stuff." Despite their considerable gulf in pedigrees in the sport, Cahill was particularly impressed with Leonard. "I liked him a lot," Cahill said. "He was a really good guy and very down-to-earth and listened a lot. I asked a lot of questions, and he was actually quite knowledgeable on the tennis side of things . . . He certainly paid attention to what was going on; he'd seen a lot of coaches work with both players."

Naomi's match practice in Nevada came against both Sargis Sargsian, a retired Armenian ATP player whom Adidas employed as a sparring partner, and her sister. "Once we started doing the point playing and the competition stuff, that's when Naomi came to life," Cahill said. "You could see the fire in the belly that Naomi had, and away they went."

Seeing her in competition mode made the strongest impression on Cahill. "Everything I said about her as a seventeen-year-old applies now: you put her on a big court against a big player and a big match in a pressure situation, that's when she rises to the top," Cahill said. That's when you see the true greatness of Naomi Osaka come out, because she loves the pressure and she absorbs it well."

At the end of a player's visit to Las Vegas, Cahill was tasked with sending an "all-encompassing" written report to Adidas executives with his assessment of their strengths, weaknesses, background, family, and coaching needs. "Then I'd obviously give a recommendation as to whether or not it's someone that I think should be wearing three stripes," he said, describing the Adidas logo. "And for Naomi, that was a definite 'yes' . . . This girl's going to be a star. Whatever you need to do to make sure that you get the deal done with her, get it done because there is no limit to her. I think that she's got everything that you need from a young player to be incredibly successful."

• • • • • • •

After his enthusiastic endorsement to higher-ups at Adidas, who would sponsor Naomi for the next four years, Cahill was ready to recommend Naomi Osaka to a second major outfitter. While Adidas and its three stripes would be on her clothing, Cahill thought the thirteen stripes of the American flag would look pretty great on Naomi, too.

Soon after Naomi, Mari, and Leonard were leaving Las Vegas, Cahill called his longtime friend and ESPN colleague Mary Joe Fernández. Fernández, a two-time major finalist, was the captain for the United States team in Fed Cup, the international women's team competition. Cahill is Australian but had been close with Fernández since their playing days; living in the States on a green card, he also liked to help American tennis prospects. "I thought it was a good idea to let M.J. know that this girl was going to be a gun, in my opinion," he said. "I said, 'Listen, I've got this young girl in Vegas who is going to be incredible. I think the upside of her is she'll be playing Fed Cup for the U.S. one day. You need to make sure you put your arms around her and look after her and put her in the system, because she could be anything."

NINE

Rising Sun

At the 2008 USTA National Clay Court Championships in Plantation, Florida, a youth tournament for Americans only, Mari Osaka competed in the girls 14-and-under division, listed as a resident of Pembroke Pines. No one would have doubted the Americanness of the Osaka sisters: they were natural-born as American citizens through Leonard's American citizenship and had lived in the United States since their early childhoods. But once Mari and Naomi started entering professional events, for which players were required to list a single nationality on tournament entry forms, they consistently affiliated themselves with Japan. When Naomi had made her professional debut in Jamaica just before her fourteenth birthday, as a dual citizen who had lived for more than a decade in the United States, it was "Naomi Osaka (JPN)" listed on the draw sheet. That pivotal decision, which was reconsidered and pondered but ultimately never changed, had profound effects on Naomi's career.

"We were talking about that a lot," Daniel Balog, Naomi's first agent, told me of the dilemma of which country Naomi should represent. "We were thinking: In case it really takes off, which market is better? And we were thinking of the United States, I'll tell you. There was definitely a lot of talk about it."

What the Osaka family had done—moving to the United States in search of advancement and self-actualization for their children in a land of unique opportunity—would be seen as prototypical of the "American dream" trope that had gained popularity in the 1930s, when writer James Truslow

Adams defined it as a "social order in which each man and each woman shall be able to attain to the fullest stature of which they are innately capable, and be recognized by others for what they are, regardless of the fortuitous circumstances of birth or position." By these aspirational measures, the Osakas' tennis dream was classically American; so, too, was their geography.

But they had lived purposefully multicultural lives in the United States, and when it came time for the family to pick a side, it wasn't automatic that they would label themselves as Americans.

. . . .

As it was for immigrants of various vocations, the United States was a popular destination for overseas tennis champions throughout the twentieth century, with many of the best switching to representing America during their careers. In the amateur era, the champion Molla Bjurstedt Mallory switched from representing her native Norway to representing the United States midway through winning her eight U.S. Open titles, spanning 1915 to 1926, after marrying American stockbroker Franklin Mallory. More dramatically, an eighteen-year-old Martina Navratilova had defected to the United States early in her career after a loss in the semifinals of the 1975 U.S. Open, requesting political asylum so she could escape the Communist regime in her native Czechoslovakia, which was exerting strict control on her tennis travel. Navratilova won all eighteen of her major singles titles as an American. Other high-profile transfers to the United States came later in careers: both Czechoslovakia's Ivan Lendl and Yugoslavia's Monica Seles acquired U.S. citizenship and switched to representing the United States as their respective countries disbanded in the 1990s.

But after the Cold War thawed out, the growing number of players who moved stateside to chase their tennis dreams at Florida academies were no longer commensurately changing their allegiances along with their addresses. Most famously, Siberia-born Maria Sharapova moved to Florida at age seven with her father, Yuri, and has lived in the United States ever since. She fit in with the locals right away, speaking English with no trace of a foreign accent and acquiring major American sponsorship deals. But though many Americans suggested Sharapova would fit right in, she remained representing Russia for her entire career. "I felt like Maria shoulda-coulda have played for the United States," Mary Joe Fernández, the longtime U.S. Fed Cup captain, told me. "But, you know, we get some; we don't get some." Sharapova rarely played for the Russian Fed Cup team, and played few tournaments in Russia, but her successes at the Grand Slam events meant she remained one of Mother Russia's favorite daughters. At the 2012 Summer Olympics in London, Sharapova was chosen to carry the Russian flag in the opening ceremony. At the 2014 Winter Olympics in her former hometown of Sochi, Sharapova was picked to carry the torch into the stadium during the opening ceremony.

Sharapova said in a 2015 interview on CNBC that the idea of switching to represent the United States wasn't something she or her family had ever seriously considered. "I would have if I wanted to," Sharapova said, "but it's never been, actually, a question in my family or in my team whether I wanted to change citizenships." Sharapova, whose sponsor portfolio never relied on any major Russian deals, said she felt tied to Russia because of its "rich culture" as well as the childhood years she spent there that she still considered formative. "I know that for so many years I was shaped into the individual I was from those experiences," she said. "And not necessarily simply the country, but the people, the mentality and the toughness and that never-giving-up attitude."

Though she never wavered from her official Russian identity, her apparent Americanization was scrutinized and lamented back in Russia. In 2018, Sharapova posted a picture of her mother and herself standing with their arms around each other in front of an artwork at The Broad, a Los Angeles art museum: one of Jasper Johns's paintings of the American flag. The image caused strong, divided reactions from Sharapova's Russian followers, who debated in the comments if the image was unpatriotic or disloyal. "Masha is no longer ours," one Russian commenter rued. "She will never return."

• • • • • • •

After Sharapova, the USTA's reputation for laissez-faire came into sharp relief in 2013, when for the first time in the forty-year history of the ATP rankings there were zero American men ranked inside the Top 20. There were, however, several players inside the Top 20 who lived in the United States, including the dual-citizen German-American Tommy Haas and U.S. permanent resident Kevin Anderson, who represented South Africa. Haas, who had lived in the United States since he was thirteen, said he wouldn't mind being counted as an American to help shore up the ranks, "In many ways I feel like I am, so maybe you guys should, too," he said.

But Patrick McEnroe, then the general manager of player development for the U.S. Tennis Association, told me that persuading foreign-born players to join forces with his federation was not something he would do in his role. "I would love for Tommy Haas to be an American, but that's his call," McEnroe said. "I know that he thought about that a couple of years ago. But at least from my perspective with the USTA, I can tell you that we don't pursue any players that have that dual citizenship. I would never go to Tommy Haas and say, 'Hey, I really want you to play for the U.S.' In my role with the USTA, I wouldn't do that."

Katrina Adams, who served as president and chairman of the USTA for two terms from 2015 to 2019, similarly told me that it hadn't been the federation's "M.O. to go after players to make them become American citizens." Instead, Adams said, the USTA gave players space to make their own choices. "That's the thing about America: you can be who you want to be," Adams told me. "I can name twenty players that grew up and trained in America while becoming Top 5 in the world representing other nations. But you are who you are. And so, yeah, [Naomi] lived in New York as a kid, but she's Japanese. And that's who she represents, and that's her choice."

· · · · · · ·

As the trend continued, it wasn't just that foreign players weren't choosing to switch to America anymore in the twenty-first century; many Americans were choosing to replant themselves on other soil, betting they could blossom more fully in less crowded crops.

After his family fled to Jacksonville in the mid-1990s as Bosnian refugees,

Amer Delić became a collegiate champion for the University of Illinois and a successful ATP pro representing the United States, reaching a career high of No. 60. But late in his career, Delić chose to switch to representing Bosnia and Herzegovina, the land he had left in his early teens. Though ranked outside the Top 200, Delić was immediately the highest-ranked Bosnian player. He later became the country's Davis Cup captain.

Alex Bogomolov Jr.'s father was a Soviet tennis coach who moved his family to Miami to start a tennis academy, where his son developed into one of America's most promising junior talents. But after twenty years in the United States, Bogomolov was convinced by Russian tennis officials to switch back to the country he had left as a child, which was experiencing a major men's tennis drought. Bogomolov, ranked 33rd, went from being the fourth-highest-ranked American to the highest-ranked Russian. He acknowledged that he was coursing an ultrarare reversal of the typical Russia–to–United States defection path. "I see the irony: 'How can anybody switch back to Russia?'" Bogomolov said. "But that's where I'm from, that's where my family is from."

Monica Puig would not have qualified for the 2016 Rio de Janeiro Olympics had she chosen to continue representing her longtime home of the United States, as she had at the start of her junior career; Puig, a longtime Floridian, was ranked 49th when the cutoff was made for the 2016 Olympics, well below the quartet of top Americans who were taking the country's four allotted spots. But because Puig had chosen early in her career to represent her birthplace of Puerto Rico, the U.S. island territory that has had its own separate Olympic committee since 1948, she was able to secure a spot in the exclusive draw under the Puerto Rican flag. Puig made the most of the opportunity: playing the best tennis of her life, she stunned the field to win Puerto Rico's first gold medal in any event in Olympic history.* The United States won forty-six gold medals in Rio de Janeiro; an additional forty-seventh won by Puig for the Stars and Stripes

---

* Puerto Rican Gigi Fernández had won two Olympic gold medals in women's doubles in the 1990s, but representing the United States.

might've gained little notice. But playing for Puerto Rico, Puig was immortalized on the island as a sporting hero.

Even Americans born in the United States have been increasingly lured away in recent years. Ernesto Escobedo, a native Los Angelino with a booming forehand, reached a peak ranking of 67th in 2017, then the ninth-best among American men. By January 2023, Escobedo's ranking had slipped to 310th, behind twenty-seven other American men. But on his way to battling through the Australian Open qualifying draw, Escobedo suddenly became his nation's top player—because midway through the tournament his flag had officially switched to Mexico, a country with no other men ranked inside the ATP Top 500 in singles.

"It's always been in me that I wanted to play for Mexico, you know? Like, always, my whole life," Escobedo said in a January 2023 interview with Mike Cation on the *Behind the Racquet* podcast. "Even if I was born in the States, in L.A., I was raised as a Mexican. I was raised with a culture, a Mexican culture, with my family, and I've always enjoyed going back to my [family's] hometown in Zacatecas."

In many ways it was an obvious choice. Escobedo had told *The New York Times* he had been embarrassed to have the American flag beside his name after the racist, anti-Mexican rhetoric of Donald Trump had been a cornerstone of his winning presidential campaign; in one memorable moment during a November 2016 training bloc, Roger Federer asked Escobedo to explain to him how Trump had won the election.

The pull of ancestral homelands has been especially strong for many Asian-Americans. Born in California to Taiwanese parents, Jason Jung represented the United States until around his twenty-sixth birthday, when he switched to representing Chinese Taipei (the name used for Taiwan in international sports). "I was like 200-something and I still felt like I wasn't getting anything from the United States," Jung told me. "I just decided to make the switch because there was no downside." The upside was clear financially: despite not cracking the ATP Top 100, as a leading athlete from Chinese Taipei Jung has received sponsorships from major brands like Taiwan Mobile, as well as additional government funding. Those incomes

have allowed him to hire coaches and physiotherapists he couldn't have af-
forded otherwise, sustaining his career well beyond what its expiration
would have been as a U.S. player. "I've been able to stay out here longer,"
he said.

Washington, D.C.–born Treat Huey said being recruited to represent
the Philippines was "the greatest thing that ever happened to me," giving
an identity and foundation to his career as a Top 20 doubles player that it
would have otherwise lacked. "If I didn't have that money I was making
playing Davis Cup three times a year, maybe I would quit before I had given
myself a real shot to make it as a pro tennis player," Huey told me. "I've been
able to financially do pretty well. Even where I was for a couple of years,
Top 20 in the world in doubles, being from the United States there's always
better players, bigger names. So I still wouldn't have been a name in tennis
or really getting any sponsorships, whereas I've done pretty well kind of
representing the Philippines."

On top of the financial support,* the moral support from smaller countries can be meaningful, too. For players like Jung and Huey: having "TPE"
or "PHI" next to their names reliably attracts local fans from those large
diasporas to their courts. "All over the world there's Filipino fans that come
out and watch," Huey said. "I've loved the support everywhere I've played.
It's been absolutely a dream come true in that sense: I've always had a
built-in fan base."

Jung and Huey are two of several Asian-American players, including
the Osaka sisters, who have chosen to represent their parents' home countries instead of the United States, sensing that their accomplishments will
be more celebrated in countries where tennis success is rarer. "I think

---

* The financial support received abroad was only possible after repaying debts to the USTA, which in-
voiced outgoing players for the financial support they had received while representing America. Jung
said he repaid somewhere between $6,000 and $10,000 to the USTA when switching to Chinese Taipei,
money he said he never realized could be reclaimed. "They had some agreements from when I was thirteen or fourteen that I signed, saying I took some grants from the USTA," Jung said. "They wanted that
money back." Bogomolov had needed to pay more to switch to Russia, reimbursing $75,000 to the
USTA on his way out. Californian Ena Shibahara told me she had repaid the USTA around $20,000
when switching to Japan.

people understand the marketability now," Jung said. "Because if you're Asian and you do well in your sport, then you're kind of an icon. I think people realize that now."[*]

Indeed, two of the biggest icons in twenty-first-century Asian sports were tennis players, and their respective paths to fame and fortune remapped the tennis landscape into which the Osaka family would enter.

· · · · · · · ·

After China's Li Na won the 2011 French Open to become Asia's first major singles champion, she rapidly became one of the wealthiest players in tennis history. Sponsors, both domestic and international, sought to capitalize on Li's popularity in the untapped Chinese market, which had little prior familiarity with tennis. Li, who won the second of her two major titles at the 2014 Australian Open, was so coveted that Nike bent its long-standing rules forbidding third-party sponsor logos on its outfits—rules that were never broken for Nike megastars like Tiger Woods, Serena Williams, Roger Federer, and Rafael Nadal—in order to retain Li on the company's roster. The WTA Tour dramatically rerouted its circuit after Li's wins: many of the biggest tournaments were moved to Asia, including to her hometown of Wuhan, a revamp fans nicknamed "WTAsia."

Alongside Li, there was also a major East Asian success story in men's tennis that played a major role in the Osaka family's future. It began when Kiyoshi Nishikori, an engineer from rural western Japan, returned from a business trip to Hawaii with a gift for his five-year-old son, Kei: a small tennis racquet. That gift changed the course of Asian tennis history. After being scouted at a tennis tryout in Tokyo when he was twelve, Kei Nishikori received financial backing from a wealthy benefactor—Masaaki Morita, a former Sony executive—and was soon off to Nick Bollettieri's IMG Academy in Bradenton, Florida, moving there on his own full-time at fourteen,

---

[*] The phenomenon spreads beyond tennis: San Francisco–born freestyle skier Eileen Gu became one of the world's highest-earning athletes after switching to representing China before the 2022 Beijing Winter Olympics; eighteen of the twenty-three players on the Philippines team at the 2023 Women's World Cup were born in the United States.

a few years before the Osaka family moved to the other side of Florida. But whereas the Osakas would navigate the Florida tennis jungle on their own, Nishikori was placed on a precisely planned path to success. Nishikori had been sent across the world to fulfill Morita's dream of creating the best men's professional tennis player in Japan's history. The mission was called Project 45, so named because the previous best ATP ranking achieved by a Japanese man had been 46th, reached by Shuzo Matsuoka in 1992. Project 45 was given enormous attention and resources by Nishikori's management team in Florida. A fourteen-person team was assembled, including coaches and agents as well as experts in media training, mental conditioning, bio-mechanics, physical training, nutrition, and yoga.

Project 45 was a resounding success: Nishikori first broke into the ATP Top 100 when he was just eighteen, having won a small ATP tournament in 2008 in Delray Beach, Florida. After an elbow-injury absence, Nishikori surged past the target of 45th, soaring into the Top 30 at age twenty-one.

The reason for IMG's intense interest and investment in Nishikori soon became apparent: *Forbes* first listed Nishikori among the world's ten highest-paid tennis players in 2013. Nishikori, then twenty-three, had never been ranked inside the ATP Top 10 and had only one major quarterfinal to his name. But as a breakout star by Japanese standards, he was lavished with attention by myriad corporations from the world's third-largest economy. Nishikori earned $9 million in endorsements that year from his predominantly Japanese sponsors, sextupling the $1.5 million he'd earned in prize money.

The music industry had used the term "Big in Japan" for decades to describe acts whose success in the country far outpaced their renown in the rest of the world. The buzz around Nishikori's earnings—frequently outpacing global stars like Rafael Nadal and Serena Williams—showed everyone in the sport just how big being "Big in Japan" could be for tennis.

When Nishikori's results improved further—he became the first Asian finalist in a men's singles major when he reached the final of the 2014 U.S. Open and broke into the ATP Top 10—his endorsements grew even more outsized. By 2016, Nishikori was included in *Forbes*'s Top 100 of all celebrities: estimated to be raking in $33.5 million annually, Nishikori's earning power put him on par on the list with acts like Maroon 5 and Ed Sheeran. His apparel deal with Japanese clothing brand Uniqlo was reportedly worth more than $10 million annually alone.

"With Kei Nishikori back then, you saw that he was an absolute superstar in Japan," said Daniel Balog, who was Naomi's agent at the time. "Obviously the Japanese market is massive if you are very good, and they're willing to really get behind you . . . And it was less competitive on the Japanese side because she was the lone star. With the United States, there's so many good players, right? You'd compete against Serena, Madison Keys—so many. So I think it was a good move; I think it was great."

There were reasons for the Osakas to be reticent about the USTA, too, seeing what they had done to the most recent Black prodigy in their care.

· · · · · · · ·

One year older than Naomi Osaka, Taylor Townsend was still years younger than most of the field when, at fifteen years old, she won the 2012 Australian Open girls' singles title. Hailing from the South Side of Chicago, Townsend won matches and admirers in Melbourne with her unexpected retro style, playing a serve-and-volley game that she had modeled off YouTube clips of fellow lefty Martina Navratilova. Townsend wore a big white bow in her hair that made her look even younger than her fifteen years, and when she smiled widely after beating Russia's Yulia Putintseva in the final, her shiny metal braces sparkled as brightly in the Australian sunshine as her silver trophy.

On the strength of her win in Melbourne and other successes, Townsend reached the World No. 1 ranking in the juniors in April 2012. But while the numbers and viewers saw a potentially transformative star in the making, the USTA saw an urgent problem in Townsend: her weight. As first reported by the late great Tom Perrotta of *The Wall Street Journal*, the USTA had wanted to sideline Townsend, who was the uninjured top-ranked girl in the world, until her conditioning improved. The federation told Townsend to withdraw from its 18-and-under national champion-ships in San Diego—a win there would have earned her a wild card into the main women's draw of the U.S. Open—and to instead go back to the US-TA's academy in Boca Raton and double her fitness regimen. "Our concern is her long-term health, number one, and her long-term development as a player," Patrick McEnroe, then the general manager of USTA player devel-opment, told *The Journal*. The USTA also asked Townsend to skip the 2012 U.S. Open, where she was going to be the top seed in the junior draw. The paternalistic USTA didn't control entries for the Grand Slam events, however, and so Townsend entered anyhow, with her mother paying her expenses.

News of the teenage Townsend being benched by the USTA quickly drew outrage from the public, as well as players past and present. Navrati-lova, whom Townsend had idolized, said the decision was "so irresponsible" and reflected "horrible ignorance." Lindsay Davenport, who like Navrati-lova had been considered overweight when she first began on the tour, echoed her anger. "I was not svelte at fifteen, and I was not fit at fifteen," Davenport said. "If they had told me I could not play, I mean, that could have ruined my career . . . You're dealing with a really difficult age for girls, and you're talking about a life-changing, detrimental step. You cannot pun-ish someone for their body type."

Serena Williams, whose own weight had been frequently scrutinized during her career, said it was a "tragedy" what she heard had happened to Townsend. "For a female—particularly in the United States [and] in par-ticular an African-American—to have to deal with that is unneces-sary," Serena said in an interview the day after she won the 2012 U.S. Open. "Women athletes come in all different sizes and shapes and colors and everything. I think you can see that more than anywhere on the ten-nis tour."

Townsend went on to win the girls' doubles title at the 2012 U.S. Open, and the USTA agreed to reimburse her expenses after the blowback to their decision. Townsend began finding success at the pro level years later, but the negative attention on her body remained a lingering challenge for her as she tried to find her place on the pro tour. "The biggest thing was just getting her to understand that she's fine," Townsend's coach Zina Garrison said after she won her first pro match at a major at the 2014 French Open. "Everybody doesn't have the same shape of our bodies. She's very clear on that now."

The Osakas witnessed this story from the beginning: ten-year-old Mari had been invited to a USTA training camp in Los Angeles in September 2006, along with other promising girls players from around the country including Townsend; eight-year-old Naomi tagged along, too. The Osakas, Townsend, and several other girls were put in a group together and came up with a team cheer to the tune "Pump It" by the Black Eyed Peas: "Hit It (Harder!)."

But aside from the fun, there was also uncomfortable scrutiny of the young girls' bodies. One parent who accompanied their child to the 2006 training camp (and wished to remain anonymous) recalled the USTA publicly humiliating Townsend, then only ten. "When we went to that camp in California, they weighed them and took their weight and announced their weight," the parent told me. "And Taylor, I don't think she was happy about that because obviously she weighed way more than the other girls already; she was also taller. And then they just dropped her because she didn't fit exactly the physique that they wanted. I just think that's cruel."

* * * * * * *

Though the USTA would continue courting the Osakas into 2015, several people told me their minds were likely made up before then. Johnnise Renaud, who trained alongside the Osakas early in their move to Florida, said she understood the Osakas' nationality decision to be "an open question" in her time with them as kids but suggested that resentment of the USTA might have been planted early for them because of the lack of support the family received early on, a sentiment she said was common among

American tennis families who felt overlooked. "Your feelings are hurt," Renaud explained. "If you've done all this work and you go to a place and you feel like you are not good enough for them, you don't meet the expectations, . . . you feel like: Why would I play for a country that's not really helping me do anything for my career?"

Harold Solomon, who coached Naomi and Mari in 2014, was one of several people who liaised with the USTA on the Osakas' behalf once Naomi's potential was clearer; he pitched the Osakas to USTA head of women's tennis Ola Malmqvist months before Cahill made his own pitch to U.S. Fed Cup captain Mary Joe Fernández. Solomon told me he thought that the USTA offered too little too late and that the support the Japanese Tennis Association was offering proved pivotal at a time when the family was struggling financially. "Japan was willing to do more things for her at the time: get her wild cards into the tournaments and help them finance a little bit," Solomon told me. "They didn't have any money . . . It might have been the thing that pushed them to Japan."

Solomon said he thought the Osakas could have been up for grabs and convinced to switch to representing the United States, but the USTA had missed that window of opportunity. "I think if the United States possibly had stepped up at the time and said, 'Look, we're willing to make this investment, we're willing to do this or send a coach with her and help pay for her expenses,' I mean, there's as good a chance as not that they would have done the U.S. thing," he said.

The Osakas' choice of Japan surprised those within Japanese tennis perhaps more than Americans. After reading a brief report of Naomi's win over Stosur in Stanford in 2014, broadcaster Florent Dabadie asked Toshihisa Tsuchihashi, a colleague who worked for the Japanese Tennis Association and would later be the country's Fed Cup captain, about who this Naomi Osaka was. "He said, 'Well, we've been watching her, but we're not sure she wants to become Japanese,'" Dabadie recalled Tsuchihashi telling him. "'Actually, she's kind of American. We approached her, even her entourage, and we thought there was no way she's going to pick Japan. So we kind of let it go.'"

• • • • • • •

Even after Naomi had already played several Japanese tournaments in 2014 thanks to wild cards she had received from the JTA, she, her family, and her agent continued to listen to what the USTA had to offer. So when Mary Joe Fernández followed up on Darren Cahill's recommendation to set up a meeting, the Osakas were ready to impress at the appointed time and place.

As it had been when Naomi first auditioned for clothing sponsors years earlier, the USTA showcase was set up nearby an ongoing major tournament—the 2015 Miami Open—but this time in considerably more luxurious surroundings: Fernández booked a court for Naomi two miles south at the Ritz-Carlton on Key Biscayne. Under towering rows of palm trees on one of the resort's green clay courts, Fernández hit with Naomi to show America's interest in her talent. Fernández, then forty-three and retired from the tour for more than a decade, knew she wouldn't be able to keep up with the teenager's power, so she brought a friend and the two drilled with Naomi two-on-one, with the USTA's Malmqvist watching from the sidelines. Fernández recalled the session as being set up casually, "just to see what I thought, give her some advice or whatever," but she was immediately impressed by the power and mindset of the unassuming teenager in a baggy pink T-shirt and black leggings. "Oh my gosh, right away you could tell she had the focus and just that champion quality," Fernández told me. "I just remember how focused, how intense she was. She reminded me a lot of Serena, you know? And when I talked to her, it was all about 'I want to serve big, and I want to hit big.' You could tell early on that she had those qualities."

It wasn't just the USTA who wanted a look at Naomi that day: Fernández's husband, Tony Godsick, an agent who had recently cofounded his own agency with his superstar client Roger Federer, was courtside with an interested eye on Naomi as well. Adidas rep Mats Merkel also attended the audition and filmed part of it for a German tennis blog. "As you can see she is quite tall but nevertheless she moves pretty well," Merkel effused in his

German narration over the pixelated footage. "Her shots are very heavy. She can still improve technically, but there's a lot of potential and I'm very happy that she's at Adidas. Right now she's on court training with Mary Joe Fernández."

The USTA ultimately offered a package to the Osakas that included access to some of their top personnel. According to Perrotta of *The Wall Street Journal,* the USTA's offer included weeks of coaching from José Higueras, who was the USTA's director of coaching, as well as time with Pat Etcheberry, the leading strength-and-conditioning coach who had worked with players like Andre Agassi and Pete Sampras. "We talked to her and we offered her some really good services," Malmqvist told Perrotta.

Balog said the decision was still up in the air after the session with Fernández. "It was definitely still circulating," he said. "But in the end, we—or the parents, I would say—decided."

The decision, Naomi has said, was ultimately made by Leonard. "I don't know the reasons for his choice," Naomi told *L'Équipe* in 2018 when asked how she had chosen Japan. "You would have to ask him."

Leonard has offered various reasons why he chose Japan for his daughters. "My two daughters were born in Japan, where I was welcomed despite the problems that my wife and I encountered," he told *L'Équipe* in 2018. "That's why I wanted them to defend this flag, as a tribute."

When I first asked Leonard about the decision in 2016, he hesitated, then cited cultural reasons. "It is just a matter of like, at home and everything that she does, the culture," he told me. "She is more close to the Japanese culture, in a way. That's a little bit what she feels comfortable with, and due to the fact that the world is very global right now, I felt like it was something that would make her feel good."

Naomi, similarly, suggested Japan was a better fit for her personality and tastes when I first asked her about the decision in 2016. "In the beginning, it kind of wasn't me that decided," Naomi told me. "Like, it was along the way. But I just kind of like the food and stuff? And, like, the city is really cool, and everyone's really nice, so. And I'm really introverted, so I feel like I fit in more there."

Naomi demurred on a follow-up question about if there had been conversations with the USTA. "I don't really know; I just play tennis," she said, giggling. "So I'm not really thinking about the outside stuff. That's kind of more, like, everyone else."

When I asked Leonard about the USTA in 2016, he made it clear he hadn't been impressed by what they had put on the table. "We've spoken to the USTA a bit," he said. "But the situation wasn't really something that made us feel like we were going to— You know, it wasn't too much more offered, really, than the situation that she was in."

After Naomi won her first major title in 2018, and many in American tennis circles questioned how the USTA had missed out on a player like her, the Osaka family explained their decision in an email to *The Wall Street Journal*. "We made the decision that Naomi would represent Japan at an early age," they wrote. "She was born in Osaka and was brought up in a household of Japanese and Haitian culture. Quite simply, Naomi and her sister Mari have always felt Japanese so that was our only rationale. It was never a financially motivated decision nor were we ever swayed either way by any national federation."

The USTA's loss would prove to be Japan's gain. "Obviously, we would've loved for her to play for the U.S.—she spent so much time in Florida," Fernández told me. "I totally understand her decision to play for Japan, but that would have been great if I had her on my team."

Soon, Naomi's chosen Japanese identity would open the door to a unique showcase, putting her back on the world stage.

Rising Star

By September 2015 it had been more than a year since Naomi Osaka's delightful debut in Stanford, and she hadn't done much to catch the attention of the tennis world since. Naomi had made steady progress, to be sure: she had reached the finals of two ITF Pro Circuit events (the level below the WTA Tour), played in the qualifying draw of a major for the first time (at Wimbledon and the U.S. Open), and cracked the Top 200 of the WTA rankings for the first time. But understandably given her modest ranking—and the tennis world's preoccupation with Serena Williams's quest for the Grand Slam—Naomi's steady but unspectacular progress wasn't gaining notice in 2015. That was going to change by year's end, however: not with the power of the ball but the ballot.

For the second year, the WTA was asking fans to vote on which four young players they wanted to see compete at a new "Rising Stars" showcase. In a statement announcing the 2015 Rising Stars event, WTA chief executive Stacey Allaster said the WTA wanted the sport's "young talent . . . to experience the WTA's grand stage, bringing the fans along to be a part of the journey."

The "grand stage" Allaster was describing was the tour's year-end championships, the WTA Finals, an exclusive round-robin tournament reserved just for the season's top eight players. As part of an investment in the Asian market, the WTA Rising Stars event had first been held a year earlier upon the WTA Finals' relocation to Singapore. Allaster had staked much of the tour's future on growth in Asia, but her "WTAsia" strategy had suffered a blow just before the first Singapore edition of the tournament in 2014: Li Na, the Chinese champion whose massive stardom had altered the orbit of the WTA calendar, retired from the sport, leaving the WTA committed to a rapidly growing footprint in Asia without a bona fide Asian star on the singles circuit. In order to reseed the soil of their new terrain, the WTA reserved two of the four spots in its new Rising Stars competition for the Asia Pacific region.

Drawing on her father's video editing skills, Naomi and her family campaigned for votes from Japan and beyond for both the 2014 and 2015 Rising Star events. In their first attempt, Naomi spoke in English (with Japanese subtitles appearing below her) as she rode on a train from Tokyo to Kofu. "Please vote for me to go to Singapore," Naomi said. "You can vote multiple times, so . . . just vote once every five seconds and then I'll be good." After that attempt fell short, the family made multiple videos the next year, in both English and Japanese. Naomi made the case for herself by holding a plush Pikachu and a colorful sign that read WTA RISING STARS NAOMI OSAKA. In a second 2015 video, bright purple sparkles flashed onscreen behind #WTARISINGSTARS and #NAOMIOSAKA, a nod to the social media hashtags that the WTA would count as votes.

When voting began on September 8, during the second week of the 2015 U.S. Open, 202nd-ranked Naomi was both the youngest and lowest-ranked of the seven nominees representing the Asia Pacific region. After the more than two million overall votes were tallied in early October, Naomi was a winner, officially a Rising Star on her way to Singapore.

. . . .

Naomi turned eighteen between the close of voting and her arrival to Singapore. That milestone freed her from the restrictions of the WTA's age eligibility rules, but she was still by far the youngest of the four players selected for the Rising Stars event. She was completely inexperienced with the various promotional activities she was roped into in Singapore, including a pretournament player party, which forced her first foray into red-carpet fashion. Naomi would headline the Met Gala seven years later, but her first attempt at gussying up for the cameras was inauspicious and exhausting. "I don't usually dress up and, like, wear high heels," Naomi explained later that week. "I stayed awake until 11:00, and I usually go to sleep at 9:00. So I was kind of, like, really tired." Naomi's outfit for the player party had been enthusiastically picked out by her mom and sister before her trip. "I was kind of surprised that it was good looking," Naomi said of the dress Mari had picked for her. "No, seriously though, she's kind of Harajuku style; it's all over the place."

Naomi also had a second chance to encounter a Williams sister in Singapore, this time meeting Venus, who was standing by at the tournament as an alternate (Serena was still ranked No. 1, but she shut down her 2015 season after a crushing upset loss to Roberta Vinci in the U.S. Open semifinals, which dashed her dreams of completing the Grand Slam). Though she had met Venus briefly before in Stanford, Naomi once again found herself speechless in the presence of one of her heroes, saying she was "just kind of creeping her out" with "the void that I left because I wasn't opening my mouth. "She was like talking and then I was like, 'Uh-huh, yeah, uh-huh,'" Naomi recalled of meeting Venus. "I don't really remember what we talked about because I was, like, really freaked out."

While the brief encounter with Venus left her starstruck, the promotional activities arranged for the quartet of rising stars gave Naomi her first significant occasion to spend time with other professional players beyond her sister. The other three players—Caroline Garcia, Ons Jabeur, and Zhu Lin—were all in their early twenties, and all had played the junior circuit. Naomi, who was three years younger than the rest and had skipped the junior circuit, arrived to Singapore as a complete unknown to them.

Jabeur, an effusive extrovert from Tunisia who had broken boundaries as the first Arab girl to win a major junior title when she won the 2011 French Open, made it her mission to "crack the code" with this quiet new person and her equally quiet father, who had accompanied her on the trip. "You know me, I like to joke with everyone, and when I see someone is shy,

I kind of push a little bit, try to make her laugh or something," Jabeur told me years later.

When Naomi was asked four years later about her memories of the Rising Stars event, it was Jabeur making the effort to get to know her that stood out. "To be honest, I just remember Ons—she was just talking to me nonstop," Naomi said. "I'm really grateful for her because, like, the amount of shyness that I am right now, back then it was way worse. For me, Singapore is Ons."

· · · · · · · ·

Since the invitational event did not count as an official tournament, matches in the Rising Stars tournament were played in an experimental format: a set could be won with four games instead of six, and coaches were allowed to sit on court throughout the match to provide constant advice to their player. Round-robin matches between the four players were played in the days leading up to the WTA Finals, on a small court about a ten-minute walk away from the main arena. Small but enthusiastic crowds of a few hundred attended most sessions. Naomi lost her first two matches against Garcia and Jabeur, but they were competitive three-setters. In her final round-robin match against Zhu, Naomi prevailed in a third-set tiebreak.

Unexpectedly for Naomi, her record of one win and two losses was enough to advance her to the finals; Zhu and Jabeur had also gone 1–2, but they had each suffered a straight-set loss, so Naomi advanced to the final for a rematch against Garcia, who had gone 3–0.

Caroline Garcia was, easily, the cream of the crop of the Rising Stars in Singapore and was almost certainly overqualified for the event. "The girl sharapova is playing is going to be number one in the world one day," Andy Murray famously tweeted as a seventeen-year-old Garcia led Maria Sharapova in the second round of the 2011 French Open. "caroline garcia, what a player u heard it here first." Garcia was twenty-two years old and ranked 35th in the world when she came to Singapore, down slightly from her career-high of No. 25. She had beaten Top 10 players seven times already in her career, had already won her first WTA singles title the year before in Bogotá, and had also qualified for the actual WTA Finals in doubles.

So when Garcia ran through the Rising Stars round-robin play undefeated, no one was surprised. Nor were they surprised when Garcia raced out to a 3–0 lead to start in the Rising Stars final against Naomi, which was the first match of the sidebar competition held in the main, twelve-thousand-seat Singapore Indoor Stadium, by far the biggest venue in which Naomi had ever played. "In the very beginning I was really nervous because it was really big," Naomi said. "Like, I've never even practiced on that court before, so just being there, I was really nervous."

But after a few games of one-way traffic against her, Naomi settled into the match. She leveled the first set at 3–3 before Garcia won it 5–3. In the second set, Garcia had four match points, but Naomi fended them each off, ultimately taking the second-set tiebreak 8-6 before running away with the third for a 3–5, 5–4(8–6), 4–1 victory. Though the invitational tournament wasn't official and didn't count toward her ranking, it was, remarkably, the first professional singles event Naomi had ever won, and she had done it in something of a trance.

"One of the biggest days of your career," emcee Andrew Krasny gushed during the trophy ceremony as he interviewed Naomi. "Four match points and you showed everybody today what a fighter you are!"

Naomi, who played nervously with her ponytail as Krasny spoke, looked surprised. "She had four match points?" Naomi asked, giggling. "Oh. Okay."

"Maybe it's better off that you didn't know," Krasny suggested, before asking Naomi how it felt to be included in the Rising Stars event.

"It's really special because it's, like, the tournament for the top people," Naomi said. "Being here makes me feel like I'm a top person—even though I'm not, really."

"Well I've got news for you, and I think everybody in the stadium will agree with me: you are one of the top people," Krasny replied. "So let's get that trophy over to you."

Naomi received the large silver plate adorned with pink tiles and posed next to Garcia and new WTA chief executive Steve Simon, her face in a clear but closed-mouth smile. "She already had that huge power on forehand and serve—it was very impressive—but she was very shy and everything, kind of like a little bit afraid to show off," Garcia told me years later. "I think at the ceremony, I lost, but I was almost the one smiling the most between the two of us. But it was definitely a good experience, and, yeah, she proved to everyone that she was definitely a rising star at that time."

Naomi's win over Garcia wound up being the last ever Rising Stars match; the event was discontinued by the WTA after two years despite accurately presaging future stardom with considerable success. Both Jabeur and Garcia would reach the Top 5 in the rankings. And Naomi Osaka would do all right for herself as well.

"Me from Europe, Ons from Tunisia, and Naomi from Japan—half-Japanese, American, whatever—it was a good mix, good different kinds of game style," Garcia said. "Obviously fans made good choices."

Years later, before a match against Garcia at the 2021 Australian Open, Naomi recalled Rising Stars as "one of the most stressful but fun things that I did" at that stage of her career. "To be surrounded by the Top 10 and see how everyone works was really fun for me, and inspiring," Naomi said. "But I would say I kind of felt like I didn't belong, like I was really trying to prove myself in a way . . . I was the lowest-ranked person there, but I felt like I really wanted to do well in order to fit in."

• • • • • • •

Just as she had during her first tour splash in Stanford, Naomi would again make some of her most memorable Singapore impressions from the podium of the interview room, where she was brought for a press conference after the trophy ceremony. A small assembled group of international reporters got their first look at her and marveled at her unfiltered answers, her self-deprecating sense of humor as she discussed meeting Venus Williams, and particularly her response to a question about bouncing back from having lost to Garcia in the round-robin stages.

"This is an American term, a recent American term, but I didn't want to be 'Meek-Milled,' like taking those back-to-back losses like that, you know?" Naomi said. "I don't like losing to the same person over and over again. So, yeah, sorry if anybody didn't get that joke. Sorry." The reference was to a rap beef earlier that summer between Drake and Meek Mill, one in which Drake had largely been considered victorious after a pair of diss tracks, the second of which was "Back to Back." Only a handful of those in the room immediately understood the reference, but Naomi's warm delivery made everyone feel like they were in on the joke.

Sportswriter Reem Abulleil wrote that Naomi's Meek Mill quip "warranted a quick visit to the Urban Dictionary website, which reminded me of how old I'm getting." But through her confusion, Abulleil was thoroughly charmed: she declared Naomi "the highlight of the WTA Finals" even though the event had just begun. "With a scary forehand and her quirky personality," Abulleil wrote, "Osaka is definitely one to watch moving forward."

ELEVEN

Translating

The four major tournaments that make up the tennis "Grand Slam"—the Australian Open, French Open, Wimbledon, and U.S. Open—distance themselves from the rest of the tour in both prize money and prestige. For the rank and file, players can often make more for losing in the first round of a major than they do for being the champion of a small tour event. For measuring the game's best, major titles are the currency with cachet. Even if they achieve high rankings—sometimes even No. 1—players who have yet to win a major title are considered unproven and unworthy of being called the best.

Naomi Osaka was ranked 127th coming into the 2016 Australian Open—there were no ranking points awarded for the exhibition event in Singapore—and still needed to play in the qualifying draw to earn one of the spots in the main draw of the year's first major. After having lost in qualifying rounds at Wimbledon and the U.S. Open in prior months, Naomi broke through in her first trip to Melbourne, winning three matches to secure herself one of the 128 spots in a major draw for the first time.

Most in the sport weren't paying any attention to her yet, of course, but the few who had seen her up close were giddy about her arrival. "She's so underground; this is, like, pre-indie label signing," my cohost Courtney Nguyen said on the *No Challenges Remaining* podcast in the week of her major debut. "She's raw, she's awkward, she's weird, she's incredibly charming. Yeah, I don't know—she just sucks you in." Nguyen, who had been one of the handful of Californian reporters to meet her in Stanford eighteen months earlier, presciently called Naomi a "multicultural potential icon" now that she was on the world stage. But while the already-hooked American media was gushing over Naomi—both *USA Today* and *The New York Times* published profiles of her during the 2016 Australian Open—connecting with the country whose flag appeared beside her name in the draw and the rankings was going to prove trickier.

With Kei Nishikori having established himself as a Top 10 player and consistent contender for major titles, Japanese sportswriters had traveled in droves for the 2016 Australian Open, the tournament that branded itself as "the Grand Slam of Asia-Pacific" and was in a convenient time zone for the Japanese market. Nishikori, who was the overwhelming focus of Japanese media attention, only played every other day at the tournament; by luck of the schedule, Naomi was scheduled to play on his off days, ensuring that a full complement of Japanese reporters were available to cover her matches and attend her press conferences.

Naomi's first major press conference came after she won her first-ever match in a major main draw, comfortably beating 104th-ranked Donna Vekić 6–3, 6–2. She was assigned to give her post-match press conference about an hour after that victory in interview room 2. The room, an office space that was converted for media use during the tournament, had space for a small dais and twenty chairs; when Naomi walked in to meet the press for the first time at a major, every seat was taken; another fifteen or so reporters stood between the chairs and against the walls. "I wasn't expecting this many people," she said as she settled into her seat at the podium.

The tournament moderator began with the standard opening line for players presumed to be bilingual: "Questions will start in English."

"Oh God," Naomi muttered in reply, visibly mortified by the realization that she was expected to publicly speak Japanese, too. "Okay . . . English only?"

. . . .

On the fateful day Tamaki first entered the shop in Sapporo where Leonard worked, Naomi's parents had been able to begin their relationship because Tamaki could speak English. Leonard wouldn't become fluent in Japanese until he had lived in the country for a few more years, but once he did it became the language they spoke in their household, and the first and only language spoken by their daughters as toddlers.

When the family moved to New York, Tamaki wrote in her memoir *Through the Tunnel,* Mari and Naomi only knew how to say "hello" in English. When they were enrolled in school, they took separate English classes but continued speaking Japanese with their mother at home, where a mix of English and Haitian Creole was also spoken. Tamaki wrote that the school's English teacher told her that speaking Japanese with her daughters was delaying their progress in learning English, so she switched to speaking English at home and even pasted English words around the home to accelerate their learning.

By the time her daughters began representing Japan when they started playing professional tournaments in their early teens, Tamaki said they had "completely forgotten Japanese." She considered enrolling them in Japanese classes on weekends, she said, but their schedules were too full with practice and matches. "After all, tennis was the top priority in life," Tamaki wrote, "so in the end, Japanese became secondary."

English is the default language on the tennis tour, with nearly every player completely fluent or at least able to answer some basic questions and converse with officials. Japanese players and media on tour, however, often have some of the least confidence in their English abilities. In a 2016 survey by Rakuten, only 8.7 percent of Japanese adults aged twenty to sixty-nine responded that they considered themselves to be "good or very good" at English; 69.6 percent said they were "poor or very poor." Naomi had only played a handful of small tournaments in Japan and hadn't faced any sizable contingent of Japanese media before this day in Melbourne. Had

Naomi been an exclusively anglophone player representing a country where English proficiency is widespread, it might have been a nonissue. But once it became clear that this new Japanese player wasn't going to be answering any questions in Japanese—becoming the only player on tour who couldn't answer questions in her country's native language—a degree of panic set in among many of the Japanese reporters packed into the room.

Asked by an American if she was daunted by the prospect of having "responsibilities to Japanese media" because of the country she had chosen, Naomi insisted that she was making an effort. "I'm, like, trying to study Japanese, but I get really nervous when I hear it," she said. "Like, it's really fast, you know? Sometimes it sounds like they're rapping. So then I'm just like, 'Oh my God, I didn't hear the first part of the question.' So then I look like an idiot, and I don't want to look like an idiot."

A Japanese reporter then playfully asked, "So which makes you more nervous: having a press conference with Japanese or playing in the Grand Slam in front of fans and the audience?"

"That's such a mean question!" Naomi responded as the room filled with laughter. "Hmm. God. No comment? I mean, I like doing interviews, though. It's, just, sometimes people don't get my jokes if it's not like an international joke, so I have to understand who's asking me the question first."

Indeed, Naomi's quirks and cultural references made even the handful of Japanese journalists who were fluent in English uncertain that they were understanding her. Aki Uchida, a veteran freelance reporter who was covering the Australian Open for Japan's *Smash Magazine*, told me there was a clear cultural chasm. "For us, it's really tough to get to know her personality," she said at the time. "She keeps making some jokes that we don't understand. It's tricky. We don't know if it's from different cultures, her personality, or could be generation gaps." One particular comment Naomi had made in her first Australian Open press conference—saying Japan's National Training Center was "pretty small" because it only had two hard courts—was met with some groans and grimaces from the Japanese press contingent. "We don't get if that is just a joke, or her honesty and she might be a little bit arrogant, or just a difference of culture or something," Uchida said. "If a Japanese had said that kind of comment, maybe we would get upset, or think it was just a pure joke. But at this point, we are wondering. We don't know."

Though Uchida said these linguistic issues made "it difficult for us to cover her," she also said the Japanese press could identify many Japanese qualities in Naomi. "She tries, definitely, to adjust to Japanese culture," Uchida said. "She bows, which looks really Japanese. She keeps saying she wants to play the Tokyo Olympics in 2020 under the flag of Japan. That kind of statement makes Japanese tennis fans quite happy. As long as she claims she's Japanese—and she wins—we are happy."

. . . .

Naomi notched one more win in the Australian Open main draw, beating 21st-ranked Elina Svitolina 6–4, 6–4. It was Naomi's best win by ranking since beating 19th-ranked Samantha Stosur back in Stanford, and in many ways more impressive. Unlike Stosur, who could go through erratic patches, Svitolina was known for her steadiness, and Naomi had needed to keep most of her hardest, riskiest shots holstered, however tempting swinging with full power would be. "Winning is fun; if I hit everything and I lose, that's not fun," she said after the match. "I'd rather be consistent and win."

Svitolina had beaten Naomi a year and a half earlier at a WTA tournament in Osaka and was struck by how much her game had matured in a short time. "She was controlling her power much, much better," Svitolina told me years later. "It really surprised me because I was remembering that first match when I played against her."

On top of the victory, the $81,119 in prize money—by far the biggest paycheck of her career, more than octuple the $10,000 she had earned for reaching the second round in Stanford—and the rankings boost that would come from reaching the third round, Naomi was touched to have gained the support of Japanese fans in Melbourne, who were turning out to her matches in increasing numbers as she racked up wins. "There was a lot of Japanese people and they were actually cheering for me," she said after

the match. "So I was, like, really happy . . . I always think that they're surprised that I'm Japanese. So like the fact that there was, like, Japanese flags
and stuff, it was really touching." She had "JPN" next to her name in the
draw and on the scoreboard, but Naomi had never felt like people recognized her Japaneseness so instantly.

In the interview we did that year in Melbourne for my *New York Times*
feature on her, I asked Naomi if she ever wondered where she fit into the
world. "Well, I know for sure I'm Japanese," she replied. "Like, there's no
doubt about it. It just—I don't know—in the beginning, I was just trying
to fit in, but then I realized that being myself is more normal. So just like
the fact that they come and cheer just makes me [feel] happy, and like, accepted." Though she was satisfied by her own sense of national identity, she
told me she wasn't content to remain unable to speak Japanese. "I'm really
trying to work on it, and I feel, like, really sad that I can't interact with
more Japanese people," she said. "I'm kind of, like, apologetic, in a way, so
I'm studying."

· · · · · · ·

Naomi's third-round match offered a grand stage—the Australian Open's
showcase Rod Laver Arena, a fifteen-thousand-seat stadium—and a marquee opponent: two-time Australian Open champion Victoria Azarenka,
a formerly No. 1–ranked player. The lights and cameras were bright, but the
action was brief: after auspiciously breaking Azarenka in the opening game,
Naomi was quickly drummed out of the third round 6–1, 6–1. Naomi was
bothered by an abdominal strain that made her serve less powerful but
found a silver lining in the decisive defeat. "I can take this as a good experience," she said. "If I were just to have beaten her, I don't think I would learn
as much."

Wim Fissette, then Azarenka's coach, saw Naomi as "a flashy, inconsistent player" with obvious strengths and weaknesses that could be exploited.
"You knew that she was going to hit some aces, but also you knew that she
wasn't moving really good," Fissette told me. "So if you could put her on

defense, like she would be in trouble and also that she would make a certain amount of unforced errors. That was Naomi for a number of years."

· · · · · · · ·

Naomi's next encounter with a large Japanese media contingent came four months later at the second major on the tennis calendar: the French Open at Roland-Garros. This time, she felt ready to give speaking Japanese a shot. "It's entirely up to you; I was told you didn't want to," moderator Catherine Whitaker said as she ended the English portion of Naomi's post-match press conference. "Ooh, yeah, let's try this," Naomi said, taking a deep breath. The first Japanese question was about her first-round opponent, Jelena Ostapenko, whom she had just defeated.*

"Um . . . dammit," Naomi replied, drawing laughter from the room. "No, because I want to answer in English, but I'm trying—okay, here we go: [speaking Japanese and giggling] like . . . how do you say, like, 'if I focus on myself'? [speaking Japanese] Yeah. Oh my God, I'm so sorry . . . Okay so, she's strong, but if I focused on myself—was that even your question?" The reporter then clarified by adding more in Japanese, and Naomi responded in English that Ostapenko has a good backhand. A second question came in Japanese, and Naomi quickly began answering in English—"I was practicing my backhand a lot, because I feel—oh my God, I'm sorry"—before switching to her intended Japanese. "Because it's weak compared to my forehand before," she said, reverting to English once more and giving a full, detailed explanation of her backhand tactics. As the Japanese questions continued, her answers to questions asked in Japanese drifted more and more into English. This would, ultimately, become the default for the remainder of her career: Japanese media would ask their questions in Japanese, and Naomi would respond in English, the same way she often communicated with her mother.

---

* Ostapenko would go on to win the French Open the following year.

. . . .

While Naomi's technique of giving responses in English proved challenging for Japanese print reporters, it was especially difficult for Japanese television broadcasters who wanted to interview her for their domestic audiences.

Florent Dabadie, a Frenchman who had gained fame in Japan when he was hired to be the translator for the Japanese national soccer team—which had hired a French coach for the 2002 World Cup—anchored many broadcasts for Wowow, the premium cable channel that held the rights to the tennis majors on Japanese TV. "[Naomi] was really keen on coming after her matches to say hello to the part of her mother's family that are in Japan," Dabadie told me. "She became very popular because she was very genuine. We could really tell that she really loved Japan."

Dabadie said that Naomi spoke Japanese in a way that a typical twelve-year-old girl might on topics with which she was comfortable. "She would be able to speak no problem, fluently for casual things or for things that she wanted to say," he said. "If you're forced into a technical or tactical question, she obviously didn't have the tools—and neither do I, because Naomi and I probably have the same level of Japanese language, so I completely understand."

Though Naomi was more comfortable in English, it left Wowow's viewership lost; when Dabadie translated her answers back into Japanese for viewers, it ate up half of the limited time they had with her on-screen. After several tournaments of struggling to find a solution, Wowow ultimately set up a simultaneous interpreter back in their Tokyo studios to do live dubbing of Naomi's answers, an unprecedented expense for a domestic broadcaster covering one of their own players.

There were also challenges beyond the technical: unlike typical Japanese players, who would politely entertain even the most bland, mundane questions, Dabadie said Naomi would quickly become visibly detached when topics weren't engaging, unable to feign interest. "It was really a good lesson for us because all the [other] Japanese players are very polite; even if you do a horrible job as a journalist, they would politely answer you at length," Dabadie said. "But her, no. If we messed up our questions, she would kind of shut down."

At the end of the 2016 season, Naomi took months of Japanese lessons, and began 2017 giving entire press conferences in Japanese. But after Naomi saw how her imprecise Japanese answers were often misconstrued in print, she reverted to English to avoid misunderstandings, and rarely spoke Japanese in public again. In a later interview with *WTA Insider,* Naomi explained that her reticence to speak Japanese in public was "a perfectionist issue" most of all. "I know what I want to say in my head and I know some of the words to get there, but I might not know the correct grammar," she explained. "So usually I would just say it in English—even though my English isn't that good."

Dabadie said answering in English seemed to feel more authentic for Naomi than forcing herself into discomfort by succumbing to pressure to assimilate. "In Japan, you really have to show your Japaneseness," he said. "And I think she was not at ease about building a character which was not true and just doing that, you know, either for business or popularity."

TWELVE

Close

■

The 2016 U.S. Open was Naomi Osaka's first main draw appearance at the Billie Jean King National Tennis Center, the sprawling facility in Flushing Meadows where she and Mari had often played during the years of their childhood spent on Long Island. Naomi, entering the tournament ranked 81st, had earned a spot in the main draw for the first time.

Her first U.S. Open match was against 28th-seeded CoCo Vandeweghe, a twenty-four-year-old who had been hyped as a Next Big Thing in American tennis for close to a decade. Vandeweghe, who had developed a reputation as a spiky, pugnacious competitor, won the first set 6–4 and shouted a loud "Let's go!" once she had reached her chair, as Naomi was walking by her.

Naomi wasn't as loudly aggressive, but cranked up her own inner soundtrack: she began silently singing to herself—"Don't Hurt Yourself," one of Beyoncé's rockiest, fieriest tracks off the *Lemonade* album she had released months earlier—and took control of the match. Naomi was handling everything Vandeweghe was throwing at her, both during points and between them. When Vandeweghe held serve with an ace midway through the match, she pointed and shook her finger toward Naomi, but Naomi was unshaken.

On Naomi's first match point late in the third set, Vandeweghe hit a strong kick serve that bounded up toward Naomi's left shoulder. Naomi leapt to her left and hit a backhand return to the middle of the court.

Vandeweghe wound up for a big backhand reply to punish the soft reply but dumped her shot into the middle of the net, ending the match. Vandeweghe cracked her racquet in anger and frustration and walked up to the net to shake Naomi's hand without it. As a pouting Vandeweghe opted against shaking the hand of chair umpire Fergus Murphy, Japanese supporters in the front rows unfurled flags and painted paper fans to wave for their winner, joined by the hearty applause of what had swelled into a standing-room-only crowd around Court 13.

Few in attendance that day were likely to have known that Naomi had closer roots to the region than nearly any player in the draw, though before Naomi had even finished putting away her racquet, the commentator on the tournament's TV broadcast of the match dutifully reminded viewers watching at home that Naomi was a dual citizen of both the United States and Japan.

. . . .

After her loss, a sullen Vandeweghe did something no opponent of Naomi's would—or could, plausibly—ever do again: claim she hadn't heard of her.

"She's done well at the Slams before; what stood out to you in her game in particular?" I asked Vandeweghe to begin her post-match press conference.

"I mean, she was kind of unknown to me," Vandeweghe said of Naomi. "So the fact that she's won matches at Slams is a surprise to me, because I hadn't, relatively, heard about her."

The U.S. Open's website and app seemed not to have taken much notice of Naomi, either: across the scoreboard from Vandeweghe's smiling face, Naomi's name was accompanied by a blank rectangle and the text NO BIO PHOTO.

. . . .

Though Naomi's first main draw win at the U.S. Open did not garner much notice beyond the hundreds of fans around Court 13 on that Monday afternoon, it portended several things that happened two years later in Naomi's most dissected U.S. Open win, against Serena Williams in the 2018 U.S. Open final.

First, Naomi had been completely unfazed by her opponent's getting into protracted arguments with the chair umpire and other outbursts of emotion, something that would rattle many players. "When she started complaining and stuff, it's never really that good, unless you're McEnroe or something," Naomi said. "I don't know if that works for you. But yeah, I just tried not to think about it too much."

Naomi also showed that her own brand of power tennis could match and beat the game's biggest hitters, perhaps because she could tap into the best. When she had been in difficult positions, including staring down triple break point in the third set, Naomi had told herself a simple mantra that awakened a superpower within her.

"I just thought: 'What would Serena do?'" Naomi explained by breaking into English during the Japanese portion of her press conference.

"You picture yourself hitting like Serena?" asked the Japanese reporter Aki Uchida.

"Yeah, a little bit because she always aces, like, when she's down," Naomi explained.

"So just imagining or picturing yourself doing that is enough to really actually make it?" Uchida asked with audible disbelief.

"Yes," Naomi replied, laughing while remaining entirely serious about what she was saying.

• • • • • • •

Naomi's second-round match at the U.S. Open offered a new sort of pressure: she was expected to win on paper for the first time in her career in a Grand Slam main draw match, facing 103rd-ranked Duan Yingying. Naomi won 6–4, 7–6(3), but admitted that being a favorite was an unfamiliar, uncomfortable feeling. "This match, it felt like I was expected to win a little bit, and that made me nervous," Naomi told a growing crowd of reporters in what was her first-ever press conference held in the main room at the U.S. Open. "The next match should be fun."

The next match would be the biggest of Naomi's career so far; it would not be fun.

. . . .

Naomi's third-round match at the 2016 U.S. Open was her first time reaching the biggest stage the sport had to offer: Arthur Ashe Stadium. Opened in 1997 and named after the civil rights icon and best Black male player in professional tennis history, the U.S. Tennis Association had wanted to prove that their new stadium was the best by making it the biggest. With a capacity of 23,771, Ashe was larger than any NBA or NHL arena, and by far the largest tennis-purposed stadium in the world; the second-largest, Stadium 1 at Indian Wells, lagged far behind at 16,102; the main courts at the other Grand Slam events topped out around 15,000. Seats in the vertiginous upper deck of Ashe, where Naomi had sat as a child with her family, offer nearly aerial views of the distant action below, with players' faces inscrutably small; the cavernous seating bowl can make even the biggest star feel tiny standing on the court.

Naomi was playing on Ashe because of her opponent: No. 8 seed Madison Keys, the powerful twenty-one-year-old American who had been positioned as the primary heiress apparent to the Williamses. Like Naomi's first-round opponent CoCo Vandeweghe, Keys had been touted as one of the brightest prospects in American tennis for nearly a decade. But where Vandeweghe was bristly and polarizing, Keys was positioned as an affable, surefire bet.

Keys and Naomi had much in common. Like the Osakas, Keys's family had relocated from their home in Rock Island, Illinois, to Florida to pursue her tennis more fully. Both could blast the ball with colossal force from a young age; the challenge was harnessing that power into a reliable weapon—"Madison at the age of fourteen can hit her serve or her forehand as big as most of the girls, and some of the top girls, on the pro tour," John

Evert had told Keys's hometown newspaper the *Quad-City Times* in 2009. Both were biracial with Black fathers, and both tennis journeys had been sparked by seeing the Williams family on television.

But the differences between their journeys to Ashe that day were just as striking. Unlike the Osaka sisters, who were put onto tennis courts by their parents when they were toddlers, four-year-old Madison Keys had spotted Venus on television herself, during a broadcast of Wimbledon in 1999, and was entranced by Venus's white Reebok dress with blue trim.

"It was a cutout dress, very racy, and it showed her back," her mother, Christine Keys, told me. "[Madison] was just walking through and she goes, 'Oh, can I get one of those dresses?' I said, 'Well, you have to play that sport.' She said, 'Oh, okay! Let's do that!' Two weeks later, she goes: 'Hey, when am I going to get that dress? And the stick?'"

Keys made a big noise with that stick, winning the 12-and-under division at the Junior Orange Bowl. She was spotlit as a bright prospect before she was even a teenager. "At twelve they said she was going to win a Slam by the time she was eighteen," Christine Keys told me. "How unfair is that?"

That hype had come from the machinery around Keys. Whereas the Osakas had operated in something of a void between worlds, fully part of neither the Japanese nor the American tennis system, Keys had been a blue-chip prospect in American tennis circles from a young age. When the family relocated to Florida, they did so to enroll Madison at the Evert Tennis Academy in Boca Raton. On Keys's fourteenth birthday, she turned professional and signed with IMG's Max Eisenbud, the agent who had made Maria Sharapova the world's highest-paid female athlete. Two months later, given a wild card into a 2009 WTA tournament in Florida, she became the youngest player to win a WTA main draw match in fourteen years. From that first match onward, she was kitted out in Nike, like all of Eisenbud's biggest clients.

Unlike the Osakas, who scrimped and scrounged to pay for their daughters' tennis dreams, Madison's parents, Rick and Christine Keys, were both attorneys who earned an ample, steady income that made pursuing Madison's dreams less perilous and pressurized. "The bottom line is that this would not have happened if we couldn't afford it," Rick Keys told *The New York Times* when his daughter made her U.S. Open main draw debut in 2011.

That privileged background hadn't made life in the spotlight easy: comments about her weight caused Keys to develop an eating disorder as a teen, which hampered her tennis. "I let other people change how I felt about myself," Keys told *Behind the Racquet* years later, "and that hurt the dream I've been working towards since I was four years old."

. . . .

On this Friday in New York, another major difference between Naomi and Keys was experience. Keys had played on Ashe three times in her career before; Naomi was playing in the world's biggest tennis stadium for the first time. Leonard sat in the front row of Naomi's box in sunglasses and an Adidas cap and shirt, nervously chewing gum. Tamaki and Mari were sitting next to each other in the second row. Representatives of her racquet sponsor, Yonex, and coaches from the Japanese Tennis Association filled out remaining seats.

Naomi started the match by breaking Keys's serve, but Keys broke back to level the score at 2–2. Keys broke again in the twelfth game to take the opening set 7–5. The second set remained on serve until the ninth game, when Naomi broke and then held to take the second 6–4. The two big hitters, who struck unreturnable serves, winners, and errors early in rallies, kept the pace of the match brisk. It took only an hour and sixteen minutes to finish the first two sets; the third would be the one to be remembered.

Ashe began to fill up slowly but surely as Keys was pushed into a third set; fans around the grounds took notice of the close score and were curious to get a look at this little-known player who was pushing one of America's greatest hopes. And when the five-digit crowd caught a glimpse of Naomi, they saw her soaring. Naomi had won eight out of nine games to put the match all but out of reach for Keys, going up a double-break lead in the third set, 5–1. Naomi was one game from beating a Top 10 player for the first time, and one game from reaching the fourth round of a Grand Slam event for the first time.

Keys held for 2–5, setting up Naomi with her first of two chances to serve out the win. Naomi was four points from the biggest win of her career, but the winds swiftly changed direction when Keys won a flashy point with a pair of lunging volleys, rallying the crowd inside Ashe behind her. "That really fired me up, and helped me start getting on a roll," Keys said of the point. Roll she did, with the thousands of American fans around and above rolling alongside her. There were cheers for Keys and cheers of "USA!" as the American grew more visibly confident.

And on the other side there was Naomi, who was looking toward her box more and more, visibly stressed and distressed. After one wild miss, Naomi looked back to Leonard, who smiled broadly, trying to get her to relax. But around the island of support for Naomi, the masses in Ashe were growing more excited by the apparent momentum swing. They began cheering every point Keys won, including a double fault by Naomi that put her down break point. Keys broke, and then held, narrowing Naomi's lead to 5–4. "It really started freaking me out when she was, like, going 5–2, 5–3, 5–4," Naomi said after the match.

The momentum was lost but Naomi still had another chance to serve for the win up 5–4. She missed a forehand long on the first point. On the second, she hit a soft second serve that Keys punished, ripping a forehand return winner fast past Naomi's outstretched backhand, which again ignited the crowd. Naomi pulled the brim of her white visor low over her face to hide her eyes and exhaled with slow, cool breaths. Her father and others in her box clapped to try to keep her spirits up. Naomi seemed to steady herself and won the next two points to even the game and put herself two points from victory. At 30-all, it looked as though Naomi might earn a match point when Keys's return clipped the net. But instead of falling back, the return sprung off the tight steel net cord and leapt forward and sideways, landing short and drawing Naomi forward. On the biggest point of her career so far, Naomi was suddenly at the net, where she was least comfortable. Keys hit a forehand toward her, and Naomi stiffly scooped at a forehand volley. Before the ball had even landed, Naomi began to shriek, knowing it was sailing far beyond the baseline. She turned and covered her mouth with her hand as she stared toward her corner in despair, taking sharp, choking breaths.

Naomi missed a forehand on the next point to give Keys the game and level the score at 5–5. She wiped at her eyes with the sweatband on her wrist, catching the tears that were forming before they fell. The match was now even, but to look at Naomi, it seemed lost. When she missed a return on the first point of the next game, Naomi swiped angrily at the court with her racquet. Keys, positive and walking tall, won a fifth straight game to take a 6–5 lead in the third.

"That's part of the sport: when you see the other person getting nervous or overwhelmed . . . you've really got to put the pressure on her," Keys later said.

Naomi steadied herself enough to hold to force a third-set tiebreak, but the momentum stayed firmly with Keys. Keys closed out the win on her first match point, tracking down a first big forehand from Naomi before the second missed, ending the match 7–5, 4–6, 7–6(3). Keys threw her arms up in the air and squealed with delight; Naomi managed a smile as the two shook hands at the net. Keys dropped her racquet at her chair and walked back out to the court to wave to the crowd, pump her fists, and shout a triumphant "Fuck yes!"

Naomi, on the other side, slung her racquet bag over her shoulders and walked off the court. In her press conference, Naomi admitted she had felt lost as she neared victory. "I was just pushing it back, seeing what she would do, if she would hit it out or not," Naomi said.

Keys, who said it had been the greatest comeback of her career "hands down," had kind words for Naomi, whom she called a "great player" with a bright future. "There are a lot of weapons that are going to get her very far," Keys said. "Yeah, I have no doubt she will be around and winning lots of matches."

The difference maker, Keys believed, had been experience. "Being in that situation before, having lost some tough matches—it happens, you know?" Keys said. "It just makes you stronger."

Consoling as it was meant to be, Naomi disagreed with that sentiment. While she acknowledged that it was her first full year on the tour, she didn't think that was a reason to be losing. "I wouldn't really say it's 'new,' though, you know what I mean?" she said. "Because a court is a court no matter where you go." Talent, Naomi believed, should be enough. "Experience is good and whatever, right?" she concluded. "But not having experience, if you're good enough, it shouldn't really matter."

. . . .

Max Eisenbud, Keys's agent, had sat in the second row of Keys's courtside box in the corner of the stadium. As he watched Naomi up close, he turned to someone beside him and said, "That girl's going to make a lot of money someday."

As he knew, that day was coming soon. Eisenbud was head of IMG's tennis division, and his agency had been making plays for Naomi all year. During their courting process, IMG had given her a wild card into the Miami Open, a tournament the behemoth corporation owned, to show the power they wielded in the sport. Stuart Duguid, who had recently joined IMG, would be Naomi's agent. But because Naomi still had time left on her contract with Octagon, the announcement had been delayed for several months.

Daniel Balog, who had plucked Naomi from obscurity three years earlier, said the attention she was getting from competing agencies as she gained the world's attention was only natural. "What I can say is it's a tough business, it's a cutthroat business," Balog told me years later, sadness still clear in his voice. "In the end, players come and go all the time. And the player just decided to part ways and go elsewhere, where she is right now.

Honestly, looking back on what she has accomplished, I feel very proud of myself to have been there, to have been able to identify her from the start. I feel proud to be part of this journey at the beginning."

IMG had two deals with Japanese sponsors ready to launch for Naomi upon the announcement of her signing: the television channel Wowow and the food conglomerate Nissin, founded by Momofuku Ando, the inventor of instant ramen. Both companies had also previously partnered with Nishikori; the two players would appear together in campaigns for both.

Naomi told Egyptian reporter Reem Abulleil that signing with IMG had made her "want to push myself more to do better so that I feel like their choice was justified." Her first chance to prove that, fittingly, was at her country's biggest tournament.

· · · · · · ·

Though it had been downgraded slightly when the tour began shifting resources toward China, the Toray Pan Pacific Open in Tokyo remained a prestigious event on the WTA Tour, attracting nine of the Top 20 for the event. Ranked 66th, Naomi needed a wild card to enter the draw, but once she had a spot she made it the best tournament of her career, giving the local fans and media an extended opportunity to get to know her game and her desire to be Japanese. Naomi beat 34th-ranked Misaki Doi, Japan's highest-ranked female player at the time, 6–4, 6–4 in the first round. In the second round, she beat 12th-ranked Dominika Cibulková 6–2, 6–1. In the quarterfinal, she beat qualifier Aliaksandra Sasnovich 6–3, 7–6(6). In the semifinals, she beat 20th-ranked Elina Svitolina 1–6, 6–3, 6–2 to book a spot in the final, becoming the first Japanese woman to reach the final in Tokyo in twenty-one years. She lost the final to former No. 1 Caroline Wozniacki 7–5, 6–3.

Coverage of Naomi during her run in Japan focused on both her prodigious talents and her Japaneseness, including her efforts to improve her Japanese language skills. "Especially if I want to play the [2020 Tokyo] Olympics, I feel like if you represent Japan you have to at least speak

Japanese," she told NHK, the Japanese national broadcaster. "I would be very happy if I got chosen to play."

. . . .

Naomi started 2016 ranked 144th; with her run to the Tokyo final, she cracked the Top 40 for the first time. That steep rise, coupled with her increasingly obvious star power, earned her the WTA's Newcomer of the Year award. Adjusting to life in the spotlight would be the next challenge.

THIRTEEN

The Social Game

Aside from reaching the first WTA final of her career, Naomi Osaka took another major step that would shape her path to stardom while she was in Tokyo in September 2016: at her new agent Stuart Duguid's suggestion, Naomi created a Twitter account for herself.

Naomi had been on social media before, with an Instagram account she posted on for her friends and family. But this was her first move toward a public-facing, branded account. Naomi had called herself a "child of the internet," but this was the first time the internet would get a chance to meet its daughter up close and personal. "This isn't as complicated as I thought . . . 10/10 on IGM," she wrote in her first tweet, joking that she'd give Twitter an elusive perfect score on the popular video game review site.

Naomi's early tweets were in a mix of English and Japanese. She shared pictures of gifts given to her by fans in Tokyo, including a map of the best places to play *Pokémon GO* around the city, the popular mobile game Naomi had been playing along with much of the rest of the world since the summer of 2016. "Pretty soon I'm gonna have to #pokemonstop," she wrote. She showed her internet savvy early, posting a photo of herself holding a piece of paper with her account name written on it but making sure that the paper was translucent to thwart would-be meme-makers from photoshopping unwanted messages into the image.

By 2016 many tennis players and celebrities had Twitter presences that were carefully controlled by their managers or other social media consultants. But though Naomi would also occasionally post things about her sponsors, her authentic voice could be readily read through her posts, particularly her penchant for sharing her most awkward moments. "I almost liked someone's post from 2 months ago," she wrote with a screaming emoji. "Omg my thumb slipped and almost ruined my life. I'm never stalking again. #died." Naomi's posts were much like those of anyone else her age. She shared her love of video games like *Skyrim,* retweeted memes from anime, gushed over her idols Beyoncé and Serena, posted pictures of her family and her dog, and captioned photos with quotes from *Mean Girls.*

Through it all, Naomi posted repeated reminders that no one should consider her to be cool. "Just a public disclaimer I wanna tell you guys . . . Well, I'm weird," she wrote. "I know it, my family knows it, and my 2 friends know it. #okpeaceout." When sharing ostensibly impressive things about herself posted by others, Naomi often hedged to make clear that she wasn't doing so from a place of high self-regard. For example, in April 2017 when she shared a video interview of herself posted by the WTA, she added "embarrassing" in Japanese, "omg #cringe #megacringe #ultracringe" in English, and a spate of embarrassed emojis.

. . . .

Naomi's arrival on Twitter was hardly a viral sensation, but within her first three weeks on the platform she had reached five thousand followers, presumably mostly from the devoted tennis fans who had already seen her on court and read about her personality in articles and interviews. As her online community was adding more digits, Naomi often tweeted about her desire to break through her shyness and make real-world connections. "Do you ever want to say hi to someone but you've never said hi to them before, and now it's too late," she wrote, adding crying emojis. When a user encouraged her to "just go ahead and say 'hi,'" Naomi's reply was similarly simple: "But I'm scared lol."

Because all of her studying since moving to Florida had been online, and most of her time socializing was only within her own family, Naomi struggled with meeting new people. She also chalked up some of her shyness around her peers to essentially being a transfer student into the pros, joining the players her age on tour after they had already spent years getting to know one another and forming bonds at the various age-group events that the Osaka family had skipped. "I think all the other girls my age, they're probably all friends because they played the juniors together and I didn't," Naomi told reporter Reem Abulleil in early 2017. "So I'm kind of like a strange person on the side trying to get in."

When the 2017 season began, Naomi found a way around this, using Twitter to communicate with the players she was too afraid to verbally break the ice with in the locker room. "You guys I'm gonna randomly tweet people questions and statements that I've always wanted to say," Naomi announced. "Lol hope they respond."

Naomi's first target was a contemporary of hers: Ana Konjuh, a Croatian who was also nineteen and had beaten her a few days earlier in the quarterfinals of a WTA event in Auckland. "@anakonjuh lol hey!" Naomi began. "Totally weird random question but, how do you have such perfect eyebrows [crying laughing emoji]?"

Konjuh replied an hour later. "Hey!! good genetics haha?! But I have to keep them in shape with regular appointments so .. come visit me in Croatia I'll take you with me."

About a week later, Naomi posted a photo of herself with her face made up for a sponsor event. "The makeup artist asked me what I wanted to do with my brows, so I told her to 'Give me the Konjuh' @anakonjuh [crying laughing emoji]."

Konjuh told me years later that, outside of their online eyebrow consultation, she hadn't interacted much with Naomi. "I wouldn't say that we're close or something that we'd call 'friends,' because I haven't seen her outside the tour," Konjuh said. "I mean, I can give her any advice she wants. She can just DM me again, and it's going to be like the old days."

• • • • • • •

Naomi's next attempt to reach out to a player over social media was more daringly across the WTA-ATP aisle to Taro Daniel, a Japanese player with whom Naomi had recently played mixed doubles at an exhibition event in Japan.

Daniel's ranking hovered around the No. 100 mark, but he stood out in the ranks of Japanese tennis. Like Naomi, he was multicultural with ties to New York: he was born in New York City, to a fully Japanese mother, Yasue, and an American father, Paul, who has half-Japanese and half-English ancestry. Aside from being a quarter White and having an English surname, Daniel stood apart by towering above the rest of his diminutive Japanese compatriots at six foot three, with flowy, boy band–worthy hair that had made him the matinee idol of Japanese tennis.

Naomi had been shy and quiet in Daniel's presence, as she was with nearly everyone else at the event. "We played the exhibition, right?" Naomi recounted soon after on the *WTA Insider* podcast with Courtney Nguyen. "We didn't talk at all. I served an ace, he'd be like, 'Good job,' right? That's it. Yeah, like, literally, we just did, like, high fives. And then: never talked."

But days later, after a reporter had asked her a question about him, Naomi said she worked up the courage to "be gutsy" with Daniel. "I'm about to tag the person the question was about. Gonna be awkward because I never talked to them. #pray4me," she wrote as a prelude, before sending the main-event tweet: "Okay so, a reporter legit asked me how did I feel playing exhibition dubs with @tarodaniel93 because he has a lot of fangirls," Naomi wrote, appending a "LOL" and a series of anguished, moribund, and laughing emojis. "Omg did I really just tweet that," Naomi wrote minutes later. To Naomi's considerable horror, Daniel saw the tweet and replied just over an hour later: "I didn't know I had fan girls?? Loll." Many hours later, Naomi sent Daniel a GIF of the "Why you always lyin'?" meme by Vine star Nicholas Fraser.

Though she had used the @ function on Twitter, which sent the message directly to Daniel's account, Naomi said she had held out hope that he somehow wouldn't notice it. "I was really hoping he wouldn't see that, like it would be buried in all of his mentions or something?" Naomi told Nguyen as both laughed. "And then I was like, 'Oh my God, I have, like, anxiety now. There's so much stress!' And so I decided that if I'm going to be this weird, I might as well go all the way. And then I pressed 'Follow.' And that one day of not knowing if he was going to follow me was the most stressful situation I've ever had in my life."

Daniel, indeed, followed her back, which eased her tension but set up future challenges. "But now, what do I do when I see him in person?" Naomi asked Nguyen. "Like, 'Hey, I'm sorry for not talking in person and [then] mentioning you on Twitter, nice to meet you?' That's kind of creepy though, don't you think? He's a guy, too! That's, like, weird!"

"You've created a situation for yourself that you're going to have to figure out how to get out of," Nguyen replied.

"I kind of regret my life a little bit." Naomi sighed with a resigned fatalism that left both laughing.

· · · · · · ·

Naomi often directly acknowledged the disconnect between her online and irl (in-real-life) personalities. "I like how I'm completely unable to hold/engage in conversations in real life, except for the occasional, 'H-hey,' I manage to stutter out," she wrote in May 2017. When Daniel had the biggest win of his career, beating Novak Djoković at Indian Wells in 2018, Naomi lamented being unable to congratulate him when she saw him in person. "It's kind of weird, because I can talk to him on Twitter, but I can't talk to him in real life," she said. "Because literally he would be coming and I would [nod] and then we would just pass. I don't know. I tried to say 'congratulations' but all I did was [nod]. Like, I don't understand."

Psychologists researching the interplay between shyness and technology have shown the positive effects that online social networks can have on fostering connections for shy people, who often feel more comfortable in social interactions that don't take place face-to-face. In a 2010 article by Marquette University researchers Levi Baker and Debra Oswald published in the *Journal of Social and Personal Relationships*, they enumerate reasons why shy people can achieve greater social interaction on "computer-mediated communication." Behaviors that foster intimacy, like disclosing personal things about themselves, are less inhibited online. Shy people also feel greater control over how they present themselves during online interactions because they can take as much time as they want to construct and revise messages, rather than feeling a need to say the exact right thing instantly, as one would in a face-to-face conversation. They can also access other resources during an online interaction, such as looking up information about a topic or their recipient's interests and recent activity, which can make finding an amenable topic much easier. Social networking services also lack most nonverbal reactions, meaning there are fewer negative or ambiguous cues for shy individuals to detect that might deter them, and therefore they are more likely to express themselves more freely without being disconcerted by registering a negative reaction from the listener. Emotional intent can also be clarified in online communication by emojis, of which Naomi is a frequent user. "I'm very bold on the internet, and not face-to-face most of the time," Naomi later said. "If it's face-to-face, then I'm kind of like 'Ehhhhh . . . I don't know.' It's different."

• • • • • • • •

The exception to Naomi's in-person shyness was, perhaps ironically, when she was speaking with many people at once, which she did with increasing frequency as her post-match press conferences grew more popular. Naomi was the inverse of most others on tour: where many players would exhale and unclench after stepping down from the podium and happily make casual, off-record conversation in the corridors, Naomi was at her most loose and light on the podium, on the record, and then might clam up if idle chatter was attempted afterward. Something about the formal structure of the press conference format, which followed a clear Q&A pattern and had few awkward silences, made Naomi feel safe and secure to share her honest feelings with little inhibition. Many of Naomi's coaches later said they learned to start reading and watching her press conferences because she was often more revealing during tournaments when talking to a crowd of reporters than she was in more intimate conversations with her own team. "I don't want to sound rude to you guys, but when I sit here, it's like you guys aren't real people," Naomi once said with a smile. Rather than multiplying the pressure, she explained, speaking to a full room gave her a feeling of safety in numbers. "If I'm talking to someone one-on-one, it just stresses me out," she explained. "[But] if I tell [a room of reporters] a joke, fifty-fifty chance at least three of you are going to laugh. I don't know if it's a pity laugh, but at least it's a laugh, right? If it's one-on-one, and that person doesn't laugh, like, I just want to leave."

Naomi's press conferences became famous for their quirks and unpredictability. Once, when the German reporter René Denfeld asked her where her mind wanders during matches, Naomi veered toward a part of the culture no one could have predicted: "You know there is that commercial that says, 'If you or a loved one has been diagnosed with mesothelioma'? That's all I could think about for the whole practice."

· · · · · · ·

While the greatest hits from her press conference answers were being compiled into YouTube videos by fans, Naomi's peers in the locker room still often felt like they couldn't get to know her. When I asked about Naomi, many players told me they felt blocked from chatting with her by her omnipresent headphones. This was a "barrier" by design, Naomi would admit. Sometimes there was music playing in them, sometimes not, but her headphones were always a first line of defense against unsolicited social advances. "It gives me an excuse to, like, not interact with someone if I don't want to," she once explained.

The players Naomi shared locker rooms with, therefore, usually only understood her personality if they followed her online.

At Indian Wells in 2017, before a rematch of the previous year's U.S. Open thriller, Madison Keys was asked by broadcaster Mary Carillo if she had gotten to know Naomi's personality. "Have you ever talked to Naomi?" Carillo asked. "Do you read her stuff? Do you see how funny she can be?"

"I see her tweets and stuff," Keys replied. "And it's hilarious, because she walks around the locker room and she's really shy and she's really reserved. And then I'll see someone retweet something, and I'm just like, 'All right! There we go!' So it's really cool to see that; I think it just shows that maybe the way that we are around our competitors, in this environment, is not always the way that we actually are."

Keys said that she had attempted conversation with Naomi when they had trained together at their shared base of the Evert Tennis Academy in Boca Raton, with limited success. "I mean, me being like the outgoing personality, I'm trying to talk to her," Keys recalled. "And she's like, '. . . Okay!' In her head I'm sure she's like, 'She's a total freak.'"

Naomi saw Keys's comments days later and responded, naturally, on Twitter. "Omg no, please talk to me. I am nice. @Madison_Keys," Naomi wrote with anguished and laughing emojis. ". . . Lol my internet and real life personality are so different, this is terrible."

"Lolololol let's chat in Miami," Keys replied, with a kiss emoji.

"Aaaand this encounter is already making me nervous #introvertproblems," Naomi responded. "Lol see you in Miami!"

"We just followed each other so we're basically best friends already," Keys assured her.

. . . .

Even after becoming No. 1 and winning Grand Slam titles and growing her profile and visibility, Naomi's shyness around her peers hardly abated. At the 2019 U.S. Open, Naomi laughed and smiled when discussing Daniil Medvedev, the lanky Russian whose mischievous mockery of antagonistic crowds during his post-match on-court interviews had gone viral. "It's just so funny," she said of Medvedev's trolling. "The sarcasm is beautiful."

Naomi frequently liked and shared Medvedev's moments on social media from that tournament onward, including during the ATP Cup event in the first week of the 2020 season, so I asked her about him. "Yeah, he's very interesting to me," Naomi said of Medvedev. "I've never talked to him in real life, but just like the things that I see on the internet about him." Naomi then turned the inquiries on Medvedev back around to me. "Have you ever, like, interviewed him?" she asked me. "Is he interesting?"

"Yeah, he's an interesting guy," I replied. I then thought of all the things she and Medvedev had in common: both were avid gamers, both were in their early twenties, both were hard-court aficionados, and both were refreshingly honest and devoid of clichés in their interviews. "You should meet!" I suggested as I connected dots in my mind between the two. "You have lots of opportunities—you're in the same places all the time."

"Yeah, I don't really talk to people, Ben," she reminded me with a smile. "I don't know what to tell you."

FOURTEEN

Into Venus's Orbit

After climbing more than 150 spots in the rankings in 2016, and crack- ing the thresholds of the Top 200, Top 100, and Top 50 in succession, Naomi's second full season on tour was a stereotypical sophomore slump. Naomi started the 2017 season ranked 40th and ended it having backslid to a ranking of 68th. Her win-loss record was a middling 18–22. She didn't reach the semifinals of any tournament; her only two quarterfinals came in her first and last events of the year at the lowest level of the WTA Tour. She struggled with a persistent abdominal injury. She lost all four main draw matches she played on the red clay of Europe, including a first-round loss at the French Open to Alison Van Uytvanck that was, remarkably, her first- ever first-round main draw loss at a major. That loss to Van Uytvanck was part of one of two five-match losing streaks Naomi endured during the season. Naomi was able to improve much of her game under Australian coach David Taylor, who added structure and discipline to both her prac- tices and her match play, but the gains were often offset by the loss of the element of surprise: Naomi was becoming a fixture on the tour on her second lap around the circuit, and opposing players and coaches not only were no longer caught off guard by her power; they knew where to find her weaknesses.

But despite the largely lackluster results, there were also several mile- stones for Naomi during the 2017 season. The first came at Wimble- don, where Naomi played in the main draw for the first time (she had lost in Wimbledon qualifying in 2015, and an injury at Birmingham had cut short her grass court season in 2016). Naomi won her first-round match against Sara Sorribes Tormo and then played her second-round match against Barbora Strýcová, a canny Czech who had nicknamed Naomi "the Shinkansen," the Japanese name for the country's bullet trains. Strýcová lacked Naomi's locomotive power, but her crafty all-court game and variety was well suited to the grass; she would make the Wimbledon semifinals two years later. After a derailment in the second set, Naomi got back on track for a 6–1, 0–6, 6–4 victory. It completed a remarkable set for Naomi, reaching the third round on her debut at each of the four majors. "I feel like everyone pays more attention to the Grand Slams, and maybe, like, subconsciously, like, I try harder?" Naomi said after her win. "I'm not saying that I don't try in the other tournaments, because that would be very bad." Naomi's reward for reaching the third round was not just the $111,678 but the priceless chance to fulfill a dream: getting to play against a Williams sister.

Venus was the only Williams at Wimbledon in 2017; Serena was a little less than two months away from giving birth to her daughter, Olympia. At thirty-seven, Venus was in the midst of an unexpected resurgent season. She had made a surprise run to the final of the Australian Open that January, the first time she had reached the final there in fourteen long years. The reappearance turned into yet another family reunion: it was Venus's ninth and last major final against her sister. Serena won it 6–4, 6–4 for her twenty-third (and ultimately final) major title. Venus was one of the few people inside Rod Laver Arena who had known Serena was nearly two months pregnant on court; she later joked that it was unfair to play two against one.

Naomi hadn't known she would play Venus until she was told in her press conference; she let out an excited "oooooh" at the news. "Well, I'm kind of honored, because I don't think I would have started playing if Venus and Serena weren't, like, there for me growing up," Naomi said. "Yeah. I mean, it's kind of weird to hear that she, like—maybe she even talked about me?" Venus had, indeed, briefly talked about Naomi. "Yeah, I have seen her play before," Venus said. "I think we play a really similar game."

Naomi clarified that she was "more of a Serena person" but that Venus, who was Mari's favorite, had also loomed large in their childhoods. Naomi had nearly gotten to play Venus at her first tournament of the year in Auckland, but Venus had withdrawn before their match. Facing Venus at Wimbledon, where she was a five-time champion, was an entirely more special proposition. "I'm really humbled to be able to come here from watching her on the TV," Naomi said. "I'll just try my best and hopefully not get too, like, nervous."

There would have been plenty of reasons for nerves: the match received more attention than any Naomi had played to that point. Not only was it a third round at a major against a legend of the sport, but the narratives linking them were irresistible: the thirty-seven-year-old veteran against the nineteen-year-old who was half her age and saw her as a role model. Venus had played her first Wimbledon match, several reports mentioned, four months before Naomi was born. The match was played on No. 1 Court, Wimbledon's second-largest venue, seating over twelve thousand. Venus raced out to a quick start, going up 4–1 after just sixteen minutes. But Naomi steadied and leveled the first set at 4–4, eventually forcing a tie-break with a backhand down the line that she punctuated with an equally fearless "C'mon!"

There was little separating the two as they traded big serves and powerful groundstrokes, but Venus played the big points better: she took the tie-break 7-3, then broke midway through the second set to put herself up for good. Venus finished with an ace down the T past Naomi's outstretched backhand on match point to close out the win, 7–6(3), 6–4. "She played an amazing match today," Venus said of Naomi after. "She really played a match that was worth—she deserved to win. But these sorts of matches are always so close."

Asked if she saw any similarities between her opponent and her sister, Venus demurred but complimented Naomi again. "I think she definitely has her own style," Venus said of Naomi. "It's so awesome to hear she's inspired by Serena, and she's made it her own. It's cool to hear."

Naomi said after the match that she had tried to think of Venus "as a normal person," down from the usual pedestal she'd put her on, so she wouldn't be overwhelmed by the occasion. "This is sort of a dream of mine, to play her—I can check that off my list," she said. "I actually feel like it's better that she beat me because I can learn more from her, and there's something more I can look forward to."

· · · · · · ·

Naomi had more big moments once the tour shifted back to hard courts. At the Canadian Open in Toronto, Naomi reached the third round, where she faced top-ranked Karolína Plíšková in her first tournament as the WTA No. 1. It was the first time Naomi had ever played against a No. 1–ranked player, and she proved herself up for the challenge, winning the second set in a tiebreak to force a third. Just when things were looking bright on the scoreboard, however, Naomi called her coach, the Australian David Taylor, onto the court for a coaching time-out.

"Good, well done," Taylor said as he arrived, before delivering nearly a minute of peppy tactics to Naomi. Taylor then asked Naomi how she was feeling, and the smile soon disappeared from his face.

"Mmmm, I may have made my ab thing a little bit worse, but that's okay," she told him.

Taylor, knowing how much Naomi had struggled with her abdominal injury during the season, was blunt in his direction: "If it hurts you, stop," he said. "If you have pain there, that's it, unfortunately." Taylor, an exacting veteran coach who had been on the tour for decades and coached Samantha Stosur to her 2011 U.S. Open title, reminded Naomi how she had mishandled the injury by pushing through it in the clay season. "You made it worse by doing that," he said.

"This is a grim conversation," Naomi said, laughing nervously.

"Naomi, you've got to be realistic," he said. "That was inexperience. The second time you do it, it's not inexperience."

"But I'm so close," Naomi said, understandably bargaining as she grieved the win that had felt within reach. She then stood up and demonstrated her service motion to test out her ab. "I'm fine, it's fine, no, it's fine," she said.

Now it was Taylor's turn to laugh. "Are you kidding?"

After playing one more game, in which Plíšková broke her serve, Naomi gave in to prudence and stopped the match, 2–6, 7–6(4), 0–1. "Having to withdraw really hurt my feelings, especially since I was playing the No. 1 and I felt like I was doing really well," she later said.

· · · · · · ·

Naomi arrived to the U.S. Open with a feeling of unfinished business. She was excited to get to wear items from Adidas's colorful U.S. Open collection, a collaboration with Pharrell Williams, and fans were excited that Naomi had landed in one of the blockbuster matches of the first round against sixth-seeded Angelique Kerber, the defending U.S. Open champion who had been ranked No. 1 for much of the year.

On a rainy day that halted play on outdoor courts at the U.S. Open, Kerber and Naomi played under the closed roof of Ashe, holding the tournament's undivided attention. Forty-fifth-ranked Naomi was 0–9 against Top 10 opponents in her career, and she was returning to the stage of her unforgettable collapse against Madison Keys a year earlier, but there was a popular premonition that she could trouble Kerber, who had been struggling under the spotlight of the No. 1 ranking and hadn't won a single title all year. "Upset on paper; based on form, maybe not as surprising," Courtney Nguyen later said on the *WTA Insider* podcast.

The two started on level terms. With Naomi serving at 2–2, Kerber earned a break point, but Naomi stayed patient and won consecutive long rallies to swing the game in her favor. Soon, it was Kerber who seemed to be buckling under the moment: her fifth double fault, with a second serve that she dumped into the net at just 66 miles per hour, gave Naomi her first break point. Naomi hit a backhand return hard down the middle that Kerber could only send into the net in reply, breaking for a 5–3 lead in the first set. Kerber earned two break points in the next game and got Naomi on the run on the second break point with a strong forehand down the line that Naomi barely reached, sending up a high, floating return to set up Kerber's putaway. But when Kerber was slightly tentative, allowing the ball to bounce before hitting it and giving Naomi time to reset, Naomi stunningly turned the point back in her favor, guessing correctly which way Kerber would hit and hitting a forehand winner as the crowd roared its approval. It was the most dramatic encapsulation of what Naomi had been doing for the whole match: pouncing whenever Kerber gave her anything she could attack. Naomi took the first set 6–3 to put the defending champion a set from elimination.

Kerber won the third game of the second set, but it would be the last she put on the board. Kerber could have played better, commentator Rennae Stubbs said as the match got out of reach, "but this is just a buzz saw she's run into." The only chance Kerber had, Stubbs said, was "if Naomi Osaka starts to remember what happened last year on this court." The nightmare wouldn't recur: instead of sputtering, Naomi accelerated through the finish line, pounding winner after winner to put the match out of reach. Hitting ten forehand winners in the second set, Naomi reeled off the last four games in a row to close out the 6–3, 6–1 victory over the defending champion in just an hour and five minutes.

It was a victory full of firsts for Naomi. It was her first win over a Top 10 opponent, her first win in the biggest stadium of a major, and her first time making headlines at a major for a win. "It means a lot, especially because of the last time I was here," Naomi said in her on-court interview. "This court hasn't really been a fond memory." It was a sonic boom of a result, but it was also the result of a steady crescendo of growth, Taylor told me in the minutes after the victory. "I think she's really matured a lot, and she had a better balance of playing the right shot at the right time," he said. "And when an aggressive player has a clearer understanding of when to hit the right shot, then they're very dangerous with anyone."

What Naomi had been unclear on was how she should react to her first big-stage win at a major, which she had marked with a fist pump and a smile. "I feel like there's something wrong with me, because I'm not as excited as I thought I would be," she said. "Like, I was thinking about it on the court: If I win, what would I do if I won? I was like, 'Hey, maybe I should throw the racquet and scream or something?' But then when I actually won, I didn't do anything, so I was kind of sad about that. This is something when you're little you dream about: playing on Arthur Ashe against a great champion. And then everyone asked me, 'Why don't I show emotion?' But I really want to—but I can't, you know? But yeah, it's really special for me."

Naomi would again reach the third round of the U.S. Open, losing a tight three-setter to powerful veteran Kaia Kanepi. She would play Kerber twice more that season, losing both times, including a first-round loss in Tokyo, where she was returning for the first time since her breakthrough final a year earlier, then another first-round loss in Beijing.

Naomi's year ended with another more rewarding rematch: in the second round of the Hong Kong Open, Naomi got to face Venus Williams once more. Venus, now ranked No. 5, served for the first set at 5–4, but Naomi broke, starting a run of eight straight games that turned the match sharply in her favor. After leading 5–0 in the second, Naomi ultimately defeated Venus 7–5, 6–2 for her first win over a Top 5 opponent. "She played well," Venus told reporters. "I made a few errors at 5–4 and after that she played pretty flawless. I can only give her credit."

Naomi got more than credit from the win. As she had learned to do throughout the year, she shared her truest feelings after the win for a tweet: "Today I accomplished one of my dreams."

. . . .

Naomi had many more dreams, of course. After the season, having parted with David Taylor, she found a new guide to reaching them. To be more like Serena—and to beat Serena—Naomi would pull herself closer to her idol's orbit than she ever had been before, learning from the one man who had spent more time on court with Serena than anyone outside her own family.

FIFTEEN

Footsteps

Like many male coaches in women's pro tennis, Sascha Bajin hadn't been much of a pro tennis player himself. Though, like the players he would most famously coach, his father had put him on the court at a young age.

Born in 1984 in Munich to a German mother, Aleksandar "Sascha" Bajin was trained by his Serbian father, a hard-driving, demanding tennis coach, from age four. As a child, Bajin played junior tournaments around Europe, gaining some decent results. When he was fifteen, his trajectory was derailed by tragedy. As he described in his 2019 book, *Strengthen Your Mind: 50 Habits for Mental Change*, his grandfather, a wealthy property owner in Serbia, died after being poisoned. When Bajin's father was driving back home from Serbia to Germany shortly after that, he crashed into a highway barrier and died. Serbian police said his father had fallen asleep at the wheel, but Bajin called the back-to-back deaths "shady circumstances" and said he still questions "what the truth is about my father's death." Shaken by the back-to-back tragedies and having lost his guiding force in the sport, Bajin's results middled and his motivation to pursue a career as a player waned. His best singles ranking was 1,149th in 2007 when he was twenty-two, and his total career prize money was just $2,054.

To make ends meet as he earned his certification to become a tennis coach—a program that takes three years in the German tennis system—Bajin worked side jobs around his tennis club stringing racquets, building courts, and bartending. Unexpectedly, Bajin was abruptly catapulted from his unremarkable path in the recreational levels of the sport to the top of the WTA Tour: Jovan Savic, a family friend who had been a hitting partner and traveling coach for both Serena and Venus Williams, was looking for someone to train with Serena in Munich during her preparations for the 2007 French Open. "There was a specific type she wanted: someone a little bit younger who is a good player who has no private life, no family, nothing, and is willing to work hard," Bajin said in 2022 on the *Craig Shapiro Tennis Podcast*. Bajin matched the description, and Serena was impressed. After she hit with him for four days in Munich, Serena asked him to join her at the French Open; he would rarely leave her side for the next seven years.

When the twenty-three-year-old Bajin arrived to twenty-five-year-old Serena's team, her tennis still operated like a family business, even though her parents had begun to recede from her day-to-day coaching. Bajin moved in with Serena and Venus; Serena's assistant Valerie Vogt and physiotherapist Esther Lee also lived in the house. Bajin's official title was "hitting partner," but he became much more. Estimating that he spent roughly 330 days out of the year with Serena, Bajin served as an eager errand boy and loyal bodyguard, accompanying Serena almost anywhere she went after threats from stalkers—a recurrent problem for decades of women's tennis stars—increased around her Florida home. "She'd always know: 'There's Sascha, he'll have my back,'" Bajin told me. He also became a frequent plus-one for Serena at star-studded events; he caused a tabloid stir when he alleged in 2012 that Dennis Quaid had stolen his date after one of Serena's karaoke parties. More enjoyable, he said, were visits to Oscar parties and the tour bus of Pharrell Williams (no relation). Forever close in Serena's orbit, Bajin slowly gained a degree of fame of his own by proximity; by his seventh year with Serena, he was photographed shirtless for *The New York Times Magazine* by celebrity photographer Ryan Pfluger for a profile of "Big Sascha," the nickname Serena's agent Jill Smoller had teasingly given him for his gym-made physique; in a tour full of men with athletic string-bean builds, Bajin's bulging bulk cut a unique figure on the tennis court.

Bajin and Serena, who have both described their unique relationship as brother-sister, remained playful with each other as they reached their thirties. At its peak, Serena made an elaborate effort to catfish Bajin with a fake profile of a woman named "Heidi," complete with a French phone number; Bajin only found out when he tried calling "Heidi's" phone and heard it buzzing in Serena's bag.

Their goofy lightheartedness was accompanied by some of the best tennis of Serena's career. Serena had been outside the Top 10 just before linking up with Bajin, but with him in her corner she returned to the No. 1 ranking and won ten more major singles titles, increasing her haul from seven to seventeen and launching herself into Greatest Of All Time conversations. (Serena also won two Olympic gold medals and seven major doubles titles with Venus during her time with Bajin, the sorts of monumental feats that only she could reduce to a parenthetical.)

Between the wins, there was also loyalty through adversity. Four days after winning Wimbledon in 2010, Serena was in Bajin's hometown of Munich to celebrate. As she described it, on a night out, Serena cut her feet badly on broken glass as she walked out of a restaurant. The injury cut a tendon in her right big toe that required surgery and forced her to wear a cast and walking boot for months. The prolonged immobilization not only kept her off tour; it ultimately caused blood clots that moved to Serena's lung, causing a life-threatening pulmonary embolism that she said had her on her "deathbed." Though she was sidelined and off the court for long stretches, Bajin remained in her employ and by her side throughout.

Though they had a good thing going, things changed on a professional front for Bajin in 2012, when Serena brought on Patrick Mouratoglou, a French tennis coach and entrepreneur with his own namesake academy in France. Though Bajin had never officially been given the prestigious title of "Serena Williams's coach" despite his long tenure in her team, Bajin effectively had filled the coaching vacuum in Serena's team for years. With Mouratoglou on the scene, Bajin felt demoted. "From 2012, when Serena hired Patrick Mouratoglou as her main coach, my position had been very blurred," Bajin wrote. "When Patrick wasn't around, Serena and I worked on her game. And then when Patrick was around, I went back to just hitting balls back and nothing more, and that was very difficult for me."

Mouratoglou, a savvy self-promoter who used Serena's successes to put himself and his academy on the map, got more and more attention and credit for Serena's success, and Bajin felt himself receding. "If I was sacrificing so much, and doing good work, I wanted acknowledgement for that, and credit for what I was doing," Bajin wrote. When it became clear that Serena was sticking with Mouratoglou at the end of the 2014 season, Bajin decided he had to leave Serena's team after more than seven years by her side. "She had been the biggest part of my life for so many years," he wrote, "and it felt like a breakup."

Not knowing where his next employment might come from, Bajin printed up flyers advertising his coaching services that he planned to distribute around Palm Beach Gardens to local club tennis players. But to his surprise and relief, his services were quickly in demand. Two days after his split from Serena, he got a call from Victoria Azarenka, one of her chief rivals, asking him to join her team, again as a hitting partner. "I'm doing a little more than just hitting balls, but I don't care about the title," Bajin told me as he began working with Azarenka. "As long as Victoria knows what work I put in, I'm good with that. Call me a gardener if you want, I don't care."

Working alongside Azarenka's head coach Wim Fissette, Bajin quickly found success anew. But not long after Azarenka had swept the "Sunshine Double" at Indian Wells and Miami—including a win over Serena in the Indian Wells final—Azarenka told Bajin she was letting him go with no explanation; it wasn't until three weeks later that Bajin learned on Twitter that Azarenka was pregnant.

After a brief stint with Sloane Stephens, who was sidelined by a foot injury, Bajin got another job as a hitting partner with Caroline Wozniacki and worked with her through the end of the 2017 season. Wozniacki ended her work with Bajin following her win at the year-end WTA Finals in Singapore. Three days after that split, Bajin's phone was ringing again. This time, at last, he was considered for a head coaching job. But after a run of working with players who had been ranked No. 1, this call was inquiring about his interest in a young player ranked outside the Top 50.

. . . .

Naomi hadn't been looking to follow in Serena's personnel footsteps. By the end of the 2017 season she had largely grown tired of the often superficial comparisons made between Serena and herself, and she didn't want to be seen as a copycat. But Serena's agent Jill Smoller, who also worked at IMG, heard that Naomi was looking for a new coach after parting with David Taylor and recommended Bajin to Naomi's agent, Stuart Duguid. Duguid called Bajin, and soon he was driving down from Palm Beach Gardens—where he still lived—to Boca Raton, where Naomi now lived with her parents and trained out of the Evert Academy. "The first time we practiced, I just was, like, 'Oh, I'm nervous,'" Naomi said soon after. "He was with Serena for such a long time; I really like Serena."

The trial session was quickly derailed, not by nerves but by a ligament. Within the opening minutes of hitting with Naomi, Bajin landed awkwardly on his right foot as he ran for a ball and fell. "Because he's really big, I thought he was joking, because he had the ankle guards on," Naomi said. "He just turned really red."

"I was in a lot of pain, and I should have immediately stopped," Bajin, who had torn a ligament in his ankle, later wrote. "But I already knew I liked Naomi and I was convinced I could help her, and I really wanted to keep going. I didn't say anything at the time, but of course Naomi had noticed that I was limping around the court, and she asked her dad if I was going to be okay. I think she felt bad that I was in so much pain."

Despite being so hurt that he couldn't use his right foot to drive—making for a harrowing trip down I-95—Bajin returned to practice with Naomi the next day. "The reason I go over the top is that it allows me to prove a point," Bajin said of his playing through pain. "I want to show my players that they are the most important person in my life, that they really are my number one priority."

Impressed by his dedication and positivity, and with her parents' encouragement, Naomi hired Bajin to be her full-time coach. Bajin described the offer from Naomi, then ranked 68th, as a "huge pay cut" from what he had been paid by Wozniacki to be a hitting partner, but Naomi had given him what he had long wanted: a chance to be a head coach on tour.

. . . .

Much of Bajin's advice for Naomi was the same as other coaches had told her: he wanted her to be more thoughtful about when to deploy her biggest weapons, playing a more high-percentage brand of tennis. "I don't have to blast it 100 percent, sort of," she explained early in their partnership. "Like, picking and choosing when to go for it." Bajin also continued a focus on improving her fitness, bringing in trainer Abdul Sillah to help Naomi enter the best shape of her life as she began her twenties. "We went old-school style," said Sillah. "We would do some sprints in front of her house on the street, like at six in the morning. I would mark up with cones: 100 meters, 150 meters, and we're sprinting. And the neighbors would come out, waving and stuff like that. But she was working, and she never complained once." Naomi also went on a strict diet before the 2018 season. "It's going to sound kind of extreme, but during the off-season, I was eating boiled foods," Naomi said. "I would boil chicken and broccoli and stuff like that, and I wouldn't eat any carbs. That was mainly just to trim down."

Where Bajin differed from Naomi's various previous coaches was in his focus on her personality: if he could get her out of her shell, he believed, he could unlock tremendous potential. Bajin said that before he began working with Naomi, he had assumed she was a "diva" for always trying to avoid eye contact when they'd pass each other in tournament corridors. When he got to know her, he realized that her reticence came from shyness, and so he worked on purposeful goofiness to get her to loosen up. "I wanted to help her to be more open, and not to be so afraid of the world, and not to worry whether people were looking at her," Bajin wrote. "I wanted to show her that it's okay to make a fool out of yourself." To that end Bajin designed challenges and games between himself and Naomi at the end of practices, where the winner would pick a mildly embarrassing punishment for the loser. When Bajin lost one several months into their partnership, Naomi took his phone and commandeered his Twitter account to post the most embarrassing tweet she could conjure: "Tbh @justinbieber is my favorite singer, kinda embarrassing but it's 2018 now- new year new me. (And also pink is my favorite color) p.s: magenta is my 2nd favorite color."

When Naomi lost one of the contests during a training session in Tokyo, Bajin had her dance in the middle of the crowded Shibuya Crossing. "That was a lot of fun, but it also taught Naomi the important lesson that if people are looking at you, and even laughing at you, that's not such a big deal," Bajin wrote. "You soon won't care so much what other people think about you. You'll no longer be so self-conscious and so awkward around other people."

Making Naomi feel less inhibited and self-conscious, Bajin thought, would make her play more freely on court, no longer burdened by negativity when things weren't coming easily to her. "She's such a perfectionist that she just gets down on herself and is too hard to herself," Bajin said. "So I have to be the contrast. If she's too negative and too down, then I have to go and say it's okay. The world is round, the grass is green, everything is all right. But in general she is more hard on herself than she should be. She's doing her thing, she's doing great."

Naomi was quickly won over by Bajin's attitude and warmth, including the effort he had made to connect with her by watching *Death Note,* one of her favorite anime shows. "He's a really positive and nice person, and he makes everything really fun, and he's very entertaining," she said months into their partnership. "Seriously, there's nothing I don't like about him."

· · · · · · ·

Though his track record with Serena was his calling card, Bajin was consistently clear that he wasn't attempting to turn Naomi into a clone of her idol. "She's her own person," he said months into their partnership. "I believe that if you step in someone else's footprints, you don't leave your own behind."

When people said they saw similarities between Serena and Naomi as players, Bajin would insist the shared characteristics between the two women were mostly limited to superficial things about their appearance—shared "big hair," he said. "Two very different individuals who have different playing styles," he later wrote. "Yes, their games might look similar, but they have different techniques, different footwork, and they each have different shots that they like and rely on in tough situations."

But as Bajin told *The Body Serve Podcast*, his experience with Serena was still a useful measuring stick. "I had the pleasure and great honor of hitting with Serena every day for eight years, and that's probably one of the best balls you're going to get from the other side," he said. "So I can kind of feel and know how far away her shots are from the world's greatest."

. . . .

Having a famous (within tennis, at least) face in her corner added some attention to Naomi as the 2018 season, her third full lap on the tour-level circuit, got underway. Naomi started her season at the Hopman Cup, a mixed-team exhibition event in Perth, pairing with Japan's men's No. 2 Yuichi Sugita. The highlight was a rare chance to play one of the best in the men's game: Japan was drawn into the same group as the Swiss pair starring Roger Federer. Unusually for a mixed doubles pair, where men almost always serve first, Naomi served first in the first set against Federer and Belinda Bencic. The choice paid off: Naomi won most of her points serving toward Federer, and even aced him in the third set with an off-speed 87 mph serve that hit the sideline and swung wide past his forehand. As the sellout crowd—most of whom were there to see Federer—cheered, Naomi raised her arms in triumph and twirled happily. The Swiss pair won the short-format match in three sets, but not before Naomi managed to peg Federer with a volley, drawing a comically exaggerated growl of pain from the superstar, who was weeks from winning the twentieth and final major title of his career.

Ranked 72nd at the start of the Australian Open, Naomi beat 16th-seeded Elena Vesnina in straight sets in the second round to reach the third round at a major for a sixth time. The third round had been Naomi's ceiling at majors so far in her nascent career, posting a 0–5 record. Her opponent for her sixth attempt to break through to the fourth round—a benchmark known as reaching the second week of a major—was a local favorite, 18th-seeded Ash Barty of Australia. Barty would be a clear favorite by ranking and in crowd support for the Saturday afternoon match, but she recognized how her opponent could prove dangerous. "Naomi is a great chick and can certainly give the ball a rip when she's got time," Barty said approvingly.

Rip, she did. Naomi dominated with her superior firepower early and often, breaking Barty in the opening game of the match to give herself a lead that she never relinquished. Barty had four break points in the first set, including two in the final game, but Naomi saved them all to take the first set 6–4. Naomi again broke Barty in the opening game of the second set, and then again in Barty's second service game of the set to give herself a commanding 3–0 lead. Naomi secured the second break in uncharacteristic fashion, showing off her improved fitness and footspeed to outlast Barty with defense and counterpunching. Never broken in the match, Naomi closed out the 6–4, 6–2 win with her twelfth ace to reach the second week at a major for the first time. Though it had been a considerable upset loss on paper for the home favorite, Aussie commentators were thoroughly awed by Naomi's level. "Sometimes you just have to say 'Too good,'" commentator Liz Smylie said. "Sometimes you just have to tip your hat to your opponent," Barty agreed in her press conference.

It was Naomi's first win in front of a partisan crowd on a big stadium at a major, a skill that would come in handy later on that year. "I feel really happy, but also I'm kind of sorry, because I know you guys really wanted her to win," Naomi said in her on-court interview. The Australian emcee then thanked her for being a "gracious and humble victor."

Asked if breaking through to the fourth round of a major for the first time was something "special or important" for her, Naomi demurred. "I feel like last year it would have been, but this year I'm really trying to focus on certain things," she said. "I'm grateful, but, like, I don't want to stop here, if you know what I mean."

Naomi's reward for reaching the fourth round was a match against the top-ranked player in the world, No. 1 Simona Halep. The two stayed on level terms through the first part of the first set, and Naomi had four break points to pull ahead with Halep serving at 3–3. But from there the top seed steeled herself and ran away with the match, closing it out 6–3, 6–2. The loss was brisk, but Naomi left Melbourne with $182,097 in prize money for reaching the fourth round, the biggest payout of her career.

Back on the cusp of the Top 50, Naomi kept her progress rolling in the Middle East. She won two matches in qualifying to reach the main draw in Doha—the last time she would compete in a qualifying draw in her career, and then reached the quarterfinal in Dubai. But it was in a desert on the other side of the world where her biggest breakthrough yet would soon come.

· · · · · · ·

With a ninety-six-player field and one of the most lucrative purses on tour, the BNP Paribas Open in Indian Wells, California, had earned the moniker of the "Fifth Slam." With the Williams sisters having ended their boycotts a few years earlier, all the world's best players reliably came to compete for a champions prize of over $1 million.

Naomi, who had never won an official tournament at any level of professional tennis, drew one of the most accomplished champions on the tour for her first-round match: Maria Sharapova, a five-time major winner and former No. 1 who was third only to the Williams sisters in most major titles won among active players on tour. Parts of Sharapova's origin story resembled Naomi's: born in Siberia, Sharapova began training on public courts in Sochi before she moved with her father, Yuri, to Florida at age seven. With little money, father and daughter bounced between coaches around Florida, often with dubious financial arrangements. Throughout her many coaches, Yuri remained a constant. Sharapova was signed by IMG at age eleven, quickly and presciently identified as a potential marketing sensation. By sixteen, she had won her first WTA title and was appearing on American talk shows. At seventeen, she won Wimbledon, stunning the heavily favored Serena Williams in the final and launching Sharapova into superstar status that included spending more than a decade as the world's highest-paid female athlete. She lost that status abruptly: Sharapova served a fifteen-month ban after testing positive for meldonium, a drug that she contended she had taken legally for nine years and had not realized that the World Anti-Doping Agency (WADA) had added to its banned substances list before the start of the 2016 season. Though her reputation took a hit, Sharapova remained a powerful presence on the tour even after her ban and was still treated as a star attraction, but a string of injuries and inconsistent results had kept her far from reentering the Top 10 in the post-ban phase of her career.

As an ardent Serena fan, Naomi said she had watched "literally every match" Serena had played against Sharapova, of which there had been twenty-one at that point. Though Naomi was rooting for Serena in those matches, which had been dominated 19–2 by Serena, she admired Sharapova's composure during their contests. "I just remember being really impressed by her, because you would never know what she was thinking," Naomi said of Sharapova, waving her hand in front of her face to show unflappability. "She never really got upset or anything and she was always fighting. I always thought that was really cool, and I thought if someone could combine her mentality with Serena's, that would be really awesome. I actually took a lot from her, and I try to learn from her, too."

Taking what she had learned from both, Naomi quickly proved ready for the moment as the night session match began at Indian Wells, racing out to a 4–1 lead in the first set. Sharapova leveled the score at 4–4, but Naomi, undaunted, regained control and took the opening set 6–4. The second set followed a similar script: Naomi led 4–2, only for Sharapova to fight back and level at 4–4. But once again, Naomi did not wobble in the face of the resurgent star and closed out the 6–4, 6–4 victory. "I feel like before, maybe, if she came back from that I feel like I probably would have gotten really upset," Naomi said after her victory. "I'm just really happy I was able to win and sort of change the way my mentality works . . . I was just thinking that I would be really disrespectful to start getting angry. I'm playing against Sharapova, and who do I think I am to start getting angry playing her? Everyone knows that she fights for every point, so I just tried to tell myself that if I fight for every point, too, then it would be an equal match."

Sharapova ended her four-year partnership with coach Sven Groeneveld shortly after the loss. Groeneveld told me he believed Sharapova had played a great match but had underestimated the quality of the player who had beaten her that night. "I actually said, 'We're not giving enough credit to this player,'" Groeneveld said of Naomi. "'She's very, very good, and you got beaten today by a better player.'"

The win over Sharapova was a bucket list item for Naomi. "There's basically three people I wanted to play: it was Venus, her, and Serena," Naomi said in her post-match press conference. "So I've ticked two people off, and now I'm just waiting to play Serena, so I'm really looking forward to that."

Later in her press conference, a reporter asked: "Naomi, can you imagine yourself as a really, really big champion, holding up the biggest trophies in the game?"

"It would be so sad if I said 'no,'" Naomi replied, laughing.

· · · · · · ·

To lift the crystal trophy at Indian Wells—one of the most prestigious and certainly heaviest in the game—Naomi would need to face a wide range of opponents, posing various challenges that would test her completeness as a player.

After beating Sharapova, Naomi was dealt another veteran stalwart in her second-round match at Indian Wells: Agnieszka Radwańska, a slight but crafty Pole dubbed as "the Ninja" for the subtle lethality of her off-pace shots. But Naomi was patient and prudent throughout, keeping her footwork precise to adjust to the unusual spins off Radwańska's racquet and closing out an ultimately uncomplicated 6–3, 6–2 victory. "I was just trying to be mentally really calm, and just go for it when I had it," she said.

The next match would require a different sort of calm. Naomi was dealt a less heralded opponent: 100th-ranked Sachia Vickery, who had pulled off a stunning upset win over No. 3 Garbiñe Muguruza the round prior. Naomi would have the new pressure of being the favorite, and playing against one of the speediest defenders on tour, but would also struggle with Vickery rushing between points and hearing jeers from Vickery's support team in the front row of the stadium. Seeing Naomi looking visibly bothered and upset, Bajin came down for an on-court coaching visit and urged her to take control of the match by pausing the match whenever she felt herself growing uncomfortable for whatever reason. "If that guy bothers you, put the racquet up," Bajin told her. "Don't let these guys bother you. If there is something, put the racquet up." Naomi won 6–3, 6–3, achieving a far tougher triumph than the score line would indicate. Asked what the key to her victory was, she responded that she had been "just trying not to get irritated."

In the next two rounds Naomi faced one of the game's elite defenders, the ultra-fit Maria Sakkari, and one of the game's elite power players, "ace queen" Karolína Plíšková. Her offense was good enough to beat Sakkari's defense, and her fitness lasted over three sets; against former No. 1 Plíšková, Naomi was able to use her increasingly improved speed and anticipation to reach Plíšková's powerful shots and send them back into the opposite corner with interest.

In the semifinals, just her second at the WTA level after her run in Tokyo eighteen months earlier, Naomi drew a rematch against Simona Halep, the current World No. 1 who had dismissed her with ease in the fourth round of the Australian Open two months earlier. The improvements Naomi had made in the short time were apparent. She was playing with more margin and moderation on her shots; when she did swing with full power, she added topspin so that balls that might have sailed long instead dipped into the court.

With five wins under her belt, the most she'd ever had in the main draw of a tournament, everything was clicking for Naomi. After just thirty-three minutes, she had taken the first set 6–3 over Halep, punctuating the decisive score with an ace on set point. Then, unusually, she called down Bajin for a coaching visit, looking concerned and uneasy.

"Why that face?" Bajin asked when he arrived to her side. "You just won a set against the World No. 1."

"My timing is messed up," she replied, sounding dejected.

"Okay, how do we fix it?" he said, rhetorically.

"Move my feet?" Naomi replied.

"Of course," Bajin said, soon adding that she needn't change anything at all. "Just keep doing what you're up to: it's perfect," he said. "And no more negativity on court. Don't feed her anything."

Naomi faked a mopey shrug and Bajin laughed. "No, no, no, we can do that after," he said, smiling. He had convinced Naomi that perfection wasn't necessary from her to beat the best in the world. With her confidence redoubled, Naomi won the second set in even more dominant fashion, completing a 6–3, 6–0 victory over Halep in just over an hour. She had reached the biggest final of her career by beating the current World No. 1 for the first time in her career.

In a typical contrast between her tennis confidence and her social hesitation, Naomi had again known how to win, but she hadn't known how to celebrate. "When I was playing the match, I was thinking, Okay, when I win, I'm going to throw my racquet and just be super happy . . . I'm going to be that extra," she explained afterward. "Maybe I'll even cry a little bit just to soak it in. But, I didn't. I was just sort of more relieved that it was over. And then, by the time that it took for me to realize that I won, I couldn't throw my racquet because it's been, like, a good ten seconds."

. . . .

Counting back to her debut as a thirteen-year-old at that small tournament in Montego Bay, the 2018 BNP Paribas Open in Indian Wells was the 110th officially sanctioned tournament of Naomi Osaka's professional career. One hundred and nine times previously, Naomi had gone to a tournament and lost. She had made six finals but lost them all, all at smaller tournaments with thirty-two-player singles main draws. Suddenly, in her 110th tournament, Naomi found herself at one of the biggest venues in the sport left standing at a place that had been bustling with hundreds of players a week earlier but was now desolate. The end, she discovered, was lonely.

"There's, like, nobody here," she said after reaching the final. "As it goes on, there's less players and stuff. It's kind of cool, but also a little bit, like, sad." There was an upside to having the place nearly to herself, she added: the Indian Wells player restaurant always had plenty of sushi in stock for her.

The other player left standing in the women's singles draw was another rising twenty-year-old, the Russian Daria Kasatkina. Like Naomi, Kasatkina had also mowed down a murderer's row to reach the Indian Wells final, beating reigning U.S. Open champion Sloane Stephens and then three former No. 1–ranked players: Caroline Wozniacki, Angelique Kerber, and Venus Williams. Kasatkina won not with power but with remarkable finesse, able to precisely direct and bend the ball with a variety of elegant strokes, opting for flowy flair over full-on firepower. Born just five months before Naomi, Kasatkina's path had been more conventional: she had won the 2014 Roland Garros girls' title to clearly establish herself as one of the best in her generation. When she first saw Naomi at a lower-level tournament on the ITF Pro Circuit, Kasatkina told me, she was struck not only by her obvious power but by a certain "charisma" she saw in Naomi. "I don't know how to explain it, but when you see the person on the court, you feel like, okay—this is not a regular player," Kasatkina told me. "She's going to be something else."

The 16,100-seat main stadium of Indian Wells is the second-biggest tennis stadium in the world, behind only the U.S. Open's Arthur Ashe Stadium; on the day of this final its massive capacity included many famous faces, including billionaire Bill Gates and various Hollywood celebrities who had driven east for the weekend's tennis. Early on it seemed like Kasatkina, who had won eight pro titles to Naomi's none, was handling the occasion better. Naomi struggled to control her shots; she gave Kasatkina a break point at 3–3 in the first set by hitting her sixteenth unforced error of the young match.

As Naomi walked to the baseline after the miss, Tennis Channel play-by-play announcer Brett Haber asked his color commentator, the Hall of Famer Tracy Austin: If she were "building a tennis player," which of the two players' skill sets would she choose? "Gosh, that's really difficult to call, but I think I would go with Kasatkina," Austin replied, mentioning Kasatkina's "terrific feel" and "soft hands" as reasons for her choice.

Naomi couldn't hear the commentators in the booth, but what came next felt like her counterargument: she hit a sliding 100 mph ace up the center of the court, curling past Kasatkina's outstretched forehand, and shouted a loud "C'mon!" to win what might have been the highest-stakes point of her career to date. Naomi didn't stop there: she won the next two points to hold, then four of the next five points to break, and then four of the next five points again to hold, taking the crucial first set of the final 6–3.

"At least for the moment, it's power over artistry," Haber said in the booth, summing up the first set. Naomi had power, to be sure, averaging 74 miles per hour on her forehand in her previous six matches at Indian Wells. Not only was this tops among the women; it was only barely slower than Roger Federer's 76 mph forehand average on the men's side during the tournament. But for Haber to sum up Naomi's winning as merely "power" completely missed the path she had taken to her imminent arrival as a champion. She had the power since she was a young teenager, bombing serves and forehands over 100 miles per hour when she won her first match on the tour back in Stanford four years earlier. What was different now was her control: Naomi had harnessed her power and was deploying it with masterful moderation. When she was hitting the balls past players like Kasatkina, Halep, and Plíšková, she was still hitting them yards within the sidelines after having opened up the court with a previous shot. Both the placement of her shots and the score lines she had reeled off in the late stages of the tournament—6–2, 6–3, 6–3, 6–0, 6–3—were showing just how much margin Naomi could win with now that she'd learned to control her power when it mattered most.

The transformation was a testament to both her tactical and her physical development: because she was in the fittest shape of her life, Naomi didn't feel the same urgent need to keep points short. If a rally was going to extend, instead of panicking with a high-risk shot to end the point for better or worse, she was ready to dig in and run, even in the seventh match of the tournament. Later, Naomi would say the most surprising part of the tournament would be how she hadn't felt fatigued at the finish line. "I didn't get as tired as I thought I was going to," she said. "Whenever I see players winning Grand Slams or Indian Wells or Miami, I always think, 'Wow, they must get very tired,' because it's back-to-back matches, seven of them. I was kind of surprised by myself."

The second set of the final is more decisive than the first. Kasatkina, now the visibly nervous and uncomfortable of the two, double-faults on break point in the first game, and Naomi races out to a 5–1 lead. At 5–2, an hour and ten minutes into the final, Naomi holds the first championship point of her career. She hits a hard 117 mph serve that Kasatkina barely blocks back over the net. Running forward to reach the return, Naomi scoops it back across the net, and Kasatkina tries to lob it over her head. Quickly but calmly, Naomi takes several steps backward and then takes the ball out of midair with her backhand, slinging the ball onto the deep edge of Kasatkina's court, hitting the baseline.

Naomi clenches her first and smiles toward her team. She looks downward, then looks back to her box with a moment of doubt, double-checking that her final shot did indeed land in even though chair umpire Jennifer Zhang has already begun announcing "Game, set, match: Osaka. 6–3, 6–2."

Naomi and Kasatkina clasp hands at the net and Kasatkina moves in for a hug, which Naomi accepts with her typically stiff shyness. Naomi smiles and waves to all sides of the stadium, then runs over to the corner where her team is gathered. She hugs Sascha Bajin, then her strength and conditioning coach Abdul Sillah, then her physiotherapist Natsuko Mogi, then her agent Stuart Duguid. And there's more people there for her, too— from her sponsor Nissin, from the Japanese Tennis Association; as the camera lingers on them, it becomes clear to everyone watching at home just how big an operation Naomi Osaka, Inc., has already become in preparation for this moment: the biggest and most prestigious professional singles title ever won by a Japanese player, male or female. Kasatkina, by contrast, had traveled to Indian Wells with only her coach and her brother. The only person missing from Naomi's box is Leonard, but he's nearby: he's developed the habit of anxiously pacing or biking around the neighborhood rather than nervously sitting and watching Naomi.

Naomi then sits and waits as the tournament sets up the podium for the trophy presentation. Kasatkina gives pleasant remarks in her runner-up speech and then there is a long, corporate speech by Jean-Yves Fillion, the chief executive of BNP Paribas USA, the tournament's title sponsor. Fillion filibusters, speaking for nearly five minutes; his long remarks include a shout-out to Larry Ellison, the billionaire tournament owner who is seated in the front row wearing a hat that says LANA'I, the name of the Hawaiian island of which he owns 98 percent. By the time Fillion finally cedes the floor to Naomi, she has forgotten everything she has prepared to say. Her mind blank, she now has to speak in front of thousands in the stadium and millions watching on television. She begins:

> Um, hello (giggles). Hi, I'm Nao—oh, okay, never mind. I would like to thank (giggles) the tournament director? Um. And then, the WTA and the staff and the physios. Oh, whoops, sorry—I would like to thank Dasha (giggles). I would like to thank Dasha for being super nice and also being a really cool person to play against. I'm pretty sure we're going to play a lot of finals and stuff later. So, hopefully. And then I would also like to thank Dasha's team, because they're super nice too? (Giggles.) Um. And. Yeah. Congrats. I mean. Yeah, congrats. I would like to thank my team, um, for putting up with me, and yeah, that's basically it, and also supporting me (laughing). I would also really like to thank Sascha—hey! (waves). And my dad—he's not here. And my mom and my sister, they're watching in Florida, so, hi. Um. Did I forget? I would like to thank my sponsors, too (giggles). Adidas and Nissin and Wowow and, uh . . . Yonex! (double thumbs-up). Okay. Did I forget? Who did I forget. Oh, and the ball kids and the umpires. The ball kids are super awesome. This is probably going to be like the worst acceptance speech of all time (giggles). And then I would like to thank all of you guys for coming and watching this match. Thank you very much (claps). Um, yeah, I think that's it? Thank you very much.

By the end, the crowd was laughing along with Naomi. "That was cute—it was a little uncomfortable," Tennis Channel's Brett Haber said as Naomi stood next to the trophy, flinching as streamers were shot out of cannons while "Chandelier" by Sia played in the stadium. "The good news for Naomi Osaka is she's likely going to have a lot of practice at giving acceptance speeches during trophy ceremonies going forward."

"The thing is I prepared and everything, and I knew what I was going to say in which order," Naomi later explained in her press conference. "But then when he called me, I freaked out. And then I just started saying whatever came into my mind first, which is why I think I kept, like, stopping halfway through my sentences, because I just remembered something else I had to say. So, yeah, that was pretty embarrassing."

The moment was understandably overwhelming: Naomi had been playing tennis tournaments since childhood, and had ended almost all of them on a loss. "I don't really know what's going on right now," she said. "I really feel like I have another match I have to play tomorrow? And it didn't really sink in that I won."

"So, yeah, I'm just trying to, like, 'Woohoo!'" she said, pointing the trophy out to herself. She was successful there, too. "I'm happy," she concluded, smiling.

There was another new experience for Naomi to look forward to in the hours after her win: her first trip on a private jet. With no options for direct commercial flights, the trip was deemed more of a necessity than a luxury for her to make it to Florida as soon as possible for the fast-approaching Miami Open, where she would play her first match in the very different Florida conditions in less than seventy-two hours. Naomi and Kasatkina and their teams were sharing the plane and splitting the cost; Naomi hoped they could share some conversation, too. "I'm going to try not to listen to music—I'm going to see if she's going to talk to me," Naomi said, eagerly explaining her plan. "I'm going to see how that works out."

When asked if she had a specific conversation in mind, Naomi revealed that she had less strategy for facing Kasatkina on the plane than on the court. "I don't know how to start conversations; I don't know what you're supposed to say to someone that you've not really talked to before," Naomi said. "So it's not like I have a certain conversation. I just think it would be cool to talk to her."

At that admission of that inauspicious ambition, Naomi dissolved into laughter. "I'm so weird; it's so bad. Oh my God."

Alas, the conversation did not take off for Naomi in the air, Kasatkina told me years later as she recalled the flight. "It was quiet," Kasatkina said, laughing. "It was very quiet."

· · · · · · ·

The discussion of the private jet and all the photos of Naomi posing with the crystal trophy—both on the court and then with a Japanese flag in front of a desert mountain backdrop—were public. But for Naomi, her most meaningful victory that day stayed within her family.

The $1,340,860 awarded to the Indian Wells champion nearly doubled Naomi's previous career earnings of $1,483,053; add in bonuses from sponsors for winning the prestigious event and climbing the rankings—as well as the future sponsorships such a victory ensured—and Naomi had comfortably more than doubled what she had earned in seven years in just seven matches.

Naomi didn't crave any of the bacchanalian celebrations or spending expected of championship-winning athletes; rather than pop champagne, she went to see the newly released movie *Black Panther* in theaters. What the money meant to her was much more personal: the opportunity to repay her mother and to free her from the grind she had been living ever since she met Leonard, ever since she broke away from her family, ever since they dreamed of raising their daughters to be tennis players, ever since they moved to America to chase that dream. While Leonard had been on the court with Naomi and Mari, it was Tamaki who was working long hours at multiple jobs to continue earning for the family, subsidizing their dream.

Even with their daughter having found full-time coaching in Sascha Bajin, Leonard still often traveled the tour with Naomi while Tamaki stayed in Florida and worked. Her latest job was working for Mitsubishi

Motors in an office in Miami, a lengthy commute of about forty-five miles from the family's home in Boca Raton through heavy traffic; Tamaki startled her daughters by telling them how she had often drifted off mentally while on the road day after day, sometimes not remembering how she had made it home after arriving.

Tamaki was only forty-seven, younger than a typical retirement age, but Naomi was determined that she shouldn't have to work any longer; with memories of her mother leaving for work at 4:00 a.m. and returning at 9:00 p.m. seared into her, Naomi had made it her "goal in life" to achieve what she saw as her mother's freedom.

"When I was younger, she couldn't really come to any of my matches or my practices because she was the one providing; she was working, because tennis isn't a cheap sport," Naomi said in 2022. "She would literally work all the time, and there were days that I didn't see her because she would go to work so early and come back so late. And I knew that one of my main goals when I was starting to play tennis was: I want to be able to make it so that my mom doesn't have to work this hard. So when I finally accomplished that goal, it was really emotional for me, because I always dreamed that I would be able to do that . . . For me, that was a really priceless moment."

. . . .

There was one more priceless moment coming on this day for mother and daughter: as Naomi rode in the car on her way to the Palm Springs airport several hours after winning the Indian Wells final, Bajin saw news of the Miami Open draw flash across his phone. When he told Naomi, she was ecstatic and immediately called Tamaki.

"Mom, guess who I'm playing in the first round in Miami? Serena!"

SIXTEEN

Welcome to Serena

Serena Williams and Naomi Osaka almost certainly shouldn't have been playing each other in the 2018 Miami Open's first round, a stage of the competition reserved only for unseeded players. Had the draw come out after the WTA rankings were updated to include Indian Wells results, Naomi would have been seeded 22nd among the 32 seeds and gotten a bye into the second round. And the name "Serena Williams" in unbolded font on a draw sheet looked like a printing error. Serena had been the No. 1–ranked player in the world less than a year before, having won her professional record twenty-third major singles title at the 2017 Australian Open without dropping a set while already nearly two months pregnant.

But because she had barely played in the past year, and rankings are made on a rolling fifty-two-week basis, Serena's had fallen from 1st to 491st entering the 2018 Miami Open. The rules regarding seedings for returning mothers hadn't been a major flash point when other new moms had returned to tennis in past years, but because it was Serena, the obscure rule became a major cultural talking point in the spring of 2018, generating hue and cry from a wide cross section of social and traditional media, and even inside the White House. "This is ridiculous," tweeted Ivanka Trump. "@SerenaWilliams is a formidable athlete (best ever!) and loving new mother. No person should ever be penalized professionally for having a child! The #WTA should change this rule immediately."

While no one would argue that there were 490 better players on tour than Serena, nor would many tennis insiders say Serena was the world's most likely to win a tennis match in March 2018 after everything she had gone through in the past six months. Serena's entire pregnancy had been smooth, allowing her to continue strength training just weeks before her due date. But when she went to the hospital to have labor induced on her due date, everything began to go wrong for Serena: her labor did not begin as it should have, and her baby's vital signs began showing signs of distress. As Serena's own stress and pain also increased, doctors made the decision to deliver the baby by cesarean section, an option Serena had wanted to avoid because of the longer physical recovery required and also the risks that any surgery posed due to her history of blood clots. Sure enough, after the birth of her daughter Alexis Olympia Ohanian Jr., Serena began to struggle breathing and felt a familiar, crippling pain: a blood clot had moved to her lung and formed a pulmonary embolism. Serena had had her first pulmonary embolism seven years earlier and recognized the signs, but her doctors were slow to react. Serena demanded they do a CAT scan with dye to check, and sure enough, the pulmonary embolism was found. Serena likely only survived her hospital stay because she was familiar with her medical condition and had asserted herself; she likely would have died in the days following giving birth otherwise. Serena's ordeal led to increased attention on the stark racial disparities in childbirth: Black women were three times more likely to die during childbirth than White women.

The near-death experience and resultant recovery—Serena had also had another blood clot in her leg, which required an operation—postponed Serena's return to the tour, but it did not lower her standards for herself. She wanted to pick up where she left off, feeling a sense of unfinished business and a desire to show her strength to her newborn daughter. "She's the reason why this all means even more than it did before," Serena said in the introduction to her 2018 documentary series *Being Serena*. "Still, there's no escaping the fear. The fear that I might not come back as strong as I was."

Serena pulled out of the 2018 Australian Open, which had been her planned return date before complications set in, but returned to singles competition just six weeks later than expected at Indian Wells, where she had ended her boycott three years earlier. Serena returned to considerable fanfare; her husband, the tech entrepreneur Alexis Ohanian, bought billboards around the town that declared Serena the "G.M.O.A.T.": "Greatest Momma of All Time." With considerable crowd support, Serena won two matches before losing in the third round to her most familiar opponent: Venus.

Serena would later say she should have pulled out of Miami, where she was scheduled to play her next match nine days later. Her self-confidence was at the lowest in her career, in large part because she had struggled to shed weight in the months since her daughter's birth. Serena was still breastfeeding her five-month-old daughter, Olympia, which was well within the recommendation of organizations like the American Academy of Pediatrics, but seemed to be undermining her hard work on her fitness, to the frustration of her coach Patrick Mouratoglou. In a scene in *Being Serena,* which tracked her struggles to regain her fitness with remarkable candor, a scale showed Serena's weight at 205 pounds, 30 pounds over her officially listed weight of 175 pounds. Serena also later acknowledged other struggles with what she called "postpartum emotions."

On this hot, sunny day in Miami, where she began the second tournament of her comeback, Serena took the court wearing all black, including leggings that reached past her knee, covering most of her legs, as well as a sleeve over her right forearm. She chugged water on changeovers.

While her idol battled sudden self-doubts and uncertainties, Naomi had newfound confidence: she had never been fitter and had never played better tennis than she had in the past weeks. She had just won the first title of her career, beating a bevy of top players.

Naomi and Mari had often gone to Key Biscayne to see the top pros practice and compete up close. Naomi had watched Serena many times at Key Biscayne; now, for the first time, her very favorite player was staring back at her across a net. Naomi had been in dominant, imperious form at Indian Wells, and her seven-match winning streak was the longest of her life, but facing Serena was something entirely new for her. "Because she's the main reason why I started playing tennis, and, just, I have seen her on

TV so many times and I have always been cheering for her," Naomi explained after the match. "So for me to play against her—and just sort of try to detach myself a little bit from thinking that I'm playing against her and just try to think I'm playing against just a regular opponent—was a little bit hard for me."

There was someone else special in the stadium, too: Serena's father, Richard Williams, who sat in the lower bowl in a gray baseball cap. Richard, seventy-six, didn't travel much anymore due to health issues; where he had once sought the spotlight, he now was reluctant to make public appearances, not feeling like his former self. But if his daughters were on a tennis court in South Florida, for practice or a match, odds were Richard Williams would be there.

· · · · · · ·

On the heels of her breakthrough win at Indian Wells, there were more pockets of fans for Naomi than before: four women held up letters that spelled out OSAKA GO; others hanging a Japanese flag off the railing in front of their seats. But Serena, who was an eight-time champion at Key Biscayne, still had the majority of the stadium behind her. "If I was watching I'd be cheering for Serena, too," Naomi said. "I didn't really mind it at all."

With the stadium roughly half full for this off-peak Wednesday afternoon session, Serena gave the crowd plenty to cheer for as the match began. She held to love to open the match, pounding a 113 mph serve down the T on game point, then took her signature long walk around the far-side net post without breaking stride. On Naomi's first service point, Serena punished a 75 mph second serve, swinging out on a forehand down-the-line winner, taking a fifth consecutive point to start the match. But Naomi did not panic: on the sixth point, she bent low to hike a backhand crosscourt winner behind Serena, a bit of skill that left Serena softly clapping her left palm against her racquet strings in appreciation, saying "Good shot." Naomi saved a break point with a body serve at Serena at 113 miles per hour and held to level the match.

The two were level at 3–3 in the first set when Serena suddenly seemed to hit an early wall just twenty-five minutes into the match. Serena was torpid, slow to react to Naomi's shots, lacking her usual first-step explosivity. Serena could make clean, crisp contact when the ball came right to her, but even slight movements were shaky. Naomi wasn't hitting the balls into the corners, but still Serena was late reaching them, and soon Naomi had a 0–40 lead on Serena's serve. On her second break point, Naomi hit a searing shot that caught Serena completely unprepared: the ball ricocheted well out of play, giving Naomi a 4–3 break advantage.

After Naomi held for 5–3, Serena raced out to a 40–0 lead on her own serve. While some players might have let the game go so they could refocus for the opportunity to serve it out themselves, Naomi conceded nothing. At 40-15, Naomi crunched a forehand return winner and shouted "C'mon!" On another later game point, Naomi cracked a backhand winner down the line and shouted another "C'mon!" On the next point, Naomi did it again, with another backhand winner to earn a set point. She clinched the first set after sprinting into a corner to send a crosscourt forehand back catty-corner; Serena, slow to reach it, sent her reply well wide, giving Naomi the opening set 6–3. It was the story of the match and the moment: Serena was too often slow and late; Naomi was as ready as she could possibly be.

No one knew better what would come next from Serena than Naomi: whenever Serena trailed in a match, she would make her presence known across the net in increasingly obvious and unmissable ways, reminding her opponents exactly whom they were considering beating. Her grunts grew louder and longer. When she hit an ace in her first service game of the second set, Serena's grunt became a moan that lasted all the way until the ball had struck the wall behind Naomi's outstretched arm. She then shouted a "C'mon" of her own when she saved a break point.

Naomi wasn't intimidated; she was thrilled. "Because sometimes she plays matches where she doesn't say 'Come on' at all, and that's a little bit sad," she explained after the match. "Because you think: Do you think she's trying? So, yeah, I just wanted her to say 'Come on' once, because I knew that maybe she would be trying a little bit. So once I heard the first 'Come on,' I was like, 'Yeah!'"

Serena was indeed trying as the second set began, and both were producing moments of glittering play. At 1–1 Serena dug into Naomi's serve and earned a break point, but Naomi saved it. The game extended onward, with both Serena and the crowd seeming more engaged than before. Then, suddenly, Naomi hit two back-to-back aces to abruptly end the threat. When asked about the game in her post-match press conference, she explained a mantra she had discussed before, albeit now with more proximity than ever before. "This is going to be really bad, but sometimes when I am in a really hard position when I'm serving, I'm, like, 'What would Serena do?'" Naomi said. "But I was playing her? Yeah, I was literally just thinking 'What would Serena do?' Because you know how sometimes she aces people in really bad positions? I was trying to do that. It worked out."

The one-two punch of consecutive aces seemed to be a knockout combination, taking Serena's second wind from her. Naomi broke for a 3–1 lead, and Serena grew uncharacteristically pouty and sarcastic. "Honestly, you couldn't be worse," Serena muttered to herself after a missed return. "I mean, hello." Serena's dour defeatism was in sharp contrast to Naomi's relentless positivity, saying "C'mon" after nearly every point she won.

When Naomi held for 4–1 with another forehand winner, a "C'mon" and a fist pump, she had won eight of the last nine games. Naomi was not only beating her idol Serena—she was routing her. Normally, players were humbled in their first meeting with Serena; this time, it was the fan who was feasting.

Serena served again down 2–5 in the second set. She hit a wild forehand error, then a double fault, then a bad backhand error. Serena saved Naomi's first match point with a body serve that Naomi deflected long.

On Naomi's second match point, Serena hammers down a 112 mph serve, which Naomi only barely blocks back high over the net, landing short in the opposite court. Serena has ample time—too much time, perhaps—to set up her next shot, and she shoves what should have been an easy putaway shot well long, drawing gasps and screams from the crowd. Naomi looks down at the ground, looks toward her box, and walks calmly toward the net. Serena widens and rolls her eyes while shaking her head, making unmistakably clear her disgust at her own performance in a 6–3, 6–2 loss that has taken just an hour and seventeen minutes. Naomi quickly jogs to the net so as not to make Serena wait and bows her head toward Serena as she approaches. The two shake hands—Serena tells Naomi a quick "thank you"—and then shakes hands with chair umpire Marija Čičak. Naomi turns back and walks out onto the court with a sigh to wave to the crowd around the stadium, not allowing herself to smile—whether she forgot or chose not to is not clear.

Less than a minute after match point, Serena is walking off the court with her bag over her shoulder and adding a twirl to her stride that allows her to regally wave to the crowd on all sides. Rather than any of the normal post-match routines—shower, physiotherapy, mandatory press conference—Serena walks off court and keeps walking. She walks straight from the stadium court down the tunnel—"I get it; oh I get it," says Venus as Serena strides past her—to the VIP parking area, where Serena, still in her sweaty tennis clothes, gets into her parked Lincoln Navigator and drives. Serena runs a stop sign in the parking lot and keeps going, more than an hour north up I-95 to her home in Palm Beach Gardens some eighty-six miles north.

Around the time Serena has put rubber to the road, Naomi is doing her on-court interview. "I'm very grateful that I was able to play her, and it's even better that I was able to win," Naomi says. "I kind of wanted to impress her."

Hours after the victory, Naomi posts a photo of their handshake on social media.

"Omg," the caption reads.

SEVENTEEN

Charleston

There are two ingredients to becoming a big star in women's tennis in the 2010s. The first is to win a big tournament; the second, more crucial step is to beat Serena on a big stage.

Naomi Osaka does both within a four-day span in March 2018, and a star is born. Riding the wave of her twin triumphs, and the spotlight on her personality that the extended time on center stage earned her, *GQ Magazine* commissions a feature profile titled "Naomi Osaka Is the Coolest Thing in Tennis," sending editor Kevin Nguyen to Boca Raton to interview her. In the first major coverage she has gotten outside of the sports pages, *GQ* celebrates Naomi's quirky press conferences and trophy speeches and explores her love of video games. Naomi does a lengthy photoshoot for the magazine in various outfits; readers are informed that her Burberry hat is $350 and her Burberry jacket is $990.

"Everything came quite fast," Naomi later said. "You actually achieve multiple dreams at one time sometimes. It's like you're checking off a checklist that you didn't even know was a checklist."

. . . .

Two days after her triumph over Serena, Naomi loses in the second round of the Miami Open to fourth-ranked Elina Svitolina, ending her win streak at eight matches.

Ten days later, she's back on court for the first tournament of the clay season: Charleston, South Carolina, a genteel tournament with a country club feel. Though smaller than Indian Wells or Miami, Charleston is one of the oldest tournaments on the WTA Tour, the biggest women's-only tournament in the United States, and a favorite for many players for the laid-back southern hospitality.

In Charleston, Naomi is a bigger marquee attraction than ever before. Fans in the stands now know who she is. They've watched her, they've liked her, and they want to watch more.

Naomi wins her first match over Jennifer Brady and her second over Laura Siegemund, both in straight sets. After she beats Siegemund, on-court interviewer Nick McCarvel begins the traditional post-match Q&A with Naomi for the fans watching on television and in the packed stands of the Althea Gibson Court, asking her what she is happiest with about the win. But Naomi isn't happy.

"I guess just winning?" Naomi replies. "I was kind of upset throughout the whole match, to be honest. So I'm just really glad I was able to win today."

McCarvel then asks if she was especially satisfied that her improved fitness and speed allowed her to track down so many of Siegemund's drop shots. "Um, sure?" Naomi replies. "I actually don't really—like, I hear your questions? But I'm not really paying attention that much."

"Okay, fair enough," McCarvel says, quickly pivoting to how great the fan support was for her on this court. "In the last couple weeks since Indian Wells, obviously a lot of pressure, a lot of expectations," McCarvel says, and Naomi nods. "But how much have you paid attention to this new attention?" he asks. "And is it different at all?"

"Um, well, I'm not really paying attention to anything," Naomi replies. "I'm like super tired all the time, and I feel like everything has gone by really quickly. So I'm just really trying to just focus on my matches here, and I'll think about the other stuff later."

. . . .

Naomi has lots on her mind in Charleston. She accomplished her biggest goal, allowing her mother to retire, weeks earlier. "I felt really happy and really proud because I knew that this is a dream that I've had since I was little," Naomi said. "At the same time, it was a bit weird because I had to shift to another goal, and that was quite hard for me for a while."

Naomi, twenty years old, feels like her life's work is complete and isn't sure how to keep living. "I just woke up one day in Charleston before one of my matches and I was just thinking, like, What is the point of my life?" Naomi later said. "I was thinking, Should I just go buy a farm and grow, like, crops? I know that's the primitive-ish life, but I'm wondering if that could spark something in me again. And I was sitting there, but then I had to go play my match . . . I was thinking in my head, like, Wow, I hope this girl beats me so I don't have to be here anymore . . . I didn't really know what it was. I just thought maybe I was just super tired and burnt out."

Naomi can't hide her feelings during her third-round match against Julia Görges. When she calls Bajin out to the court for a mid-match coaching timeout during a second-set changeover, already down a set and a break, Bajin quickly voices his concern.

"You're giving it to her, Naomi," Bajin says. "From the outside—I'm just going to be honest with you now—from the outside it looks a little bit like somebody is forcing you to be here."

"And I don't want to be here," Naomi confirms, flustering Bajin.

"But you're here now!" he replies. "Why do we work? You want to be the best player in the world? This is where you prove it . . . You can beat her even with just 75 percent . . . You can do it, Naomi. Come on, you've got three people in the box who all believe in you, who are behind you and support you."

At the mention of the people there to support her, Naomi's tears intensify, and she pulls down her visor to cover her face.

"You can do this, Naomi," Bajin reiterates. "After this tournament, we get a couple of days off. But we're here now and we're trying to make the best out of it, okay? You give me a promise that you're going to be a little bit positive."

"I can't!" Naomi protests.

"Yes, you can," Bajin says, still trying to reassure her with repetitions of his belief. "You can. I know you can. I know you can. I know you can. I know you can, Naomi. We all know you can. And if you don't, then that's fine with me, too. But we've put in the work."

Naomi, still sobbing, then has a question for him. "Why is this so depressing?" she asks.

The umpire calls "Time" to signal the end of the ninety-second changeover.

"What is depressing?" asks Bajin.

"I can't," Naomi replies. "Like, this place."

Confused and out of time, Bajin leaves her with a last assurance. "You can do it, Naomi," he says once more. "Forget about that place. Go to your own happy place."

. . . .

Naomi comes into her press conference after the straight-set loss, still sullen. "I've never been in this position before," she says. "I do know that what I felt today was like a new feeling, though. What I felt today I've never felt it before."

"Can you articulate how you felt?" a reporter asks.

"I don't know how to explain it, but, like, kind of depressed," Naomi replies. "But, like, it comes in waves . . . It kind of started yesterday. Like, yesterday I just woke up and I was really depressed, but I don't know why."

After a few more questions, a reporter asks: "With your tournament over and getting to have a break now, what's the first thing on your mind that you want to do?"

"Nothing," Naomi replies.

"Just nothing?"

"Yeah."

Asked about the clay tournaments ahead in Europe, Naomi says she takes little solace in her two wins in Charleston. "I'm just an okay player that was able to play okay," she says. "Like, I am so sad right now. I don't really want to think about other tournaments. Yeah. I'm sorry."

Naomi is asked if she understands why she feels this way.

"Yeah, I don't really know," she replies.

EIGHTEEN

Collision Course

∎

It had been a forgettable summer for Naomi Osaka. Seeded for the first time at major tournaments, Naomi matched her previous year's results when she lost in the third round of both the French Open—where she lost to Madison Keys for the third time—and Wimbledon, where she lost in the third round to eventual champion Angelique Kerber. After playing and losing one match for the Washington Kastles of the exhibition league World Team Tennis, Naomi failed to make a dent at any of the three WTA hard-court tournaments she played. At the Citi Open in Washington, D.C., Naomi lost in the second round to Magda Linette. In Toronto, she lost in straight sets in the first round to Carla Suárez Navarro. In Cincinnati, Naomi again lost in straight sets in the first round, this time to Maria Sakkari.*

Naomi's cooling off reduced the heat of the spotlight on her heading into the U.S. Open. Because of concern over her slumping results, *The New York Times Magazine* moved the cover story it had commissioned about Naomi for the Sunday before the U.S. Open off the cover. The article, an excellent look at her multicultural existence—"living on the hyphen" in the words of writer Brook Larmer—ran inside the magazine instead, paired with an arresting photograph of Naomi in front of a beige backdrop in a simple white tank top and visor that allowed her curly hair to dominate the frame. For the photoshoot in Florida, the magazine had flown hair stylist

---

* It would be the last time Naomi would lose back-to-back first-round matches for four years.

Yoichi Tomizawa down from New York to brush out Naomi's black-to-gold ombre hair high above her white Adidas visor and wider than her shoulders, making her look more majestic than she ever had before. It was an image worthy of the cover, but there were growing doubts at the magazine that Naomi was capable of justifying that showcase with her results at the upcoming U.S. Open.

Naomi herself was admitting doubts, too, but she found a way past them by sharing them with the world. Two days after her loss to Sakkari in Cincinnati, after which she had cried alone in the locker room, Naomi posted a screenshot of her Notes app to Twitter:

> Hello umm so this is like a lil update post haha

> So the last couple weeks have been really rough for me, I haven't been feeling the ball right and it's thrown me off a lot to the point where I started getting really frustrated and depressed during my practices. I had a lot of pressure entering the hard court swing because I felt a lot of expectation on me from Indian Wells and I didn't feel like the underdog anymore (which is a totally new feeling for me)

> If anyone was following Cincy you would know my match I lost but I feel like it was a step in the right direction, things weren't working the way I wanted but I finally felt that fun feeling playing tennis that I haven't felt since Miami. So I'm really happy/excited about that and I wanted to share my feelings with you guys. Update finished, see you in NY

In her own quiet way, and with the benefit of hindsight, Naomi had announced herself as ready once more to make noise in New York. But few people at the time were listening, because the loudest drumbeat in tennis, once more, was around Serena Williams.

. . . .

In her second major back from maternity leave, Serena had reached the final of Wimbledon, losing to Kerber; she was again marching through a major draw at the U.S. Open to the delight of media, sponsors, fans, and Naomi. "It's no secret that Serena is my favorite; I've watched all of her matches in the U.S. Open this year," Naomi said during the tournament. "I'm just really grateful that she's playing again. I'm grateful that I got the opportunity to play her in Miami; I hope I can play her here. That would kind of mean we have to meet in the finals."

Playing on the days when Serena wasn't, Naomi found her rhythms in New York. Each morning, she ate a bagel with smoked salmon. And each match, she played some of her best tennis. Naomi's first-round win, 6–3, 6–2 over 146th-ranked Laura Siegemund, took only an hour and eighteen minutes. Her second-round win, 6–2, 6–0 over 162nd-ranked Julia Glushko, was done in just fifty minutes. Naomi was into the third round for the sixth consecutive major; this time had been the easiest of them all.

Naomi's third-round match was even more emphatic than her first two, blanking 33rd-ranked Aliaksandra Sasnovich 6–0, 6–0 in just fifty minutes. It was the first "double bagel" Naomi had won since beating sixty-five-year-old Gail Falkenberg back in 2013, and it was a loud warning shot to the field about her level before the biggest challenge yet.

. . . .

There were obvious similarities between Naomi Osaka and her fourth-round opponent Aryna Sabalenka. Both had climbed from outside the Top 70 to inside the Top 20 over the course of the season. The tennis world was bullish on the big-hitting Belarusian: Sabalenka would be voted WTA Newcomer of the Year at the end of the 2018 season, the same award Naomi had won two years earlier

Unlike Naomi, who had made her big leap in March at Indian Wells and had come into New York cold, Sabalenka was the red-hot player in women's tennis in the lead-up to the U.S. Open, reaching the semifinals of Cincinnati and winning her first WTA title at the Connecticut Open in the two weeks before. Since the start of August, Sabalenka had scored five wins against Top 10 opponents.

Sabalenka had done it all with ferocity; the roaring tiger tattoo on her forearm was an appropriate logo for her primal play. Sabalenka cut a predatory presence on the court, a bruising behemoth who barked bellicosely with every belt of the ball. She was a ball basher in the most beautiful sense of the tennis term, swinging as hard as she possibly could on most every thunderous swing. In order to beat Sabalenka, who was becoming a force of nature in the summer of 2018, Naomi would have to weather the storm.

The match between the two highly touted twenty-year-olds was the marquee match of the fourth round of the U.S. Open, and the stakes were high. Not only would the winner be into her first major quarterfinal; she would be a heavy favorite to go even further, as they were the only two seeded players remaining in the bottom quarter of the women's draw.

The roof of Louis Armstrong Stadium, the U.S. Open's newly rebuilt second stadium, was open for the afternoon match, letting the heat into the stadium unabated. Naomi started hot, too, breaking twice to take the first set 6–3 over Sabalenka in thirty-one minutes. But Sabalenka, who had won more matches in the last month than anyone, soon found her range and her confidence, breaking Naomi twice herself to go up 4–1 in the second set. Sabalenka took the second 6–2 to force a third after an hour and eleven minutes.

Because of the oppressive heat, there was a ten-minute break for both players to cool off indoors before the third set. When they came back, Sabalenka picked up where she had left off, gaining speed like a boulder rolling downhill. Naomi shrieked as she went down break point in the third game, and after Sabalenka pounced on a second serve to break for a 2–1 lead, Naomi put a towel over her head and pressed her hands to her face, taking deep breaths.

Sabalenka, who had been the more aggressive, assertive player, seemed to be in full control of the match. But on that changeover, the thought occurred to Naomi: Sabalenka had never won a match in a big stadium at a major; Naomi had. "For once in my life, I actually think that I was the player with more experience, which is very odd for me to say," Naomi said afterward. "But I know that she just sort of recently started coming onto the Grand Slams and stuff. I feel like there were moments that I kind of knew what to do."

Sabalenka began to wobble, and Naomi slowly but surely took control. On Naomi's fourth match point, Sabalenka double-faulted, ending the fireworks show from both with a dud. But despite the anticlimax to Naomi's 6–3, 2–6, 6–4 win there was catharsis. As Sabalenka chucked her racquet to the side, Naomi sobbed softly as she walked to the net. After they shook hands, Naomi sat, covered her face with her towel, and cried some more. She was still fighting back tears when she spoke to on-court interviewer Andrew Krasny, having finally reached her first major quarterfinal.

"I was just thinking I wouldn't forgive myself if I managed to lose that," she said.

. . . .

Naomi was inexperienced at this stage of Grand Slams, but Sascha Bajin had been there many times with Serena. Knowing how prone Naomi was to overthinking, he wanted to get her mind off the tennis. "You can't escape tennis in New York in August," Bajin said. "You just can't. Serena was on every billboard, she was on every TV commercial." Bajin knew the best way to counteract this was alternate programming. Because her hotel room's television was incompatible with her PlayStation, Bajin found an electronics store and bought Naomi a new fifty-five-inch TV, carrying it three blocks through Manhattan back to the hotel. "I wish she was more into books than PlayStation—it would have been easier to carry a few books a couple of blocks than a fifty-five-inch TV," Bajin joked. "But, you know, it worked." After Naomi beat Sabalenka, he called the hotel's concierge to get the new television set up in Naomi's room as a surprise for when she returned that night.

And so the night before her first major quarterfinal, Naomi stayed in her hotel room, playing *Overwatch* on one TV and watching Serena beat Karolína Plíšková on the other. Their paths were drawing closer, but Naomi still wanted to watch and cheer on her favorite player.

· · · · · · · ·

Naomi's long-awaited first Slam quarterfinal wound up being one of the most forgettable matches of the tournament. Her opponent, Lesia Tsurenko, had struggled physically in the heat and humidity during her grueling three-set win in the fourth round, and had nothing left to give when it came time for her own first major quarterfinal. Even in the warm-ups, when she swung and whiffed on an overhead, it was clear Tsurenko would be little opposition. Naomi rolled, nearly unimpeded, 6–1, 6–1 in just fifty-eight minutes. Winning a quarterfinal—and becoming the first Japanese woman to reach a major singles semifinal since Kimiko Date in 1996—was a bigger step, but there were none of the emotions like after her fourth round.

The women's singles semifinal matches were played back-to-back in the Thursday-night session as the two halves of the draw converged on the eleventh day of the tournament. Serena was up first, and she rolled 6–3, 6–0, over Anastasija Sevastova to book her spot in her second straight major final. In order to face her idol, Naomi would have to do something she'd never done before: beat Madison Keys.

Not only had Keys won their scarring third-round encounter two years earlier, coming back from 1–5 down in the third set, but she'd won their next two meetings as well, including a straight-set win in the third round of the 2018 French Open. On this fourth occasion, Naomi played with a newfound focus. Trained to weather power by surviving the Sabalenka match, she knew when to push and when to pull back against the similarly aggressive Keys.

The biggest revelation of the match was what Naomi did under pressure, saving all thirteen break points she faced. "I kept thinking, 'Okay, there will be a let-up, somewhere I'll be able to get back in it,'" Keys later recalled. "[But] even on any of the break points that I had, I had no shot. I walked away obviously very disappointed, but at the same time to play someone who was playing at that level . . . I think she deserved it."

Naomi's final service game lacked the drama of her others. Up 40–15, she hit a hard body serve at Keys, who could only shank the ball into the stands to complete Naomi's 6–2, 6–4 win. Naomi laughed with delight, smiled, and threw her arms briefly above her head as she looked toward her box.

"Thirteen break points faced, thirteen break points saved—how did you do that?" ESPN's Tom Rinaldi asked Naomi in her on-court interview.

Naomi smiled and laughed. "Um, this is going to sound really bad? But I was just thinking: I really want to play Serena."

After the cheers from the crowd subsided, Rinaldi asked a follow-up: "Why?"

"Because she's Serena!" Naomi said again. "Like, what do you mean?"

Rinaldi later asked Naomi if she had a message for her mom, who was watching courtside.

"Mom, I did it," Naomi said. "I love you. Thank you."

Tamaki, who had rarely watched Naomi's matches in person, gave two thumbs-up, and the crowd cheered once more.

Rinaldi then made a more unusual follow-up suggestion: "And perhaps, given how much it was in your mind, and how much you said you wanted it, a message to Serena?"

Naomi paused only slightly before answering: "I love you?"

The disarming declaration of love was perhaps the furthest thing from trash talk there had ever been in the lead-up to a major final, and it sent the entire stadium, Naomi included, into fits of laughter.

. . . .

Asked about Naomi after her own semifinal, Serena said that she could draw positives from having faced her in Miami already. "It was good that I played her, because I kind of know how she plays now," Serena said. "I mean,

I was breastfeeding at the time, so it was a totally different situation. It was what it was. I mean, hopefully I won't play like that again. I can only go up from that match."

Naomi said it felt "surreal" to get to face Serena again. "Even when I was a little kid, I always dreamed that I would play Serena in the final of a Grand Slam," she said.

Naomi was then asked: "How did that dream match come out?"

"You already know," Naomi replied, grinning. "You're just asking me. I don't dream to lose, so . . ."

. . . .

In one of her many interviews in advance of her first major final, Naomi was asked if she had surprised herself with her run at the U.S. Open. "Not really that much?" Naomi replied, showing a sudden self-assurance. "I feel like there's a certain mindset I have when I play. When I have that mindset, I always win."

NINETEEN

Boiling Point

To understand the 2018 U.S. Open final, you first need to understand the acoustics inside Arthur Ashe Stadium.

Whereas Wimbledon's Centre Court prides itself on a reverent pin-drop hush, a piano could be dropped from the upper deck inside Ashe and hardly be heard landing over the sound of 23,771 New Yorkers who never shut up. The din is worst at court level, where every sound from every side swirls together. Communication inside Ashe is muddled at nearly any volume, quadruply so since the 2016 addition of the retractable roof, which keeps sound waves inside, rebounding and distorting. Even for those sitting courtside in the front row about ten feet behind the players' benches, it's nearly impossible to understand any of the players' conversations with the chair umpire. It's clearer from home; broadcast microphones can now pick up almost everything for viewers watching remotely. But for players and spectators alike, when you're inside Ashe, and something happens, you probably won't understand right away what's going on. It's a cauldron of confusion, all the more so when the lid is shut.

And on the afternoon of Saturday, September 8, 2018, with intermittent rain in the forecast, the pot lid was staying closed, and the turmoil roiled within.

· · · · · · ·

Even without knowing what chaos lay ahead on that fateful afternoon, there was plenty of reason to stress for Naomi, who was playing in her first

Grand Slam final. The 4:00 p.m. start gave Naomi plenty of time to fret beforehand, starting when she woke up already sweating. "I was so nervous and my heart was racing the entire day," she said. "I think that wasn't good for my health. And, I don't know, like I couldn't eat anything. Like I felt like I was going to throw up."

Naomi's nerves were apparent as she warmed up on Ashe with Bajin two hours before the final. As Naomi missed ball after ball into the net during the warm-up, she asked him if perhaps the net was higher than usual that day. Bajin, who himself had had two sleepless nights in a row as he prepared for his player to face the woman he had considered family for eight years, stayed relentlessly positive. At Naomi's suggestion, the two spent extra time in the warm-up working on Naomi's returns, helped by Bajin's keen understanding of Serena's serving patterns. There was off-court preparation in the hours before the match, too: Bajin showed Naomi video highlights of her win over Serena six months earlier in Miami to help remind her what patterns worked in their matchup and to allow her to visualize beating Serena again.

Despite being ready on a tennis level, Naomi still felt overwhelmed by the occasion. So to calm herself down on the morning of the final, she repeatedly called Mari, who was an ocean away in France as she traveled between lower-level tournaments. "She was just telling me to think of it as just another match," Naomi recalled. "And then I would yell at her: 'You're crazy! This is a Grand Slam final!'" Mari decided that the best way to calm down her sister was to distract her. "Since she's in Paris, she was like showing me these random croissants and baguettes to try to take my mind off of it," Naomi said. "And it kind of worked."

· · · · · · ·

As Naomi gazed at distant croissants, most eyes at the U.S. Open were trained firmly on Serena Williams, considered the clear favorite to win the match. Serena had been the oddsmakers' top favorite to win the Open since it began; Naomi had started as a forty-to-one long shot, about the seventeenth favorite. Serena hadn't lost at a major to a player ranked as low as 19th-ranked Naomi since her loss to 43rd-ranked Roberta Vinci three years earlier. And though Serena had lost her first match against Naomi, that was almost seen as a positive, so adept was Serena at avenging her losses. In fact, only four players had ever won their first two matches against Serena.

There was considerable cultural momentum around Serena, too. Serena was taking on a greater stature as a public figure than ever, centering motherhood and empowerment in such a way that she believed—as did so many of her admirers—that she now was playing for far more than just a twenty-fourth Grand Slam.

Serena, one match from completing a triumphant return to the top of the sport just a year and a week after giving birth to her daughter, was certainly dressed for something beyond tennis as she took court for the final against Naomi. Virgil Abloh, the pioneering Black fashion designer who founded his Off-White brand and was artistic director for Louis Vuitton's menswear, teamed with Nike to make 2018 U.S. Open outfits for Serena called—you guessed it—The Queen Collection. The centerpiece of the collection was an asymmetrical black dress with one long sleeve and a layered tulle skirt that fanned out like a ballerina's with every swirl of Serena's racquet. As with everything about Serena by this point, the dress was designed to radiate beyond the confines of sports, earning her coverage in non-sports publications weeks before the U.S. Open. "It's always been my dream to wear a tutu," Serena told *Vogue*. "The dress is feminine, but combines her aggression," Abloh said in *Elle*. Nike had made a matching black tutu many sizes smaller for Serena's daughter, Olympia. Serena posted a photo of Olympia wearing it after her semifinal, with the caption "Did Momma win?" The tutu dress was not designed with a mass market in mind, but if anyone else wanted to buy one, it retailed for $500 and paired with the $900 leather bomber jacket that Serena wore onto the court. In Abloh's typical style, "LOGO" was written above the Nike swoosh on her chest, and "SERENA" was written on the sleeve of her left forearm—yes, those quotation marks were included for both, as they were on the inscription on Serena's bag: "AKA QUEEN."

Serena answered to "Queen" more and more by 2018. In a pretournament Beats by Dre ad, Serena wears a deep blue chemise with large puffy sleeves befitting a Tudor monarch, and a dome of bulbous black petticoats that swish with each sashaying step. The brief sequence, in which more than a dozen dancers line up and bow to Serena, ends with a Nefertiti-esque cylindrical gold crown* being placed atop Serena's head as the Nicki Minaj song "Majesty" purrs obediently: "Whatever you say, Mrs. Majesty." Minaj herself, wearing her own crown, then appears on-screen to shout, "Now watch the Queen conquer!" before the text "Queen of Queens" flashes on-screen below Serena's face with a rhyming verse beneath: "Never before was more greatness foreseen / Than in the eyes of the woman who made herself Queen."

Naomi's outfit at the 2018 U.S. Open was black as well, but similarities to Serena's custom tutu stopped there. Naomi wore a simple black visor, black skirt, and black tank top with a square neckline, accessorized with color-pop hot pink wristbands that matched the hot pink heels on her white Adidas shoes. The Adidas outfit was not unique to Naomi; several other Adidas-sponsored players wore the same getup at that year's U.S. Open. To dress up the plain outfit somewhat, Naomi wore pearl stud earrings and a gold chain with a single pearl on it around her neck. The blond ends of her hair were wrapped in a loose bun, and she was ready.

The U.S. Open had attracted its typically eclectic roster of A-listers in the stands to see Serena vie for her twenty-fourth major title. There were actors—Adrien Brody, Pierce Brosnan, Kevin Hart, Taraji P. Henson; there were singers—Sara Bareilles, Alicia Keys, Kelly Rowland, Vanessa Williams; there were television personalities—Andy Cohen, Trevor Noah, Dr. Oz, Robin Roberts; there were fashion icons—Vera Wang, Anna Wintour; and there was a large swath of Winter Olympians—Wayne Gretzky, Adam Rippon, P. K. Subban, Lindsay Vonn, Jakub Voráček, Shaun White.

---

* The shape of Serena's crown also resembles the headgear seen earlier that year on Angela Bassett's Queen Ramonda in the 2018 film *Black Panther*, work for which costume designer Ruth E. Carter became the first African-American to win an Oscar for Best Costume Design.

After Deborah Cox sang "I'm Every Woman" and "America the Beautiful" in a pre-match ceremony, a court-size American flag was stretched out across the net. The two players were each given a bouquet of pink and purple flowers to carry out onto the court, a strangely bridal tradition still entrenched at some tournaments for women's finals; men are not given flowers. Naomi, as the lower-ranked player, walked out first—"From Japan: Naaaaomi Osaka!"—to flashing lights, techno music, and considerable applause. "From the United States: Serena Williams" received at least twice as much twenty seconds later. Once she reached her seat, Naomi took off the red headphones she had used to block the sound. After a brief chat between the players and chair umpire Carlos Ramos, Serena won the coin toss and elected to serve first, then she and Naomi posed alongside Billie Jean King at the net for pre-match photographs. It was time to begin.

. . . .

The first point of the final was a long one. Serena's improved fitness since their last match in Miami had been a major discussion point before this rematch, but Naomi's had only gotten better, too. And now that she was fitter and quicker, Naomi could be more patient than ever before during rallies, allowing her to extend rallies and take fewer low-percentage risks when out of position or out of breath. Her footwork was more dynamic and purposeful, especially resetting between shots. Adding to her speed, her anticipation of Serena's shots was preternatural: almost none of Serena's opponents had ever watched so much of her play.

Serena won the first game, and Naomi held to win the second. In her second service game, Serena wobbled for the first time, double-faulting down break point to give Naomi an early 2–1 lead. Naomi, out of the gates, was the clear better player, and she was executing Bajin's game plan for facing Serena: making the thirty-six-year-old move side to side whenever possible, without taking undue risks. At 2–1, 30-15, Naomi hit a sharply angled crosscourt backhand that left Serena screaming "Aaahhh!" as she reached far to her left to wrangle it, in audible anguish at being pushed beyond her limits so soon. Naomi hit an ace on the next point to go up

3–1 and gave her own shout of "C'mon!" to announce her own presence. Serena hit another double fault and soon Naomi led 4–1, having won four straight games. The deejay inside Ashe played Alicia Keys during the changeover. "This girl is on fiiiiiire!" she sang.

Time was already running out for Serena early in the match, and she knew it. For all her general excellence, and her reputation as a battler, Serena had not come back to win a major final after losing the first set since 2005, holding a 2–7 record when dropping the first set overall. It wasn't just Serena who struggled to come back: the twenty-three previous U.S. Open finals had also been won by the woman who won the first set.

So, down 1–4, Serena dug in. She screamed her loudest "C'monnn" of the match as she struck a forehand down-the-line winner, and the crowd, eager to help her turn the tides, roared with her. Serena earned a break point, but Naomi saved it with a 117 mph ace, and then hit another big 117 mph serve out wide past Serena's backhand to hold for 5–1. Once Naomi had pulled ahead, it was easy for commentators to find reasons why she was winning. Thirty-six-year-old Serena and twenty-year-old Naomi had the second-biggest age gap in a women's Grand Slam final in the Open Era*; every other match in the top five of biggest gaps had been won by the younger player.

Serena held for 2–5, and then Naomi held again to take the first set, finishing with a 117 mph body serve right at Serena, which the veteran could only dump back into the net. Naomi led 6–2 after just thirty-three minutes. As weak as Serena's stats were after losing the first set of a major final, Naomi's first-set stats were very strong: when winning the first set in 2018, she was 31–0. But closing out a first major final was a skill Naomi hadn't yet proved, and finishing off Serena in front of a crowd desperate for her to prevail wasn't going to be easy. ESPN's announcer Chris Fowler asked color commentator Chris Evert how much harder it would be for

---

* The biggest age gap was seventeen-year-old Monica Seles winning the 1991 U.S. Open final over thirty-four-year-old Martina Navratilova; the 2019 U.S. Open final between thirty-seven-year-old Serena and nineteen-year-old Bianca Andreescu set a new record a year later.

Naomi to win the second set than the first. "If she's playing against an angry, upset Serena Williams?" replied Evert. "Really hard."

Evert was suggesting that Serena would be upset that she was losing—which, of course, she would be. But the scoreboard would be only one of many sparks in an emotional explosion just minutes away from detonating in this final.

· · · · · · ·

ESPN's roving reporter Pam Shriver hustled to Serena's coach, Patrick Mouratoglou, for an interview between sets that aired after Serena won the first game of the second set. "I think she's surprised by the quality of the tennis of Naomi, and she's started rushing a bit too much," Mouratoglou said. "But I'm sure she'll find a way in the second set." Though citing Serena's low first-serve percentage as an issue, Mouratoglou heaped praise on Naomi, who he said was on her A-game. "She's super good on the big points, she's very solid from the baseline, she doesn't miss, she loves pace," he said. "You have to play smarter and not give her too much angle and attack her when you have the right ball—which is difficult when you are a bit under stress. But Serena will find a way." What Serena wouldn't have expected to find, however, was that Mouratoglou would soon find a way to insert himself into the match itself.

Despite the tough situation his player was in, the loquacious Mouratoglou was happy to talk to Shriver. Mouratoglou, a handsome forty-eight-year-old with mutual affection for the camera, had an academy bearing his name in his native France; he wore the M-shaped logo of the academy on his black T-shirt as he sat in the second row of Serena's courtside box in the northeast corner of Ashe. With Serena under his wing, Mouratoglou had built a larger media profile than any tennis coach since Richard Williams. Mouratoglou's results had justified the attention, guiding Serena to her last ten major titles. Mouratoglou was ready for the success: in 2012, the year he first started working with Serena, he was already traveling on tour with his own personal PR manager, an unheard-of companion for a coach on tour. Mouratoglou's appetite for attention and penchant for self-promotion drew reliable eye rolls from his peers, but he was appreciated by the press as a ready spigot of information and insight into the often watertight ship that was Serena. Though for what happened next, Mouratoglou didn't want to be seen.

With Naomi serving up 40-15 in the second game of the second set, Serena took a long look across the court to her box. Mouratoglou, seeing her look his way, held both his hands in front of him, palms facing each other and thumbs pointing up. He shoved his hands back and forth several times, indicating Serena should be moving forward. The match, forty-two minutes old, would not be the same again.

Before Naomi could serve, a voice quickly interjected across the public address system: "Code violation: coaching. Warning, Mrs. Williams."

There was little immediate reaction from the crowd or commentators, but Serena immediately registered what had happened. Coaching from the stands was forbidden in tennis, and it was not something Serena had ever been accused of by an official before. Serena walked up to chair umpire Carlos Ramos and made that clear, though it seemed she had perhaps only seen the tops of Mouratoglou's hands from her vantage point about forty-four yards away on the opposite side of the court.

"The one thing I've never done is cheat," Serena told Ramos. "If he gives me a thumbs-up, he's telling me to 'come on.'" Serena quickly sounded a note of equanimity to Ramos before again emphasizing her values. "We don't have any code—and I know you don't know that, and I understand why you may have thought that was coaching. But I'm telling you, it's not. I don't cheat to win. I'd rather lose. I'm just letting you know."

"That was intense," Mary Joe Fernández, sitting courtside, said on ESPN.

As Serena turned and walked back to the baseline, Mouratoglou smirked. "What just happened?" asked Kelly Rowland, the founding Destiny's Child member who was sitting behind Mouratoglou in Serena's courtside box.

What had happened was that Ramos had hit one of Serena's most sensitive nerves by penalizing her for receiving illicit coaching, which she equated to an attack on her character. The Code of Conduct rules in tennis can be divided into two general categories: rules designed to keep players behaving in an unemotional manner to uphold the sport's prim Victorian England origins, and rules to prevent cheating. Serena had been called for many code violations over the years for outbursts of anger; those sorts of misdeeds she could rationalize as simply an expression of emotion. But Serena had never before been called for any code violation in the latter category, and so this charge wounded her like none of the penalties had before. If there was one thing Serena cared about on court, it was fairness.

· · · · · · ·

What Serena didn't understand at this pivotal moment of the 2018 U.S. Open final, however, was that Ramos was correct: the coaching rule had been broken by her coach, Patrick Mouratoglou, albeit without Serena's desire to be illicitly coached. The 2018 *Grand Slam Rule Book* said, "Communications of any kind, audible or visible, between a player and coach may be construed as coaching." Mouratoglou would admit he had been attempting to send signals to Serena, albeit against her adamant wishes. "I'm honest: I was coaching," Mouratoglou later told ESPN's Pam Shriver. "I mean, I don't think she looked at me, so that's why she didn't even think I was. But, I was." Mouratoglou justified breaking this rule by saying he was just doing what "100 percent of the coaches on 100 percent of the matches" do by flouting the rule, adding that he had never before been caught and penalized by an official. "So we have to stop this hypocrite thing," said Mouratoglou, who then gestured across the length of the court toward Bajin in the opposite box. "Sascha was coaching every point, too."

The coaching penalty didn't immediately derail the match, however: because it was her first code violation of the match, Serena was only given a warning. A second code violation would cost her a point penalty; a third code violation would trigger a game penalty.

Serena held serve for 2–1 in the second set and walked back to her chair, where she reengaged Ramos about the penalty he had called six minutes earlier. Both were conciliatory, perhaps to a fault. "Again, I can see where you may have thought that, but I want to be clear: I've never gotten a coaching violation—because I don't do it," Serena said. "You can look historically: it's not something I do. But I can understand why you may have thought that, but just know I've never cheated."

"I understand your reaction," Ramos told her, pacifyingly.

"Okay, thank you, because I'm like—" Serena held her hands to her chest and shook them to show how rattled she felt to be tarnished by the penalty. "I don't cheat."

"And I know that," Ramos assured her.

"Yeah, so thank you so much," Serena said, grateful to have been absolved.

The pleasant conversation went perhaps *too* well, however. "We had this great exchange; we were on the same page," Serena said after the match. In hearing Ramos's placatory remarks as he tried to de-escalate the situation, Serena convinced herself that, because of her powers of persuasion, Ramos was rescinding the coaching penalty he had called against her earlier. But Ramos was not undoing that call, of course; reversing a call because of a player's pleas is not something that officials do. That critical misunderstanding, very soon, would prove catastrophic to the match.

Serena rode the high of her apparently successful conversation with Ramos into her best form of the match. She dug into Naomi's serve more tenaciously than before, causing Naomi to have her first moments of visible self-doubt. When Naomi badly missed a backhand into the net to put herself down break point, she looked toward her box with a sudden panic on her face, not unlike she had two years before when her lead against Madison Keys had slipped away on that same court. Naomi fought, but ultimately lost her serve: on the fifth break point of the game, Naomi sent a backhand long to put Serena up a break for the first time in the final, at 3–1 in the second set. Much of the crowd, thrilled to see Serena clawing back, stood to cheer.

But Serena's success was short-lived. Perhaps out of respect for Naomi's powerful return, Serena was going for too much and missing serves, hitting her fifth and sixth double faults of the match. Down break point, Serena dumped a backhand into the net, giving Naomi the break and throwing away the momentum she had earned. "C'mon!" Naomi turned and shouted toward her box, holding up her fist.

"I can't serve!" Serena wailed toward her box, her face scrunched up in exasperation. When Serena turned around, she took her frustration out on her racquet, angrily spiking it down onto the court and cracking its black-and-neon-green graphite frame, warping its flat face into something resembling a Pringle.

Breaking a racquet in anger—forbidden in tennis under its gentility rules—automatically triggers a code violation from the chair umpire, and so Ramos spoke into his microphone: "Code violation: racquet abuse. Point penalty, Mrs. Williams." But over the din of the stadium, Serena did not hear his words and did not understand that her second code violation had earned her a harsher penalty.

As Serena walked back to the baseline after the changeover, Ramos announced that the score was already 15–0 because of the point penalty. But because she hadn't heard Ramos's prior announcement clearly, this point penalty was news to Serena; she erroneously thought she had accumulated only one code violation because the first for coaching had been somehow expunged.

"This is unbelievable," Serena said as she walked toward Ramos, rolling her eyes toward the heavens in exasperation. "Every time I play here I have problems. What?"

· · · · · · ·

Serena hadn't had problems *every* time she played at the U.S. Open, but she was understandably weary: Ashe had consistently been the site of her most controversial encounters with officials, incidents for which she carried varying degrees of blame.

In 2004, Serena was playing a competitive quarterfinal against her rival Jennifer Capriati in a night session on Ashe. Because of a shortage of top-level officials—three elite "gold badge" chair umpires had been dismissed midway through the 2004 U.S. Open because of their involvement in a credential-forging scheme at the Athens Olympics earlier that summer—the match was being helmed by a lower-ranking umpire, Mariana Alves of Portugal. When Serena struck an impressive backhand down-the-line winner at 40-all in the second game of the third set, Alves announced "Advantage, Capriati" as the score. "Williams," Serena said to correct her. "That was my point, the ball was in, it's my advantage." But Alves, bafflingly, said she had silently overruled the call on the previous point, saying that Serena's shot—which had landed well inside the line, and on the far side of the court from Alves's vantage point—had actually been out. "Excuse me? That ball was *so in*," Serena cried with exasperation. "What the heck is this?" Serena would go on to lose that game, and later the match. Her anger on that night was righteous: the uproar over the egregiously bad call by Alves, and several other crucial missed calls in the match, expedited the adoption of electronic Hawk-Eye technology to be used for players to challenge line calls; it was officially introduced onto the tour eighteen months later.

But at subsequent moments at the U.S. Open, Serena's outbursts of rage had been considerably less defensible. In the 2009 U.S. Open semifinals, defending champion Serena was losing to Kim Clijsters, a longtime rival who was in her first major back from maternity leave. Two points from defeat in the second set, Serena was hitting a second serve when a line judge positioned on the baseline called her for a foot fault, meaning her foot had touched the baseline during her service motion. The rare call put Serena down match point, and she suddenly snapped. "I swear to God I'll fucking take this ball and shove it down your fucking throat!" Serena said as she walked toward the line judge, a diminutive Japanese woman named Shino Tsurubuchi. "Do you hear me?" Serena continued, holding the ball up toward Tsurubuchi's face. "I swear to God. You better be glad—you better be fucking glad that I'm not, I swear."* Serena, who had never acted anything like this in a match before, was given a code violation. Serena

---

* "I've never been in a fight in my whole life, so I don't know why she would have felt threatened," Serena said of Tsurubuchi in her post-match press conference.

protested—"There's a lot of people who've said way worse," she insisted—
but because it was her second code violation of the match, having already
received one in the first set for breaking a racquet, the tirade cost Serena a
point penalty. And because she was down a match point when the penalty
was assessed, she lost the match. Serena was later subsequently fined a
record $82,500 for the incident and was put on a two-year probationary
period.

Two years later, Serena again blew a fuse while losing an important
match in Ashe. In the final of the 2011 U.S. Open, down a set and an early
break point in the second set to Samantha Stosur, Serena shouted "C'mon!"
immediately after striking a powerful forehand. But because Stosur reached
the shot, meaning Serena had shouted mid-rally, chair umpire Eva Asderaki
correctly called Serena for a hindrance and awarded the point to Stosur.
Serena looked at Asderaki and began to see red once more: "Aren't you the
one that screwed me over last time here?" Serena said. "Yeah, you are." Asderaki wasn't, however; Serena was likely confusing her with Alves, who
also wore her hair in a blond ponytail. But Serena was infuriated. "Seriously, you have it out for me? I promise you, that's not cool. That is totally
not cool. I truly despise you." When Serena won the opening point of the
next game after the booing had subsided, she jogged up toward Asderaki
and pointed her racquet at her and said, "I hate you," to which Asderaki
responded by calling a code violation for verbal abuse. Serena wasn't done
with Asderaki, delivering a monologue at her through the duration of the
ensuing changeover:

> I promise you, if you ever see me walking down the hall, look the other
> way. Because you're out of control. You're out of control. You're totally
> out of control, you're a hater and you're unattractive inside. Who would
> do such a thing? And I never complain. Wow. What a loser. You give a
> code violation because I expressed who I am? We're in America, last I
> checked. Can I get a water? Or am I going to get "violated" for a water?
> Really, don't even look at me. I promise you, don't look at me. Because
> I am not the one. Don't. Look. My. Way.

The venting didn't earn Serena any further penalties in the match, but neither did it help her play—she lost five of the next six games to Stosur to lose the match 6–2, 6–3. Serena was only fined $2,000 for this incident, but to detractors who considered her a bully with anger-management issues, evidence was mounting.

For the next seven years, however, Serena had grown more, well, serene. She won the U.S. Open the next three years in a row: 2012, 2013, 2014. Except for the heartbreak of her defeat to Roberta Vinci when she had been two wins from completing the calendar Grand Slam in 2015, there hadn't been any major incidents for Serena. But once she got a second code violation from Ramos on this day in 2018, the emotions of the past—and new ones—came flooding forward.

· · · · · · ·

"You broke a racquet," Ramos said as he explained to Serena why she had gotten a point penalty.

"Yeah, that's a warning," said Serena, agreeing so far.

"And, you got the coaching," Ramos said.

Serena, who had genuinely thought she had talked her way out of that penalty, was aghast: "I didn't get coaching! I didn't get coaching. I didn't get coaching. You need to make an announcement that I didn't get coaching. I don't cheat! I didn't get coaching! How can you say that? You need to—you owe me an apology.

"You owe me an apology," she repeated. "I have *never* cheated in my life! I have a daughter and I stand for what's right for her, and I've never cheated. And you owe me an apology. You will never do another one of my matches."

The crowd, which couldn't hear what was going on, began to boo, and then the boos grew louder. Serena walked back to the baseline and eventually held her hand up, asking the crowd to calm down.

As the anger boiled and spilled over, Naomi Osaka stood alone on the opposite side of the court, watching and waiting. There was a ball in her hand, and the title she had dreamed of was within reach.

With her 15-0 head start, Naomi won the next three points to hold at love to level the second set at 3–3. Serena was still seething, mostly from the rulings against her but also from the score. All of her previous major troubles at the U.S. Open, uncoincidentally, had occurred during matches she was losing. This time, though, with her icon status firmly entrenched, she had the thousands inside Ashe vociferously on her side, matching her anger.

"Meanwhile you have to admire the composure, really, and the maturity, with what Naomi's experiencing," Evert said on ESPN. "She's playing against Serena and the crowd at this point."

In the next game, at 30-all, Naomi blocked back a body serve from Serena with her backhand; the floating shot fell onto the baseline, catching Serena off guard as she let it pass by her. And then on the next point, Naomi cracked a forehand down the line to break for a 4–3 lead in the second set, putting herself two games from the U.S. Open title. Naomi had been the better player in the match, and particularly on the biggest points. She was four for five on converting break points, while Serena was only one for six.

Serena, while losing her grip on the match, couldn't let go of Ramos's penalizing her and tore into him anew on the next changeover. "I explained it to you," Serena reiterated. "And for you to attack my character is something that's wrong. It's wrong. You're attacking my character. Yes you are. You owe me an apology. You will never, ever, ever be on another court of mine as long as you live. You are the liar."

Serena took a sip of water, then ramped back up. "When are you going to give me my apology?" she demanded anew. "You owe me an apology. Say it. Say you're sorry. Well then you're—don't talk to me. Don't talk to me. How dare you insinuate that I was cheating."

Serena then began to rise from her chair. "And you stole a point from me. You're a thief, too!"

As Serena walked away, Ramos spoke again, for a fateful third time: "Code violation: verbal abuse. Game penalty, Mrs. Williams."

But again, Serena hadn't heard him. Naomi hadn't heard him, either. Serena got into her crouch, ready to return Naomi's serve in the eighth game which Ramos, unbeknownst to the players, had already awarded to Naomi. To make his ruling clear, Ramos waved both players toward his chair. Naomi walked up, a ball still in her hand and another tucked under her skirt, ready to serve. When Ramos told her that she had been awarded the next game because of a game penalty, and that it would be Serena's serve down 5–3 in the second set, Naomi turned to look toward her box, then softly tossed both balls across the net. She turned, put her head down, and walked away from the argument that was ratcheting up again.

As they had nine years earlier when she had threatened the line judge, tournament referee Brian Earley and supervisor Donna Kelso walked on the court. "She called me a thief, and I gave Serena a game penalty," Ramos explained to Earley. "For calling you a thief, okay," Earley replied back, echoing to make sure he understood. (Per the 2018 *Grand Slam Rule Book*, verbal abuse is defined as "a statement about an official, opponent, sponsor, spectator or other person that implies dishonesty or is derogatory, insulting, or otherwise abusive.")

"This is not right," Serena told Kelso, a veteran WTA employee whom Serena knew well. "This is not right. I called him a thief because he stole a point from me—because I never cheated."

"You know me, you know my character," Serena then said to Kelso, pointing at her heart. "And that's not right, this is not fair. This has happened to me too many times."

"She called him a thief," Earley reiterated to Kelso, one of the rare times one of the officials was audible during this exchange. All that could be heard to most viewers was Serena, and the pain in her voice.

After her dispute with Alves in 2004, Serena had not broadened her feeling of discrimination beyond herself whatsoever, saying in her post-match press conference that she would "really prefer if she not umpire my courts anymore because she's obviously anti-Serena." But seeing Ramos, the first male umpire to be involved in one of her U.S. Open disputes, and having been elevated in the past several years of her life as a symbol for women, Serena began to cite gender as an issue on the court for the first time in one of her arguments.

"But do you know how many other men, how many other *men* do things that are much worse than that?" Serena asked Earley. "This is not fair. There's a lot of men out here that have said a lot of things, and because they are men, that doesn't happen to them."

Earley was unsympathetic, however, and suggested to Serena that she should "know the risk" of haranguing a chair umpire when she had already received two code violations.

"No, I don't know the risk, because if I say a simple thing, a 'thief,' because he stole a point from me—there are men out here that do a lot worse," Serena again said, both trying to be calm and considered while having to shout to be heard over the growing din. "But because I'm a woman, because I'm a woman, you're going to take this away from me? That is not right. You know it, and I know you can't admit it, but I know you know it's not right. I know you can't change it, but I'm just saying, that's not right. I get the rules, I get the rules, but I'm just saying, it's not right. And it happened to me at this tournament every single year that I play. It's just not fair. That's all I have to say. It's not fair."

When Ramos hit the button on his tablet to officially flip the scoreboards in the stadium over to 5–3, the boos intensified even more. Venus, almost always placid when watching her sister, had stood up in the box, staring. Serena's husband, Alexis Ohanian, stood slack-jawed, shaking his head.

The boos continued to swell louder and louder. Many of the fans stood to make their displeasure even more apparent.

· · · · · · ·

As tennis analyst Jeff Sackmann would later calculate in *The Economist*, the point penalty against Serena only increased Naomi's chances of winning from 97.8 percent to 98.2 percent; the game penalty only boosted her probability of victory from 98.1 percent to 99.2 percent. "By the time the New York crowd started booing, the match was virtually in the bag," Sackmann wrote.

None of the boos at any point were aimed at Naomi. But unfortunately, that was clear to everyone but her. When Serena won the first point after the resumption, the Ashe crowd roared out loudest cheer yet. When Serena won the second point on a missed return by Naomi, the crowd roared out again. Naomi held two fingers to the carotid artery in her neck to feel her racing pulse. When Ramos called "let" on Serena's next serve, the boos picked up again; at this point, they were angry to hear his voice at all.

Serena held at love and quickly walked to the corner of the court where Kelso sat. "This is *not* fair," Serena repeated once again. "I don't care, but it's not fair. The fact is that men did this a thousand times and did a lot worse, and I've worked so hard for women. This is not fair."

Serena then sat back down and stared straight ahead. All the cameras in the stadium were focused on Serena and her dry, heaving sobs. Almost no one was looking at the player who was four points from winning the tournament.

Serving for the U.S. Open final up 5–4 in the second set, Naomi smacked a forehand winner down the line on the opening point and shouted a "C'monnnn!" 15-0.

"She's played brilliantly and she's been up to every moment," ESPN's Fowler said of Naomi, who hadn't gotten much mention recently in this two-person match. "And the thing is that if she does win this game, win this title, and realize a lifelong dream, unfortunately the match will be remembered largely for what has happened between Ramos and Serena Williams. And that's too bad."

"Yes, it will definitely take away from it," Evert concurred.

Serena hit a curling forehand winner to level the game at 15-all, but Naomi responded with a booming serve down the T at 115 miles per hour that Serena couldn't return. 30-15.

Naomi stepped back to the line and boomed down another big serve, a 113 mph ace angled so far beyond Serena's left that she didn't even bother taking a step toward it. 40-15.

Naomi now had two championship points. She got a ball from the ball kid and clenched her fist again, staying focused, intense, and intent despite everything around her. Naomi delivered another big first serve—119 mph—but Serena hit a strong backhand return back and then finished the point with a backhand winner several shots later, erasing Naomi's first championship point.

Naomi has a second championship point. Again Naomi lands a strong first serve—114 mph—to Serena's backhand. Serena stretches, lunging to her left, but she cannot reel the serve in. The ball falls meekly to Serena's left, and Serena's racquet clangs against the ground as she comes down to earth.

"Game, set, and match: Osaka," says Ramos.

Naomi looks across the court to her box, then pulls down the brim of her visor to cover her eyes as she walks toward the net. As the two women walk toward each other, the boos chorus once more.

As they meet at the net, Serena reaches out her arms.

"I'm proud of you," Serena says to Naomi.

They embrace. The boos continue.

Then they separate, and Serena holds out her arm to allow Naomi past her. But as Naomi steps by, Serena bumps into her as she turns back to look at Ramos one last time. "You owe me an apology," Serena says. And she points and repeats herself. "You owe me an apology."

Naomi walks to her chair, covering her face with her hand as tears begin to flow.

While the boos persist and predominate, there are pockets of unabashed joy. In Naomi's box, her mother and coach and team and sponsors exchange hugs. Up on the third level, Leonard is mobbed with hugs and kisses from Haitian family and friends who had packed out a suite, dancing and proudly waving Haitian flags of various sizes.

The sounds and the faces around the stadium tell a powerful story, but so does the scoreboard: Naomi Osaka had won the 2018 U.S. Open final decisively over Serena Williams, 6–2, 6–4, in one hour and nineteen minutes. Soon, the displays around the arena flashed NAOMI OSAKA 2018 WOMEN'S SINGLES CHAMPION, a recent happening that was easy to overlook given everything else that had transpired.

"She was depressed, I'm telling you, two weeks before this tournament," said Chris Evert, whose Boca Raton academy Naomi used as a pretournament training base. "She had had bad results this summer. But now, the tears of joy."

But for viewers getting a close look at Naomi, "tears of joy" seemed like an optimistic diagnosis atop an angry soundtrack. Many of the boos at that moment were for Ramos as he exited the court; normally the chair umpire stays and is thanked at the trophy ceremony, but tournament officials decided to whisk him away from the scene as soon as possible.

A communications official came out to speak to Naomi to tell her about the trophy ceremony. Naomi was reminded of the notes that were prepared for her remarks this time so she would sound less ill-prepared than at Indian Wells.

"I really do feel that she's been robbed of some of the joy of this occasion because of what happened between the chair umpire and Serena Williams," Fowler said as the wet-faced Naomi walked toward the corner where her team and mother waited for her. Naomi wiped away her tears one more time before stepping up onto the ladder the tournament had positioned in front of her box. Her team had been as confused as the rest of the crowd as the match descended into chaos, but they were now clear in their delight for Naomi.

The first hug Naomi got was from Bajin, who reached his muscly arms around her and whispered assurances and congratulations in her ear. Then came a hug from Abdul Sillah, then one from Natsuko Mogi, then from Stuart Duguid.

Then, walking down from the second row, was Naomi's mother, Tamaki. As she made eye contact with her daughter for the first time since she had won, Tamaki's own tears poured anew. Tamaki wrapped her arms around her daughter, patting the sides and back of her hair. The crowd in Ashe, seeing this moment on the large screens, cheered in earnest unison for the new champion for the first time.

As Naomi carefully climbed down from the heights of the ladder, the lights inside Ashe dimmed for the trophy ceremony. Naomi then sat back down on her bench and draped a towel over her head, blocking out as much of the stadium as she could.

"It is Naomi's moment," Fowler again reminded ESPN viewers. "But much of the story, as it always is, centers around Serena."

. . . .

Naomi had a faint smile as the lights went up on the trophy ceremony, where she stood between Serena and tournament director David Brewer.

ESPN reporter Tom Rinaldi, one of the network's most formal voices, emceed the ceremony. "Good evening, everyone, and we welcome you to the trophy celebration of the United States Open," Rinaldi began. But the crowd was in no mood even to hear the most benign platitudes. Ramos was off the court and out of sight, but again the boos rained down. So, too, did the tears from Naomi's face. Her small smile quickly faded, and she pulled the visor back down over her face to hide it from the watching world.

Serena, seeing Naomi's distress up close for the first time, put her arm around her. "You okay?" Serena asked. Naomi nodded, but the tears were still streaming. "Are those happy tears?" Serena asked Naomi with a smile and a laugh, trying to cheer up the crying champion.

USTA president Katrina Adams, the first Black woman to hold the post, then took the microphone. "Naomi, welcome to the big stage," Adams began, before pivoting to heap praise on Serena. "Serena, welcome back. These two weeks you two have showed your power, your grace, and your will to win. Perhaps it's not the finish that we were looking for today, but Serena, you are a champion of all champions. 'This mama' is a role model, and respected by all."

Adams's remarks were quickly jarring to those paying attention. It was strange for a trophy ceremony presenter to seemingly lament an outcome. "#ThisMama," also, was a hashtag used by Chase, also a major U.S. Open sponsor, in its marketing campaign around Serena. Adams plugging the slogan gave the übercorporate U.S. Open an even more crassly commercial feel than usual.

Naomi didn't seem to mind, however. She clapped for Serena along with the rest of the crowd. "Naomi, congratulations on your first Grand Slam title," Adams said to Naomi, who still looked wet-eyed and miserable. "You are indeed a champion and a force of the future." Adams then thanked the fans, who took that as a provocation to start booing again.

Rinaldi then turned to Serena. Unlike many trophy ceremonies, which give the players the microphone and allow them to make open-ended remarks, the U.S. Open conducts its ceremonies in an interview format. "Serena, not the result that you wanted tonight," Rinaldi said, understatedly. "How do you put into perspective what this match contained?"

But Serena was in no mood to answer anything. "Well, I don't want to be rude, I don't want to interrupt, but I don't want to do questions," she said. Instead, Serena wanted to talk about Naomi. "I just want to tell you guys that she played well. And this is her first Grand Slam."

For the first time, at Serena's urging, the stadium cheered in earnest for the champion. Serena, her voice quavering, had seen something in Naomi that needed help, and so she continued. "I know you guys were rooting, and I was rooting, too, but let's make this the best moment we can, and we'll get through it. But let's give everyone the credit where credit's due. And let's not boo anymore! We're gonna get through this, and let's be positive. So congratulations, Naomi. No more booing!"

Naomi exhaled as she took in the new waves of positive emotion.

"I really hope to continue to go and play here again," Serena said, tears now running down her face, too. "We'll see," she added with a sharp laugh. "It's been tough here for me, but thank you so much."

Serena accepted her runner-up plate and twirled with it.

"And now our champion, Naomi Osaka!" Rinaldi announced. And with Serena making her displeasure with the booing clear, this time the crowd cheered wildly and loudly for Naomi: twenty-six long seconds of sustained applause and shouts of approval, an audible effort to remedy the pain they had seen on her face on the screens around the stadium.

"Naomi, after the semifinal win, you said you had a dream, and the dream was one day, from when you used to sit up in the upper bowl here and watch Grand Slam tennis, that you would have a chance to play in a finals match, and perhaps even against Serena Williams," Rinaldi said. Naomi nodded.

"How does the reality compare with the dream?" Rinaldi asked, almost certainly using a question he had written before that was now deeply out of touch with Naomi's visible emotions. There was no way any of Naomi's dreams had looked or felt anything like this.

"I know that everyone was cheering for her, and I'm sorry it had to end like this," Naomi said, still gasping as she fought back tears and drawing loud "Awwwwws" from the audibly moved crowd.

"I just want to say, thank you for watching the match," Naomi said, adding a quick bow of her head. "Thank you."

"After match point you made your way over to your box and you had an embrace, a long embrace, with your mom," Rinaldi said. "What did the two of you share?"

"Well, she sacrificed a lot for me, and it means a lot for her to come and watch my matches, because she doesn't normally do that anyways," Naomi said, drawing a sudden peal of laughter from the crowd, who were cooling back down to a less volcanic temperature with Naomi's every word. "All we're missing is my dad, but he doesn't physically watch my matches; he walks around, so I'll see him later."

Naomi hadn't meant for these statements to be jokes about her parents, but again the crowd laughed, grateful for any levity. Naomi remained disarming, even through tears.

Rinaldi reminded viewers that Naomi was the first Japanese player to win a Grand Slam singles final, and Naomi bowed at the acknowledgment. "What does it mean to you?" Rinaldi asked.

"Well, it was always my dream to play Serena in the U.S. Open finals, so I'm really glad that I was able to do that, and I'm really grateful I was able to play with you," Naomi said, turning to Serena and bowing to her as well. "Um, thank you."

Again, the crowd gasped with delight, utterly charmed. Serena, though, had had enough. Whether out of discomfort for Naomi or bad feelings of her own, Serena discreetly but directly signaled to Rinaldi to stop there. "Okay, that's it," Serena told him. "That's it."

Rinaldi looked at Serena and then nodded, agreeing to wrap things up at her request. Rinaldi then announced that Kristin Lemkau of J.P. Morgan Chase would present Naomi a check for $3.8 million, more than doubling her career prize money earnings. The sum drew awestruck gasps from the crowd.

Chris Evert then handed the trophy to Adams, who handed it to Naomi, kissing her on each cheek. Naomi struggled to grip both the handle of the trophy and the check with her right hand and nearly dropped it, but once the tournament director helpfully took the check out of her hand, her grasp became firm. Slowly, then quickly, she raised the silver cup up high above her head and ball kids launched metallic red, white, and blue streamers into the air.

Once the streamers had floated down to the ground, Naomi lowered her arms, turned to her box, and smiled. For the first time all day, she looked happy.

Serena walked up to join Naomi for the photographers but turned away and walked back after just ten seconds. She was ushered back, however, to join in more photos with Evert and Adams but left again as soon as she could.

Once Serena had gone, Evert reached out to put her arm on Naomi. Naomi bowed her head to her. Evert responded in turn with a far deeper bow of her own and then moved in to hug Naomi, letting her arm linger on the new champion as she pulled away.

Naomi, now all alone on the podium, raised the trophy again and spun to all sides, and the crowd, some of whom were beginning to filter out of the stadium by now, cheered anew.

. . . .

After she had finished her posing for the photographers, Naomi walked to her bench and, suddenly curious, pulled off the lid of the U.S. Open trophy to peek at what might be within its shiny silver exterior; she closed it once she realized it was empty inside.

TWENTY

From Ashe to Wildfire

When Serena Williams had received the shiny silver platter given to the runner-up during the trophy ceremony from USTA president Katrina Adams, she held it high over her head and twirled to all sides of the cheering crowd in Ashe, a closed-lipped but clear smile on her face.

But once she was behind closed doors, Serena made her feelings about the relic of her loss clear, dumping the platter into a trash can in the locker room. As Serena took a shower, a locker room attendant pulled the platter out of the trash and set it neatly on a bench near Serena's locker.

Spotting the platter's unwelcome resurrection when she returned, Serena was incensed. So there could be no misunderstanding of her wishes again, Serena announced her disdain for the token of her loss for everyone in the locker room to hear: "I. Don't. Play. For. Second. Place," Serena said, spiking the platter away once more.

· · · · · · ·

Naomi Osaka and her champion's trophy, meanwhile, were whisked by tournament director David Brewer straight from the court to the ESPN desk just outside of Arthur Ashe Stadium for her first interview as a major champion. ESPN anchor Chris McKendry, who had already led a panel discussion on the controversies of the match before Naomi's arrival, started by affirming Naomi's win, in case she might have some doubts amid the maelstrom. "Naomi, that was a victory you earned," McKendry told Naomi, an assurance rarely deemed necessary for a player in possession of the trophy.

Asked how she had handled the pressure-packed occasion against her idol, Naomi framed it as a duty. "I just sort of thought that it would be a bit disrespectful to the audience and the opponents that I've beaten to, like, succumb to my nerves," she said.

Naomi also hadn't succumbed to curiosity about what was unfolding across the net from her. While millions of television viewers around the world had gotten remarkably clear audio of the heated dialogue unfolding between Serena and officials, Naomi said she hadn't heard any of it. "No, I didn't know what was going on, I was just trying to focus," Naomi said with a nervous giggle. "Like, since it was my first Grand Slam [final], I didn't want to be overwhelmed too much, so I wasn't really looking." When asked follow-up questions about specific moments during the dispute between Serena and Ramos, Naomi remained consistent. "I didn't really know what was going on," she reiterated.

Chris Evert responded approvingly from the far side of the panel. "That's called focus," Evert said. "You had your little blinders on, the tunnel vision, that I think helped you so much to win this whole tournament." Naomi nodded in agreement.

McKendry closed the interview the same way she had started it: trying to cheer up a sullen-looking Naomi. "You also had a lot of fun this tournament; we saw it even warming up today, you would flash a smile," McKendry said. "Can we have one more before you go?" Naomi smiled and giggled obligingly, rocking shyly to her side. "And I do hope you enjoy this day," McKendry said, before turning to the umbrella-spangled crowd on the plaza behind her. "Everybody: Naomi! She's the champion!" The crowd cheered as Naomi turned and looked, nodding slightly toward them. "You're an absolute breath of fresh air and you're a fabulous player," McKendry continued. "We look forward to seeing you for many, many more. Congratulations, Naomi."

· · · · · · ·

As McKendry was reassuring Naomi outside, Serena was making her way around the corridors inside Arthur Ashe Stadium. Unlike with her previous loss to Naomi in Miami, after which she had absconded to her car and driven off into the distance, this time Serena was eager to be heard, to have a chance to explain herself. As reported by ESPN's Don Van Natta Jr., Serena first went from the locker room to the referee's lounge—a space players almost never enter—to talk to Ramos once more. Albeit both using their indoor voices this time, Serena and Ramos spoke again for several minutes, largely repeating what they had said on court: Serena said she respected Ramos as an umpire but disagreed with his calls; Ramos said the respect was mutual, but he was doing his job. And just like on the court, Ramos did not apologize to Serena.

En route from the referee's lounge to the press conference room, the communications rep preparing her to meet the press told Serena information that complicated her case: Mouratoglou had confessed on-air that he had indeed been trying to send her signals when Ramos called the coaching violation. The admission undermined Serena's initial outrage and left her baffled.

"So I don't know, I literally just heard that, too, when they prepped me to come in," Serena said at her press conference. "And I just texted Patrick—like, what is he talking about? Because we don't have signals, we've never discussed signals. I don't even call for on-court coaching. So I'm trying to figure out why he would say that. I don't understand."

Where Serena was still confident, however, was in her own actions. When asked how she might explain what had happened to her daughter someday, Serena replied that she would tell her "that I stood up for what I believed in, I stood up for what was right. Sometimes things in life don't happen the way we want them, but to always stay gracious and stay humble. That's the lesson we can all learn from this, just like I did."

Serena was also asked if motherhood had played a role in her comforting of Naomi; she was willing to entertain the notion. "At one point I felt bad because I'm crying and she's crying," Serena said. "She'd just won, and I'm not sure if they were happy tears or they were just sad tears because of the moment. I felt like, Wow, this isn't how I felt when I won my first Grand Slam. So I was like, Wow, I definitely don't want her to feel like that.

"So, yeah, maybe it was the mom in me that was like, Listen, we got to pull ourselves together here," she added, laughing by the end of her answer.

The ninth question Serena was asked was the most high-stakes of all: Did she think the chair umpire played a part in the outcome of the match? Here, Serena was given a chance to escalate her claim of injustice and say that she had lost the match unfairly, and commensurately that Naomi had won undeservedly. She had reiterated during her press conference that she had called Ramos a "thief" because he had stolen a point from her, but did she believe he had stolen the entire U.S. Open title from her as well, making Naomi its less-than-rightful owner?

There was reason for uncertainty on what Serena's answer might be: for all the superlatives Serena had earned throughout her career, she wasn't known as a reliably gracious loser. Most infamously, when Serena lost in straight sets to Justine Henin in the 2007 U.S. Open quarterfinals—the third consecutive major at which she had lost to Henin at that stage—she said that Henin had won because she "made a lot of lucky shots."

Serena, who had swung across axes of righteousness, rage, and rationality for the last several hours, paused as she contemplated her coordinates for this final, ultimate position on if she had deserved to lose this match to Naomi. "I think that's a really good question," Serena began. "I . . . I . . . I don't know. I feel like she was playing really well. I really needed to do a lot to change that match to try to come out front, to try to come out on top. It's hard to say, because I always fight 'til the end and I always try to come back no matter what, but she was also playing really, really well. It's hard to say that I wouldn't have got a new level, because I've done it so many times in my career. So, it's a tough question."

When asked later in the press conference if she had felt bad that Naomi's first major title had been marred by the boos, Serena landed on an even more affirmative appraisal of her opponent's victory. "She played an amazing match," Serena said of Naomi. "She deserved credit, she deserved to win. At the end of the day, that's what it was."

Serena was last asked if she "could change one thing about what occurred," and her answer would set the tone for the conversation around the match for many days to come. "I don't know," Serena began after a long pause. "You definitely can't go back in time. I can't sit here and say I wouldn't say he's a 'thief,' because I thought he took a game from me. But I've seen other men call other umpires several things. And I'm here, fighting for women's rights and for women's equality and for all kinds of stuff. And for me to say 'thief' and for him to take a game, it made me feel like it was a sexist [ruling]. He's never taken a game from a man because they said 'thief.'"

Serena's eyes widened and she threw open her mouth and arms in disbelief. "For me it blows my mind. But I'm going to continue to fight for women . . . I just feel like the fact that I have to go through this is just an example for the next person that has emotions, and that wants to express themselves, and they want to be a strong woman," Serena said, her voice beginning to quaver as her thoughts came faster and faster. "And they're going to be allowed to do that because of today. Maybe it didn't work out for me, but it's going to work out for the next person."

As Serena's sister Isha and agent began applauding in the front row, Serena stood and walked off the stage, content with her mic-drop moment.

· · · · · · ·

Naomi entered the press conference room minutes later and gave the same answers she had at the ESPN desk when asked about the controversy: she hadn't heard anything that went on between Serena and Ramos, so she didn't have any comment. She also demurred when asked if the controversy had "spoiled the moment" for her, as perhaps evidenced by her tears during the trophy ceremony. "I just feel like I had a lot of emotions, so I had to kind of categorize what was which emotion."

The critical question to Naomi came well into her press conference, like in Serena's before, when the Spanish reporter Candy Rodo asked Naomi if her long-held view of Serena as her idol had been tainted. "What happened today in the final, her behavior on the court, does it change at all, tarnish at all, the image you had of her?" Rodo asked.

"The thing is, like, I don't know what happened on the court," Naomi again reiterated. "So for me, I'm always going to remember the Serena that I love, and it doesn't change anything for me. And she was really nice to me, like at the net and on the podium, so I don't really see what would change."

The controversy that rocked the match had been seismic, but Naomi's foundational admiration of Serena was unshaken. "She hugged me, and it was really awesome," Naomi said, grinning.

Naomi's continued affection for Serena became clearest when Soraya Nadia McDonald, covering the tournament for *The Undefeated*, later asked Naomi why she had felt during the trophy ceremony that she "needed to apologize for doing what you set out to do?"

Naomi smiled nervously and then held her hand up, playfully blocking McDonald from her view. "Agh, your question is making me emotional," Naomi said. "Okay. Because I know that, like, she really wants to have the 24th Grand Slam, right? Everyone knows this. It's on the commercials. It's everywhere. And, like, when I step onto the court, I feel like a different person, right? I'm not a Serena fan. I'm just a tennis player playing another tennis player. But then when I hugged her at the net . . . Sorry."

In the tornado of emotions that had swirled inside Ashe, one that had most shaken Naomi was the harsh, zero-sum reality of tennis: she had to crush her hero's dream in order to achieve her own. As she paused to collect herself, Naomi covered her face with her hand, tears beginning to well up inside her. She then rested her face on her palm and stared down at the podium for several seconds, wiping away the tears that were beginning to form. "Anyways, when I hugged her at the net, I felt like a little kid again," she said.

"Sorry," she quickly added again, wiping further tears from her face.

There was, however, also a moment in the press conference that made her feel young again for much happier reasons and showed how many people, even within the tennis media, were really paying close attention to Naomi only for the first time now that she was a major champion.

"Naomi, your last name is Osaka, you were born in Osaka, which is a bit strange because your father is Haitian," began the veteran Italian reporter Ubaldo Scanagatta. "So how come your last name is the same name of the city? But your father—you should have the last name of your father?"

Naomi smiled her broadest smile of the day, instantly flashing back to her very first press conference at Stanford more than four years earlier, and prepared to quote herself. "You ready? We're recycling a joke from 2014!" she said, beaming. "'Everyone who was born in Osaka, their last name is Osaka!' Eyyyy!"

As Naomi and others laughed, Scanagatta remained perplexed. "Is that true?" he asked.

"Nooo!" Naomi replied, laughing anew and swaying from side to side.

· · · · · · · ·

The morning after the U.S. Open final, Naomi, her agent's wife, her mother, and her publicist went to Manhattan's Dover Street Market to pick out outfits by the Japanese designer Rei Kawakubo's fashion label Comme des Garçons for her fast-approaching media tour. There would be satellite appearances on Japanese TV, an in-studio interview on the *Today* show, and then a trip to Los Angeles for more shows. The first stop on Sunday was a photo op with her trophy on a high floor of a Manhattan skyscraper, a dreary, rainy backdrop behind her, wearing a white Comme des Garçons dress. "For me, I think it's still a win?" she said when asked once more about the controversy. "So I'm just going to count it as that." Naomi's predominant emotion, however, was fatigue. "Hopefully as that wears off, then I'll start feeling more happy."

Naomi then recorded a podcast interview with *WTA Insider* in the back seat of a car between photoshoots and reiterated her weariness when asked about her thoughts since the match had ended less than a day before. "Everything is going really fast, so I haven't really had the chance to process it," she said. When host Courtney Nguyen asked Naomi if she was ready for her "life to change fairly dramatically," Naomi expressed skepticism and cautious acceptance. "I guess a part of me is," she said. "But also at the same time, I feel like it's sort of weird, the things that are happening. But, um, yeah, I guess it's more interesting if life changes instead of being the same."

As the story dominated news cycles in the following days—and completely overshadowed the men's U.S. Open final in which Novak Djoković beat Juan Martín del Potro—clear trend lines could be drawn charting the macro pattern of reactions and allegiances across the sociological and political spectrum. In broad strokes, Serena was defended by women and people of color on liberal and pop culture–focused platforms; Ramos was supported by men and White people on conservative and sports-centered outlets.

Washington Post columnist Sally Jenkins scorched Ramos, claiming his sexism robbed both Serena and Naomi of the moment. "Ramos took what began as a minor infraction and turned it into one of the nastiest and most emotional controversies in the history of tennis, all because he couldn't take a woman speaking sharply to him," Jenkins wrote. Jenkins didn't stop there: she went where Serena didn't, casting doubt on the validity of Naomi's victory. "We will never know whether young Osaka really won the 2018 U.S. Open or had it handed to her by a man who was going to make Serena Williams feel his power," she wrote.

Jenkins's quickly published column was the first volley—in the artillery sense, not the tennis sense—in a crowded cultural cross fire. At ABC's feminist-leaning all-female panel show *The View,* the studio audience broke out in applause at the very first mention of Serena's name. "I didn't see it as abusive of this chair ump, I really didn't," said Sunny Hostin, a *View* panelist of Black and Puerto Rican ancestry. "I think she took issue with the call, and I think she did what a lot of men do across the board, not only in tennis but all athletes in all sports."

The National Organization for Women, the feminist organization founded by Betty Friedan, put out a statement demanding the U.S. Open "cancel any contracts with Carlos Ramos to umpire tournaments in the future." In NOW's summation, "in what was a blatantly racist and sexist move, tennis umpire Carlos Ramos unfairly penalized Serena Williams in an abhorrent display of male dominance and discrimination. This would not have happened if Serena Williams was a man."

This notion of a gendered double standard in tennis officiating—a possible phenomenon almost no one had contemplated before Serena introduced it into the culture during the U.S. Open final—proved resonant for feminists. More than a year later, Taylor Swift directed a music video for her single "The Man" featuring a male character throwing a histrionic hissy fit at an umpire during a tennis match and going unpunished. "If I were a man, then I'd be the man," Swift sings as a ball girl rolls her eyes.

More male and conservative audiences across the table in the debate equally saw the topic as red meat. On *America's Newsroom* on Fox News, host Bill Hemmer ridiculed the notion that the match had been about "women's rights and equality," accusing Serena of "gaslighting everybody around" once the match wasn't going her way. His guest, Fox News sports reporter Jared Max, ended by looking askance at the politics of the U.S. Open crowd that had supported Serena. "When it was the Serena-Venus match about a week ago, the largest cheers that night went to Colin Kaepernick when he was shown on the screen," Max said, pausing for dramatic effect after sounding one of the network's most reliably powerful klaxons. "Same exact crowd."

The stark demographic lines down which this tennis-rules debate split caused some to reflect on their own assessments. After publishing his *Slate* piece, which included examples of Serena's pattern of trouble at past U.S. Opens, Josh Levin was disconcerted by the lopsided feedback he received from readers. "The thing that made me uncomfortable was that, in the response to the piece, I felt like there were a lot of White men who were cheering me on and saying, 'This was the best piece I read, this is so fair, this is so neutral,'" Levin said on the *Slate* podcast *Hang Up and Listen*. "And then the responses that I got from people who didn't like the piece or thought it was unfair were from people of color and women. I don't want to think that what I wrote was because I'm a White man; it is what I believe and what I thought."

Not everyone stuck to their demographic trend lines. Mary Carillo was one of the women most critical of Serena. On MSNBC, Carillo said that the "dead wrong" Serena had acted "like a bully" toward Ramos. "A lot of these people who are weighing in and saying 'double standard'?" Carillo said, exasperated. "I'm thinking, you know what? This is not the hill that you die on for #MeToo."

．．．．．．．

As Naomi sat in the *Today* green room at Rockefeller Center early Monday morning, IMG's publicist repeated her main advice for her first in-depth interview since the final: They will bait you into it, but don't say anything bad about Serena, it's not worth it. There was a considerable cultural current coursing against Serena if Naomi had wanted to tap into it, but she had no interest in doing so: despite appearing above a dramatic chyron reading "*Today* Live Exclusive: U.S. Open Winner Speaks Out," it was clear from Naomi's opening answer that she wasn't raring to make headlines. "Um, I mean, I've never been on a talk show before," she said softly, smiling. "So, um, I'm very happy to be here. And yeah, I mean, it still feels a little bit surreal, but I think it's slowly sinking in."

After a few lighthearted questions, *Today* anchor Savannah Guthrie dug into the controversy at hand. "Obviously some stuff went on on the court during the match," Guthrie euphemized. "What was going through your mind? Did you even know what was happening exactly with Serena and the ref? Could you hear it? I mean, how were you feeling in those moments?"

Naomi repeated the same answer she had given in the hour following the match: that she didn't know what was going on. Guthrie soon followed up on her initial question, pressing that Naomi must have learned in the two days that had passed what had happened between Serena and Ramos, and surely, like everyone else in America, she must have formed a strong opinion on whom to blame. "Now you've, I'm sure, read and learned what this whole controversy was about—do you have an opinion about whether the umpire did the right thing, whether Serena did the right thing?" Guthrie asked. "Now that you know the facts, what do you think of it?"

Naomi flinched backward in her chair as she answered. "Um, well, I'm not really that 100 percent sure, because I kind of haven't really had time to look too much at the news," Naomi replied. "I've been, like, going all over the place. So I can't really form an opinion right now, but, I mean, for sure, I want to watch everything, and I want to know what happened because this is sort of one of the biggest things that happened to me."

On follow-up questions about her emotions during the trophy ceremony, Naomi articulated the anguish that had been clear on her face. "I felt a little bit sad because I wasn't really sure if they were booing at me or if it wasn't the outcome that they wanted," Naomi said. "And then I also could sympathize because I've been a fan of Serena my whole life, and I knew how badly the crowd wanted her to win. So, I don't know. I was just really emotional . . . I just felt like everyone was sort of unhappy up there. And I know that it wasn't really like the ending how people wanted it to be. I know that in my dreams, I won, like, in a very tough, competitive match. So I don't know. I just felt very emotional and I felt like I had to apologize."

The U.S. Open champion's media tour of New York was a triumphant annual occasion, but this go-round was stubbornly somber; Guthrie's cohost Hoda Kotb even appeared to wipe away tears during the interview. There were moments of smiles, including when the cameras showed a waving Tamaki standing nearby in the studio, but the mood remained mournful as Guthrie ended the segment much as McKendry had days earlier, imploring Naomi to be happy. "I hope you feel good," Guthrie urged. "This is the championship trophy right there: it belongs to you. No more tears."

• • • • • • •

Naomi explained weeks later, in an interview with journalist Reem Abulleil, that she had intentionally kept herself from learning more about what had happened on court before her *Today* appearance. "I didn't want to know anything," Naomi told Abulleil. "I was going in with as little knowledge [as possible]. I mean, for me, I tried to tell my version of the truth as much [as possible]. I feel like people didn't believe me when I said I didn't know what was going on, even though that was true—I didn't turn my phone on or anything. So I hope that the talk show people thought I was telling the truth."

When Naomi had woken up the morning after the final and saw

herself—and the controversy—as the lead story on the news, she was un-derstandably overwhelmed. "I was very shocked because, first of all, that was the first time I was ever on the news; second of all, I felt like it was for all the wrong reasons," Naomi said years later. Not knowing how to process what was happening in the world around her, Naomi chose to engage with the story as little as she could for not just days, but for weeks, months, and years.

Sascha Bajin wrote that he had tearfully hugged Naomi at the U.S. Open in the moments after her win. Though it was a career peak for both, Bajin said the two never discussed the U.S. Open again after that quick post-match embrace. "This might surprise you, but that was the last time that Naomi and I spoke about that match," he wrote. "For the rest of the time we worked together, she didn't want to talk about the U.S. Open, and I respected that: it was the biggest achievement of her career to date, and it went unmentioned between us."

It wasn't for lack of trying. "Sometimes I'd slip or slide in a little com-ment about the U.S. Open, kind of trying to normalize the whole situation, and just make it look like any other tournament," Bajin told Abulleil. "But she wasn't really too fond to speak of it."

Days later, Naomi said she felt ill-equipped to measure her emotions. "For me, I don't feel sad because I wouldn't even know what I'm expected to feel?" she said. "Because I feel like since it was my first final and it was my first Grand Slam victory, overall I felt really happy, and I know that I ac-complished a lot."

Naomi first publicly articulated fuller feelings about her U.S. Open about four weeks later, after her first win at the China Open in Beijing. "I have so much tea right now, but I'm not going to spill it," she said with something like a mischievous giggle. "There's a lot of stuff I want to say about, like, how I felt and whatever. But for me, I don't know. I don't know. The memory of the U.S. Open is a little bit bittersweet. Like right after, the day after, I really didn't want to think about it because it wasn't necessarily the happiest memory for me. I don't know. Like, I just sort of wanted to move on at that point."

When a reporter asked if joy was "taking over the bittersweet feeling" with time, Naomi paused and then responded with a question of her own. "Have you ever eaten green tea ice cream?" she asked, smiling. "This is a serious question. When you bite into it, it's, like, sweet but also very strong. Like, that's how that memory feels to me. I mean, of course I'm happy that I won a Grand Slam; I don't think there's anything that can take away from that. But I don't know. I feel like—not that when I look back on it that it's a bad memory—but I feel like it was so strange, I didn't just want to think about it. I wanted to just push it to the side . . . I'm still trying to take my mind off of it a little bit."

Naomi continued processing what happened at the 2018 U.S. Open over the course of the next months and years, and her answers about it evolved.

In the first few months, she took on an upbeat tone about it in interviews. "In a perfect dream, things would be set exactly the way you would want them," she told *Time* months later. "But I think it's more interesting that in real life, things aren't exactly the way you planned. And there are certain situations that you don't expect, but they come to you, and I think those situations set up things for further ahead."

"It's kind of weird to hear people say that," she told *Vogue* when it was suggested she had a negative experience at the U.S. Open in December 2018.

"My biggest dream was to play Serena in a Grand Slam final, and for that to be the first one, I wouldn't wish it any other way," Naomi similarly told an unconvinced host during a Tennis Channel interview in March 2019. "And I was happy."

As months passed, her answers grew terse. "Do you think the U.S. Open final made you a stronger player and a stronger person, as well?" a reporter asked her in May 2019.

Her reply: "No."

Naomi was readier to expound by early 2021. "I was just going into it thinking it was a tennis match, and then I feel like everything after was something that I could have never prepared for," Naomi told *GQ*. "And I just felt super overwhelmed. Even during the trophy ceremony, I was overwhelmed. But I feel like the me now sort of understands everything that took place."

Though Naomi wasn't ready to declare the occasion "tainted," she did admit it had been overwhelming. "I would just say that it gave me a lot of experiences in one single day that maybe would have taken a lot of other people a couple of years to experience," she said.

Indeed, the inferno that was the 2018 U.S. Open had burned all involved, but it had also been rocket fuel that launched Naomi into an orbit of instant notoriety that would have been unthinkable before the tournament, and even before the second set of the final became what it was.

The embers smoldered for weeks. When *Saturday Night Live* had its season premiere in late September, they included a skit about the three-week-old controversy, featuring cast member Leslie Jones angrily interrupting Weekend Update in a Serena wig and the black Nike tutu Serena had worn during the final. "I want an apology!" Jones, quoting Serena, shouted at the camera.

"Serena Williams, everyone," Weekend Update anchor Colin Jost said, ending the bit.

"This moment is for Naomi Osaka!" Jones declared as she walked off-stage.

· · · · · · ·

Naomi did express one regret in her 2021 interview with *GQ*: she wished she could've defended Serena, whom she did not think deserved the negativity she received in the days following the final. "I never saw Serena as angry or anything like that," Naomi said. "It was a tennis match. She was expressing her emotions, but we were playing tennis. You know what I mean? [I wanted] just for everyone to stop pushing the narrative that Serena was being mean or stuff like that."

The demonization of Serena was most stark in an editorial cartoon published in an Australian tabloid, the *Herald Sun,* in the days after the final. Cartoonist Mark Knight drew Serena as hopping mad, mid-tantrum, hands curled into fists, stomping on a broken racquet with a pacifier on the ground beside her, her curly black hair looking like smoke billowing up from her exploding rage. Most gallingly for many, Knight drew Serena with thick, reddened lips, a quickly recognizable trope of racist depictions of Black people dating back centuries to the blackface minstrelsy of the 1800s.

Though Knight's depiction of Serena drew most of the criticism, the depiction of an opponent whom the umpire was addressing—"Can you just let her win?"—was also jarring. The player drawn across the net from Knight's hulking Serena was a thin woman with long, straight blond hair and lighter skin than Serena's; Breanna Edwards of *Essence* said Naomi was drawn as "a small, delicate, White-passing blonde figure," and indeed, the drawing resembled Maria Sharapova more than Naomi Osaka. The racialized depictions of both women were each dehumanizing in their own way.

· · · · · · · ·

Knight's depiction of Naomi was simultaneously wildly wrong and unintentionally meaningful: with so much attention paid to characterizing Serena and Ramos by their respective critics and defenders in the furor following the final, Naomi had been repeatedly reduced to something blank and meek in the background, a colorless canvas onto which various virtues had been projected as needed.

Amid the unpleasant history repeating, Naomi was fresh and new.

Amid the cacophony, Naomi was quiet.

Amid the discord, Naomi was pleasant.

Amid the storm, Naomi was calm.

Amid the mess, Naomi was clean.

Amid the blame, Naomi was innocent.

Even though the characteristics projected onto Naomi were largely positive, they still made her uncomfortable, especially because they were in contrast to negative things said about Serena. "If I were to put it bluntly, I know that there's a lot of people that don't like Serena, and I feel like they're just looking for someone to sort of jump on to be against her and I feel like

they found that in me," Naomi told Soraya Nadia McDonald in an interview months after the U.S. Open final. "Of course, I don't really like that . . .
I want people to go with me for the right reasons. If I'm being blunt, I feel
like that's happened a lot, like after the U.S. Open."

In her article for *The Undefeated,* McDonald further articulated the
way she saw Naomi being used as a palate cleanser for distaste for Serena
and what she had represented:

> For some, Osaka's rise marks the beginning of the end of the Williams
> era, something that can't come quickly enough. To an ugly part of ten-
> nis fandom, part of Osaka's appeal is that she's black without constantly
> reminding everyone of her blackness . . . If Serena is the boogeywoman
> who won't let anyone forget about race at large and American blackness
> in particular, then Osaka has been branded, without her consent, as the
> angel who will deliver us from such sordid unpleasantries.

Naomi not only didn't want to be an antidote to Serena; she also rejected how she was being cast as an angel, either in comparison to the demonization of Serena or independently. "After my first Slam, I was supposed
to be the 'good girl,' you know?" Naomi said in August 2021, after she had
taken several stands of her own that had made people angry and uncomfortable. "But now that I'm talking about stuff that bothers me, I think it's
confusing a lot of people."

· · · · · · ·

Days after the 2018 U.S. Open final, Black writers Kara Brown and Ira
Madison III spoke ominously, and perhaps presciently, about what the current characterizations of the two women could portend on the pop culture
podcast *Keep It.* "She did it in part for Naomi," Brown said of Serena's indignation. "I don't think specifically in that moment, but she was like: this
is a young, up-and-coming tennis player who is not White, who we're going
to see more of, and who will probably be treated as unfairly as I have been
treated. And she was like, I'm not letting this happen. And I think when

you see Naomi in that moment—and I can't speak for her, I don't know—but I think she also seems to maybe recognize that this is, maybe, her future, too. This is the kind of shit she may have to be putting up with."

"Yeah, that's a very interesting point: just the fact that Naomi right now is being positioned as being the calm and collected one against Serena, the unruly Black woman," Madison agreed. "I'm like, Wait 'til Serena and Venus are retired and out of the game. Who's the Black woman they're going to go against next?"

"Let [Naomi] get mad for unfair treatment," Brown concluded, "and see how quickly they turn on her."

· · · · · · ·

After her shock loss to Roberta Vinci in the 2015 U.S. Open semifinals when she was just two wins from the elusive Grand Slam, Serena had developed a pattern: after losing at the U.S. Open, she would retreat into a degree of hiding for the remainder of the year. While the tour rolled on into Asia, Serena alighted from the ride in New York, not playing any tournaments and making few public appearances. After she again lost the U.S. Open final in 2019 to Bianca Andreescu, her final appearance in a major final, Serena canceled a planned *Saturday Night Live* hosting gig.

Serena would have wanted to make her retreat from the spotlight as complete as possible in the days following the 2018 U.S. Open final, perhaps the most painful loss of her career. But three days after the final, Serena had an odd bit of promotional work to do for one of her sponsors, the Australian bra-maker Berlei: to boost Berlei's involvement in a self-check campaign for Breast Cancer Awareness Month in Australia, Serena had recorded a topless video of herself holding her breasts, singing a repurposed rendition of the raunchy "I Touch Myself" by the Divinyls, and she was committed to promoting it with appearances in Australian media.

Lisa Wilkinson, who interviewed Serena for Australian current affairs program *The Project*, admitted her surprise that Serena hadn't canceled on her but said that a strict precondition was set by Serena's publicist: any mention of the cartoon by Mark Knight and Serena would get up and leave.

Wilkinson did ask about code violations Serena had incurred during the U.S. Open—the publicist interrupted to curtail that line of questioning but Serena begrudgingly allowed Wilkinson to proceed—and then finished by defending herself for one final time. "Even [for] a man, like if you want to express yourself in a way where you're not using profanity, you're just being yourself, and you're at this moment you've worked for since you were three years old and you're on the cusp of this amazing moment?" she said. "If you're a female, you should be able to do even half of what a guy can do. And I feel like, right now, we are not, as it's proven, in that same position.

"But, you know, that's neither here nor there," Serena said, audibly weary to be picking at a wound that was still fresh. "I'm just trying to most of all just recover from that and just move on."

Serena concluded the interview by gifting Wilkinson a Berlei snakeskin bra. "That's gorgeous," Wilkinson said. "And it's even in my size!"

· · · · · · ·

Serena had completed the bra handoff that signaled the end of her obligation to speak about what had happened, but she still felt uneasy after returning home to Florida. "Every night, as I would try to go to sleep, unresolved questions ran through my mind in a never-ending loop," Serena later wrote.

Serena began talking to a therapist, but still she felt restless. She eventually realized she still wanted to talk about what had happened to one more person, so she tracked down a phone number and began writing a text message. She had demanded an apology from Ramos, but after time had passed, Serena now believed she might owe one of her own:

Hey, Naomi! It's Serena Williams. As I said on the court, I am so proud of you and I am truly sorry. I thought I was doing the right thing in sticking up for myself. But I had no idea the media would pit us against each other. I would love the chance to live that moment over again. I am, was, and will always be happy for you and supportive of you. I would never, ever want the light to shine away from another female, specifically another Black female athlete. I can't wait for your future, and believe me I will always be watching as a big fan! I wish you only success today and in the future. Once again, I am so proud of you. All my love and your fan, Serena.

Serena wrote in *Harper's Bazaar,* where she shared the conversation months later, that "tears rolled down my face" when Naomi's reply flashed onto her screen: "People can misunderstand anger for strength because they can't differentiate between the two," Naomi wrote. "No one has stood up for themselves the way you have and you need to continue trailblazing."

Many thought Naomi should resent Serena for overshadowing her moment. Because Naomi's love for Serena was absolute, she had given her absolution.

· · · · · · ·

Though her feelings for Serena never wavered, other parts of Naomi's mind were shaken by what happened that day. When she revealed her ongoing struggle with depression in 2021, she traced it back to the trauma of what had happened in New York three years earlier. "The truth is that I have suffered long bouts of depression since the US Open in 2018," Naomi wrote, "and I have had a really hard time coping with that."

· · · · · · ·

Naomi had little time to process what had happened at the time. By the time she had gotten the message from Serena, Naomi was already in the one place on earth where her win had been bigger news than Serena's loss: Japan.

TWENTY-ONE

The Talk of Tokyo

The rising sun reached Nemuro at 4:50 a.m. on Sunday, September 9, 2018, illuminating the small fishing town on the northeast edge of Hokkaido before anywhere else in the country. Within ten minutes of the morning light reaching his window, Tetsuo Osaka was watching another distant, ascendant star that he'd seen before the rest of Japan: his granddaughter Naomi, who was winning her first major title at the U.S. Open as a new day dawned in the country she represented.

Hours after her win, with a media storm already brewing a world away in New York, seventy-three-year-old Tetsuo had a far more tranquil media scrum outside his home on a cool, crisp day in Nemuro. "I still don't grasp that my grandchild has become the best in the world," a beaming Tetsuo told gathered reporters.

Unlike when Serena had to ask the weeping Naomi if she was crying happy tears during the trophy ceremony, there was no ambiguity around emotions caused by her victory in Japan. Naomi's face was on the front page of major Japanese newspapers for days, with headlines like "The Top Feat of a Japanese Player" and "Overnight Queen—Powerful and Stable." Long-time Japanese prime minister Shinzo Abe congratulated Naomi on her breakthrough victory and thanked her "for giving Japan energy and excitement at this time of hardship," referring to an earthquake that had hit southern Hokkaido three days earlier, killing dozens. Kei Nishikori, the longtime standard-bearer of Japanese tennis, sent Naomi a congratulatory tweet written solely in the universal language of emojis. The U.S. Open final had only been broadcast live in Japan on Wowow, a premium cable channel with limited reach, but the news of Naomi's win dominated all the biggest media platforms in Japan—print, television, Web, electronic billboards—for a full week after her win. Naomi, who had only been well known in Japan to tennis fans, was suddenly a sensation across the culture.

In various man-on-the-street interviews, a popular genre for vloggers in Japan, dozens expressed their admiration for Naomi's achievement. The average Tokyoite had little interest or understanding in why Serena had been upset or why the crowd had been booing. Some suggested, not entirely erroneously, that the American public had foremost been upset that their player was losing; one man wistfully suggested that the anger directed at a foreigner's success reflected the xenophobia that had taken over America during Donald Trump's presidency.

Thanks to a coincidence of the tennis calendar, Naomimania would soon pick up pace on the ground: the next big tournament on the WTA calendar after the U.S. Open was the mid-September Toray Pan Pacific Open in Tokyo, meaning Naomi was Japan-bound at the peak of national interest in her. Despite the facts that she had never resided in Tokyo and had only spent a few sporadic months in Japan since leaving the country at age three, Japanese media billed Naomi's arrival as a homecoming.

After a stopover in Los Angeles to film appearances on *Ellen* and *The Steve Harvey Show,* Naomi, her parents, and her managers flew to Tokyo Haneda Airport. A throng of fans and photographers were waiting for Naomi as she walked out. It was the breathless beginning of the pop star treatment that Naomi would experience for the rest of her Tokyo trip. One night in her Tokyo hotel room, Tamaki decided to run an experiment: Could she flip through all the channels without seeing her daughter's face at least once? She could not.

Naomi had already done satellite interviews from New York with major Japanese networks NHK and TBS the day after her U.S. Open win, answering some questions in Japanese—most often when talking about her favorite foods. Others she answered in English, like when a TBS interviewer asked her how it felt to be the first Japanese major champion. "I am very honored," Naomi said. "I don't know how to say that in Japanese."

There was still a ravenous appetite for more access to the new star four days after her win, so her sponsor Nissin arranged a press conference in Yokohama several hours after her arrival in the country. Nissin president and chief executive Koki Ando presented Naomi with a bouquet of flowers, and she posed for photographs in front of Nissin logos and took questions from a crowd of hundreds of reporters, more than double the number she had faced in New York.

"Firstly, I want to thank everyone for coming here," Naomi began in English, which was later translated into Japanese by an interpreter beside her on the podium. "I really appreciate all the support. And then also, I want to say, um, I heard about, like, the stuff that happened in Hokkaido, so I really wish that everyone is really safe and I send all my wishes." Flashbulbs and motorized shutters from the hoard of photographers went off at such frequency as Naomi spoke that it sounded like a steady, rustling breeze. "I've never had like—oh my God, so bright—so many people coming to a press conference," Naomi said as she answered a question on if it felt like she was dreaming. "I think for sure it's sinking in now."

As the press conference extended, one reporter asked her to send a message to Japanese fans in Japanese. Naomi, who always responded with only the most basic phrases when urged to speak in Japanese in recent years, twice said "Thank you for your support." She then added a long "Konichi-waaaaa" and said, "The sushi is really delicious." She gave a thumbs-up, and the gathered reporters laughed, fully charmed.

The rest of the nation was enchanted, too. "She is such a lovable character," Seiji Miyane, an NTV talk show host, said after his interview with Naomi. The Associated Press wrote that Naomi's "broken Japanese works as an asset, apologizing occasionally for getting the wrong word—or not knowing the Japanese word at all." When the publisher Jiyū Kokumin Sha announced its candidates for the words and phrases of the year in November 2018, they included *Naomi-bushi,* or Naomi-esque, describing her "shyly delivered, simple Japanese phrases."

Though more than 90 percent of her public speaking was in English, Japanese media and viewers often enthusiastically pointed out the Japaneseness they saw in her presentation. "She's insanely Japanese in her mannerisms, right down to the head tilt," one YouTube commenter said under a video of Naomi. The magazine *Weekly Toyo Keizai* wrote that Naomi "is not the type of person who asserts herself boldly, but she is shy and humble and that makes her look more like a Japanese." Motoko Rich, the Tokyo bureau chief for *The New York Times,* said the way Naomi had apologized for her victory during the U.S. Open trophy ceremony had "demonstrated a characteristically Japanese trait." Naoko Ohno, a Japanese tennis fan interviewed in Rich's *Times* story, said that Naomi's Japanese qualities ran deep. "Her soul is Japanese," Ohno said. "She doesn't display her joy so excessively. Her playing style is aggressive, but she is always humble in interviews. I like that."

. . . .

These declarations of Naomi's Japaneseness were particularly meaningful to Japanese people who looked like Naomi and had their own Japaneseness frequently doubted and challenged. The spotlight on Naomi meant more light than ever before was reflecting onto mixed-race people, an often marginalized and overlooked part of Japanese society. In Japan, where around 98 percent of the population is ethnically Japanese, people of mixed Japanese and foreign backgrounds are commonly called *hafu,* from the English word "half." The term *hafu* is divisive among those described by it; many parents of mixed children, particularly, do not like *hafu* because they consider it to be a pejorative like "half-breed." Thinking that *hafu* makes their children sound less than whole, some have proposed the term *daburu,* from the English "double"; instead of being only half of something, they can be fully two things.

"The way the Japanese people celebrated her made me think that the media and the people really accept her as pure Japanese," one darker-skinned Japanese woman said, before adding caveats. "I'm really happy with her achievement, but from my point of view as a half-Japanese, half-Black person myself, I don't want Japanese people to have this stereotype that we're more athletic just because we're Black . . . If the Japanese society continues to look at us only as athletic people, then they will never realize issues like racism."

Several of the most famous mixed-race Japanese celebrities had also been athletes, like the basketball player Rui Hachimura and the baseball pitcher Yu Darvish. There was also Denny Tamaki, who was elected governor of Okinawa Prefecture around the same time as Naomi won the U.S. Open, and a Miss Universe Japan, Ariana Miyamoto. But those people had all grown up in Japan and developed under a more gradually brightening spotlight, nothing like the on switch that had instantly illuminated Naomi after her major win.

Though identity politics had nowhere near the prominence in Japan as it did in the United States, Japanese people with one foreign parent like Naomi suddenly found themselves a topic of some curiosity and interest as the homogenous Japanese society was suddenly foregrounding and festooning a different-looking icon. Joe Oliver, a half-Black, half-Japanese engineer and model, was interviewed by many outlets in the days after Naomi's win and spoke of the bullying he had experienced as a child—a common theme for mixed Japanese people interviewed. "I think mixed raced people's success, such as Osaka's, can help to bring down the wall most Japanese have between people with different backgrounds," Oliver told Reuters. Oliver and others also hoped that Naomi's fame would bring attention to serious issues multiracial people who weren't sports superstars had faced, like housing and hiring discrimination. When vlogger Max D. Capo asked him how Japanese people on the street would feel about her "if you take Naomi Osaka away from tennis," Oliver's answer was quick and blunt. "Oh, she's a foreigner," Oliver said. "That's how Japanese people think."

Baye McNeil, a Brooklyn-born Black writer who has lived in Japan for nearly two decades, said that Japanese people's limited exposure to Black people—the same imprecise Japanese term for "Black," *kokujin,* is used to describe dark-skinned people from places as far-flung as Senegal and Fiji—made them quick to ascribe positive or negative stereotypes. "Whatever she does has an effect on me, because unfortunately, whatever one Black person does in Japan affects all of us," McNeil said of Naomi. "If one Black guy robs a Japanese woman, or some Black soldier rapes a Japanese woman in Okinawa, that's going to affect me. Because of the limited imagination of the racial sense of Japanese people, they can't see Black people as individuals, they see us as a monolith. And Naomi is included in that now. So whatever she does, her greatness shines on me."

McNeil devised what he calls an "ABC" rubric for measuring how Japanese someone is deemed to be by three metrics: **A**ppearing Japanese, **B**ehaving Japanese, and **C**ommunicating in Japanese. While Naomi would have low scores in A and C, he said, her B score was immense, both from her shy, deferential demeanor and her enthusiasm for Japanese pop culture staples like anime, video games, and *Pokémon.* "Initially, I think Japanese people were really charmed by her," McNeil told me. "She was kind of an ideal combination of Western and Eastern qualities. She had this shyness of the Japanese background, but she also had this aggressiveness of her Western influences. That combination is something that people really aspire to. They wish they could get that, capture it, bottle it."

Sure enough, Japanese brands were lining up to capture, bottle, and sell the essence of Naomi Osaka.

· · · · · · ·

After her general press conference hosted by Nissin, Naomi went across Yokohama to the launch of a major new sponsorship deal: Nissan, the car manufacturer, was signing Naomi to a three-year contract to become one of its most prominent brand ambassadors. Again, hundreds of photographers and reporters had gathered, this time at Nissan headquarters, to document the occasion. When Nissan's presenter began the ceremony by asking Naomi to speak a little Japanese, Naomi's eyes widened; she obliged briefly before quickly switching back to English within the first sentence. "I'm just really honored that I'm able to be a brand ambassador," she said.

"Nissan and Osaka share the same spirit in trying to change the world and become a game changer," said Nissan senior vice president Asako Hoshino. In a brief onstage conversation, Hoshino presented Naomi with one of their new youth-targeted Nissan Leaf electric models and appeared to confuse her by excitedly telling her that Nissan also had a minivan model called the Nissan Serena. Naomi delighted Hoshino, however, by telling her about the Nissan Quest minivan her father had driven during her childhood, the van into which he had fatefully loaded his daughters and driven to Florida, changing their lives forever. "Being able to be a brand ambassador now, it feels like I've come full circle," Naomi said. The pair finished the ceremony by signing a giant novelty contract—Naomi signing her name in English, Hoshino signing hers in Japanese—and posing for photos. Later in 2018, Nissan released a commemorative limited-edition car model in her honor: The "Nissan GTR Naomi Osaka Edition." Naomi picked three color schemes for the cars.

The Nissan deal was one of the biggest in Naomi's rapidly thickening Japanese endorsement portfolio. Having started the 2018 season already with sponsorship by her racquet manufacturer Yonex, Nissin foods, and Wowow television (as well as her one non-Japanese sponsor, Adidas), Naomi added four more Japanese sponsors by year's end: Nissan, Citizen watches, Shiseido beauty products, and All Nippon Airways (who paid a premium for Naomi to wear an "ANA" patch on her match outfits). Naomi's existing sponsors could already point to their partnerships with Naomi paying dividends: according to *Nikkei Asian Review,* Wowow experienced a 500 percent increase in subscription inquiries after Naomi reached the U.S. Open final, and Yonex's stock rose by 11 percent in the three days after her win in the final. Nissin stock also had a 3 percent rise.

(The deluge of cash onto Naomi even created a splash zone of earnings for those near her: making himself a billboard at her matches, Sascha Bajin wore his Yonex T-shirts with additional sponsor patches from Nissin and

Nissan. Bajin also signed a six-figure deal with a Japanese publisher to write a self-help book that would be published exclusively in Japanese.)

Before her U.S. Open win, Naomi's annual endorsement earnings were estimated at $1.5 million; that number was now rising exponentially, with buzz that Naomi could soon surpass Serena's $18 million in annual endorsement income. With the 2020 Tokyo Olympics now thought to be less than two years away, a feeding frenzy had begun among Japanese brands looking for a female face of the games. Kei Nishikori, who had earned $33 million in endorsements over a recent twelve-month period, according to *Forbes*, was frequently pointed to as the obvious analog. "We manage Kei so we know how strong that market is for endorsements—the blueprint was there," Naomi's agent Stuart Duguid told British reporters after her U.S. Open win. "There's a lot of companies for whom Kei is the male and they are looking for a female, so it couldn't be better timing."

While American tennis pundits had often side-eyed Naomi's choice to play for Japan, suggesting it had been a cynical cash grab, there was little such sentiment or skepticism in Japan. "I think among non-Japanese people, pretty much everyone feels it was a power move, it was a monetary decision, because it's the smart move," McNeil told me. "But as far as Japanese people are concerned, I haven't heard anything about any concern with sponsorship. Honestly, I don't think people think in those terms . . . I just think it's a different culture, and Japanese culture isn't inclined to think that she would choose Japanese as her nationality for financial reasons."

. . . .

While most of the spotlight on Naomi focused on what she had done days earlier, there was also sidebar speculation in Japan about what might happen thirteen months from now, on her twenty-second birthday: by law, Japanese people who have reached the age of twenty-two are no longer allowed to hold dual citizenship and are forced to expatriate from other countries if they wish to keep their Japanese citizenship.

Naomi was well known to be a dual U.S.-Japan citizen,* and the topic of Naomi's citizenship dilemma was the focus of another man-on-the-street video made by the YouTube channel Asian Boss, yielding a wide range of reactions:

"I think she should choose Japan because she's winning as a Japanese player. I think it'll be easier to play at the top level with Japanese citizenship . . . She'd have more competition in the States."

"English is her mother tongue, and she's going to spend more time in America."

"I feel like she identifies more with her American side, but Japanese people are getting overly excited about calling her Japanese. I think they just want to say that a Japanese person is succeeding."

"I'd support her, that wouldn't change. Even if she decides to go with her American citizenship, she still has Japanese blood in her. I just want to continue to support her."

One twenty-three-year-old woman in the video who had been forced to renounce her dual citizenship with Canada grew emotional as she discussed her experience. "Both countries were part of my identity, but because Japanese law makes you choose one, I feel like my identity is sort of dismissed," she said. "It's not accepted here, which makes me sad. I feel bad that [Naomi] has to choose, so I empathize with her . . . I hope there will be a day when I can get back my lost nationality."

Naomi expressed rare frustration when asked at a press conference weeks later what her citizenship choice would be. "I don't really understand why people keep asking me this," she said. "I'm pretty sure it's obvious: I'm playing for Japan. Not to be disrespectful or anything, but I don't really get where the conclusion that it's a hard choice for me or anything comes from."

Naomi did indeed keep her Japanese citizenship and continued playing

---

* In a sign of how slow Japan had been to expand its definitions of what it meant to be Japanese, Naomi wouldn't have been granted Japanese citizenship had she been born just thirteen years earlier. Before 1985, a child could only acquire Japanese citizenship if their father was a Japanese citizen, which Naomi's father was not. A 1985 revision of the law allowed either parent's Japanese citizenship to transfer onto their child.

for Japan. But like roughly an estimated million of her Japanese compatriots who have evaded the loosely enforced law, Naomi in fact kept her dual
citizenship, too: Naomi's name has never appeared on the *Quarterly Publication of Individuals, Who Have Chosen to Expatriate* published by the U.S.
Internal Revenue Service in the years before or after her twenty-second
birthday.

· · · · · · ·

Though it had long been a focus in the coverage of her in English-language
media, Naomi only occasionally got questions from Japanese media about
her multicultural background; some Japanese commenters were critical of
this trend, complaining that Naomi was asked too many basic, infantiliz-
ing questions about frivolous topics. Indeed, at her big arrival press conference in Japan, she had been asked questions about light topics like eating
ice cream and what her next post on Instagram might be, before someone
asked her to reflect on how she was changing conceptions of Japanese identity. After some confusion over the question when it was mistranslated by
the interpreter, Naomi largely demurred. "I don't really think too much
about my identity or whatever," she said. "For me, I'm just me. And I know
that the way that I was brought up, I don't know, people tell me I act kind
of Japanese? So I guess there's that."

Naomi answered similarly in a separate interview quoted by the Associated Press. "When someone asks me a question like that, it really throws
me off because then I really have to think about it," Naomi said of her
multicultural background. "I don't know. I don't really think that I'm three
separate, like, mixes of whatever. I just think that I'm me."

Coverage of Naomi in Japan was wide but not deep. Even after she became one of the country's biggest stars, domestic coverage of Naomi hadn't
been interested in probing deep dives into her family's biographical details.
Florent Dabadie, who had covered Naomi for years as a presenter for
Wowow, remarked at how many new biographical details about Naomi's
family and their time in Japan he had learned from the *New York Times
Magazine* story on her before the 2018 U.S. Open. "In Japan, they were not

really interested in this kind of background," Dabadie told me. "When she came for a tour in Japan, she was also a bit annoyed how the late shows that we also have in Japan were asking her kind of dumb questions and really pushing her on saying 'What's your favorite food?' 'What's your favorite city in Japan?' 'Why do you like Japan?' And it was becoming kind of a circus and nobody would ask her adult questions." Whereas English-language coverage repeatedly steered Naomi toward the choppier waters of social and political topics—to the repeated aggravation of her IMG PR handlers, who wished she could steer clear of politics in the way that their earlier clients like Roger Federer, Rafael Nadal, and Maria Sharapova had reliably been able to do—Dabadie was similarly annoyed that Japanese media were paddling Naomi toward the kiddie pool of fluff questions instead of asking her and her family about the issues their experience and existence raised in Japan. "I think she was a grown-up and she wanted to speak about important issues," he said. "But in Japan, sports is an entertainment, and they sometimes talk to players as if they shouldn't talk about important issues."

Though Naomi was riding a Kanagawa-size wave of public and corporate enthusiasm in Japan, not everything was smooth sailing. When Nissin commissioned an animated ad campaign featuring anime characters of both Naomi and Nishikori, viewers were shocked. While Nishikori's likeness was readily recognizable, Naomi's depiction looked nothing like her, especially the character's pale skin color that was the same shade as Nishikori's. The brand was widely criticized for "Whitewashing" Naomi, giving her the first corporate PR crisis of her career. Naomi initially demurred when asked about the controversy at a press conference but then answered more fully. "I've talked to them; they've apologized," Naomi said. "For me, it's obvious, I'm tan. It's pretty obvious. I don't think they did it on purpose to be, like, 'Whitewashing' or anything. But I definitely think that the next time they try to portray me or something, I feel like they should talk to me about it."

Another controversy over Naomi's skin tone came months later when

A Masso, a duo of female comedians, joked that Naomi "needs some bleach" and "is too sunburned." The pair apologized, and Naomi deflected the moment into a cheeky plug for one of her new sponsors. "'Too sunburned' lol that's wild," Naomi wrote on Twitter. "Little did they know, with Shiseido anessa perfect uv sunscreen I never get sunburned."

. . . .

Given all of the new and emotional experiences that Naomi had in the ten days between the U.S. Open final and her return to competition at the Toray Pan Pacific Open, it would have been fair to expect drained sluggishness on court. Instead, Naomi harnessed the ambient energy into a charge. "Coming to Japan has been really fun," Naomi said during her visit to Nissan headquarters. "Just seeing how proud and happy everyone is about how I did in the [U.S. Open], it makes me want to do a lot better during my matches."

That Naomi could be inspired to up her level of play even further was a daunting proposition for the field, but she did. Because the ten-thousand-seat Ariake Coliseum was being renovated to prepare for Olympic Games, the Toray Pan Pacific Open was being played that year in a small three-thousand-seat indoor basketball arena in Tachikawa. Naomi easily packed the stands. After getting a first-round bye for being one of the highest-ranked players in the draw—the first time in her career Naomi had earned that privilege—Japanese fans, several of whom brought homemade signs and banners to show their support, saw a quick contest when Naomi made her debut in the second round, routing former WTA No. 4 Dominika Cibulková 6–2, 6–1 in under an hour.

With broadcast cameras trained on her mother and grandparents in the stands, Naomi reeled off two more straight-set wins to extend her winning streak to a career-best ten matches and make the final. Seventh-ranked Naomi ultimately lost the final to eighth-ranked Karolína Plíšková 6–4, 6–4, but she showed that her form could be sustained even as she coped with weight and attention few other players had ever faced.

. . . .

But at her next tournament, in Beijing, Naomi suddenly felt empty again, like she had in Charleston, weeping on court during a match. "The same thing," Naomi later said. "I was in China, I was hoping this girl would beat me and I was crying on the court and whatever. And then I just kind of thought to myself, like, I don't know what this feeling is. I don't know how to describe it, and I also don't know how to fix it. So I guess I'm going to have to live with it for the rest of my life."

TWENTY-TWO

Down Under to the Top

When Naomi Osaka returned home to Florida for the first time in more than two months at the end of the 2018 season, she was a far different commodity than when she had last left. She was a major champion and Top 5 player, with earnings for the year reaching into the eight-digit range. Reporters were flying to Florida to profile her for a feature in *Vogue* and a cover story in *Time*.

But despite all these changes that had made her a global superstar and household name, twenty-one-year-old Naomi still came home to the same household, still living with her parents and sister in her parents' Boca Raton home. "My mom cooks dinner and we all go out somewhere—usually to the mall because there's nothing really to do in Florida, to be honest," Naomi said of her typical off-season day. "And yeah, I just spend a lot of time with my sister. Maybe we play video games or something? We're all enjoying each other's company." Naomi had taken immense pride and satisfaction when her earnings had allowed her mother to retire from the workforce, but she was bemused by Tamaki's inability to chill out as she continued to oversee her daughter's career and business interests. "I always ask her, 'Do you want to go somewhere?'" Naomi said of her mother. "She's like, 'No, I'm so busy! Can't you see how busy I am?' And then she would go on her computer—she has, like, an office in the house and she's always in there—but I feel like she's, like, fake being busy, like she's making herself more busy than she has to be."

Leonard was less of a busybody, but he also remained close to Naomi's career. Though he hadn't been in an official coaching role for years, he attended all of her off-season practices at the nearby Evert Academy, where Naomi's coach Sascha Bajin, her strength coach Abdul Sillah, and her new physiotherapist Kristy Stahr were preparing Naomi for the fast-approaching 2019 season. Naomi's 2018 season had ended on a down note—after qualifying for the elite year-end WTA Finals in Singapore as one of the eight best players of the year, Naomi went 0–3 in her round-robin matches—but despite the slight setback, spirits were high. The WTA had introduced a new Coach of the Year award, and Bajin ran away with the votes to be its first winner, no surprise after the transformation he had closely overseen; by his count, Bajin had spent 360 of 365 days with Naomi during their first year together. Naomi grinned broadly as she presented Bajin his trophy at her first tournament of the year in Brisbane.

Not content to be complacent, Naomi's coterie of coaches had worked on retooling and strengthening for the 2019 season, a necessity to counter the field's scrutiny of Naomi as each player saw her as a boss battle. "Other players and their coaches had been analyzing her game," Bajin later wrote. "You could see people were suddenly paying attention and trying to solve the puzzle."

Bajin and the rest of Naomi's team believed that Naomi's mental strength could be built from the outside inward: if her body was strong, it would make her mind strong, too. "If Naomi thought that she had worked harder in the off-season than any other player, and she knew that she was physically stronger, that would take away so much stress and pressure," Bajin wrote. "Then you know you don't have to play well to win matches. You know you can always outlast opponents. That gives you enormous confidence."

Naomi spent the first weeks of her training only doing physical work, not picking up her racquet. Along with keeping her on a strict diet, Sillah worked Naomi for long hours on the track and in the weight room. When Naomi arrived to Australia for the start of the 2019 season, the Japanese media quickly took note of her trimmed-down physique and asked her repeatedly at press conferences about her weight loss. "Because I want to be faster; it's not for looks or anything," Naomi said when she was first asked. "I feel like it helps me play better. I get to the ball faster, and I'm not as

Tamaki (pregnant with Naomi), Leonard, and baby Mari in Osaka in 1997.

Courtesy of Pedro Herivaux

Naomi's father, Leonard (center), became a recognizable face in Japan through his TV appearances and parlayed that into occasional endorsements; he and some friends were once hired to appear in a *Cool Runnings*–themed advertisement for a Japanese ski resort.

Courtesy of Pedro Herivaux

A USTA youth camp in California in 2006. Naomi, fourth from right; Mari, second from left; and Taylor Townsend, fourth from left.

THIS AGREEMENT is made the ___21___ day of ___MARCH___

BETWEEN Christophe Jean

AND Leonard Francois on behalf of Marie Osaka   Naomi Osaka /Tennis Players

IT IS AGREED as follows:

Both parties agree on a fixed fee of twenty percent (20%) on every tennis contract or monetary agreement on behalf of Marie Osaka and Naomi Osaka

The term of employment shall be indefinite, either party may terminate this agreement by giving three months written notice to the other party. All monetary obligations must be regulated before termination. All contract agreement assigned at time of employment will uphold until the cancellation or completion of contract.

Traveling Accommodations:

Where the Coach is required to travel with Marie Osaka and Naomi Osaka to an event training session, or other related activity the following applies:
All travel expenses must be covered prior to travel.
Exceptions will be made to this arrangement only by mutual agreement.

Reasons for Termination:

This contract may be terminated if there breach of this contract, behavior in a manner inappropriate to a tennis professional

Christophe Jean
Coach Signature

CHRISTOPHE JEAN
Coach Name (please print)

MARI OSAKA
Player Signature

NAOMI OSAKA
Player Signature

Responsible Party Signature

The 2012 contract with coach Christophe Jean signed by Leonard on behalf of his daughters.

Broward County Courts

Mari, Naomi, and Naomi's first agent, Daniel Balog, in 2014.

Courtesy of Daniel Balog

Naomi poses with the scoreboard after beating Samantha Stosur. Stanford, 2014.

Courtesy of Kevin Fischer

Naomi's selfie from meeting Serena. Stanford, 2014.

Courtesy of Kevin Fischer

Naomi addresses the Japanese media. Tokyo, 2016.

Jimmie48

Naomi, in her Pharrell Williams Adidas outfit,
crushes a forehand at the 2017 U.S. Open.

Jimmie48

Naomi giggling through her speech. Indian Wells, 2018.
Jimmie48

Naomi poses with her trophy and the Japanese flag. Indian Wells, 2018.
Jimmie48

Victorious Naomi shakes hands with Serena Williams after their first match.
Miami, 2018.

Jimmie48

Naomi clenches her fist as she takes control of the 2018 U.S. Open final.

Jimmie48

Serena pleads her case to tournament referee Brian Earley as the 2018 U.S. Open final spirals into chaos.

Jimmie48

Serena consoles Naomi during the 2018 U.S. Open trophy ceremony.

Jimmie48

Naomi holds her trophy among the debris of the 2018 U.S. Open final.

Jimmie48

Naomi, in her Comme des Garçons dress, poses for photographers in Manhattan with her 2018 U.S. Open trophy.

Jimmie48

Naomi celebrates her coach Sascha Bajin winning the WTA Coach of the Year award. Brisbane, 2019.

Jimmie48

A fan holds up the Japanese flag for Naomi at the 2019 Australian Open.

Jimmie48

Naomi wins a second consecutive major at the 2019 Australian Open.
Jimmie48

Naomi cries at her press conference while discussing Bajin's firing. Dubai, 2019.
Jimmie48

Mari Osaka plays her lone WTA main draw singles match as a wildcard. Miami, 2019.

Jimmie48

Naomi's star-studded box at the 2019 U.S. Open includes her agent, Stuart Duguid (in blue), Kobe Bryant, Colin Kaepernick, and her boyfriend, Cordae.

Jimmie48

Coco Gauff and Naomi talking after their third-round match at the 2019 U.S. Open, which became a viral moment.

Jimmie48

Naomi laments during her loss to Gauff at the 2020 Australian Open.

Jimmie48

Naomi wears a mask with the name Ahmaud Arbery, one of the seven masks she wore during the 2020 U.S. Open.
Getty Images / Al Bello

Naomi wears African and Caribbean fashions as she poses with the 2020 U.S. Open trophy.
Getty Images / Matthew Stockman

Wim Fissette consoles Naomi after a rough practice set before the 2021 French Open.
Jimmie48

Naomi holds her torch high at the Opening Ceremony of the Tokyo Olympics in 2021.

Getty Images / Ezra Shaw

Naomi, wearing her increasingly omnipresent headphones, listens during a rough press conference. Cincinnati, 2021.

Jimmie48

Naomi at the 2021 Met Gala in the Louis Vuitton outfit co-designed by Mari.
Getty Images / Rob Kim

Naomi and WTA supervisor Clare Wood
discuss a heckler. Indian Wells, 2022.
Jimmie48

Leonard takes over as his daughter's coach after Fissette's departure in summer 2022.
Jimmie48

Naomi looks distracted during her on-court interview. Tokyo, 2022.
Jimmie48

sore." When she was later asked by a Japanese reporter how much she weighed, Naomi's eyes widened. "Wouldn't you like to know?" she said, grinning. "I don't know, I haven't weighed myself in a while. And you shouldn't be asking people's weight like that."

· · · · · · ·

As successful as Naomi's 2018 campaign had been, rising from 68th to 5th in the rankings, there was one glaring weakness Bajin saw: her lack of scoreboard resilience. Though all of her matches were played in the best-of-three format, the standard for women's tennis, they might as well have been best-of-one: whoever won the first set in Naomi's matches had won the match nearly every time. When Naomi won the first set in 2018, she was an unstoppable 41–0; when she lost the first set, she was a nearly hopeless 2–19. Bajin believed Naomi's defeatedness when trailing came down to self-consciousness. "She thought too much about, 'Oh my God, I'm playing bad—what are the people in the stands thinking about me? What are the people on TV thinking about me? Oh my God,'" Bajin said years later. "She was too much concerned about all of the other stuff going around outside, rather than finding a way to actually play better, or focus on what is working on the court." All the efforts Bajin had made to get Naomi to loosen up away from the court, he said, were with the end goal to get her to be more buoyant during matches.

That quest got off to a rough start at the outset of the 2019 season. In the semifinals of the Brisbane International, Naomi grew mopey and defeatist after losing the first set 6–2 to Lesia Tsurenko. "I can't play tennis," she told Bajin. "It's not going in the court . . . I feel stressed out." When Bajin, trying to be constructive, offered to bring her a racquet strung at a different tension, Naomi said it would be no use. "No, I think that there's something wrong with my head. I'm putting myself in this situation that I'm either going to win, or die, you know?" After losing the match, Naomi apologized for having "the worst attitude" on court. "Sorry to everyone that watched," she tweeted. "I keep telling myself to be more mature but seems it'll take a while."

Naomi pulled out of her next tournament, Sydney, and went straight to Melbourne to prepare for the Australian Open. But even as she practiced well in the sunshine, Naomi still felt a lingering shadow around herself from her last showing. "After my Tsurenko match, I just had this dark cloud over me, and I felt like I couldn't do anything about it until my next match, because that's when you guys see me play tennis," Naomi said. "So I just thought that feeling was very . . . sort of icky? And I didn't really want to have regrets like that anymore."

· · · · · · ·

The players atop the women's tennis ladder were more tightly packed than ever before heading into the 2019 Australian Open, continuing the parity that had predominated ever since Serena left the tour due to her pregnancy. Eight different women had won the previous eight majors, and eleven women had a mathematical chance to leave Melbourne with the No. 1 ranking, including 4th-ranked Naomi. Bajin, however, didn't discuss the possibility with her. "I didn't talk to Naomi about her mathematical chances of reaching Number One, as how would that have helped her?" he wrote.

Naomi's tournament started smoothly with straight-set wins in her first two matches. Her mindset, she later said, was completely different than it had been in New York. "In Australia, the goal was to win," she said. "That was what I was waking up every day thinking." When she would walk down the long tunnel from the locker room to the court of Rod Laver Arena, she would tap the picture of the women's trophy, as if knocking on its door, telling it she was arriving. Naomi's confidence was so high, she called her mom, who was traveling with Mari at an ITF tournament in Michigan, to invite her to come to Melbourne, guaranteeing glory. "I was, like, 'Do you want to come to Australia? Because I'm going to win this tournament?'" Naomi later recalled. "She's like, 'No, I'm with your sister. No thank you.' I was, like, Okay."

· · · · · · ·

Wherever she watched her daughter from, Tamaki would have seen a new-found resilience in Naomi. In her third-round match, she lost the first set against the tricky Hsieh Su-wei but rallied from 2–4 down in the second set to win in three. "I think the more matches that I play like this, the tougher ones, then maybe as I go on it won't seem as hard," Naomi said after her victory. Naomi's next match wasn't any easier: playing against 13th-seeded Anastasija Sevastova, who had made the U.S. Open semifinals four months earlier, Naomi again lost the first set but rallied for a 4–6, 6–3, 6–4 win to reach the quarterfinals.

The second week of Naomi's Australian Open mapped out a steeper course than her U.S. Open run: this time, she would have to face many of the highest-ranked players in the world. Sevastova, whom she had beaten in the fourth round, was ranked 12th, higher than any opponent she had faced in New York. The rest of the way in Melbourne, Naomi would face Top 10 opponents who, like her, were in pursuit of the up-for-grabs No. 1 ranking. For all of her big wins in 2018, Naomi hadn't been at her best against the best: she had only gone 3–9 against Top 10–ranked foes in 2018, including 1–4 after her U.S. Open win. This time, there was the added pressure of being the favorite on paper: fourth-ranked Naomi was the highest-ranked player of the eight women remaining.

First up in the quarterfinals was sixth-ranked Elina Svitolina, who had recently won the year-end WTA Finals in Singapore, where Naomi had gone winless. Svitolina had beaten Naomi twice in 2018, including in Miami, where she stopped the eight-match winning streak Naomi had racked up after her title at Indian Wells and her win over Serena. But on this day in Melbourne's steamy midday heat, Naomi drew on her years of training in Florida and flourished as Svitolina wilted, reeling off eight of the last nine games for a 6–4, 6–1 win.

· · · · · · ·

If the match that followed Naomi's win over Svitolina went as expected, it would set up a highly anticipated rematch, a reprisal of the most-talked-about match of the year before, pitting Naomi against Serena Williams for the second consecutive major. Serena, who had knocked off the No. 1–ranked Simona Halep in the fourth round, was leading her quarterfinal against No. 7 Karolína Plíšková 5–1 in the third set.

While Serena was still on court, Naomi was asked in her press conference if the controversy from their match in New York would linger into a meeting in Melbourne and if she expected that Serena would have particular motivation to seek revenge. Naomi didn't take the bait. "I can't speak for her, but for me, it's always a really big privilege and an honor to play her," Naomi said of Serena. "For me, I have been watching her since I have grown up. Honestly, I feel very lucky I've gotten to play her twice already. If I do play her, I'm just going to be looking forward to it."

With *Vogue* editor Anna Wintour cheering her on from her box, Serena was one point away from booking the rematch when disaster struck. Up 5–1, 40-30 in the third on Plíšková, Serena was serving at match point when she rolled her left ankle. Serena, who like all righties lands on her left foot when serving, didn't win another point on serve for the rest of the match. Though Serena generated more match-point chances with her returns as the match slipped away, Plíšková stunningly reeled off six straight games to steal a 6–4, 4–6, 7–5 victory.

Despite the obvious impairment—later revealed to be an ankle sprain—Serena repeatedly and robustly downplayed the injury in her post-match press conference, in no mood to be branded a sore loser again, perhaps especially given how critical Australian media had been about her conduct in New York. "I think she just started playing really, really good," Serena said afterward. "I don't think it had anything to do with my ankle, per se. I just think she was just nailing and hitting shots."

* * * * * * *

Though it lacked the narratives of a rematch against Serena, Karolína Plíšková was a daunting semifinal opponent for Naomi, having beaten her in straight sets in the Tokyo final months earlier. Naomi and Plíšková were two of the best servers in the game, but as the match started Naomi seemed to be breaking Plíšková nearly at will, racing out to a 6–2, 1–0 lead. Plíšková leveled the second set, however, and kept it on even terms until the tenth game, when she pounced to take it 6–4, forcing Naomi into a third set.

The match hinged on the early games of the third set. Serving at 0–1,

Naomi saved three break points to halt Plíšková's momentum and hold for 1–1, exhaling deeply and looking up at the closed roof after she clinched the game. She rolled that momentum into the next game on her return, breaking Plíšková at love for a 2–1 advantage by pouncing on her second serves as she did all match, winning sixteen of nineteen such points. Broadcaster Mark Petchey, calling the match for the tournament's world feed, credited Naomi's coach with the effectiveness of her attack on return: "If you're Sascha Bajin, you're going to say you're the greatest coach in the world, because you've concocted a plan there that kept her to those numbers."

Naomi reached her first match point at 5–4, 40-30, and hit a curling serve down the T that landed short in the box. As it went past Plíšková, she turned to her box, clenched her fist, and smiled, only realizing seconds later that the line judge at the far end of the court had called it out. As Naomi waited for the Hawk-Eye display, she folded her hands in prayer across her racquet. When the animation showed that a sliver of the ball had indeed clipped the line, sealing her 6–2, 4–6, 6–4 victory, she smiled broadly once more and skipped giddily toward the net and toward her second major final. "I just thought I wouldn't forgive myself if I had a little dip or a moment of accepting defeat," Naomi said afterward.

· · · · · · · ·

Naomi had made it to the finals of back-to-back majors on hard courts, but the atmospheres had been entirely different. Compared to those in New York, the matches in Melbourne had been tougher competitively but less fraught. There had been considerable sympathy for Naomi among tennis fans worldwide after her tears on court in New York, and among the crowd at the tournament that branded itself the "Happy Slam" had been more of a warm blanket than the raging inferno that had surrounded her four months earlier. Not only were Australians warm toward Naomi, but there were increasing numbers of Japanese fans at her matches, particularly Japanese women. They waved flags, banners, and painted hand fans (*sensu*), giving Naomi both visible and audible support around the stadiums each time she took the court.

That Naomi could get an uncomplicated second major title as a sort of redo was a popular sentiment, but she was facing an even bigger sentimental favorite in the final. Petra Kvitová, a two-time Wimbledon champion and seven-time winner of the WTA sportsmanship award, was into her first major final in more than four years, having made a remarkable physical and emotional recovery. In December 2016, a knife-wielding robber had entered Kvitová's apartment in Prostějov, Czech Republic, under the guise of checking a utility meter. In the struggle that followed, Kvitová had grabbed the blade of his knife as it was held against her throat. Kvitová fought free but sustained deep cuts to the fingers of her dominant left hand that required hours of emergency surgery to repair tendons and nerves, and months of rehabilitation to regain use of the hand that had launched some of the world's most powerful shots. Just over two years after not knowing if she would ever be able to hold a racquet again, the twenty-eight-year-old Kvitová had regained her world-beating form, powering into the Australian Open final without dropping a set. Kvitová, too, was looking to reach the WTA No. 1 ranking for the first time in her career; whoever lost the final would be ranked No. 2.

Naomi and Kvitová had never played against each other but seemed evenly matched. Like Naomi, Kvitová was a big hitter who thrived on the biggest stages: she had played exceptionally well in her two previous major finals, both at Wimbledon, handling Maria Sharapova in 2011 and routing Genie Bouchard in 2014, both in straight sets. And as their final began, there was little between them: Naomi saved all five break points she faced in the first set, including three in a row at one point, and the first set reached a tiebreak. Naomi pounced at her first opportunity, ripping a backhand return winner to take an early 2-0 lead, and another down-the-line winner, this time on her forehand, to extend the lead to 5-1. Naomi converted her first set point soon after, taking the first set 7–6(2) and jackknifing her right leg in celebration as she clenched her fist and shouted a long, hard-earned "C'monnnnnnn!"

When Kvitová pounced early in the second set, cracking a forehand return to take a 2–0 lead, Naomi's frustration began to show. She shot forlorn glances to her team, she dropped her racquet in disgust. But within minutes, Naomi had recovered. She broke Kvitová back immediately, the first of four games in a row she won to take a 4–2 lead in the second set.

Two more holds later, Naomi's lead had carried to 5–3. When she got to 0–40 on Kvitová's serve, "Championship Point" graphics flashed around the arena. After an hour and thirty-two minutes, Naomi was one point from her second major title and the No. 1 ranking. Kvitová saved the first championship point with a scorching inside-out forehand winner, and Naomi applauded the shot with her racquet. On the second, Naomi's forehand erred long, and she glanced up at her box quickly. On the third, her backhand return missed. Kvitová held to take the game, but Naomi was still up 5–4, with a chance to serve out the victory. Then Naomi seemed to panic. When Kvitová's first shot of the game was a return-winner, Naomi threw her hands up in disbelief. When Naomi double-faulted, she smacked her shoe with her racquet. When Naomi lost the game with a loose forehand error, she angrily spiked the ball into the court and covered her ears to block out the cheers of the crowd, who were excited to see the match continue. Instead of finishing with a flourish, Naomi had grown more tentative, decelerating her swings. Instead of attacking, she seemed to be hoping Kvitová would miss. When Kvitová correctly challenged to overturn what had looked like a winner for Naomi, Naomi looked at her box in despair at how her fortunes were reversing. Kvitová held for 6–5.

"She's struggling, Osaka here, to keep it together emotionally," broadcaster Mark Petchey said on the world feed.

"She's looking more like a twenty-one-year-old now," Chris Evert said on ESPN as Naomi lost her composure.

On Kvitová's first set point, Naomi missed a first serve and then angrily swatted the ball into the net. On her second serve, she double-faulted, sending a match that had been within her reach to a third set. Naomi's face was tear-streaked and her eyes were red by the time she made it to chair umpire Louise Azemar Engzell to ask to leave the court. Naomi put a towel over her head and walked off.

"It just seems like nothing is going her way right now," Petchey said.

"It's tough to have a positive perspective if you're Osaka. This would be a monumental effort if she were to win this from here."

• • • • • • •

As the sage Mary Carillo often says, the toughest thing in tennis is to "come back from ahead." To have had a lead and lost it, ceding scoreboard advantage and momentum while accruing disappointment and regret, can be the toughest situation in a tennis match.

From late in the second set to early in the third set Kvitová won twelve points in a row. Naomi needed to find a way to dig back into the match, to stop the landslide from sweeping her away completely after she had been so close to the pinnacle of the sport. "Of course I felt very disappointed and sad when I had those three match points, and I tried to tell myself there's nothing I can do about it, but you always have these doubts," Naomi said after the match. "I just told myself that it's a final and I'm playing against Petra—she's a really great champion—so I have to keep fighting. I can't let myself act immature, in a way. I should be grateful to be here. So that's what I tried to do."

Naomi turned it around, not by doing more but by doing less. To stop herself from boiling over, she dialed down her emotions as simply as if turning the knob on a stove. After the match, Naomi said she had been able to "dissociate [her] feelings." "You know how some people get worked up about things?" she said. "That's a very human thing to do. Sometimes I feel like I don't want to waste my energy doing stuff like that. I think about this on the court, too. Like in the third set of my match today, I literally just tried to turn off all my feelings. So that's why I wasn't yelling as much in the third set."

There was something almost machinelike about Naomi with her feelings turned off, she admitted. "I just felt kind of hollow, like I was a robot, sort of," Naomi said later. "I was just executing my orders. I don't know. Like, I just did what I've been practicing my whole life in a way. I didn't waste any energy reacting too much." Naomi said that the experience of switching into power-saver mode had felt like an out-of-body experience at times. "I do realize that I'm the one that made all those shots and it was like the decision making on my part," Naomi said the next day. "But at the same time it feels—I don't know—like I was just watching myself from a computer, in a way."

It was easily noticed by those watching in the arena, too. "She shows emotions but right now Osaka is like a poker player: stone-faced," Chris Fowler said on ESPN. Naomi's new quiet, stealth mode was lethal on the court: she held for 1–1 to stop Kvitová's run of five straight games, then broke for a 2–1 lead, then held again for 3–1. When Naomi couldn't convert three break points at 4–2, she wasn't rattled; she held to love in the next game to extend her lead to 5–3.

Light rain began to fall as Naomi served for the match up 5–4 in the third. The retractable roof over Rod Laver began to close; if Naomi wasn't quick, the match might be suspended. Naomi hit an ace to start the game. Then she hit a forehand winner. Then another hard shot up the middle that jammed Kvitová. It was triple championship point again, nearly an hour after the first occasion. Naomi missed a forehand long on the first one, but on the second she hit a strong serve down the T at 114 miles per hour. Kvitová reached to her left with her forehand but couldn't get her racquet around the ball in time to corral it back into the court. Naomi, now a two-time major champion and the World No. 1, crouched to the ground. The tears were fewer this time, with no doubt they were joyful.

· · · · · · ·

Naomi's run to her second major title had been remarkable and history-making. She was the first woman in Australian Open history to win four three-set matches en route to the title. Naomi was the first woman to follow up her first major title by winning her second at the very next major since Jennifer Capriati in 2001. Naomi was the first Asian singles No. 1, female or male, in tennis history. The previous biggest jump someone had made to No. 1 in fifty-two weeks was from No. 17 (Dinara Safina and Karolína Plíšková); Naomi had shattered that record, having soared to No. 1 from down at the depths of No. 72 a year earlier.

The win also meant that a gamble had paid off: Naomi's Adidas contract had lapsed at the end of 2018, but her agents had waited to sign her to a new apparel deal, thinking her price would skyrocket if she could win in Melbourne. When she did, it did. Nike, which had flown Naomi and her family on a private jet from Florida to their headquarters in Oregon during their courting process, with Nike cofounder Phil Knight meeting Naomi personally, signed Naomi to the biggest contract of her career, worth more than $10 million a year. It was bigger than just the number: Nike bent its rule prohibiting third-party patches on its outfits, allowing Naomi to keep her Japanese sponsors' patches.

· · · · · · · ·

After her fourth-round win, Naomi had told incredulous on-court interviewer Sam Smith that she never got recognized when walking the streets of Melbourne. "No? I'm not like that," Naomi insisted. "I don't think they care." In her press conference later, I asked Naomi why she didn't think anyone cared about her, and she made it clear it was a status for which she was grateful. "People that are famous like that, I feel kind of bad for them," she said. "Because you can never really truly enjoy going outside and stuff. So, for me, I feel kind of lucky that I'm unknown."

When I heard Naomi call herself "unknown" after everything that had happened in the previous four months, my eyebrows must have raced upward.

"What was that eye thing you did just now?" Naomi asked me, grinning at my lack of a poker face.

"I don't know if I agree you're unknown anymore," I replied.

"I'm a ghost," she said, smiling. "You don't see me."

But days later, after winning her second major and rising to the No. 1 ranking, there was no plausibly denying that Naomi was a global star. This time, the post-final focus would be entirely on her—no need to discuss the runner-up or the chair umpire. "You say you're not getting carried away with the fame, but there's plenty of people here who will be wanting a piece of Naomi Osaka," Australia's Channel 9 host Tony Jones told Naomi during her first media appearance after the final.

The "pieces of Naomi Osaka" being taken from her as she made her long media rounds around Melbourne Park in the hours following the final seemed to be eroding her. In her speech after being presented the trophy by Li Na, the only other Asian woman to have won major singles titles, Naomi was just as halting as after her win at Indian Wells, but in a way that seemed less whimsical and more genuinely uncomfortable. "Hello? Uh, uh, sorry public speaking isn't really my strong side, so I just hope I can get through this," Naomi began. She had looked at notes reminding her what to say before her speech but had forgotten them once she reached the microphone. "I forgot to smile," Naomi said afterward with a laugh. "I was told to smile and I didn't."

Though she had now spent years in the spotlight, public speaking hadn't gotten easier for her. "Of course I would love to be better at talking," she said afterward. "In the first place, I don't even talk normally in my day-to-day. I might speak, like, ten sentences."

In her press conference, Naomi seemed tired and even cranky at already having spent hours talking, no doubt not helped by the opening questions that foregrounded the U.S. Open final. "Apparently you're unable to win a Slam without some drama," the first question began. Another asked her to "talk a little bit about the difference between how it felt in there tonight compared to how it felt in Flushing," and another asked her to compare it to the "bittersweet, not the happiest" memory she had from her previous major win. The easy narrative for Naomi's second major win was that it had been a redemption from the awkwardness of the first, but Naomi didn't engage with that storyline: Naomi was tired of thinking about the U.S. Open, and also just tired, having played a long, exhausting match to finish a long two-week tournament. As she moved from television studio to television studio, from podium to roundtable, stretching past midnight, Naomi's fatigue was more visible. "Now I'm just so tired," Naomi said in her press conference. "I don't know how anyone is awake right now."

Once she finally finished all the post-match obligations, Naomi called her mom at around 2:00 a.m. "She didn't even say congratulations—she just yelled at me to go to sleep," Naomi said on the *WTA Insider* podcast the next day. "So I felt really loved."

· · · · · · · ·

Part of Naomi's fatigue and weariness, the public learned weeks later, had been about what had been happening inside her team. She had dropped a hint during her post-final press conference when asked what advice Bajin had given her before the match. "I didn't talk to him," Naomi said, then laughed nervously. "Yeah, no, like we haven't really been talking, to be honest, like before any of my matches here. He would tell me, like, one thing, and then I would be, like, Okay. That was it."

The day after the final, Naomi called a team meeting in Melbourne. Naomi confronted Bajin, breaking the weeks-long silence between them, putting him on the spot about what she'd heard about his off-court relationship with another player. Bajin, who had encouraged Naomi to hit with this player at tournaments despite her much lower ranking, denied it repeatedly, and the group dispersed. The next day, when Bajin came back and admitted it was true, Naomi told him that her trust had been broken.

Bajin traveled back to Florida with Naomi and held one more practice with her days after the final; it ended with Naomi in tears. Later that evening, Naomi's agent, Stuart Duguid, called Bajin.

The next time Naomi would make headlines, two weeks after her triumph in Melbourne, it would be because the new World No. 1 had fired the coach of the year.

TWENTY-THREE

Heavy Is the Head

The new No. 1 shocked the tennis world two weeks into her reign. Fifteen days after her win in Melbourne, Naomi announced she had fired the man who had coached her from No. 70 to No. 1. "Hey everyone, I will no longer be working together with Sascha," Naomi wrote on Twitter. "I thank him for his work and wish him all the best in the future."

"Thank you Naomi [praying hands emoji]," Bajin replied on Twitter. "I wish you nothing but the best as well. What a ride that was. Thank you for letting me be part of this."

The surprise firing generated rampant rumor and speculation in tennis circles. What could have happened to make the ascendant No. 1 player fire the recently named WTA Coach of the Year immediately after winning their second major together? "The foundations of tennis have been rocked," announcer Jason de la Peña melodramatically declared as a panel discussion of the breaking news began on Tennis Channel.

"It really doesn't make a lot of sense on paper," said Lindsay Davenport. ". . . We've heard a lot of shockers in player-coach relationships not working out: this is the top for me." Davenport thought it was clear, at least, that the split couldn't have been "tennis related," given Naomi's on-court success. "Something pretty drastic had to have happened behind the scenes," she said.

The breakup with her coach just after making history was undeniable news, but Naomi's team wanted to insulate her from questions on the subject when she rejoined the tour for a WTA tournament in Dubai two weeks later. Duguid canceled a planned pretournament interview with CNN when it became clear Bajin would be a topic. At her pretournament press conference in Dubai, a WTA moderator tried to cut short the Bajin line of questioning. But while she didn't give many details about the split in her answers, nor did Naomi want to duck the topic. "It's okay, I'm just trying to figure out what I should say," she told the moderator, allowing the discussion to continue.

Naomi had begun by mentioning one of the most common theories swirling around the split: that there had been a disagreement over Bajin's pay. "I know everyone thinks it was a money-related issue, but it wasn't," she said. "For me, that's one of the most hurtful things I've ever heard. I travel with everyone on my team, I see them more than my family. I would never do that to them."

Naomi also alluded to her decision in an interview later that day with *WTA Insider*. "The biggest thing is I don't want myself to think that to be successful I have to put success over happiness," Naomi told Nguyen. "Because if I'm not happy being around certain people, I'm not going to torture myself, especially since Charleston and Beijing . . . This is my life. I'm not going to sacrifice that just to keep a person around. I have to be happy with where I am at in my life. I feel like I worked really hard—maybe not for twenty-one years, but for seventeen years—to be No. 1 and to win Grand Slams."

. . . .

After directionless practices with no coach at the helm, Naomi lost her first match in Dubai, 6–3, 6–3 to Kristina Mladenovic. Naomi admitted the attention around her split with Bajin during her first tournament as the No. 1 had been difficult to handle. "It's a little bit hard because I feel like people are staring at me, and not, like, in a good way," she said.

"I don't think I necessarily understand what position I'm in, in a way, because last year I wasn't even anywhere close to this ranking," she soon added. "People didn't pay attention to me, and that's something that I'm comfortable with." As she finished that thought, Naomi's voice suddenly caught, and she giggled nervously. "I don't know why I'm crying," she said.

"Are you okay?" the WTA moderator asked. "Do you want five minutes?"

"I don't know why this is happening," Naomi said.

"Shall we step outside?" he again offered.

"It's cool," she said. "It's done now."

A reporter then asked one more follow-up about the attention she was getting.

"Yeah, I don't really like attention," Naomi said. "It's been a little tough."

. . . .

Naomi hasn't spoken publicly about her specific reasons for firing Bajin. But when the book he had signed a deal to write for a Japanese publisher came out months later, I asked her at a press conference if she had read it, and her eyes widened at the question.

"Man, you're shady," Naomi said. "Man, you're shady. I haven't read it. Don't plan on reading it."

Naomi made several other major life changes shortly after reaching the No. 1 ranking. She abruptly left her parents' home in Boca Raton and relocated cross-country, moving into the first of her several Los Angeles area mansions. "I never thought I was young until a electrician came to my house and asked me if my parents were home," Naomi later tweeted. "He said, 'This is a nice house, what do your parents do?'"

Naomi had moved to Los Angeles both for independence and business: she wanted to take a more hands-on approach to her growing roster of corporate sponsors, and brands could more easily meet with her in Los Angeles than in Boca Raton. Duguid and his wife, Carly (who took on a managerial role in an unofficial—and later official—capacity for Naomi) lived in the area and became a surrogate family of sorts for the young megastar. "When I first moved out here I didn't know anyone, so I would always go bother them," she said. "So they were like my mom and dad or like my aunt and uncle."

Around when she moved into her own home for the first time, Naomi also had another first: her first date. "Your girl doesn't get out much," she said, admitting the late milestone.

The first date, with the up-and-coming rapper Cordae, started a relationship that endured. Born Cordae Amari Dunston, he was then known by the stage name YBN Cordae as a member of the since-disbanded Young Boss Niggas rap collective. How Naomi and Cordae first connected isn't clear. "Trying to put together a coherent timeline of their romantic backstory is tough," *GQ*'s Mark Anthony Green conceded years later in a gushing profile of the couple's "puppy love." What is agreed is that their first date was at a Los Angeles Clippers game at the Staples Center. Cordae said years later that he didn't know Naomi was a tennis player when he first met her. "I could only give you Venus and Serena Williams, you know?" he said of his prior tennis knowledge. "Because they're just a part of the culture."

Naomi's family took time to adjust to the new relationship. "We talk to each other about everything," Mari said in an interview months later. "But recently she found someone to replace me, and that's what I don't like so much." After initially being taken aback to hear her daughter was dating a rapper, because of the negative stereotypes she had in mind, Tamaki said she thought of her own father's prejudices when he heard his daughter was dating a Black man. "I myself have been listening to hip-hop since I was young and am familiar with it, but I thought that listening to hip-hop was different from dating people in that industry," she said. "I suddenly realized and changed my prejudice."

. . . .

The next tournament for Naomi offered a new experience that most players have well before they reach No. 1: her first time as defending champion at a tournament. By Indian Wells, Naomi was feeling better about herself and her team. She had hired a new coach who, like Bajin, also had ties to the Williams family: Jermaine Jenkins, Venus's former hitting partner. The new partnership got off to a strong start: Naomi took advantage of an immediate chance to avenge her Dubai loss, beating Mladenovic 6–3, 6–4 in her opening match at Indian Wells. In her second match, she beat recent Australian Open semifinalist Danielle Collins 6–4, 6–2.

Naomi's match in the round of 16 presented a familiar foe: Belinda Bencic, whom Naomi had beaten back at that $25,000 tournament in Alabama in 2013 when she was just fifteen and Bencic was the World Junior No. 1. Naomi's win over Bencic that day was what had caught the attention of her first agent, Daniel Balog. Six years later, Naomi was such a star that it had cost Bencic *her* agent: Duguid, who had also represented Bencic, had to cut her from his roster once his Naomi workload left him too busy to handle any other clients, and so Bencic was passed off to another IMG agent.

In their first official meeting in six years, Bencic seemed ready to settle those scores, and quickly: she broke Naomi early and often, dominating her for a 6–3, 6–1 victory in just an hour and six minutes. But despite the abrupt end to her title defense, Naomi left Indian Wells in positive spirits. "With that score line I would usually feel very depressed and sad," Naomi said, "but I feel pretty good right now, because I think—given the circumstances—I tried my best and I don't really have any regrets."

· · · · · · ·

As one coach exited and another one arrived, an old one also resurfaced. As Naomi signed more and more contracts of her own after reaching No. 1 in 2019, bringing her earnings into the tens of millions, Christophe Jean still hung on to the contract he had made seven years earlier.

Jean had never received any money from the contract on which Leonard had signed over 20 percent of his daughters' future earnings. But he had kept tabs on the family's growing income. Jean told me he had checked back with Leonard to remind him of the contract after several of Naomi's public high-water marks, including in 2014 when she earned $10,000 for reaching the second round of Stanford, and again four years later when she earned $1.34 million for winning Indian Wells.

Though the Osakas had a reputation for stinginess, Naomi's most recent coaches—Cyril Saulnier, David Taylor, Sascha Bajin—had all been paid their agreed amounts without issue. But even as the money began to roll in by the millions, there was no remedial pay for Jean or Patrick Tauma, the past coaches they had left unhappily empty-handed.

Eddie Sposa, the director of tennis at Pompano Beach Tennis Center where Jean had trained the Osakas for years for free, urged his employee Jean to seek what Sposa believed he deserved for the years of work he had seen him do with the family. "They should've taken care of him," Sposa told me. "Take care of my boy. He's the one that worked hard every day. It's not right."

Leonard, however, was adamant that he wasn't going to give Jean a dime, growing more irritated as Jean continued to pester him as Naomi's career soared. "He got mad and then he told me, 'Fine: get a lawyer,'" Jean told me. "Because he knows the contract wasn't that good. He found out, and then he told me, 'Get a lawyer.'"

After Naomi won the 2018 U.S. Open, Sposa introduced Jean to a local attorney, his next-door neighbor Christopher Hahn. They filed his lawsuit on February 7, 2019, twelve days after Naomi won the Australian Open. Getting 20 percent of everything Naomi had ever earned was a long shot, they recognized, but they thought she now had enough money to give Jean *something*, maybe even just a percentage of what she had earned before her eighteenth birthday. Jean had wanted to sue only Leonard, but to his dismay, he was told he also had to file against Naomi; Jean even had to sue Mari, who had made little money in her career, because her name was also on the contract. "I didn't want to do it, because Mari, I'm telling you, she was like my daughter," Jean said. "I love her. I don't want to put her name out there like that. I did it because her dad makes me so mad."

Naomi and the rest of her family did not comment on the lawsuit. "I'm not allowed to say anything—I'm unable to make a comment," Naomi said when asked about the suit in a press conference, the rare occasion of her needing to give a canned answer to a question at a press conference instead of showing her normal spontaneity.

The Osakas brought in a heavy hitter to swat away the suit: Alex Spiro, a New York lawyer who later gained fame as Elon Musk's personal attorney.

Spiro ripped and mocked Jean's claim in a statement to *The South Florida Sun Sentinel.* "While it comes as no surprise that Naomi's meteoric rise as an international icon and inspiration would lead to some false claim, this silly, imaginary contract that Naomi never saw or signed—which purports to give away part of herself at the age of fourteen—is particularly absurd," Spiro said.

Broward County circuit judge David A. Haimes agreed and ultimately dismissed the lawsuit. "Because no court ever approved the subject contract, and Naomi Osaka and Mari Osaka, who were minors, disavowed said contract, the court holds that the subject contract is not valid or enforceable," Haimes wrote in his ruling.

The loss in court did not surprise Jean and his allies; they had known a contract that a parent had signed on behalf of minors was likely unenforceable. But still, there was disappointment that some sort of justice couldn't be done to show appreciation for Jean's time and effort, especially given the immense success Naomi had found. "Contract, no contract; it's just karma," Sposa told me. "She's the highest-paid female athlete in the world. Drop him a check for fifty grand: he's happy. Fifty grand wouldn't be a blink of an eye for her, you know?"

Though disappointed that the lawsuit had failed so completely, Jean consistently reiterated that his effort had been more about respect and recognition than money. Just a simple "thank you" for his work, he said, would be enough. "That would mean the world to me," he said. "Sometimes you don't even need money. Money's important, but money's not the first thing... That would be good [enough] for her to come to me today and say 'Christophe, I'm sorry for what we did, what I did, too, because I know you've been working with me and then we did that to you. We did not even say thank you.' Even if she doesn't pay me, then I'm going to feel good about it, because that's big for someone who changed your life forever, you know?"

· · · · · · ·

Jean's lawsuit wasn't the only document on which Naomi's and Mari's names appeared together at that time. For the first time in years, they would compete in the same tournament.

TWENTY-FOUR

Mari's Shot

When Naomi was asked about her sister by interviewers, as happened more frequently as Naomi's basic biography became known, their questions rarely included any details about Mari beyond that she was also a tennis player. But though they would have listed the same occupation on forms, Naomi's and Mari's careers shared very little in common by early 2019.

On January 28, 2019, the day Naomi's ranking had risen to first, Mari's ranking dropped to 332nd, down from a career-best of 280th eight months earlier. Mari played almost exclusively on the ITF Pro Circuit, the minor leagues of women's tennis, where most players fail to break even. A 2013 study by the International Tennis Federation estimated that a woman would need to be ranked 253rd to break even with minimal travel, lodging, equipment, and coaching expenses (most in tennis thought the threshold was actually closer to 120th). Ranked well below those marks, Mari's finances were well in the red, her expenses far exceeding her paltry earnings. In the entire 2018 season, Mari had earned just $15,002 in prize money; Naomi had earned $6,394,289 in prize money that year (more than 400 times as much), and many millions more in endorsements.

"I thought about money a lot," Mari later told me. "The cost of everything was adding up. I was just leeching off others to chase a tennis dream. It started to really hurt after a certain point of not making money." Even though Naomi's earnings had secured her family financially, Mari still felt like she was letting them down. "She took that burden off of me but all I felt was guilt," Mari told me. "I felt as the older sister that it was supposed to be my position to provide."

Mari's progress was also slowed by battles with injuries to "almost every joint"; her knee was the most troublesome, but she also had trouble with her Achilles tendon, her shoulder, and both wrists. The tension she felt from the pressure to succeed, she told me she later realized, was likely the root cause of her physical breakdowns. "I was always tight and nervous; I definitely think I caused those injuries on myself," Mari said. "I assumed that people had certain expectations of me and it translated into fear constantly."

As she struggled with a shoulder injury at the start of the 2019 season, Mari lost 6–0, 6–0 in her first match as a challenger in Newport Beach. Her second match was a 6–1, 6–4 loss in the first qualifying round of an ITF tournament in Michigan. She then took two months off, resting to make sure she was ready for the opportunity that had been circled on her calendar for months.

· · · · · · · ·

Shortly after Naomi's U.S. Open win, her management company IMG told the Osaka family that they were gifting Mari a wild card into the 2019 Miami Open, a top-level WTA event just one step below the majors, as a thank-you to the family.

A ticket into the Miami Open main draw, her first WTA singles main draw, was a massive opportunity for twenty-two-year-old Mari. The prize money for just the first round, $16,425, was more than Mari had made the entire previous season. If she won her first-round match, she'd add another $10,000 to that haul, and her total prize money would roughly double every round after that.

There was no obscuring that Mari was only getting this chance because of her sister's success rather than her own performance on court. "We know she'll also be a draw," James Blake, the tournament director of the Miami Open, told me. "Naomi has so many fans; Mari is going to hopefully gain some of those fans by association."

Blake also admitted his own personal experience had made him "pretty partial": his own older brother, Thomas, had reached a career high of 264th, 260 spots behind his own career-high of fourth. "He got some wild cards, definitely, with the Blake name," Blake told me. "He really appreciated them. Mari has thanked me, her parents have thanked me. They realize that this is a big opportunity for her. We'll see how she does . . . We gave her this one opportunity, and if she doesn't do well, she'll go back to the drawing board. Luckily she's got a sister to measure herself against—although it's a pretty tough task to measure yourself against the No. 1 in the world."

Though she teased Mari, as she had done for years, Naomi was sincere about hoping she would be able to make a habit of playing at this level with her. "For me it would be a dream," Naomi said. "Because I don't really talk to that many people, and she's the nicer one in this relationship, so it would definitely mean a lot."

· · · · · · · ·

Though Venus and Serena were the most famous pair of tennis siblings, wide rankings chasms between siblings were far more common on tour. Naomi's opposite number atop the men's ladder in early 2019, ATP No. 1 Novak Djoković, has two younger siblings who also played tennis, but both had largely given it up by 2019. Marko Djoković had peaked at 571st, while Djordje Djoković topped out at 1,463rd. Novak Djoković told me that it had given him "satisfaction and peace" that his brothers had both chosen to step away from the sport rather than continue to struggle in his enormous shadow as a national hero of Serbia. "Because if you're part of the same sport, naturally, everyone will compare you to your other siblings," Djoković told me. "It's not ideal, especially if your other sibling is the best in the world."

Marko Djoković had gotten dozens of wild cards during his playing career, including four into ATP main draws where he lost in the first round each time. But though his ranking was never near as good as Mari Osaka's, his wild cards didn't generate the negativity that hers did. Tennis blogger

David Gertler dragged the Miami Open's choice at LastWordOnSports .com with the unsubtle headline "Mari Osaka Wild Card an Embarrassment" and stated "nepotism at its finest" as his diagnosis. "I understand that we should not be mad at Osaka for accepting it, but hopefully even she realizes how ridiculous this is," Gertler wrote. "She just lost easily in qualifying for an ITF event. When she played a Challenger event earlier this year, she couldn't win a game! This isn't hard, everyone. Someone like this shouldn't be near the qualifying draw, let alone the main draw of an event of this magnitude."

· · · · · · · ·

Mari landed a fortunate first-round draw, facing one of the other lowest-ranked players in the draw: 205th-ranked Whitney Osuigwe, who had also been given a wild card by IMG. Despite the low rankings of both players, the stands on Court 6, which accommodated about five hundred people, were full before warm-ups had ended, with many more ticket holders waiting outside the gates in hopes further space might open up. Tamaki sat in the second row in a wide-brimmed straw hat. She texted Naomi, who had planned on coming, that it was too full for her to attend, so Naomi watched the biggest match of her sister's career on TV instead.

Mari looked ready for the occasion, with her blond hair tied up in a striking puff atop her dark roots, and wearing bright red matching shorts and top from Yonex. "We wouldn't offer that to other players with her ranking," Yonex executive Nori Shimojo later told me of Mari's sponsorship. "That family name has to be Osaka to get that offer."

Like Naomi's game had many times, Mari's game also elevated on the bigger stage. But still, she was outmatched: Osuigwe quickly won the first two games of the match, breaking and holding in just four minutes. The third game was long, ten minutes, but again Osuigwe prevailed, putting herself up 3–0 and stoking early concerns that Mari might be blanked once more. But Mari was able to get on the board when Osuigwe hit consecutive double faults and then held for the first time to narrow the lead to 3–2. Osuigwe then quickly won the next three games to take the first set 6–2.

Mari started the second set well, breaking Osuigwe early and extending her lead to 4–2. But when she was serving at 4–2, 30–all in the set, Mari's momentum halted: she won just one of the next fifteen points, succumbing to a 6–2, 6–4 defeat in a match that had lasted an hour and twenty minutes. "It's been a fine display from Osuigwe, but it will not stop the questions that have come quietly about whether Osaka should have received a wild card to this tournament," the WTA commentator said as the match slipped away.

. . . .

As Blake had predicted, Mari's match had generated considerable interest; she was brought into the main interview room for a press conference where reporters from local, national, and Japanese outlets waited for her to describe her experience. "There were so many people watching," she said. "I was super nervous, but it was fun. It would be funner if I had won, but, you know, you can't get everything."

Many of the questions to Mari, as expected, related to Naomi, both about the childhood matches against each other that Naomi had often discussed and about Naomi's more recent success. "She's doing so amazing," Mari said. "Like, it's almost our dreams coming true that we have been working for our whole life."

Almost.

Mari was then asked if she felt like she "had big shoes to fill" because of Naomi's successes, or if she was able to keep her own journey separate. "My own journey is separate, but of course I tend to compare a little bit, so it's frustrating," Mari said. "But, you know, not much I can do about that."

Mari chuckled, then abruptly began crying. "Sorry, I just came off the court," she said.

The WTA moderator asked Mari if she would like to step outside of the room to compose herself for a few minutes, and she accepted. When she returned, she answered a more upbeat question about the positives she could take from the experience. "I played this match with no pain, which I haven't done in such a long time," Mari said. "It feels really good, like I can keep moving forward from here."

Mari then did something her sister couldn't do: answered several questions from Japanese reporters in fluent Japanese.

. . . .

Mari wouldn't get any other wild cards into WTA events, but her Miami Open appearance was remembered as a prime example of nepotism in tennis. The practice continued unabated elsewhere: in February 2020, 1,292nd-ranked Petros Tsitsipas received a qualifying wild card into an ATP tournament in Dubai where his sixth-ranked brother, Stefanos, was one of the star attractions. A nineteen-year-old Bulgarian tennis fan named Krasimir put up a poll for his followers on his Twitter account, @LobDownTheLine, which tallied hundreds of votes. Krasimir offered two options for "which wild card is more embarrassing," Petros Tsitsipas's in Dubai or Mari Osaka's in Miami.

Hours later, Naomi responded from her own Twitter account to Krasimir's tweet with a third suggested answer. "Your existence is embarrassing," Naomi lashed back in reply. "Don't mention my sister ever."

Naomi deleted her tweet shortly after; Krasimir, who told me he never expected a superstar player to see his tweets, soon deleted his poll as well. "I completely understand that she wants to protect Mari," he said. "And let's be honest, Mari is in that situation because of her sister."

TWENTY-FIVE

Shooting Stars

When Naomi lost 4–6, 7–6(4), 6–3 to Hsieh Su-wei in the third round of Miami, it ended a remarkable streak: it was the first time in sixty-four matches that she had lost after winning the first set. Mari, also in the tournament, got an unusually close look at her sister's agony. "She stayed in the locker room crying forever," Mari later said. "But the thing is, she'll pop right back in a week. You just gotta give her time. And then she'll fight harder because of it."

Naomi had exited before the quarterfinals in her first three tournaments as the No. 1, but her fortunes began to improve when she traveled to Europe for the clay season. In her first match at the Porsche Grand Prix in Stuttgart, a lucrative indoor tournament, Naomi won a rematch against Hsieh to put her into the quarterfinals. There, she won a protracted battle over 25th-ranked Donna Vekić, winning 6–3, 4–6, 7–6(3) in two hours and eighteen minutes. After the physical victory, the sort of grinding win on clay that sent a signal to the field that Naomi was ready to scrap on the clay, Naomi was asked by reporter Anita Stahl how she pushed through moments where she was struggling.

"You know what?" Naomi said with a mischievous look. "I'm just going to say it, because, you know what? Whatever. I might get in trouble, but it's okay: I don't understand why people are saying I'm having a bad season if I won Australian Open, right? Last year I didn't win Australian Open. Sure, I didn't win Indian Wells, but I still thought I did pretty good there and Miami, and then I'm here now. Sometimes I hear people say like, 'Naomi's kind of struggling there,' and I'm like, 'Yoooo . . .'"

The answer was revealing of Naomi's underlying confidence—and how much she had paid attention to rumblings about her underwhelming recent months—but not relevant to the intended question. "Sorry, I should have been specific: I meant within the third set, when you were down," Stahl clarified.

"Oh! Pfff." Naomi laughed, throwing her head back.

Albeit with asterisks due to her two injury withdrawals, Naomi compiled a strong 7–1 record on the red clay in her French Open buildup. She arrived in Paris having won the last two majors in a row. As the World No. 1, she was going to be the top seed at a major for the first time. Though those statuses could have imbued her with a natural, organic confidence, Naomi felt unsure how to act in her new role.

To compensate for that insecurity, she decided to perform preeminence on and off the court at Roland Garros. In her pretournament press conference, Naomi was talking a much bigger game than she ever had before, declaring her intention to win the title, despite never having reached the fourth round on her three previous appearances there. "I don't want to be here thinking 'I want to get to the quarters,'" she said in her pretournament press conference. "Of course I have never been that far here before, but my end goal is to win, of course." Naomi went further than that, openly speaking about setting her sights on achieving the Grand Slam: winning all four majors in one calendar year. "It would be really cool to win everything in one year," she said. This goal was at once obvious and outrageous: no one had won all four major titles in a year for more than three decades, since Steffi Graf in 1988. Only two women had even won the first two legs of the Grand Slam in a year in the previous twenty years, Jennifer Capriati in 2001 and Serena Williams in 2015. Serena, whose bid was stopped by Roberta Vinci in the 2015 U.S. Open semifinals, had dodged questions about the elusive feat even as she got within two matches of it; Naomi was talking about it despite still being twenty-one long matches away.

Naomi later admitted that she had felt a need to act like something other than herself because of her ranking at Roland Garros. "I've never really seen someone with my kind of vibe become No. 1," she told Simon

Briggs of *The Sunday Telegraph* after the tournament. "At first, I was trying to figure out who I can mimic or portray as much as possible. I was trying to be intimidating, to look serious. And during my whole French swing that was what I was trying to do."

When she took court for her first match, however, it became clear Naomi had only psyched out herself.

· · · · · · · ·

Naomi's first opponent at Roland Garros was 90th-ranked Anna Karolína Schmiedlová, the sort of opponent a top seed is expected to dismiss with ease. And sure enough, the first set was 6–0 after just twenty minutes—but in Schmiedlová's favor. It was the first time Naomi had lost an opening set 6–0 in nearly three years, and it was entirely her fault: Schmiedlová didn't hit a single winner in the set; every point she won was from an Osaka error. "I think this is the most nervous I have ever been in my entire life during a match," Naomi said after.

Schmiedlová was within two points of victory five times in the second set—it would have been only the second-ever first-round upset of a No. 1 seed in French Open history—but Naomi steeled herself: she broke Schmiedlová twice to stay in the match, then took the tiebreak 7-4. After hitting thirty-two unforced errors through the first two sets, Naomi hit only four in the third, ultimately running away with a 0–6, 7–6(4), 6–1 victory, her fifteenth straight match win at a major.

Naomi listed the "logical reasons" for her to have felt nervous. "First time playing a Grand Slam as Number One; Won the last two, so I kind of want to win this one really bad; I have never played on Chatrier before, this was my first time," she listed. "And, yeah, I kind of feel like I'm having the thought of wanting to prove myself again."

· · · · · · ·

Naomi's second-round encounter against 43rd-ranked Victoria Azarenka was circled as the can't-miss match of the first week of the tournament. A two-time Australian Open champion and former No. 1, Azarenka had been ranked outside the Top 10 since her return from maternity leave two years earlier. But Azarenka had maintained her reputation as one of the fiercest big-stage battlers in women's tennis, a fiery competitor who stood firmly on the baseline, a hooting grunt punctuating her every shot. In Naomi's most highly anticipated match since reaching the No. 1 ranking, she said she felt like the "challenger" taking on the veteran star. "I'm still kind of new at this," Naomi said with a smile.

The occasion felt considerably less fraught than the first round—a loss to an accomplished player like Azarenka wouldn't be nearly as disastrous—but Naomi was slow getting on the scoreboard once more. Azarenka raced out to a 4–0 lead and stayed in front even as Naomi found her range. Up 6–4, 4–2, Azarenka was two games from what would have been her biggest win in years. But Naomi, it seemed, had forgotten how to lose major matches. "I have this mindset that I feel like I can win if it gets down to the wire," Naomi explained afterward. "I probably shouldn't wait until the last minute."

Sure enough, when the match had nearly swept her away, Naomi turned the tides. She saved a break point that would have put Azarenka up 5–2 in the second, then saved three game points that would have put her up 5–3. "She has obviously a lot of confidence playing right now in those moments," Azarenka said after the match.

From down 6–4, 4–2, Naomi won ten of the next twelve games to put herself up 5–1 in the third. Naomi now had a comfortable lead but allowed herself to entertain the notion of calamity when she turned in a shaky service game. "You know what I started thinking about? I was thinking about the [2016] U.S. Open against Keys, the tragic match," Naomi said. "I was like, 'Yo, I'm going to do this again? For real?'"

Naomi stopped the skid before she got too near the cliff's edge, completing the 4–6, 7–5, 6–3 victory, her sixteenth-straight win at a major. After the match, Naomi was asked if she felt she had lessened the pressure on herself by winning two tough matches to reach the third round. "It's not outside pressure; it's more like *I* feel like I have to win," she said. "I acknowledge that's kind of a toxic trait, but, like, it's gotten me this far, so . . ."

· · · · · · ·

Naomi figured to have an easier test in the third round against 42nd-ranked Kateřina Siniaková, a Czech with leonine blond curls who was better known for her success in doubles and who had never before won a third-round singles match at a major. Yet again, Naomi lost the first set. In the second set, Siniaková broke again for a 3–2 lead, then held for 4–2, then had a point to go up a double break. As she prepared to serve, Naomi squinted and frowned, staring at major defeat up close for the first time in nearly a year. She didn't recognize what she saw, and she didn't quite seem to know how to react to it. Naomi hit her first serve into the net. She then stared some more, a mixture of confusion and disgust, and hit a second serve that floated well past the service line for a double fault. The crowd sighed and groaned. Minutes later, Siniaková threw her arms up in the air and squealed with delight at having knocked off the tournament's top seed 6–4, 6–2.

For the first time in eleven long months, Naomi had lost a match at a major, but only after first having lost the sensations she'd so often enjoyed at majors. She arrived to her press conference still wearing her lavender match dress after nearly an hour of wallowing in post-loss inertia, explaining that she had fatigue and headaches from the stress of the event, feeling a "weight" on herself throughout. "I have had a feeling that was different to every other Grand Slam that I have played," she explained, "because usually I find it very freeing and fun, and this time around I was kind of tense the entire time."

It was the highest-profile loss of Naomi's career so far; asked to measure her disappointment, she said "from one to ten, I'm like at a hundred right now." But when she switched from numbers to words, she struggled for an appropriate way to articulate her sadness without overstating her state of mind. "I don't want to say I feel 'depressed,' but I do," she said. "I think it's a natural part of life, especially if you train super hard for moments like these and then you don't perform how you want to. I feel like saying that 'I'm depressed' is a very strong statement. Because I felt that way before, and it's not as extreme as that. So I would just say I'm very disappointed in how I played, and I wish I could have done better."

Naomi's passing mention of having experienced depression went nearly unnoticed in the moment; the tennis world was instead swept up in the exit that same day of Serena Williams, who caused further waves by going straight from the court to the press center after her loss and demanding to do her press conference immediately, which caused the Austrian player Dominic Thiem to be evicted from the interview room podium in the middle of his own press conference to clear space for the impatient superstar.

In hindsight, someone—anyone—paying attention to Naomi's mention of depression would have proved prescient: the next time she was in Paris two years later, her mental health would become the talk of not only Roland Garros but the world.

. . . .

Naomi had never made it past the third round of the French Open in her three previous appearances, but still the loss to Siniaková felt different. It was her first time being the main character at a major, her first time being the top seed, her first time being the player everyone wanted to beat. Climbing and beating players ranked above her was something Naomi had been doing her whole career. But especially because she had skipped the ITF junior circuit—and hadn't been particularly successful playing among kids her age when she first started—Naomi had no experience being on top, of being the hunted, a realization that became suddenly stark in the light of her loss to Siniaková.

As Naomi sat in the Roland Garros player restaurant across from Duguid after the loss, she wondered aloud how the greats did it. How did they handle knowing that every opponent would bring their best each time they stepped on the court? How did they accept that wins were expected while each loss would be headline news? Naomi didn't have the answers that could only be gained with years of experience at the top. She wondered who might be able to share their wisdom. The most obvious mentor might have been Naomi's lifelong role model, Serena, but Naomi still found herself petrified around her idol. "I still feel a bit shocked whenever she reaches out," Naomi said of Serena later that summer. "I don't say 'Hi' to her or anything, because I get so nervous. And she always seems like she's doing something important, so I don't want to interrupt. I really want to talk to her about life and stuff, and how she manages to do things on and off the court, but I don't want to be disrespectful to her and try to talk to her like she's my mentor while she's still playing. I'm kind of just chilling on that."

Someone outside tennis, therefore, would be a better mentor. Naomi and Duguid had another idea whom to ask: LeBron James, whom Naomi had briefly met at a Lakers game earlier that year when her Nike deal was rolled out. When Duguid reached out to one of LeBron's agents, however, he was rerouted: the better mentor, the agent knew, was another NBA legend.

· · · · · · · ·

Kobe Bryant had retired from basketball three years earlier, ending a twenty-season career that included eighteen All-Star selections, five championship rings, two Olympic gold medals, two finals MVP awards, and one regular season MVP. From the time he was drafted—straight out of Lower Merion High School in suburban Philadelphia without playing in college—Kobe was a singularly ambitious presence in the league, a focused, tenacious competitor who blurred the lines between self-confidence and selfishness, gaining simultaneous reputations for cold-blooded clutch play and showboating ball-hogging. Tellingly, one of his biggest rivals was his own teammate on the Lakers, star center Shaquille O'Neal, with whom he struggled for power and spotlight on the championship-winning, dynastic team.

A 2003 rape charge in Colorado against Kobe, dropped during jury selection, ultimately did little to derail Kobe's legacy or trajectory with the public. Because he played his entire career with the Lakers—and won a fourth and fifth title for them as the team's undisputed superstar after O'Neal had departed—Kobe became a Los Angeles institution and was recognized and revered league-wide as a proven winner. Kobe also gained praise for his vocal support of women's sports, including the WNBA, the league that he said the second-eldest of his four daughters, Gianna, hoped to join. Kobe coached Gianna's youth basketball team, which was part of his Mamba Sports Academy. After he retired, Kobe began to broaden his interests. He narrated an Oscar-winning animated short, *Dear Basketball*. Kobe was also, in a timely twist, publishing a young adult novel in the summer of 2019, *Legacy and the Queen,* which centered on a tennis-playing girl with magical powers.

Once he and Naomi were back stateside, Duguid received an email address for Kobe's manager and sent a message asking if he might be up for meeting Naomi. Within twenty minutes of emailing her, Duguid received a reply: Kobe would meet with Naomi at his office in Newport Beach at 9:00 a.m. the next morning. Duguid and his wife, Carly, picked Naomi up the next morning to drive her to Orange County. When they got to their destination, to her shock, the Duguids told Naomi she was going into the building on her own to talk to Kobe adult to adult, peer to peer, champion to champion.

The first time they ever met, Naomi and Kobe spoke for two hours; when she walked out of the building she told Duguid it was the most valuable two hours of her life. "I remember telling him I wanted to be like him, and his response was 'No, be better,'" Naomi later said of Kobe. "I will never forget that."

Kobe gave Naomi his number, and the two stayed in frequent touch by phone. He called her Little Sis and she called him Big Bro. "He was like the older brother/uncle that I wish I always had," Naomi later said. "He was someone that, no matter how busy he was, for some reason he always picked up the phone when I called him."

• • • • • • •

With her new mentor's number in her phone and his words in her mind, Naomi returned to Europe for the grass court swing in England. Tennis had first been played on grass in its Victorian England beginnings—the sport was originally called lawn tennis—and grass was once the surface used at three of the four majors. By 2019 it was a largely marginal surface on the tour, taking up only a month of the calendar. But despite its scarcity, grass took on an outsized importance in the tennis consciousness: it was still the surface at Wimbledon, the spiritual home of tennis.

Pundits from Britain and elsewhere looked at Naomi Osaka and saw a likely Wimbledon champion: her game was built around a big serve and flat, powerful groundstrokes, the weapons considered most conducive to grass success. The comparisons often made between Naomi and the Williams sisters also augured success at Wimbledon: Venus had won five of her seven major singles titles at Wimbledon, while Serena had triumphed there seven times. "Of course people are saying I could do really well here, and that's sort of what I'm aiming for," Naomi said before her first grass court match of 2019. "But I think I kind of have to learn how to get comfortable."

Her limited results on grass had been promising. She had made the final of her very first grass tournament, an ITF event in Surbiton, England, in 2015. In her two previous appearances in the Wimbledon main draw, she had lost third-round matches to eventual finalist Venus Williams in 2017 and eventual champion Angelique Kerber in 2018.

But instead of those strong showings, Naomi seemed to dwell on her inexperience and injuries on the surface. Unlike most top players, who had played on grass events while competing on the junior circuit, Naomi had stuck to hard and green clay courts in the United States. Because of its sometimes-slick surface, grass requires a certain type of precise footwork that even veterans sometimes find tricky. In 2016, Naomi had slipped and injured herself on the slick surface at a warm-up event two weeks before Wimbledon, forcing her out of the major tournament, one of the few times an injury had derailed her thus far in her career. That memory could have been supplanted by her more recent successes, but Naomi seemed unable to focus on the positives once she got onto the surface, where now more was being expected of her than ever before.

Despite those insecurities, Naomi's campaign on grass began auspiciously. She battled to win her first match in Birmingham, 6–1, 4–6, 6–3 over 33rd-ranked Maria Sakkari. "I feel like there's a process that needs to happen that I'm developing," Naomi said. "But I would rather it come at a quicker rate."

It didn't come quickly, or perhaps at all, in Naomi's second match in Birmingham. Her opponent was 43rd-ranked Yulia Putintseva, the fiery five-foot-four daughter of a Soviet judoka who treated her tennis like a combat sport. Putintseva hadn't been successful on grass—she'd lost all seven matches she'd played on grass against Top 50 opponents in her career—but she came out against Naomi smelling blood. Putintseva had won the pair's one previous meeting in Tasmania the year before, and she raced out to a big lead in the first set, hitting a taunting drop shot return winner on break point to extend her lead to 4–0 that felt like the tennis equivalent of a knockdown. Putintseva soon completed a tidy 6–2, 6–3 win, her first career victory over a World No. 1.

Naomi took the loss to Putintseva hard and did something she had never done before: skip her mandatory post-match press conference. "That was the first time, and I felt really bad about it after," Naomi said weeks later. "But at the moment I was just like, 'I don't even think I can articulate sentences well enough to do the press conference, so I don't even see the worth of trying.'" Naomi said she couldn't even bring herself to talk with her team in the hours following the defeat. "It was kind of rough," she said. "But I think that loss, it was so shocking that it was actually kind of good for me."

Naomi lost more than the match in Birmingham: Ash Barty, who had won the French Open earlier that month, won the title in Birmingham as well to slingshot past Naomi into the top spot in the WTA rankings, ending Naomi's reign atop the ladder at twenty-one weeks and knocking her down to No. 2. There was more bad news for Naomi that week: the draw for Wimbledon had come out, and she would be facing Putintseva again, in the first round. There was some reason for optimism, however, that a change of fortunes was afoot: throughout her career, Naomi had always been much stronger at major events, particularly out of the gates: in her thirteen major appearances, she had a 12–1 record in the first round. And twice already that year she had beaten an opponent (Mladenovic, Hsieh) in an immediate rematch of a defeat.

Naomi and Putintseva were chosen to play their first-round match on Centre Court, the sport's fifteen-thousand-seat cathedral, the lone women's match given that honor on the tournament's opening day. Naomi began positively. She broke in the third game with a swinging backhand volley winner and a loud "C'mon!" to put herself up 2–1. But Putintseva, as ever, was ready for the fight. With "C'mons" of her own, and a deluge of drop shots, she leveled the first set and pushed it into a tiebreak, which she won 7–4. At 2–2 in the second set, Putintseva hit another drop shot return winner on break point, as she had in Birmingham. After Hawk-Eye confirmed that the shot had caught the line, Putintseva raised her fists in the air and giddily skipped to her chair; across the net, Naomi could only look sad and roll her neck, trying to loosen the tension that was suffocating her more and more. "Normally I love Grand Slams, I love playing on the big courts," Naomi said weeks later. "But for some reason when I was there, I wasn't enjoying it at all. Like, I was playing my match on the Centre Court in Wimbledon, and honestly, I would have rather been anywhere else."

Putintseva swiftly put Naomi out of her misery, reeling off the final three games to complete the 7–6(4), 6–2 upset win. She dropped her racquet to the ground and ran to the net to shake Naomi's hand, sealing just the second first-round loss at a major in Naomi's career in fourteen main draw appearances. "I don't want to open all my secrets against her," Putintseva told me years later when I asked about the key to her back-to-back wins. "But definitely I was mixing it up, and she's playing kind of flat."

Naomi didn't skip her post-loss press conference as she had in Birmingham, but neither did she seem ready to talk: she came into the interview carrying a towel and still wearing her white match dress and even her visor and the sweatbands on her wrists, having been unable to muster the energy to change out of her sweaty clothes in the half hour that had passed since her elimination.

Naomi's answers were short, mumbly, and uncertain. "How hard is it not to have that in my head?" she repeated after a question about facing

Putintseva again soon after a recent loss. "Very hard? I don't know how to answer that."

Another reporter suggested her split from Bajin had "correlated in a change of form" in the months without him—indeed, she had started the season 9–1 with him but was 13–7 since their split. Was there a link?

"I don't think it's related at all," Naomi tersely replied.

How, the reporter then asked as he tried to find a more positive angle, would she go about "restoring your confidence in the next few days to pick yourself up?"

"I don't know," Naomi replied. "There's answers to questions that you guys ask that I still haven't figured out yet."

As tears began to well in her eyes, a BBC reporter asked another question: "Has it been difficult to get used to the new level of fame that you have? You've pretty much become a global superstar over the past twelve months by winning in Australia and New York."

But before he had finished his question, Naomi turned to her left and softly asked a question of her own to the moderator who sat beside her on the dais: "Can I leave?"

"You would like to leave?" the moderator asked.

"Because I feel like I'm about to cry," Naomi responded, her voice just above a whisper.

"Okay," the moderator replied. "I'm sorry, we have to leave it there," the moderator told the room.

With permission granted, Naomi stood up and walked out of the Wimbledon interview room.

No one could have guessed the finality of her departure that day: Naomi Osaka wouldn't return to Wimbledon the next year, or the year after, or the year after that, or the year after that.

. . . .

Naomi returned to Los Angeles, the city she had called home for months, once more after Wimbledon. She threw out the first pitch at "Japan Night" at Dodger Stadium. She attended a launch event for Kobe's book in

Newport Beach, and the two hit some balls together. Though Kobe was one of the greatest basketball players ever, his athleticism did not translate to tennis: in a video Naomi later posted of them playing, all three of Kobe's shots were mishits. "He wasn't THAT bad at tennis," she wrote. "haha love you bro."

· · · · · · ·

Naomi would rejoin the tour at the Canadian Open in Toronto, a little over a month after her Wimbledon loss. But first, she wanted to therapeutically empty her mind into her Notes app:

> Okay so, leaving to Toronto tomorrow and I wanted to get some things off my chest before the hard court swing begins. The last few months have been really rough for me tennis wise, but thankfully I'm surrounded by people I love and who love me back (hopefully hahaha). In that regard I'm very thankful because whenever things go wrong I blame myself 100%, I have a tendency to shut down because I don't want to burden anyone with my thoughts or problems but they taught me to trust them and not take everything on by myself. Unexpectedly though the worst months of my life have also had some of the best moments cause I've met new people, and been able to do things that I've never even considered doing before. That being said I can honestly reflect and say I probably haven't had fun playing tennis since Australia and I'm finally coming to terms with that while relearning that fun feeling. I've put so much weight on the results of my matches instead of learning from them which is what I "normally" do. Having this time to reflect and think (from losing in the 1st round lololol), I've learned a lot about myself and I feel like I grew so much as a person in this past year(s) so I'm really excited what the future looks like on and off the court. See you in the US swing- Update finished [smiley face].

Naomi was feeling better both in her mind and under her feet as the tour returned to hard courts for the remainder of the 2019 season.

After a first-round bye, Naomi advanced through her second-round match in Toronto after just a set when her opponent, Tatjana Maria, retired with an injury. In the third round, she faced Polish qualifier Iga Świątek, an athletic player with a whipping topspin forehand and a traveling sports psychologist. After nearly two hours of the two going toe-to-toe in baseline exchanges, Naomi prevailed 7–6(4), 6–4. Naomi was left very impressed by the young Pole, whom she called a "crazy good mover" with a "quite spinny" forehand. Unbeknownst to her, Świątek would be the next new player to reach the WTA No. 1 ranking a little under three years later, moving into the top spot after beating Naomi in the 2022 Miami Open final.

But in the short run, Naomi had a quarterfinal to play against a player with whom she was far more familiar. As Naomi reasonably phrased it in her on-court interview in Toronto, Serena Williams had essentially birthed her career: "She's like my tennis mom."

Though there had been a close call at the next major—Serena had been up 5–1 in the third set in her Australian Open quarterfinal, one game from booking a rematch—Naomi and Serena hadn't played each other since their controversial U.S. Open final eleven months earlier. The smoke from that inferno of a match hadn't fully dissipated nearly a year later: Serena had published a first-person essay about the match in *Harper's Bazaar*, and ESPN was coming out with an hour-long documentary, *Serena vs. the Umpire*. But despite the past being prologue, the stakes and the temperature this time would be considerably lower in all ways. There was no twenty-fourth major title on the line for Serena or any breakthrough coronation for Naomi. Because of Ash Barty's loss earlier in the tournament, Naomi had already secured a return to the No. 1 ranking regardless of what happened in Toronto. What was on the table, if she wanted it, was a chance for Naomi to run up the score on her idol: with a win, Naomi would be the first player in two decades to win her first three matches against Serena: Venus and Arantxa Sánchez-Vicario each took their first three matches off Serena when the future G.O.A.T. candidate was still a teenager who hadn't yet won her first major.

Though it would be their third meeting, Naomi said playing Serena always felt like a "once-in-a-lifetime opportunity" for her. Serena, perhaps ominously, was eager to get to face Naomi again, too. "I've been actually looking forward to playing her for a while," she said.

When it came time for the match, Serena indeed looked like the more motivated of the two, playing the more positive, proactive tennis. Serena was being more aggressive and hitting harder—her average of 69 miles per hour on groundstrokes well outpaced Naomi's 62 miles per hour. In part due to the winds, and perhaps more because she just didn't seem to want to show up Serena, Naomi was playing some of the most timid tennis of her career. While Serena was gritting her teeth and growling to herself in exhortation between points, Naomi didn't seem to have any hunger and almost seemed to be conceding the match to her idol as something of a peace offering. Naomi Cavaday, the color commentator on the WTA feed, was baffled by Naomi's passive play, saying it was "totally different" from how she had played against Świątek the round before. "Even if she makes some errors, it's fine, she's just got to try to do something," Cavaday said. When the match was over, with Serena winning 6–3, 6–4, Serena had hit twelve aces to Naomi's zero, and thirty-one winners to Naomi's five. The two shook hands at the net and smiled at each other.

Unlike New York eleven months earlier, when both were in tears on the court, this was an evening of considerable contentment. When Serena was asked in her on-court interview how it felt to play someone who had called her a "Tennis Mom," she was ready with a joke: "Ehhh, I'd say more like 'Tennis Grandma,'" Serena said, drawing laughs from the crowd. "That was very nice of her to say 'Mom.'"

Naomi admitted after the match that she had been "a bit too defensive," but she hardly seemed disappointed to get to lose to Serena for the first time. "Actually, this is how I thought the first time I played her in Miami was going to go," Naomi said. "So in a weird way, losing today, I accomplished my dream. I know that sounds kind of weird, but if there's anyone in the world that I would want to lose to—of course I would never want to lose, but—I don't mind losing to her, because I learned a lot."

In her post-match press conference, Serena was asked if, had she played as well as she did on that night, she would have beaten Naomi in the U.S. Open final a year earlier. She didn't take the bait. "I don't know," Serena demurred. "I think she was supposed to win that and she deserved to win New York . . . It was her moment, and I don't—I don't know."

· · · · · · · ·

Naomi jammed her leg on a serve during her quarterfinal in Cincinnati, ending her final U.S. Open warm-up tournament. She took the court in New York with a brace on her left knee, but more attention was on the outfit she wore. The custom orange-black-and-white ensemble, made in collaboration between Nike and the Japanese brand Sacai, had different versions for her day and night matches. A year before, Naomi had worn the same Adidas outfit as several other players at the U.S. Open while Serena's tutu was written up in *Vogue*; this time it was Naomi getting the *Vogue* treatment.

As she had in Paris, Naomi felt gripped by nerves in her opening match as the top seed, this time with the added pressure of being the defending champion, needing three sets to beat 84th-ranked Anna Blinkova in Arthur Ashe Stadium. "Yeah, I'm kind of really glad that's over," she said.

The second round saw Naomi's A-list status confirmed in a new way for her: the stars were turning out in her box, most meaningfully her new mentor. Kobe Bryant coincidentally came to the U.S. Open the same day as Naomi's boyfriend, Cordae, brought his friend Colin Kaepernick, the star NFL quarterback who had been without a team since his polarizing kneeling protests of police violence during the pregame national anthem. The two inactive California sports stars clasped hands and embraced once Kobe arrived at Naomi's box for her second-round match against Magda Linette, which was being held on the secondary Louis Armstrong Stadium. The star-studded corner, ironically, was the only U.S. Open match that Naomi played outside Arthur Ashe Stadium between the 2018 quarterfinals and the 2022 U.S. Open, a relegation that caused security concerns as Kobe navigated his way through the grounds to Armstrong. Naomi won in straight sets this time, which she said was in part motivated by her guests. "I really didn't want them to sit in the sun too long, honestly," she said.

In his media rounds at the Open to promote his book, Kobe often spoke fondly of Naomi. He told the *Los Angeles Times* that he and Naomi had "been hanging out quite a bit" together. "She's so sweet," Kobe said.

What had most struck Kobe watching Naomi live, he said, was the loneliness of the athlete by herself on the court; even though he had been a singular superstar, he had always had four other guys wearing the same jersey as him whenever he's on court. "You have an idea of it when you see it on TV, but when you're in person . . . they're really isolated, right?" he said of tennis. "There's no teammate out there that can cover for blown coverage. It's just you. And when you're in person and you're watching them perform, that is extremely evident."

The character at the heart of the book Kobe was promoting was a girl named Legacy, a tennis player who had special powers to change the dimensions of the court and the air around her as she played. But aside from the fantasy element, Kobe had chosen tennis as Legacy's sport because he wanted the character to have a "more inner" struggle. "It is just you out there, facing these external challenges that then challenge you internally," Kobe said.

* * * * * * * *

The third round would be the climax of Naomi's tournament, pitting her against a newcomer who was quickly challenging her as the biggest young name in tennis. Fifteen-year-old Coco Gauff had been the youngest in the women's singles draw at Wimbledon 2019 when she drew a first-round match against thirty-nine-year-old Venus Williams, the oldest. Venus was undoubtedly past her prime, but she was still a five-time Wimbledon champion, and when Gauff beat her 6–4, 6–4 in front of a capacity crowd at No. 1 Court, she slingshotted to instant celebrity; no one had ever been crowned the "next Serena" quite so quickly.

Gauff lost in the fourth round of Wimbledon to eventual champion Simona Halep, but enthusiasm for her was still at a fever pitch when she arrived to the 2019 U.S. Open the next month. By winning her first two matches in three-set thrillers against unseeded opponents, Gauff set up the most hotly anticipated third-round match in years: on a Saturday night in Ashe, the teen prodigy would face the top seed and defending champion, Naomi Osaka.

No women's match generated more anticipatory hype all year than the Osaka-Gauff third-round meeting. "This one really does feel large, doesn't it, for a first-week encounter?" Mary Carillo said on Tennis Channel. "Naomi Osaka, the two-time Grand Slam champion . . . but Coco Gauff seems like a bigger deal than anybody this week."

"It's been twenty years since we've seen a player—and that was Serena, and maybe Venus a few years before that—take our world by storm," Lindsay Davenport agreed. "They're able to get fans that aren't necessarily tennis fans interested in our sport, and that doesn't happen all that often. Coco has that magic factor about her . . . It happened so quickly for Osaka that all of a sudden, wow, there's a bigger story on the other side of the net right now."

The sensationalized showdown was a mismatch, as perhaps it always should have been forecast to be: Naomi raced out to a 3–0 lead and hung on to take the first set 6–3. Just thirty minutes later the match was over, with Naomi bageling Gauff to close out a 6–3, 6–0 win in just an hour and six minutes. For whatever fireworks had been expected on court, the match was a dud on the scoreboard: Gauff had only managed to hold serve once in seven attempts. The next minutes, however, would redeem the occasion.

After the two embraced at the net, Naomi, seeing the tears in Gauff's eyes, went over to Gauff's chair as the defeated teenager was beginning to pack her bag and told her that she should join her for the on-court interview, an occasion almost always reserved solely for the winner in matches before the final.

"These people are here for you," Naomi told her.

"No, it's fine. I'm going to, like, cry the whole interview," Gauff replied.

"No, I think it's better than going into the shower and crying—you have to let these people know, like, how you feel," Naomi countered, touching her chest.

Gauff eventually relented to Naomi's urging. Still in tears, she joined

Naomi for the on-court interview with ESPN's Mary Joe Fernández, still wiping away tears.

"Coco, this crowd absolutely loves you. Wipe those tears away," Fernández said as the crowd and Naomi applauded.

The crowd cheered again, happy to have an emotional moment that the match itself had not conjured. "She did amazing, and I'm going to learn a lot from this match," Gauff said of Naomi. "And she's been so sweet to me. So thank you for this. Thank you."

Naomi walked up to hug Gauff once more as she walked away, and the crowd's cheers grew even louder.

"You're a class act," Fernández told Naomi, before asking her, "What's it like now being the veteran, mentoring someone like Coco?"

"I don't think I'm a mentor," Naomi replied before turning around to face Gauff's corner. "You guys raised an amazing player. I remember I used to see you guys—I don't want to cry—"

It was now Naomi's turn to wipe away tears. "This is an emotional night, everybody!" Fernández announced.

"I remember I used to see you guys training in the same place as us," Naomi said once she had regained her composure. "And for me, like the fact that both of us made it, and we're both still working as hard as we can, I think it's incredible, and I think you guys are amazing. I think Coco, you're amazing." Gauff, who had waited and watched Naomi's interview, hugged Naomi once more as she walked off the court.

After the ugly, angry scene of the previous year's U.S. Open final, the moment between the two young women was seen as a healing balm for the tournament. "I have never seen anything like that in my life," ESPN's Chris Evert said moments later.

Gauff, already understanding how the moment was being received, was full of praise for Naomi in her post-match press conference. "After the match, I think she just proved that she's a true athlete," Gauff said of Naomi. "For me the definition of an athlete is someone who on the court treats you like your worst enemy but off the court can be your best friend. I think that's what she did tonight."

Naomi said the gesture had been "instinctive" after seeing how sad Gauff was when they met at the net, adding that she wanted her to be able to leave the court on a positive note with fans who might not see her post-match press conference. "Honestly, like, I know that you guys are kind of coming at her with love, too, but I feel like the amount of media on her right now is kind of insane for her age," Naomi added. "I just want her to, like, take care of herself."

· · · · · · · ·

The emotional moment instantly went viral, shared across non-sports media as a feel-good moment between the two young women of color.

Vogue: "Naomi Osaka and Coco Gauff's Post-Match Moment Shows Sportsmanship Is Well and Alive."

Glamour: "This U.S. Open Moment Between Naomi Osaka and Cori 'Coco' Gauff Is the Definition of Sisterhood."

Elle: "Naomi Osaka and Coco Gauff's Viral Emotional Exchange After the US Open Is So Touching: A Video That Everybody Should Watch Today."

Women's Health: "Why We're Obsessed with This Moment Between Naomi Osaka and Cori 'Coco' Gauff at the U.S. Open."

The moment was rapturously well received, but when I asked Gauff about it years later—when she had reached the ripe old age of eighteen—she didn't see it so fondly in hindsight. "Honestly, I don't even remember the moment so much, because looking back, I was definitely, like, having a panic attack on the court," Gauff said. "I was hyperventilating and everything, and I think it was just so much for me. I felt like I'd disappointed people because I didn't give them the match that they wanted. In that moment I remember just not even feeling upset about the loss, just about that I didn't fulfill everyone's expectations."

Gauff had been ranked 140th and playing against the No. 1 but told me she had let herself believe the pre-match hype fomented by media and promoters. "I wish, going back to that moment, that I didn't put so much pressure on myself," she said. "Because that was my first U.S. Open, and I didn't even really get to enjoy it."

· · · · · · ·

After the excitement of the first three rounds at the U.S. Open, the fourth round was an unfortunate familiar feeling for Naomi: a third loss that season to Belinda Bencic, 7–5, 6–4. Though Naomi was upbeat in the wake of the defeat, it was a tough one on paper. Naomi would lose the No. 1 ranking once more, ending her second stint at the top spot after just four weeks, for a total of twenty-five weeks, roughly half a year, in the top spot. Naomi would win more big tournaments in her career, but she has not yet gotten back the top spot in the rankings since.

Naomi made another change after the defeat, ending her partnership with Jermaine Jenkins. After starting the year 9–1 with Bajin, Naomi had gone 20–9 under Jenkins and had exited before the quarterfinals at the three majors she played and before the semifinals at all other events. News of their split was considerably less surprising than of the Bajin breakup months earlier. "I'm super grateful for the time we spent together and the things I learned on and off court but I feel like now is an appropriate time for a change," Naomi wrote in a brief statement announcing the split.

Naomi had her sights on a new coach, Wim Fissette, but for the remainder of the season she was going to take it back to the old ways, being coached by her father, Leonard. Fittingly, the first tournament for the father-daughter pair was in Naomi's birthplace of Osaka. The Toray Pan Pacific Open, normally held in Tokyo, had relocated to Osaka for one year due to renovations happening to the Tokyo stadium in preparation for the next year's Olympics. With Leonard watching from the sidelines, instead of pacing nervously around the grounds as he normally did, Naomi won her first title on Japanese soil. The father-daughter duo's next tournament was an even bigger triumph. At the China Open in Beijing, a tournament on par with Indian Wells in the WTA tier system, Naomi beat recent U.S. Open champion Bianca Andreescu in the quarterfinals, defending champion Caroline Wozniacki in the semifinals, and No. 1 Ash Barty in the final.

The ten wins across Osaka and Beijing were the longest streak of Naomi's career, and it carried her into the WTA Championships, which had relocated from Singapore to Shenzhen, China. After winning her first match in round-robin play against Petra Kvitová, Naomi withdrew from the tournament due to a right shoulder injury, ending her season on a down note, but also on an eleven-match win streak. She wouldn't pick up a racquet for nearly a month as she healed, but the pause gave her plenty of time to reflect and find gratitude for the wild ride.

"2019 was probably the best year of my life," Naomi wrote in an early November tweet. "Even though at times it really tested me. I learned a lot this year and I realized I have great influence over the things that can happen to me. Excited for the things in 2020 (both on and off the court)."

The year 2020 would challenge Naomi—and the rest of the world—in ways she couldn't expect. But even before the pandemic changed everyone's way of life, her world would be rocked.

· · · · · · · ·

After a run to the semifinals of the Brisbane International in the opening week of the season, which extended her winning streak to fourteen, Naomi suffered a shock loss to Gauff in the third round of the Australian Open on January 24, 2020. For a second time, Naomi hadn't come close to defending a major title. Her world ranking fell from 4th to 10th.

Two days later, after she had returned home to Los Angeles, she suffered a far greater loss: on his way to his daughter's youth basketball tournament, Kobe Bryant was killed when his helicopter pilot became disoriented and crashed into a fog-cloaked hillside in Calabasas, California. He was forty-one. Kobe's thirteen-year-old daughter, Gianna, was also killed, as were all seven others on board, including the pilot.

News of the crash, and rumors that Kobe had been aboard the helicopter, spread on social media before official confirmation. Naomi texted Kobe, knowing he always texted her back right away. When no reply came, Naomi knew the news must be true.

They had known each other for less than eight months, but Naomi was devastated by the abrupt loss of the mentor she had cherished. In footage later used in her Netflix documentary, Naomi filmed herself reacting to Kobe's death, showing the camera the lock screen of her phone, which was a picture of the two of them together.

Naomi allowed herself to be wracked with guilt, feeling as though she had fallen short of meeting her mentor's expectations by losing in Melbourne. "I'm feeling like I let him down," she said. "I'm supposed to carry on his mentality in tennis, and here I am."

Naomi said she had thought about texting Kobe after her loss in Melbourne, asking him how to deal with the situation, but she had hesitated. "Then I didn't text him that because I didn't want to feel like a loser," she said. "And now, I'll never have the chance to talk to him again."

As she had at other inflection points of her life, Naomi took to her Notes app to try to spell out her feelings, writing a message addressed to "Big bro":

> Hey . . . I don't really know what to do so I'm writing you this letter.
>
> Thank you for being you.
>
> Thank you for inspiring people everywhere, you have no idea how many hearts you've touched. Thank you for being so humble and not acting as big as you are. Thank you for caring and checking up on me after my hard losses. Thank you for randomly texting me, "You ok?", cause you know how fucked up my head is sometimes. Thank you for teaching me so much in the short time I've been lucky enough to have known you.
>
> Thank you for existing.
>
> You will forever be my big bro/mentor/inspiration. Love you.

. . . .

For her first match since Kobe's death, Naomi traveled to Spain to play a Fed Cup tie on clay. Her body was present, but her game, mind, and heart seemed to be missing: she lost bleakly, 6–0, 6–3, to Sara Sorribes Tormo. It would be the last match Naomi would play for more than six months; the coronavirus was soon to stop the sporting world in its tracks.

When Naomi returned to the tour, she had not only found her game, her mind, and her heart; she found her voice like never before, and an entirely new purpose.

TWENTY-SIX

Staying In, Speaking Out

Naomi Osaka spent the first weeks of the Covid-19 pandemic doing the same things many others were doing in their sudden confinement. She expressed shock and bewilderment at how quickly her world was changing (using a GIF of *SpongeBob SquarePants* entrepreneur Mr. Krabs). She shared her gratitude for healthcare workers on the front lines of the little-understood pandemic ("I hope that everyone is well and safe," she said in a video for Global Citizen). She embraced inactivity ("Sorry I haven't been active recently. I've been real busy doing nothing") and assessed the stark shift in her life and its current limitations ("First it was hot girl summer, now it's homebody spring"). She started a TikTok account and did some dances. Sometimes, the relatable things Naomi did had their own unrelatable twists. She played video games online (but in her case, it included a celebrity Mario Tennis tournament where she was partnered with model Hailey Bieber, a fellow IMG client and the wife of pop superstar Justin Bieber).* She started cooking more, and came up with a new steak, shrimp, and onion risotto recipe that she dubbed "RisottOsaka" (the recipe was later published by *Glamour*).

But most of all, Naomi had time during the shutdown to let her mind wander in ways it hadn't before. The forced stoppage was Naomi's longest break from tennis since she was three years old, and when her body was at

---

* Naomi played in the charity Mario Tennis tournament on behalf of Hope for Haiti's Covid response efforts in her fatherland.

rest, with no tournaments on the horizon, she had time and space to explore her thoughts in ways she never had before. "Quarantine is making me overthink so many things that never even crossed my mind before," she wrote on the last day of March 2020.

With time to think, Naomi found herself coming to a new conclusion: no longer could she accept her well-documented shyness as a barrier to self-fulfillment. "I'm done being shy," Naomi wrote on Twitter. "It's really a waste of my time. I could've shared so many ideas by now, I could've had convos with so many different people. All the things I could've learned [face palm emoji] but no I'm over here actually putting my own limiter on myself." Naomi further illustrated this resolve with a teardrop-shaped name drop, recounting a time when she was too nervous to hold a conversation Jay-Z had begun with her—"the convo came to a screeching halt GOD WHYYYYYYY [crying emojis]."

Naomi was determined to strengthen her social skills the same way she had improved her tennis: practice. While millions were reconnecting with friends and family over Zoom and other video chat media during the pandemic, Naomi was making public connections with some of the tennis players who intrigued her most.

The most meaningful connection came in the form of an invitation from Venus Williams for Naomi to join her for one of her Instagram Live workout sessions. "A real winner on and off the court, and a super awesome, amazing person," Venus said as she introduced Naomi. With Serena and thousands more watching and commenting, Venus asked Naomi various questions as she led them through stretching exercises of increasing intensity, including what she most missed about playing tournaments. "I would say being around my team," Naomi answered. "Honestly, I don't really have a group of friends outside anywhere, so they were kind of my common interaction." Venus, supportive of Naomi throughout the call, assured her that she had also been too focused on tennis to have many outside friends when she was twenty-two.

Naomi was also proactive in setting up her own connections, inviting Gaël Monfils, Frances Tiafoe, Stefanos Tsitsipas, and Iga Świątek to join her for public calls. In most cases, these Instagram Live conversations were the longest conversations she'd ever had with each player. Naomi staged the interactions in the conversational format with which she had the most experience: interviews. On a small notepad, she prepared questions for each player, ranging from their favorite tennis memories to their favorite ice cream flavor.

Often, Naomi surprised her guests with her candor.

"Honestly, I feel like I want to, in the end, not be known for being a tennis player," Naomi told Świątek.

"Oh," Świątek replied. "That's going to be hard."

"It's going to be super hard," Naomi agreed. "But like, tennis is such a short time in our lives."

· · · · · · ·

Though she wanted to expand her social circle, Naomi wasn't just interested in learning to be chatty around new people. She finished her "done being shy" declaration with a pledge that, once she stuck to it, would change the course of her life: "I won't pass on opportunities to speak my mind anymore."

Many of the thoughts Naomi began sharing were borne of frustrations that had long been pent up. And so where she had once been consistently self-deprecating and abashedly awkward on social media, Naomi's posts in the spring and summer of 2020 became more pointed, exasperated, and defiant.

Naomi spoke out when the reception to her posting photos of herself in swimsuits received mixed reactions. "I just wanna say it's creeping me out how many people are commenting @ me to maintain my 'innocent image' and 'don't try to be someone you're not,'" she wrote. "You don't know me, I'm 22, I wear swimsuits to the pool. Why do you feel like you can comment on what I can wear?"

In a TikTok video, Naomi posed in front of two Google results for definitions of words she felt were often misunderstood in relation to her, saying she "just wanted to clarify this one more time for the people who don't understand" their meanings. "You see this?" she began, waving her hand in front of the first definition. "This is 'eth-nici-ty.' Okay? Read it, figure it out, get into it." Naomi then gave a fake, sarcastic gasp as the slide behind her changed, and pretended to clutch at pearls. "And then this— what is that? That's 'nationality'! It's different from ethnicity! Oh my God, I'm truly shook. What? What?"

It was fatefully in May 2020 that Naomi Osaka had committed to making her thoughts known. And by the end of that month, Naomi's thoughts—like those of millions of Americans—would be consumed by what had happened about fifteen hundred miles northeast of her Los Angeles home, on the pavement of the intersection of East Thirty-Eighth Street and Chicago Avenue in South Minneapolis.

· · · · · · ·

On the evening of Monday, May 25, 2020, a forty-six-year-old Black man named George Floyd purchased cigarettes at the Cup Foods convenience store in South Minneapolis, where he was a frequent customer. After the transaction was completed, a cashier and store manager became suspicious that Floyd had bought the cigarettes with a counterfeit $20 bill, walked out to Floyd's parked car, and asked him to come back inside to return them. When Floyd refused, a third employee called the police and told the 911 operator that Floyd was "awfully drunk" and "not in control of himself." The 911 dispatcher sent two Minneapolis police officers to the scene.

Once the policemen intervened, the minor infraction turned tragic. Within seconds of arriving, one of the police officers pulled out his gun. He reholstered it but within minutes yanked Floyd out of the driver's seat of his car. After handcuffing him and talking to him on the sidewalk, officers walked Floyd to their police vehicle. Increasingly distressed, Floyd fell to the ground as he reached the police car and told officers he was having trouble breathing and was claustrophobic, resisting being put inside the police car. A second and third police vehicle arrived as backup, the third carrying Derek Chauvin, a White police officer who had already been the subject of seventeen complaints. After Floyd was forcefully wrangled into the back seat of the police vehicle through one door, Chauvin pulled Floyd back out the door on the opposite side and onto the asphalt of the street beside the car, where he laid facedown on the pavement, with Chauvin's left knee planted firmly on the back of Floyd's neck while two other officers put additional weight on his torso and legs. "I can't breathe, man, please," Floyd soon cried out. "Please, please let me stand! Please, man, I can't breathe." One of the officers radioed for emergency medical assistance to the scene, but despite those recognitions of severe distress, Chauvin kept his knee on Floyd's neck for another seven minutes. "I can't breathe," Floyd again said. "Please, the knee in my neck. I can't breathe, shit." One of the officers responded: "Well, get up and get in the car, man," and Floyd responded, "I will—I can't move." But Chauvin did nothing to relent, keeping Floyd pinned to the ground by his neck. "Mama, Mama!" Floyd called out, his grunts increasingly labored. "I can't."

According to analysis by *The New York Times,* Floyd can be heard telling officers that he "can't breathe" sixteen times in less than five minutes, but his repeated pleas—and soon the pleas of bystanders watching the scene as Floyd lost consciousness—went ignored.

Eventually, an ambulance arrived on the scene, but Chauvin still kept his knee planted on Floyd's neck. "Get off of his neck! Are you serious?" the bystanders shouted. An EMT checked Floyd's pulse, but still Chauvin's knee remained planted on Floyd for nearly another minute, until directly instructed by an EMT to remove it; Chauvin's knee had remained on Floyd's neck for over eight minutes. Floyd's lifeless body was lifted onto a stretcher, loaded into the ambulance, and driven away. Within three blocks of driving away, the EMTs on the ambulance called for further backup, as they saw that Floyd was in full cardiac arrest. He was pronounced dead at an emergency room.

The Minneapolis Police Department's initial statement on the incident was titled "Man Dies After Medical Incident During Police Interaction," an egregiously euphemistic synopsis easily disproved once videos of the incident circulated. Autopsies ruled Floyd's death a homicide. All four officers who responded were fired, and Chauvin was charged with second-degree murder. Once the videos of his arrest and murder circulated, outrage over his death sparked across the Minneapolis area and around the United States.

Floyd was not the first Black man killed by police, but the excruciating video showing Chauvin's callous cruelty ignited an outcry like nothing heard before, including from a young woman who had promised herself she wouldn't be silent anymore.

· · · · · · · ·

On May 27, two days after Floyd's death, Naomi shared two videos of his murder. The next day, she retweeted her boyfriend Cordae's tweet of a quote from Martin Luther King Jr.: "There comes a time when silence is betrayal." Over the next several days, Naomi would call out that silence in her own words, sharpening her words each time:

"Just because it isn't happening to you doesn't mean it isn't happening at all."

"It's funny to me that the people who wanna wear chains, blast hip hop in the gym, attempt to get dapped up, and talk in slang are suddenly quiet right now."

"When you tweet about the lootings before you tweet about the death of an unarmed black man [four clown emojis]"

"I see people been ghost on twitter for a week when the events first started unfolding, but as soon as the looting started they sure are quick to give us hourly updates on how they're feeling once again"

"I'm torn between roasting people for only posting the black square this entire week . . . Or, accepting that they could've posted nothing at all so I should deal with this bare minimum bread crumb they have given."

· · · · · · ·

Some of Naomi's strongest words in the days after Floyd's murder came in response not to the silence of others but those who thought she should be silent, too. Naomi's voice was one among many in a chorus from sports and culture in the wake of Floyd's murder, but there was still considerable resistance among many who had followed Naomi as a tennis player and now didn't care to hear her opinions, telling her to stick to her lane in a way that echoed an infamous conservative commentator.

In 2018, Fox News commentator Laura Ingraham played a clip of LeBron James and Kevin Durant lamenting their growing numbness to President Donald Trump's repeated racist comments in an interview with ESPN's Cari Champion. "Must they run their mouths like that?" Ingraham asked once the clip ended. ". . . It's always unwise to seek political advice from someone who gets paid $100 million a year to bounce a ball. Oh, and LeBron and Kevin? You're great players, but no one voted for you. Millions elected Trump to be their coach. So keep the political commentary to yourself. Or, as someone once said: shut up and dribble."

As the protests gained momentum in the wake of Floyd's death, Ingraham's abrasive, mocking "shut up and dribble" clip from 2018 was mashed up with her more supportive recent comments on New Orleans Saints quarterback Drew Brees speaking out against Kaepernick-style protests. James shared the video of the stark contrast in a post that was retweeted over 140,000 times. Naomi also joined in, tweeting, "This you tho @IngrahamAngle?" with a GIF that appeared to show Ingraham giving a Nazi-style salute onstage at the 2016 Republican National Convention.

Naomi then articulated her own repudiation of Ingraham in a post that was retweeted more than twenty thousand times: "I hate when random people say athletes shouldn't get involved with politics and just entertain," Naomi wrote. "Firstly, this is a human rights issue. Secondly, what gives you more right to speak than me? By that logic if you work at IKEA you are only allowed to talk about the 'GRÖNLID'?"

As Naomi grew stronger in her conviction, and got more and more support and encouragement in the days that followed, she began clapping back at the persistent dissenting voices with the sort of force she had previously only shown with her racquet.

When Naomi shared news of a Black Lives Matter march being organized in her birthplace of Osaka, Japan, a Twitter user named David Bechard, whose profile photo showed an older White man posing next to a giant salmon, chidingly responded to her that "sports and politics do not mix." Naomi replied: "I hope that fish eats you."

Another tweeter named S.Ladin responded, "There is no racism in Japan. Do not make a disturbance." Naomi responded with a screenshot of an article about the Japanese comedians who had apologized the year before for racist jokes that Naomi "needs some bleach" because she's "too sunburned." Naomi had publicly laughed off those comments when they were made in late 2019, but now she was ready to bring them out as receipts. Another tweeter named Chloe Thomas responded to Naomi's post with "RACISM IS NOT ONE SIDED. STICK TO TENNIS." Naomi responded with a favorite meme, a photoshopped cover of the fifth installment of the popular wizardry series that had been changed to read "Harry Potter and the Audacity of This Bitch."

Naomi often deleted her most cutting tweets after they had been up for minutes, hours, or days, recognizing that she was potentially playing with fire by torching people, including Japanese people, online. "Live view of my agent whenever I open Twitter," she posted with a meme of a nervous Kermit the Frog. Naomi slowly became less combative as the summer wore on—"I'm gonna be a peaceful person now . . . my twitter fingers be itching tho," she wrote. As Naomi later said, there was a concern that her messaging could get lost in translation in the country she represented. "I think athletes are scared of losing sponsors whenever they speak out," she said. "For me, that was really true, because most of my sponsors are Japanese. They probably have no idea what I'm talking about, and they might have been upset. But there comes a time where you feel like you gotta speak on what's right and what's important."

. . . .

Naomi had been more than just a keyboard warrior. She had almost always had her schedule completely dictated by the tour, but she used the break to go where she most wanted to be. "The quarantine was a curse and a blessing at the same time because it gave me the opportunity to travel and process things with my own eyes," Naomi later said. So in the days after George

Floyd's death, Naomi and Cordae had flown on a private jet to Minnesota to join the protests there in person, not telling anyone on her team that she was going until after she'd already arrived. She said the experience in Minnesota, where she "saw everything" in person instead of through a screen, was life-changing. "Everyone was so passionate," she later said. "There were constantly things going on and people talking to each other about who's organizing this rally and things like that. I thought it was really powerful."

In a later interview with *Highsnobiety*, Naomi said that before she went to Minnesota, she had preferred to let people who were "more articulate" talk rather than speaking herself. "It was definitely something surreal for me," Naomi said of being on the ground during the protests. "And I just started thinking, 'Even if one person cares about what I say, then maybe that person will show another person.'"

In an essay for *Esquire* published weeks after her trip to Minnesota, Naomi described her experience and articulated support for political causes like she never had before. "I support the movement to defund the police," Naomi wrote. "By that, I don't necessarily mean to eradicate them altogether. Some of their funding—like payment plans to cops who have been convicted of crimes—should be re-allocated to social measures within the community: Education, housing and youth programs, which are so often neglected. We need to take a holistic approach to our communities and to keeping each other safe."

Naomi acknowledged that being willing to speak out like this, and lend her name and her voice to overtly political calls for action, was something entirely new for her. She titled the essay "I Never Would've Imagined Writing This Two Years Ago."

TWENTY-SEVEN

Stop and Start

Belgian coach Wim Fissette had guided several players to the No. 1 ranking and wins at nearly every big tournament in a decade coaching on the WTA Tour, but for him, the true sign he'd made it was when he got hired in late 2019 to work with Naomi Osaka. Fissette told Dutch reporter David Avakian that getting hired by Naomi felt like he had "arrived at the pinnacle" of his profession. Though he had worked with major champions and former number ones before, Fissette said working with Naomi was his peak because she was more than "just well-known among tennis lovers," but a "global star" and "world figure."

Naomi had finished 2019 strong, riding an eleven-win streak when Fissette came aboard. But after a productive offseason together before the 2020 Australian swing, in which Fissette said he was largely observing and learning how his new player operated, their first trip together had a rocky finish: not only did Naomi lose meekly to fifteen-year-old Coco Gauff in the third round of the Australian Open to end her title defense there, but she absconded from Australia after the loss without talking to anyone on her coaching team. "That was tough," Fissette said. "For me, we're together in good and bad moments. That's why we are a team."

About ten days later, the two reunited in Spain, where Japan was playing a Fed Cup tie. Though Naomi lost her match, her communication with Fissette improved considerably. "That was actually one of the best weeks ever, because we spoke about the whole situation and how she felt," Fissette said. "She was super open."

As they were training in her Los Angeles base in preparation for the upcoming Indian Wells tournament, Fissette sensed Naomi was close to her best, despite her ranking having slipped from 1st to 10th. "I felt extreme motivation from her side," he said. "And honestly, I can't prove it, but I would bet that she would have won Indian Wells. Honestly she had such a high level, and after the Australian Open she really wanted to show 'Okay, I can still do it. I'm Naomi Osaka.' She worked really hard for that. So I was impressed by the level she had and also the mentality. And then Covid happened."

After players had already arrived and begun practicing and other promotional activities, Indian Wells was canceled on the eve of the tournament at the advice of local health authorities due to a first positive coronavirus case in the region, making it one of the first major sports events to be canceled. Three days later, the NBA postponed its season due to the positive test of Utah Jazz center Rudy Gobert, and the worldwide shutdown of sports leagues and all other public activities quickly snowballed. As more and more tennis tournaments began getting postponed and canceled, with no resumption date apparent, Naomi's global team dispersed back to their respective home countries.

The pandemic scrambled the 2020 tennis calendar. The French Open was postponed from its typical late May start to a late September start. The 2020 Tokyo Olympics were postponed to 2021. Wimbledon, which had the remarkable foresight to have purchased pandemic insurance, canceled its 2020 edition entirely.

Despite New York City being one of the hardest-hit regions early in the pandemic, the U.S. Tennis Association was determined that it could host the U.S. Open with its ordinary late-August start date, albeit with extraordinary measures. The tournament would be completely closed to spectators, played in front of empty stands. The Cincinnati tournament, the main warm-up event normally held two weeks before the Open, would be held the week before on the U.S. Open grounds in New York. Players would be required to stay within a "bubble," unable to explore the city as they often did while staying in Manhattan.

With a tournament again on the horizon, Fissette searched for a way to get back from Belgium to California. "I was super ready," he said, "because I felt that was a time that we could really build something." Fissette ultimately found an exemption to travel restrictions for athletes that allowed him to travel to the United States. He flew from Belgium to California via Dublin and New York; he said his transatlantic flight had only two other passengers.

When he reconnected with Naomi in Los Angeles, after she had already begun speaking out and finding her voice, he found a player who was refreshed and reenergized. "Naomi is someone who was born with a tennis racquet," Fissette said. "She always had tennis. Tennis, tennis, tennis. Having a two- or three-month break was actually really good for her. I felt that she really missed the game and the training; it made her really aware that she loved the game."

Fissette worked on fine-tuning Naomi's technique on her groundstrokes with a focus on footwork. They made her second serve less attackable. They hired a new strength-and-conditioning coach, Yutaka Nakamura, who had worked for years with Maria Sharapova, to elevate her athleticism. "We had so many weeks where I'd say, 'Hey, this is a fantastic moment, because when do you have three months to develop?'" Fissette said. "'Normally you have your preseason for, like, three or four weeks. Now, we have three months. We can develop your game; we can bring your game to the next level. That is our goal; this is our opportunity. We have to use it.'" Even though the tour would resume on hard courts, Fissette carved out some time to practice on clay, knowing there would be little turnaround time between the U.S. Open and the postponed French Open.

The setup was also unique because Fissette, Nakamura, and a personal assistant were all living in the house with Naomi during her pandemic training block. In the same places nearly 24/7, the group shared meals and bonded with pandemic-safe activities, including hikes in the nearby hills. "It was to be safe, and it was really helpful," Fissette said. "We did a lot together."

Fissette said that Naomi was a "really chill" and "super easygoing" roommate, but also one who was eager to make sure everyone was comfortable. "She always wants to take care of people," he said. "It's very important to her that everyone's doing well and healthy and happy." Though under one roof, the group also gave each other space to be alone. "Naomi is also a person that needs some time for herself," he said. "So every day she isolated herself a little bit in her TV room or in her room and spent some time just by herself." Fissette also gained an appreciation for how involved Naomi, who was named the world's highest-paid female athlete that year for the first time, ahead of Serena, was in her various business partnerships. "She always comes up with ideas; she's always drawing something or working on something," he said. "We were always practicing starting from early in the morning, we'd be back in the house around two or three, and then she would be doing her other stuff as well."

Naomi has described her voracious appetite for sponsorships and partnerships as, in part, a sort of adult education to give her a more well-rounded range of expertise. "I grew up playing tennis, so there are so many fields that I don't have that much knowledge on," she said.

Her commitment to outside interests, Fissette told me, was in part for Naomi to calm her concerns about what might lie after tennis. "She said her biggest fear is that at one point she would stop playing tennis and she would not have a plan of what to do after," he said.

· · · · · · · ·

After months of anticipation, it was time to travel to New York for the U.S. Open and the Cincinnati lead-up tournament. "I'm just grateful to be here; I'm happy that there's a tournament that's going on that I can play," Naomi said as she returned to the tour. Though no one was watching her from the stands, Naomi noticed different looks on the faces of her peers in the locker room than she'd seen before the pandemic, before she'd been named the world's highest-paid female athlete, before she'd started speaking out. "People were always looking at me differently, but now people are just kind of looking-looking," she said. "It's a different vibe."

Naomi's first match in more than six months pitted her against crafty

Czech Karolína Muchová. Naomi won in three sets and said she found the empty stadium less distracting than she'd anticipated. She beat Dayana Yastremska—who was now being coached by Sascha Bajin—in the second round in straight sets in the silent stadium.

The quiet wouldn't last much longer. Two days later, another violent moment in the Upper Midwest would shatter the fragile peace in the world of sports, bringing voices including Naomi's back to calling out for justice.

· · · · · · · ·

On Sunday, August 23, 2020, Kenosha, Wisconsin, police officer Rusten Sheskey shot Jacob Blake seven times, four times in the back and three times in the side. Blake, who had outstanding warrants for his arrest, survived the shooting but was paralyzed from the waist down. The wounds were fresh and new in a country already ailing from the George Floyd killing. The seven shots into Blake echoed throughout the country as video of the shooting went viral in the following days, sparking protests and unrest both in Kenosha—where teenage civilian Kyle Rittenhouse fatally shot two people with his assault rifle—and inside the bubbles where pro sports were being played.

On the day after the shooting, stars inside the NBA's bubble in Orlando—where about 80 percent of players were Black—used their time at microphones to address the most recent violence. "We said we're going to speak on social injustice, and the things that continue to happen to our people—it's not right," Chris Paul of the Oklahoma City Thunder said in an on-court interview he dedicated to Blake. LeBron James, the league's biggest star, also addressed the fear of the Black community at length in his remarks. "For Black people right now, we think you're hunting us," he said.

By midweek, the talk gave way to unprecedented action, and athletes leveraged their power against the machinery of sports as they never had before. On the afternoon of Wednesday, August 26, the Milwaukee Bucks, who play their home games about forty miles north of where Blake was shot in Kenosha, stayed in the locker room during warm-ups for a game that had been scheduled to begin at 4:00 p.m. The game was ultimately postponed, as were the league's two later games that day. The day of disruption became an existential threat to the NBA season, with some teams including the Clippers and eventual-champion Lakers seriously floating the idea of abandoning the entire remainder of the playoffs. The Bucks' disruption was taken seriously both within the league and in wider political circles; that day, the team had a conference call with the attorney general and lieutenant governor of Wisconsin. Former president Barack Obama ultimately liaised with the players during their shutdown, and advised them to leverage their position to get guarantees from owners, who were overwhelmingly White, wealthy, politically conservative, and well connected. Those concessions, ultimately, included pro-democracy innovations such as turning NBA arenas into polling places for the 2020 election. What the NBA players had done didn't fit within the bounds of their collective bargaining agreement, but whether it was defined as a boycott or a wildcat strike, they had used their power as labor to stop the league with an abruptness never before seen, for a cause that had never before triggered the cessation of a major professional sports league.

The Bucks' protest was followed not only within the NBA's bubble in Orlando—where no games were played for another two days—but in leagues around the country: all games in the WNBA were also postponed for that day and the next; some games in Major League Soccer and Major League Baseball were postponed, too. The National Hockey League bubbles in Canada also followed suit.

Tennis officials in New York had taken notice of the NBA stoppage as news of it flashed across their screens, too. They wondered how it might affect the U.S. Open, which was set to begin in five days. They didn't predict, however, that one tennis player would force them to confront the issue within hours.

· · · · · · ·

Having taken court in New York at 1:00 p.m., Naomi Osaka was midway through her quarterfinal match against Anett Kontaveit when the Bucks' protest became apparent. After trailing 4–6, 0–2, Osaka pulled out a victory over Kontaveit—a rising star who would reach No. 2 in the WTA rankings two years later—4–6, 6–2, 7–5, finishing the win just after 3:00 p.m. Naomi wasn't asked anything about the protests in her post-match press conference, which focused on lighter questions about the match and memories of playing in Cincinnati—"Have you ever been to the Cincinnati Zoo?"—rather than any political fare.

But even if no one thought to ask her, Naomi was aware of what was happening in the NBA and was ready to make a stand of her own. "During the entire quarantine, I was seeing a lot of things happening, and I always thought in my mind it would be nice if someone started something in tennis," Naomi later said on ESPN. "And honestly, I'm more of a follower than a leader and I like to follow things. So I was just waiting and waiting. But then I just realized that maybe I would have to be the one to take the first step. And yeah, that's kind of what happened."

Naomi chose to articulate her message in the medium with which she was most comfortable. So as she had many other times before at inflection points in her career, Naomi took to the Notes app on her iPhone, but this time with a new urgency.

Before screencapping and sending out the statement, however, Naomi wanted to tell her team. After returning to the rented house they were sharing, Naomi texted those with her—coach Wim Fissette, strength coach Yutaka Nakamura, physiotherapist Natsuko Mogi, hitting partner Karue Sell—asking the four of them to meet her in the living room in a few minutes. Sell said he could sense Naomi was somewhat nervous as she began telling them she was quitting the Cincinnati tournament, which as a WTA 1000 event was the highest level of the tour below the majors. "She's not confrontational; she doesn't want to disappoint the team," Sell told me. But any initial hesitancy quickly gave way to decisive resolve: Naomi told her team that she had decided to withdraw from the tournament, joining the protests happening in the NBA.

"When I heard that, I dropped my jaw, to be honest," Nakamura told me. "All I was thinking was we're here for the tournament, the Cincinnati

Open, then also to prepare for the U.S. Open . . . But she was thinking of totally different things at the same time."

Sell said the news was initially jarring to the team. "Obviously we were working hard: we're in the semis of a 1000, Cincinnati; I think most players would go into a semifinal of a 1000 with a broken foot," Sell said. "But for her, again, there's certain things that are more important."

Fissette told me the decision had "come out of nowhere" for him. "It wasn't, like, 'What do you guys think about it? Should I or should I not play?' No, no, the decision was made."

Initial shock gave way to acceptance, however, through both empathy and necessity. "I was shocked, yes, but as a coach, what do you do with that? You support her," Fissette said. "'Okay, Naomi, that's your decision. Of course we're proud of you taking a big decision like that, to support something that is definitely right. And yeah, okay, we're behind you.' I mean, what can you do? You're a few days away from starting the U.S. Open that you want to win and you believe that she can win. You want to have a positive vibe, of course, going into that U.S. Open."

For Fissette and the others, the decision was especially shocking because of the monthslong buildup to the tournament: Naomi's first tournament back from the pandemic stoppage had been a target as the team trained and lived together in isolation in Los Angeles all spring and summer, and now it was suddenly called off. "Everyone was putting in so much work; like, I was away from home for like ten weeks in a row, I couldn't go home because there was a risk that possibly I couldn't come back," Fissette said. "And then you finally get to a tournament and then that happens. Of course in some way it's a big disappointment; on the other way, yeah, it was also a super brave moment from her, and of course I have full understanding, also, for that."

Sell said the team also grasped that there were parts of Naomi they might not readily comprehend when it came to Black Lives Matter. "We don't know how it is; she knows," Sell, a Brazilian, told me. "I'm White; the rest of the team is either White or Japanese. We don't understand, so there's certain things that we have to support."

Fissette discussed the decision with Duguid, who was the one core member of Naomi's team who wasn't with her in New York. "I remember Stuart saying, 'You know, Wim, maybe in two weeks' time we look back and we say, Hey, this was probably the best decision ever,'" Fissette recalled.

· · · · · · ·

Duguid was less surprised than the others: he had expected Naomi to join the protest once he saw news of the Bucks' boycott on the ESPN news ticker on the bottom of the screen as he watched her match that day. Duguid was fully supportive but asked Naomi to wait to post her statement for ten minutes so he could give heads-ups to the tour, the USTA, and Naomi's sponsors so they wouldn't be blindsided by her announcement and withdrawal.

When Duguid told the tour of Naomi's decision, they asked if she could wait another thirty minutes so that the various stakeholders could coordinate their reaction. Negotiations then began in a series of high-level conference calls including Duguid, USTA chief executive of professional tennis Stacey Allaster, and WTA chief executive Steve Simon; because it was a combined tournament, ATP chief executive Massimo Calvelli was also on the call to represent the men's tour. The call turned into a series of calls, lasting hours. The officials, nervous about the knock-on effects Naomi's withdrawal might have, pressured Duguid for Naomi to reconsider her withdrawal. Eventually, they had a counteroffer for her: the whole tour would stop for a day, and the tournament would resume on Friday.

When Duguid presented this offer to Naomi initially, she was skeptical, having already resolved to withdraw. But as they spoke, she realized her individual stance might be quickly passed over if the tournament proceeded on schedule without her. By agreeing to the stoppage, she would ground the entire sport for a day, and also return on Friday, ensuring two full days where the message she wanted to send would dominate the tennis news cycle.

As she contemplated that decision, the calls dragged on; the initial ten-minute delay Duguid had asked her for had devolved into hours of waiting. Eventually, while yet another call was being held, Naomi decided not to wait any longer: to make sure that her original message got across, and unsure what other machinations and distortions it might be fed through if she waited for someone else, Naomi posted her self-written statement on Twitter at 8:53 p.m. while calls were still ongoing.

> Hello, as many of you are aware I was scheduled to play my semifinals match tomorrow. However, before I am an athlete, I am a black woman. And as a black woman I feel as though there are much more important matters at hand that need immediate attention, rather than watching me play tennis. I don't expect anything drastic to happen with me not playing, but if I can get a conversation started in a majority White sport I consider that a step in the right direction. Watching the continued genocide of Black people at the hand of the police is honestly making me sick to my stomach. I'm exhausted of having a new hashtag pop up every few days and I'm extremely tired of having this same conversation over and over again. When will it ever be enough? #JacobBlake, #BreonnaTaylor, #Elijah Mcclain, #GeorgeFloyd

Naomi's announcement was foreseeable for those who had followed her finding her voice in recent months, but the act was still staggering: Naomi, known for her shyness and deference, had never before done anything to disrupt the sport of tennis like this.

More than two hours later, the USTA, WTA, and ATP came out with their own joint statement, which didn't mention Naomi.

> As a sport, tennis is collectively taking a stance against racial inequality and social injustice that once again has been thrust to the forefront in the United States. The USTA, ATP Tour, and WTA have decided to recognize this moment in time by pausing tournament play at the Western & Southern Open on Thursday, August 27. Play will resume on Friday, August 28.

The tours' statement didn't mention her by name, but it was still obvious what had happened that evening: Naomi Osaka had single-handedly caused the sports of men's and women's tennis to shut down for an entire day.

And while there wouldn't be any matches on that next day, there would be more talk about Naomi Osaka than ever before among other players, on both the men's and women's tours.

Naomi's individual impact was indeed hugely outsized: while the stoppages in other sports were ascribed to entire teams or leagues, Naomi got sole credit for what had happened in tennis, and full praise from the many who supported her. "Naomi Osaka, thank you so much for the past forty-eight hours," ESPN's Chris McKendry told her when she appeared on the network days later. "For being a leader, and finding your voice."

· · · · · · ·

While she received near-universal praise for her actions in the media, opinions about what had happened inside the locker rooms were considerably more mixed. Naomi didn't attend the tournament site that next day, but her protest—and the way the tournament had followed her lead—was the topic of the day. Unlike in the NBA and WNBA, where decisions had been publicly made team-wide and league-wide, Naomi Osaka was getting sole credit—or blame—for sparking the stoppage in tennis. And unlike those leagues, with strong Black majorities in their player base, Naomi was the only player of color left among the four women and four men whose semifinal matches had been stopped.

Six of the seven other players were European; the one exception was Milos Raonic, a Canadian. Raonic, like Naomi, had immigrated to North America as a three-year-old, along with his parents and older siblings, from Montenegro. Raonic was one of the last players to finish his quarterfinal match the day before, coming off court about an hour after Naomi had made her statement. When I asked him for his reaction to her stand, which he hadn't seen before coming into his post-match press conference, Raonic, who had seen reports of the NBA stoppage before taking court, was immediately and effusively supportive. "Real disruption, I think that's what makes change," Raonic said. He then dismissed a suggestion from another reporter that something like wearing a Black Lives Matter patch on his shirt could effectuate change. "I'd be glad to wear a patch, but I think bigger changes need to happen," Raonic said. "A bigger demonstration needs to happen and a bigger disturbance needs to happen."

That disturbance was realized roughly an hour after Raonic's comments when the next day's play was postponed and all players remaining in the draw were telephoned with the news that they wouldn't be playing the next day for this unprecedented stoppage.

The European players, far less attuned to happenings in American politics, were largely shocked and confused by the decision. Many were angry, especially with the U.S. Open so close on the horizon.

Though no players publicly dissented on the day of the stoppage, several players took their complaints to tour and tournament officials. Anxiety in the bubble during this unprecedented mid-pandemic tournament was high, and for many the disruption caused eruptions. Even some players who weren't in the draws in Cincinnati, like Feliciano López, took the opportunity to complain to officials about how they could disrupt the tournament on such a whim. The two other major champions still in contention in the Cincinnati draw, Novak Djoković and Victoria Azarenka, both independently lodged the same complaint to officials: no one would ever stop a tournament for something unrelated to the sport happening in their respective home countries of Serbia and Belarus, so why should something happening in America disrupt a tournament? Djoković, famous for his meticulous planning and preparations, was particularly upset that there would be one fewer day between the end of the Cincinnati tournament and the start of the U.S. Open.

"I disagreed with that, totally," Roberto Bautista Agut, one of the ATP semifinalists that week, later told me. "I felt that was not fair, and we had less rest between Cincinnati and the Slam. I think that was not a good choice for the tournament . . . The ATP schedule shouldn't depend on what she did; we have to be for ourselves, and I think it was not a great choice."

. . . .

Though all remaining players were affected by Naomi's declaration and how the tournament responded, the most directly affected was Naomi's semifinal opponent, Elise Mertens. Naomi had been ready to forfeit her semifinal match, giving Mertens a free pass into the final and the additional 235 ranking points and $77,999 in prize money that would come with advancing another round. But when the tournament agreed to delay play by a day and Naomi stayed in the tournament, those potential gains were lost to Mertens.

Many players who thought their opponent had withdrawn only for the tournament to make unprecedented concessions on their behalf to keep them in the competition might feel hoodwinked. But Mertens, a well-adjusted twenty-four-year-old Belgian who is one of the few players who consistently seems happy to be playing tennis, was glad the match was back on after hours of uncertainty. To play against Naomi, Mertens told me, was a privilege and great preparation for the fast-approaching U.S. Open. "I was just happy to play that match against a top player," she said. "If I would've been in the final, that would be good, too, but I know the reason why she didn't play and I didn't want to be like, 'Okay, let's get that walkover!' No, I really respected it, and of course I wanted to play."

Mertens said she had been following the news about the protests happening across America while she had been home in Belgium during the summer—"It's a very big country so it's all over the news"—so she could understand why Naomi had made her stand, to an extent. "I definitely understood where it's coming from," she said. "I don't know if I can 100 percent understand, because, you know, I'm White. But I definitely understand."

Mertens wasn't inclined to complain and also said she didn't think anyone would listen to her even if she had, since she didn't have the clout of being a major champion like Naomi, Azarenka, or Djoković. "I haven't won a Grand Slam in singles yet, so I just have to follow through with everything they gave me," Mertens said. "I just try to adapt to the situation. It was definitely not ideal, I think, for the ones who had to play [U.S. Open matches] on Monday. But on the other hand, we have to respect the reason why she did it. And I don't think she wanted to create such chaos; that's definitely not her."

• • • • • • • •

As her rescheduled semifinal against Mertens approached a day later, Naomi still had misgivings about agreeing to play after her initial declaration. "Last night was really stressful," Naomi said after the match. "I woke up sweating. I had a really bad stomachache, and I think it was from nerves. I know why: it's because I feel like in my brain I felt like I had to win this match and there was no possibility of losing it. I think I just put a ton of pressure on myself, and I just really wanted to back up my previous statement."

Naomi's tension was obvious to her team. "We had to tell her, 'Hey, well, you're not going back on your decision; the tournament gave a global signal and postponed the matches, so your message has arrived," Fissette said. "'You did what you wanted to do, and now you can just play.' But yeah, she was very stressed about reactions."

More outsized attention was focused on Naomi than it ever had been at a tournament outside of Japan. Though the grounds were devoid of fans, photographers and videographers swirled around Naomi as she walked from the locker room to the court. "I've never seen so many cameras with her, walking to the match," Fissette said. Not that Naomi was showing any misgivings about her message: as she walked onto the court, she wore a black BLACK LIVES MATTER T-shirt with a picture of a clenched fist—a decades-old symbol of Black Power—across its front.

Naomi showed no tension when the match began, racing out to a 6–2, 2–0 lead. Mertens fought to level the match, but Naomi won 6–2, 7–6(5) to book her spot in the final.

• • • • • • •

Because there was no need for geographic proximity to attend a press conference in the pandemic era, journalists from all over the world, dozens more than had been there after her previous match, Zoomed into Naomi's press conference. "Of course I feel extra pressure now that there's more eyes watching me," Naomi told reporters. "Honestly I don't recognize some of you guys, so 'hi,' I guess."

Naomi said it had been both "hard and easy at the same time" to decide against playing. "I felt like I needed to raise my voice," she said. "If withdrawing from a tournament would cause the most stir, then it's something that I would have to do."

Naomi didn't agree that she had been "brave," however. "I just feel like I'm doing what I should be doing," she said. "Yeah, so honestly, when people say 'courageous' or anything, I don't really resonate that well with it. I just feel like this is what I'm supposed to be doing in this moment."

Naomi said she hadn't anticipated how much attention she would get for her statement. "Honestly when I posted it, I just thought it would make rounds in the tennis circle," she said. "I wasn't aware, like, the reach that it would get. So if I'm being completely honest, it was a bit frightening for me, and I had to turn off my phone because I get really anxious whenever I see people talking about me. But then, honestly, I did put myself in that situation, so that was kind of stupid. But, yeah, I would just say I didn't expect the response that I got."

Naomi's anxiety had taken a physical toll, too: late in the match against Mertens she had aggravated a minor injury in her left hamstring that would keep her out of playing the final the next day. "It's always the same thing: if you're stressed, then injuries happen quickly," Fissette said.

Victoria Azarenka, who had won the other semifinal, would be handed the trophy without having to hit another ball. The lack of a final was a disappointment for the tournament, but what Naomi had done had generated far greater interest than anything that happened on court that week.

Azarenka, who had been the player most aggravated by the tournament's delay, refused to answer questions in her press conference about the one-day delay Naomi had caused. "Why not?" said Azarenka. "Because I want to talk about tennis."

TWENTY-EIGHT

The Names on Her Lips

Because the United States had gained a global reputation for handling the coronavirus pandemic poorly in 2020, many highly ranked women opted out of the trip to New York, leaving the draw markedly depleted. Only one of the seven Top 10 players based outside the United States, third-ranked Karolína Plíšková, had chosen to make the trip to New York. That left the top four seeds for the U.S. Open as Plíšková at No. 1, fourth-ranked Sofia Kenin at No. 2, eighth-ranked Serena at No. 3, and ninth-ranked Naomi at No. 4. Bianca Andreescu, the defending champion who had beaten Serena in the 2019 final, had also decided against playing the tournament, leaving Naomi as the most recent U.S. Open champion in the field.

Naomi's first-round match at the 2020 U.S. Open, against her Japanese compatriot Misaki Doi, was scheduled for Monday as the last match on the first night session in Ashe. In normal years at the Open, night sessions were the times Ashe sizzled with energy, packed with thousands of noisy New Yorkers who only grew louder as they swilled more and more Grey Goose Honey Deuces as the night progressed. But in this surreal year, conditions were reversed: Ashe was mildly bustling with people during the day session, with many top players lingering and watching from the vacant suites they had been allotted, but by nighttime most everyone had gone back to their hotels, leaving the world's biggest tennis stadium deserted and desolate. Most of the seats in the stadium's lower bowl were tarped off; in the first three rows of seats behind the north baseline, there was a collection of Black Lives Matter–inspired artwork displayed, titled "Moving Black Lives to the Front."

While the backdrop of artwork had gained some notice, Naomi Osaka was about to foreground the cause in a new, unexpected way.

. . . .

"From Japan, 2018 U.S. Open champion Naomi Osaka," growled stadium announcer Andy Taylor as Osaka walked on the court, carrying a bag, her racquet bag, and a fanny pack, and wearing her Beats headphones. While Naomi's name flashed to the beat of techno music on electronic screens around the cavernous confines, a different name was written in bold, all-caps letters across the black mask she wore on her face: BREONNA TAYLOR.

Breonna Taylor's name was new to Ashe but familiar to those who had followed the Black Lives Matter movement in the summer of 2020. Taylor was a twenty-six-year-old Black woman who was killed in Louisville, Kentucky, in March of that year, after police executing a "no-knock" search warrant (which had been obtained under false pretenses) had burst into her apartment with a battering ram in the middle of the night. Kenneth Walker, Taylor's boyfriend, feared a break-in once the front door came off its hinges and fired his gun once, hitting a police officer in his thigh. Police officers returned fire, blindly shooting into the apartment, striking Taylor five times and killing her.

ESPN interviewer Tom Rinaldi did not mention the name on Naomi's mask when conducting his pre-match interview with Naomi, instead asking two anodyne, presumably prepared questions about how she had spent the days since her withdrawal from the previous final and the occasion of playing at the U.S. Open.

Mary Carillo, who was calling the match for the U.S. Open world feed, was better able to read the mask and the moment. Carillo, who was inside Ashe alongside color commentator Chanda Rubin, began her broadcast by necessarily explaining to viewers who Breonna Taylor was. "Naomi Osaka has become a fervent activist for Black Lives Matter," Carillo said after briefly summarizing the circumstances of Taylor's death. "Are you surprised that she walked on the court making a statement before she ever swung her racquet, Chanda?"

"Not surprised, because this is the Naomi Osaka we have been seeing since the murder of George Floyd," Rubin replied. "She has been speaking out, she has been finding her voice. She went to Minneapolis after the murder during some of the protests just to get a sense and a feel for what was going on . . . She has really been stepping up and speaking out. And that's not easy to do when you're also trying to perfect your craft and compete at the highest level."

"'I'm done being shy,' she announced," Carillo quoted Naomi as saying for viewers. "This is a woman who has been [shy] in the past several years . . . She can at times seem socially awkward. But, boy oh boy, have things changed. Naomi Osaka, coming to realize her own personal power."

Rubin, who had been the top Black American player in women's tennis in the mid-1990s before the Williams sisters' ascendancy, later told me it was "amazing" seeing the first moment Naomi walked out onto the court with her mask. "For me, as a person of color, as a Black person, Black female, Black tennis player . . . when I saw it, I just thought it was remarkable," Rubin said. "It took bravery and single-mindedness to basically own that and say: 'This is what I'm going to do, and whatever happens in this match is what happens in the match.'"

Rubin was well aware of how risk-averse and distraction-averse players and coaches are on tour, which made her appreciate Naomi's choice even more. "So often we look at stepping out onto the tennis court and everything having to be a certain way with our routines," Rubin said. "That was something she thought of, that she felt was important enough to put alongside whatever importance the match had for her. And I thought, for me, that was just tremendous respect."

Naomi won the match in three sets and put her mask back on for her post-match interview with ESPN's Rennae Stubbs. After asking her about her injury and her serve, Stubbs addressed the words across Naomi's face. "I notice the mask, Breonna Taylor," Stubbs began. "We know how you've been fighting this fight now for at least this week, it's been a social issue that you have brought to us. Are we going to see more different names, or is this the name that you're going to come out with every night?"

"No, actually," Naomi replied. "So, I have seven. And it's quite sad that seven masks isn't enough for the amount of names. So hopefully I'll get to the finals and you can see all of them."

Stubbs later told me she was "blown away immediately" by what Naomi had said. "I have a bit of a sixth sense when I do commentary," Stubbs said. "I get these moments. And just right away, I was like, 'Oh my God, she's going to win this tournament.' She manifested those seven wins, really, by doing what she did and putting herself on the line. But it also put a big spotlight on her that she was now going to be not only a tennis player, but she was going to be in the spotlight for other things and be responsible for those. And she's not known to be somebody who puts herself out there like that, so it was a big, big two weeks for her."

Rubin, watching from the booth, similarly marveled at Naomi stating her goal aloud, well aware how difficult it was to make it through seven matches at a major. "Knowing all of that and still stepping out with that kind of commitment, it was remarkable," Rubin told me. "And I think, still, one of the most incredible wins for me at any tournament because of it." Rubin also marveled at how Naomi's confidence didn't remotely read as cockiness. "It wasn't really bragging; it didn't come across that way," she said. "She's just got this way about her, Osaka does . . . It was just very quietly stated, like: 'I'm prepared, and it means that much to me that I've prepared for each match. Hopefully, I'll make it there. But even if I don't, this is still important.' It was a really neat way to see someone call attention to what is such a serious subject and what remains something we have to keep addressing."

Naomi elaborated in her post-match press conference that night that "awareness" was her stated goal. "I'm aware that tennis is watched all over the world, and maybe there is someone that doesn't know Breonna Taylor's story," Naomi said in her post-match press conference.

It worked. One Japanese viewer said that she googled "Breonna Taylor" as Naomi walked on court, thinking it was the name of an exclusive new fashion designer. When she read Taylor's story, she was shocked.

. . . .

Naomi had the idea to make the masks only about two days before her first match; Duguid had them made by a printing company in Los Angeles and shipped to her as soon as possible. Duguid, who had also acted as an intermediary during Naomi's withdrawal the week before, gave her full credit for both ideas. "Both of those things were like 100 percent her idea, nothing to do with me," he later said. "That's what made it so special: they were not preconceived ideas; they were just genuine, from-the-heart moments that were done in the heat of the moment."

Fissette and the rest of Naomi's team in New York hadn't been in the loop on her mask plan. "Again, we didn't know anything about it until we saw her walk on the court," Fissette told me. "Of course, that's who she is: she likes to keep things to herself and surprise everyone—maybe because she doesn't want to hear an opinion?"

Fissette quickly realized that the masks would amp up the attention, and therefore the pressure, on his player. "All eyes are on you; that's not making it easier, I would say," said Fissette. But as he saw her tournament progress, he saw that pressure powering her. "Thinking back, it was unbelievable," he said. "I think it was a big extra motivation for her, and I think it helped her in difficult moments."

In her post-match press conference, Naomi was asked how she managed the pressure of "playing for" a political cause. "A lot of people ask me if I feel more stressed out ever since I started speaking out more," she replied. "To be honest, not really. At this point, like, if you don't like me, it is what it is, you know what I mean? I'm kind of here for pride. Like, I don't have to be here, you know? And so for me, I'm just here to, like, hopefully beat people."

. . . .

While the mask that she had worn hadn't bothered him, Fissette was unhappy with what he had seen during Naomi's first-round match itself, during the 6–2, 5–7, 6–2 victory, perhaps too casual about facing the

81st-ranked, five-foot-three Doi. "I had a good feeling about her winning the tournament, but the first match, I thought that was mentally not good," he said. "I had a conversation after that match with her because I wasn't happy with her attitude."

Fissette also wanted Naomi not to dillydally during matches because she was carrying an injury; indeed, Naomi's hamstring had become more painful as her match against Doi stretched beyond the two-hour mark. In order to win the U.S. Open, he knew, Naomi would have to be more efficient in order to manage both the pressure and her injury. But Fissette also, perhaps counterintuitively, thought that a way to make Naomi more disciplined was to keep her away from tennis as much as possible. And so they resolved: for the first time in her career, to manage her injury and her mind, Naomi wouldn't practice on her off days during the U.S. Open, using those days solely for resting and recuperating.

· · · · · · ·

With her left thigh heavily taped—as it would be for every remaining match at the tournament—Naomi looked much sharper in her second round, easily dismissing Camila Giorgi 6–1, 6–2. Naomi was still hurting—"I feel like I want to be the player that you can't tell I'm in pain," Naomi said in her post-match interview on ESPN—but the match and her injury were again a sidebar to the story of the second name she wore across her face as she entered Ashe: ELIJAH MCCLAIN.

McClain was a twenty-three-year-old Black man who died after an encounter with police in Aurora, Colorado, in which police had used a since-banned carotid chokehold and injected him with ketamine; he had a heart attack en route to the hospital. McClain had died more than a year earlier, in August 2019, but his story had gained renewed attention amid the national scrutiny of police violence toward unarmed Black people. McClain was discussed as a kind, gentle soul in protests a year later; a photograph of him playing his violin for stray cats at a Petco store went viral. During his encounter with police, McClain described himself as an introvert. "No one can really paint the narrative that he was a bad guy because they had so many stories and so many warmhearted things to say about him," Naomi said after the match, adding that his story hadn't garnered as much attention. "For me, today was very special . . . I wanted to represent him very well."

Naomi's activism was generating attention not only with American audiences but also in Japan, where the media was tasked with explaining why their country's superstar had these names on her face. When she was asked by a Japanese reporter after her second-round win about what she hoped international viewers would gain, Naomi had some of her most direct words yet. "Google the name," she implored. "Research the story. Find out exactly what's going on. Racism isn't just an American thing; like, it's all over the world. It affects people literally every day. I don't know, I'm just trying to spread the story and spread awareness. I feel like it's helping. I hope it's helping."

· · · · · · ·

Naomi, as usual, hadn't talked to many other players at the Open; on top of her usual in-person shyness, social distancing measures in place because of the pandemic—and the private suite that she and her team had to themselves—allowed her to literally wall herself off like never before. But though they weren't coming face-to-face with her, Naomi hoped that the masks she was wearing had started players talking among themselves.

There was one player at the Open whom Naomi knew had already been moved by what she had done in New York: Stefanos Tsitsipas. "Stefanos was really interesting," Naomi said, smiling as she often did when trying to describe him, "because as soon as he heard it, he texted me asking questions." Tsitsipas, who had been assigned a next-door suite inside Ashe, had worn a Black Lives Matter T-shirt while in the stadium. "He didn't get that from me," Naomi said of Tsitsipas's shirt, "but I'm super proud of him. I'm very glad that his first response when everything started happening was to ask me questions."

. . . .

Naomi's third round, against feisty eighteen-year-old Ukrainian Marta Kostyuk, became her trickiest match of the first week. After winning the first set, Naomi was within a few points of winning the match in a second-set tiebreak when a lucky stab volley by Kostyuk won her a crucial point. When Kostyuk won the tiebreak a point later, Naomi angrily spiked her racquet across the court.

Kostyuk held in a marathon third game to take a 2–1 lead in the third set, and then held a 0-40 lead on Naomi's serve in the next game. Naomi saved the first two break points with strong serves; on the third, however, she got away with a limp 76 mph second serve that Kostyuk completely mistimed, sending a return into the net and then squealing with anguish. Naomi saved two more break points to hold, and the match swung abruptly from there: Kostyuk would not win another game in the match, and Naomi prevailed 6–3, 6–7(4), 6–2. "She could have lost that match," Fissette recalled. "I think Kostyuk played a really good match, but she choked a little bit . . . We escaped that match, I feel."

. . . .

Naomi had worn the name AHMAUD ARBERY on court for her third round, and the name TRAYVON MARTIN on court for her fourth, which she won 6–3, 6–4 over 14th-seeded Anett Kontaveit. Both had been shot and killed by aggressive civilians who erroneously suspected them of wrongdoing simply for walking through their neighborhoods while being Black.

"I remember Trayvon's death clearly," Naomi wrote on Twitter after wearing the name of the seventeen-year-old boy whose 2012 death had happened a few hours north of where she lived in Florida. "I remember being a kid and just feeling scared. I know his death wasn't the first but for me it was the one that opened my eyes to what was going on. To see the same things happening over and over still is sad. Things have to change."

After she won her quarterfinal 6–3, 6–4 over Shelby Rogers, Naomi went to the ESPN desk for a post-match interview that brought an unexpected revelation. During the interview, ESPN host Chris McKendry told Naomi to look at the on-set video monitor, where she would learn, for the first time, that what she was doing on court in New York had been reaching the families of those she had named on her masks.

"I just want to say thank you to Naomi Osaka for representing Trayvon Martin on your customized mask," Sybrina Fulton, Martin's mother, said in the first of two video messages that ESPN played for Naomi. "And also for Ahmaud Arbery and Breonna Taylor. We thank you from the bottom of our hearts. Continue to do well, continue to kick butt at the U.S. Open. Thank you."

Fulton's message was followed by a second video from Marcus Arbery Sr., Ahmaud's father. "Naomi, I just want to tell you thank you for the support on my family," Arbery said. "And God bless you for what you're doing. You're supporting our family. With my son, and with my family, I really, really appreciate that. And God bless you."

Naomi held together her emotions in the moment but allowed the weight of the messages to hit her once she left the set. In her press conference, I asked her what it meant to know she had reached the affected families. "Yeah, actually I was just trying really hard not to cry," she said. "But for me it's a bit surreal, and it's extremely touching that they would feel touched by what I'm doing. For me, I feel like what I'm doing is nothing. It's a speck of what I could be doing. So yeah, it was really emotional. After I saw it, at first I was a bit in shock, but now that I'm here and I took the time, I'm really grateful and I'm really humbled."

Naomi, who had stayed quiet beyond posting photos of herself in the masks during the tournament, commented further on Twitter that evening. "I often wonder if what I'm doing is resonating and reaching as many people as I hope," she wrote. "That being said, I tried to hold it in on set but after watching these back I cried so much. The strength and the character both of these parents have is beyond me. Love you both, thank you."

Sheneen McClain, mother of Elijah McClain, whose name had been on Naomi's second mask, also expressed gratitude for Naomi's highlighting of her son. "I had been so stressed out because of the lack of public awareness about my son's murder and when I saw Naomi Osaka showing her support for Elijah's justice, it was overwhelming!" McClain said. "That's one of the ways that I knew my prayers had been answered!"

. . . .

ESPN's presentation of grateful comments from relatives of victims had been a high point in the media's engagement with Naomi's efforts, but other moments were considerably clumsier. Many sportswriters, particularly those from outside the United States, had rarely had to discuss the Black Lives Matter movement in their reporting. The broadcast crews, which largely consisted of former players, often lacked the language to discuss the topic of racialized violence against Black people, a facility that had never before been required for the job of analyzing a tennis tournament.

Chanda Rubin told me she didn't "remember a lot of conversations" around Naomi's masks happening among broadcasters inside the bubble off-air during the 2020 U.S. Open. "It's a very uncomfortable subject, still, for a lot of people," Rubin said. "And in tennis, a predominantly White sport—I mean, that's just the nature—everybody kind of defaults to the norm, which is you focus on the tennis and you have your side conversations with people you know and trust. And apart from that, you just kind of keep going on, business as usual."

Interviews with a winner were usually uniformly upbeat and chipper across the sports media industry. But for those tasked with interviewing Naomi on court after her wins, asking her about the name across her face required an ability to change the tone and tenor of the interview. When that tone did not shift, it was cringeworthy and discordant.

ESPN's Rennae Stubbs, who had been the first person to ask Naomi about her masks in the on-court interview following her first match, said there was a desire among broadcasters to do justice to Naomi's efforts to fight for justice. "We wanted to do right by her; we tried to do right by her, anyway," Stubbs told me. Stubbs's enthusiasm for Naomi's activism, however, jarred with the subject matter after Naomi's quarterfinal win, when she took a disconcertingly jovial tone about predicting the names on Naomi's mask, seemingly gamifying the tragedies.

"I've been trying to guess what name is going to be on the mask every single day," Stubbs told Naomi, who was wearing a GEORGE FLOYD mask. "I was wrong about today. Are you going to give us a foretelling about who is going to be in the next match?"

Naomi replied that she didn't have a plan in advance, and picking which mask to wear on a given day was more about "a feeling I have inside."

"Okay, well we can't wait for that feeling, and for that next mask," Stubbs replied.

Stubbs, who was criticized for her playful tone, later told me she had been trying to show her enthusiasm for Naomi's project, overcompensating in an interview where both people had their faces obscured and were standing a considerable gap apart due to social distancing, but admitted to me that it had "sounded very insensitive."

"It's a big lesson for me that I learned over that period of time," Stubbs said. "You have to be more sensitive to how you talk about racial divides in this country, and so I just think she did a good job of bringing that to light."

ESPN was much more deliberate the next time they spoke to Naomi on court. ESPN's Mary Joe Fernández conducted the subsequent interview with Naomi after her semifinal win. After a string of normal conversational questions about the match, Fernández took out a piece of paper with a written question on the topic to make sure she didn't similarly misfire when it came time to address Naomi's mask, reading a written question that still managed to approach the topic in a somewhat upbeat way: "Naomi, perhaps more than your tennis, your activism has received worldwide attention. What has been most gratifying for you as you raise awareness for social injustice?"

· · · · · · ·

As they had two years earlier, both Naomi and Serena had made it to the semifinals of the U.S. Open, putting them one round away from a hotly anticipated reconvening of their controversial final. Their presence deep into the tournament had been a blessing for the embattled tournament: though attendance from top women's players had been meager at the U.S. Open, the biggest stars had persevered. The men's draw, meanwhile, had been shaken by the shock disqualification of top-seeded Novak Djoković, who had been ejected from the tournament after hitting a ball in annoyance that inadvertently struck a lineswoman in her throat. His departure left the men's draw without any past major champions.

While the U.S. Open generally has room to shine in late August and early September, this edition was a more crowded sporting landscape than ever before. The 2020 U.S. Open was competing against not only baseball but also the postponed playoffs of the NBA and NHL, which are normally held in the springtime. Through the quarterfinals, U.S. Open TV ratings were down by 47 percent from the year before. The one U.S. Open story able to cut through the crowded sports sections—because it also touched on the news dominating headlines across the media landscape—was Naomi and her masks.

Naomi's sixth and penultimate mask, which she wore as she walked onto the court for her semifinal, bore the name of PHILANDO CASTILE, a thirty-two-year-old Black man who was fatally shot by a police officer during a traffic stop in Minnesota in 2016, slowly dying as his girlfriend livestreamed the video of the shooting's aftermath on Facebook. The officer who shot Castile five times at close range was acquitted, but Castile's family won nearly $3 million in a wrongful death lawsuit.

Unlike the 2018 semifinal schedule, when Serena had booked her spot in the final first, this time Naomi's semifinal match was first up in the Thursday night prime-time session. There were only about 150 people in the stadium for the match, but one new arrival was notable: Cordae had flown into New York and sat courtside wearing a hoodie with a quote from Outkast rapper André 3000: ACROSS CULTURE, DARKER PEOPLE SUFFER MOST. WHY?

Naomi's semifinal opponent was 28th-seeded Jennifer Brady, a Pennsylvanian who was in the final four at a major for the first time. The retractable roof over Ashe was closed due to rain, giving the two power players pristine indoor conditions for their match. While some matches at the Open had felt sterile or cold without the crowd, the battle between Naomi and Brady felt somehow pure: unimpeded by crowds or ambient noise, the two women cracked powerful shots at each other that echoed through the stadium, producing sweet, clean hitting that popped off the court and off the screen.

Women's semifinal night at the U.S. Open was designated to honor the fiftieth anniversary of the Original 9, the nonet of women led by Billie Jean King who had formed their own professional tour in defiance of the U.S. Tennis Association's wishes in 1970; those founding mothers would have been proud of the quality on display from the two young women taking center stage. With unflappable serving, the two combined for nineteen aces against only three double faults. There were no breaks in the first set; when it reached a tiebreak, Naomi's familiarity with the occasion seemed to steady her, and she ran away with it 7-1. Brady claimed the first break of the match and held on to take the second set 6–3, but Naomi turned the tables in the third, finally earning her first break points of the match and converting to pull ahead 3–1. Naomi sealed the win five games later, hammering down a 116 mph serve that Brady's outstretched forehand could not corral, closing out a 7–6(1), 3–6, 6–3 victory and booking a spot in her third major final.

While fans and pundits gushed about the quality of the match, Naomi expressed some faint surprise that her best effort had been effectively matched for most of the match: "Normally if I focus that much, then the match potentially could be over in two," she said. "But I felt like it just kept going on. Honestly, it was a bit fun because [of] that quality of an opponent."

Naomi's fun was just getting started. After she won her semifinal, she went up to her suite to watch her favorite player, Serena, play her semifinal against Victoria Azarenka. Naomi had watched Serena on many of her off days during the Open and was still just as excited to watch her even when she loomed as an opponent. Naomi's persistently positive attitude toward Serena was at odds with the obvious narratives building around this highly anticipated rematch, given the ugliness of the 2018 final between the two.

But when Naomi was asked if the memories of that match would have any bearing on a rematch, Naomi insisted she didn't "linger in the past" when it came to Serena. "Honestly the only reason I would think about it is because other people bring it up," she said. "For me, this is the reason why I practice for so many hours. This is literally my dream when I was little: to play against Serena in Grand Slam finals."

. . . .

Because the fanless stadium was so scarcely populated, an accurate visual census was possible: broadcaster Nick McCarvel counted 147 people—mostly tournament personnel and off-shift production crew—inside Ashe, filling less than 1 percent of the 23,771-seat stadium. Naomi, wearing her black Kobe jersey, was one of them for much of the match. Though she had struggled in major finals, including losses in the 2019 Wimbledon and U.S. Open finals, Serena had won all four semifinals she had played in convincing fashion since her return from maternity leave, by the set scores of 6–2, 6–4, 6–3, 6–0, 6–1, 6–2, 6–3, and 6–1.

When Serena won the first set 6–1 over Azarenka, she looked well on her way. Serena had won all ten of her previous matches against Azarenka at majors, including the finals of the U.S. Open in 2012 and 2013. Serena was sharp, focused, and just three sets from that elusive twenty-fourth major title. But Azarenka, unlike Serena's recent major semifinal opponents, was undaunted and high on confidence from her ten-match win streak that had included her title in "Cincinnati" the week prior. She dug into Serena's service games, breaking midway through the second. As Azarenka found her footing, Serena grew louder, both in her grunts during rallies and her heavy breathing between points, which was unusually audible in the empty stadium. To anyone watching—or listening—it became clear to see: there would be no rematch of the final from two years earlier. Serena could not roar her way back. Azarenka took the second set and continued to level up from there: in the third set, she hit twelve winners and just one unforced error. On match point, Azarenka hit an ace. Serena, nowhere near reaching it, could only challenge the call. As she walked up to the ball mark, she could see that it had just caught. "Dammit," Serena said softly, a second before Hawk-Eye confirmed the call, completing a 1–6, 6–3, 6–3 victory for Azarenka and booking her into a major final for the first time in seven years.

. . . .

There would be no rematch of the 2018 U.S. Open final after all, but there was no shortage of storylines and stakes as Naomi Osaka and Victoria Azarenka prepared to face each other in the U.S. Open final.

Azarenka had won the Australian Open twice early in her career, in 2012 and 2013, feats that vaulted her to the No. 1 ranking. After being knocked off the top spot by a resurgent Serena, who beat her in the U.S. Open finals in those years, Azarenka appeared on her way back to the top in early 2016, when she reeled off titles in Brisbane, Indian Wells, and Miami to start the season. Naomi had played Azarenka during that hot streak back in her first major main draw at the 2016 Australian Open; Azarenka had thumped her 6–1, 6–1.

But like Serena would be a year later, Azarenka was sidelined months later, in the midst of playing some of the best tennis of her career, by an unexpected pregnancy. After giving birth to her son, Leo, in December 2016 in California, Azarenka returned to the tour in mid-2017. She was soon sidelined again, this time by a custody dispute with Leo's father, Billy Mc-Keague. The legal battles were prolonged and contentious, involving both American and Belarusian courts. Azarenka, unwilling to travel without her child, played a very limited schedule in ensuing years. When she played, she uncharacteristically struggled with her self-belief in crucial moments of tight matches, like when she failed to close out the second-round match at the 2019 French Open against top-ranked Naomi despite leading 6–4, 4–2. "Vika was struggling the whole year with confidence," Fissette recalled. "Her personal issues brought her confidence completely down."

Fissette had been Azarenka's coach during her two previous matches at majors against Naomi. For their third meeting at a major, he would be in the opposite corner—with Azarenka's blessing.

After Naomi lost to Belinda Bencic in the fourth round of the 2019 U.S. Open, continuing a disappointing run of results under Jermaine Jenkins, Duguid had contacted Fissette, asking if he would be interested in coaching Naomi. Fissette was still working with Azarenka, who was still competing in the doubles draw in New York. "I loved working with Vika," Fissette said. "I felt like my job wasn't finished: I wanted to win Slams, because Vika is one of the best ever. She was so, so fun to work with. On the other hand, she had private issues, and it wasn't certain how much she was going to play. She was not in a good spot, privately, and it was uncertain how her career would be."

The ongoing custody dispute had continued to rankle Azarenka's career. After Fissette had traveled with Azarenka to Wuhan, she had pulled out of that tournament due to related personal reasons; she wouldn't play again that season, and she'd also miss the next year's Australian swing. With Azarenka's career outlook hazy, Fissette told her of the offer he'd received to coach Naomi. "I had an open conversation with her: 'Vika, I know it's really tough for you right now, but I also have to think a little bit about myself,'" Fissette recalled. "'I have the opportunity to work with someone like Naomi. I love working with you. But on the other hand, if you don't know how much you're going to play next year or if you're going to play, then it's better for me to move on, right?' We had a really good conversation about it. And a week later, Vika called me and said, 'Well, Wim, I really have no idea what's going to happen next year, so I give you all the chances for the rest of your career.'"

As Fissette went on to work with Naomi, Azarenka went five months without touching her racquets. "It was pretty close," Azarenka said of her contemplating quitting tennis. "But what kept me in the game is my desire to go after what I want."

When she arrived to New York for the Cincinnati–U.S. Open bubble, Azarenka hadn't won a match in over a year. "Vika, I think she started the Cincinnati tournament with absolutely zero confidence," Fissette said. "Her game was absolutely not there. And then I saw her getting better every single match. And I know, if Vika gets confident, how good she is."

On top of whatever resentments or frustration she may have still held from Naomi having stopped play for a day, Naomi's withdrawal from the Cincinnati final two weeks earlier had made the first title Azarenka had won in more than four years a considerable anticlimax. "Very excited about that," Azarenka said of getting another appointment to play Naomi. "I'm as excited as I was last week. I'm sure this time we're going to get to play and it's going to be a great match."

．．．．．．．

Though there was still much to play for, Naomi had already accomplished a major goal by reaching the U.S. Open final: she would get to wear all seven masks she had brought, which she said had been a "very big motivating factor" during the tournament. "I wanted more people to say more names," she said after the final.

The seventh and final mask Naomi wore as she walked onto Ashe for the final bore the name TAMIR RICE. Rice, a twelve-year-old Black boy, was killed in Cleveland in 2014 by Timothy Loehmann, a White police officer. Police had received a call that a juvenile was pointing a "probably fake" gun at people in a public park. As he arrived to the scene, Loehmann shot Rice out the window of the police cruiser before the vehicle had even come to a complete stop; the gun Rice held was an airsoft toy. The Rice family received a $6 million settlement from the city of Cleveland in 2016.

Naomi had completed that part of her mission by making it to the end of the tournament, but the goal to lift the trophy was still very much at hand. After playing in the loudest U.S. Open final ever, Naomi would now try to win the quietest final ever. The U.S. Open invited staff from around the grounds inside the stadium to watch the final, but no more than 2 percent of the seats were filled. Cordae was again in the stands, this time wearing a shirt that said DEFUND THE POLICE. After the first time he was shown on the TV broadcast, directors made sure to only show him from the neck up.

Naomi served to open the match and was quickly broken. She stopped, exhaled, and nodded before crossing to the other side. Azarenka then held, not missing a first serve. Naomi got on the board with a hold for 1–2 in the first set, but Azarenka responded with another hold of her own, again without missing a first serve, finishing the game with a forehand winner down the line, punctuating her 3–1 lead by punching the air in triumph.

Azarenka was firing on all cylinders, picking up where she had left off in the semifinals against Serena. Serena, perhaps, had been the perfect preparation for Azarenka going into a match against Naomi: she was ready to handle power. And now that she had finally beaten Serena at a major on her eleventh attempt, she appeared to be playing with a newfound freedom. Her normal weaknesses, her forehand and serve, looked like strengths. Naomi, by contrast, was playing nowhere near the sterling standard she had shown against Brady in the semifinal, seemingly lacking direction and purpose in her shots. "Naomi was very passive in the beginning, and Vika was just doing whatever she wanted to do," Fissette said.

Naomi, broken again in the fifth game, draped a towel over her head as she sat through the changeover down 1–4, already well behind after just seventeen minutes. When she missed a forehand in the next game, she clanged her racquet down onto the ground in frustration, its hollow rattles echoing throughout the empty stadium. Naomi was capable of playing better, but she also needed some help. So when Azarenka finally missed a first serve for the first time in the match in the following game, Naomi quietly clenched and pumped her fist, relieved that Azarenka's improbable perfect streak was broken.

But still, Azarenka was well ahead, and Naomi was a shell of the player she had been against Brady. "This is woeful," Mary Carillo said in the commentary booth. Azarenka broke for a third time to take the first set 6–1 in twenty-seven minutes. The match wasn't over, but history said it might as well have been: the last twenty-five straight U.S. Open women's finals had been won by the player who won the first set.

The second set didn't start with much reason for hope: Azarenka held, and Naomi was broken for a fourth time to go down 1–6, 0–2. "We often think of tennis as marathons; Azarenka is on the verge of turning this into a sprint," said play-by-play announcer Ted Robinson. "You can't say it's over, but for Osaka, it is Yogi Berra time: it's gotten late early." Indeed thirty-seven minutes into the match, Naomi was already just thirteen points from defeat, with Azarenka serving at 40-30. The conversation had become not if Azarenka would win but if she might make it one of the quickest major finals ever. Azarenka had hit fifteen winners and six unforced errors, while Naomi had the inverse: six winners, fifteen unforced errors. Azarenka had made more than 90 percent of her first serves, turning her weakness into an unforeseeable weapon. "I just thought it would be very embarrassing to lose this in under an hour, so I just have to try as hard as I can, and stop having a really bad attitude," Naomi said after.

Desperate to somehow change the momentum, the idea Naomi came up with midway through the second set to change the match went completely against her attacking instincts as a player: she decided to make the match into a track meet. "Maybe we should just take turns running side to side and that's how I win?" Naomi said after the match. "Which isn't pretty, but I feel like maybe it would have gotten the job done."

Naomi started mixing in slower, loopier shots, and sure enough, Azarenka started missing. When Naomi did attack, she started hitting more shots down the line, instead of her usual cross-court.

Naomi earned her first break point of the match soon after and converted when Azarenka wildly missed a backhand long. Now down 1–2 in the second set, Naomi was back on serve. From there, she was able to hang tough, keeping the set level with two more holds to get to 3–3.

After how poorly Naomi had started, the elevation in her game seemed to unnerve Azarenka, who began to start doubting herself and making more errors. Down break point, Azarenka guided a backhand wide, giving Naomi a 4–3 lead, her first advantage of the match. "Vika got nervous a little bit, finally made a few errors," Fissette said. "Then it completely, completely changed."

As Azarenka drifted wayward, Naomi began finding her range. After hitting no aces in the first set, she hit five in the second, and won it 6–3 to force a third. The momentum didn't stop there: Naomi broke to take a 3–1 lead in the third, winning a baseline rally on break point and shouting a loud "C'monnn!" in triumph.

After Naomi held for 4–1, she earned four more break points in the next game. But with her back against the wall, Azarenka suddenly found some range and held. Now Naomi seemed to be feeling the nerves of the occasion once more. After getting out to a 40-15 lead when serving at 4–2 in the third, Naomi lost four straight points to hand Azarenka a break. She cocked her racquet back, ready to smash it in anger, but opted to shriek instead.

Naomi was faltering but so, too, was her opponent. The choice Naomi had made midway through the second set to make the match more physical was paying dividends: Azarenka stayed standing during the ensuing changeover to avoid cramping; the ten matches she had played in the previous three weeks were finally catching up to the thirty-one-year-old. Naomi got the best of the toughest baseline rallies in the next game and broke when Azarenka badly mistimed a forehand on break point to go up 5–3, putting herself one game from the title.

Two years earlier, Naomi had gotten within one game from the title because of a game penalty given to Serena Williams. She had to block out the noise of twenty-two thousand screaming New Yorkers as she closed out the U.S. Open title, the loudest and angriest major final in tennis history. This time, with no sound to drown out her thoughts, Naomi only had to battle Azarenka and her own nerves. Naomi's second championship point became one of the best rallies of the match: the two traded blows, pulling each other from corner to corner of the court, until, on the thirteenth and final shot, Azarenka's backhand finally hit the net, her trademark hooting grunt turning into a scream of despair as Naomi shouted her own cathartic relief.

There would be no tears this time: Naomi briefly held her hand to her face, exhaled deeply, and looked skyward as she slowly walked toward the net. Instead of an embrace, the two tapped their racquets, the pandemic-approved greeting, and smiled.

Hugs abounded in the stands, however, with Fissette, Nakamura, and Mogi all coming together to celebrate, and then waving to Cordae and Sell to join them. "Can I go up there?" Naomi asked the WTA manager standing on the court, who went to check for an answer. As she waited for a reply, Naomi got another idea of where to go.

Naomi walked back out to the middle of the court, looked up, and then got down on the ground, lying flat on her back. "I was thinking about all the times I've watched the great players sort of collapse onto the ground and look up into the sky," Naomi explained afterward. "I've always wanted to see what they saw. For me, it was really an incredible moment. I'm really glad I did it."

· · · · · · · ·

The trophy ceremony lacked nearly all the tears of the previous occasion—though Azarenka had cried a bit before it began, disappointed that her third U.S. Open final appearance wouldn't be "the charm" as she'd hoped. Still, even without the angry masses raining down boos, it was still easily the second-strangest U.S. Open trophy ceremony to that point: because of the pandemic, players picked their own trophies up off a table instead of being handed them, staying socially distanced from the array of masked officials who were spaced across the playing surface.

When it came Naomi's time to make a speech, she was composed and ready with her thoughts organized, a far cry from the twenty-year-old girl who had stumbled and sputtered at the microphone at Indian Wells two and a half long years before. Naomi congratulated and thanked Azarenka, who she said had inspired her when she had watched her on TV years earlier. She then thanked her team for believing in her, and then in quick succession thanked the WTA, tournament organizers, the ball staff, ground crew, USTA, sponsors, and "all my people back home—my mom, my dad, my sister—I wouldn't be here without you guys."

Soon enough, the red, white, and blue streamers would fall on Naomi for a second time, and Coldplay's "A Sky Full of Stars" would echo through the stadium as she lifted her trophy, later joined on court by her team for group photos.

The lasting memory from the ceremony came before those Kodak moments. In the interview portion that followed her speech, ESPN's Tom

Rinaldi asked Naomi about the activism that had been the major storyline of the tournament. "You said from the beginning you had seven matches, seven masks, seven names," said Rinaldi. "What was the message you wanted to send, Naomi?"

Naomi quickly turned the question back on Rinaldi: "Um, well, what was the message that you got? [That] was more the question. I feel like the point is to make people start talking."

· · · · · · ·

Naomi had resoundingly accomplished her goal: people had started talking around the world. By the time she had reached the final, Japanese TV was running segments explaining to viewers who people like Tamir Rice were and what had happened to them. Baye McNeil, the Black writer living in Japan, told me he marveled at how deep the Sunday morning programs got into the victims' stories. "They took time to explain each of these children and people who were murdered, the stories of racism—this is unprecedented stuff," he said. "This was unheard of. So she made a significant change, you know? That morning, Japan had Black Lives Matter for breakfast, and they never had it before. It was a strange meal. Yeah, I'll never forget that day. I'll never forget that morning. That was the morning I said, 'Oh, wow, maybe Japan has a chance to actually live up to its truest potential' . . . I do think that there's a good chance, because of people like Naomi Osaka who use their influence, use their notoriety, use their fame to push along the idea that we're all humans here. That was the impact of what she did, and I'm so proud of her. I'm really moved, and really just in debt to her willingness to show generosity. Just beautiful stuff."

· · · · · · ·

Though the people whose names had been on her face were being discussed far and wide, the world was also talking about the woman behind the masks more than they ever had before. And because she had won, it was all positive. Had Naomi Osaka lost in either her Cincinnati match against Mertens or at any stage of the U.S. Open after the stands she took and the masks she wore, she would have been undoubtedly subjected to endless criticism, both from right-wing media and old-school voices within the sports media echo chamber, telling her to "stick to tennis" because being distracted by her activism had caused her to lose. If Marta Kostyuk had converted her chances in the third round, or if Jennifer Brady had won that battle, or if Azarenka had finished the rout she started, Naomi would have heard ad nauseum that her failing was not just losing but a lack of focus on the task at hand and an inability to stay in her lane.

Naomi's only option, if she wanted to keep those voices silent, was to win the U.S. Open. So, she did.

. . . .

Days after her win, Naomi spoke with Billie Jean King, the first female athlete to embrace mid-career activism on a similar scale. "When I see you, it makes me really happy," King told Naomi. "Because you can make such a difference. I was thrilled that you did something."

"I wouldn't have gotten this platform if I wasn't where I am right now, and I'll say that is thanks to you," Naomi told King. "So thank you very much for the things that you've done."

Naomi knew that the tennis champions with the most cultural impact weren't necessarily the ones who won the most. When the USTA renamed the U.S. Open grounds in King's honor in 2006, it wasn't because she had won the most—many players had won more—but because of her advocacy for women and the LGBT community. Similarly, Arthur Ashe hadn't won the most, either, but his pioneering as the first Black man to win major tennis tournaments was what the USTA wanted to foreground when they named their new stadium after him in 1997.

In tennis, particularly in America, the most important champions were the ones who redrew lines outside the court.

TWENTY-NINE

Ancestors

Just as the atmospheres in Naomi's first and second U.S. Open finals had been starkly different, there was also a remarkable contrast between her first and second U.S. Open trophy shoots. Two years before Naomi had gone to the boutique of a Japanese designer to pick out a dress; this time she looked toward the West African diaspora, wearing a patterned, ruffled dress in bright orange and a headwrap made from Ghanaian kente cloth. "You already know I had to bring out the headwrap for this one," Naomi tweeted.

Naomi's leaning into her Blackness was celebrated by many Black communities. "It's the way Naomi Osaka is giving me everything Tiger Woods wouldn't," Twitter user @shizzyshane215 wrote in a tweet that shared Naomi's trophy photo and was retweeted more than 18,000 times. "She's constantly reminding you all that the 'B' in Blasian stands for BLACK."

While Naomi had often experienced gatekeeping and scrutiny regarding her Japanese identity, the Black community in the United States had claimed Naomi as one of their own, particularly after the summer of 2020. After she won the U.S. Open, Naomi received a tweet from former First Lady Michelle Obama: "So proud of you, @NaomiOsaka!"

As Naomi found her voice in 2020, she also changed how she spoke about the Haitian roots of her Blackness. In her first years on tour, Naomi generally spoke about Haitianness in the context of living with her grandparents in New York, her love for the cuisine, and the generosity she had received from the Haitians she'd met.

Naomi and her family had made the long trip to Japan frequently from around the time she was eleven, both to visit Tamaki's parents and later to play tournaments. But though it was a much shorter flight from Florida, Naomi didn't travel to Haiti for the first time until she was an adult, making her first trip shortly after her twentieth birthday, in late 2017.

Naomi's first visit to Haiti had preceded her breakthrough season, which she later said wasn't a coincidence. "It's a very humbling experience to go back, because you see so many people that they don't have much, and then you go back to your house and everything that you take for granted," Naomi said. "You start appreciating it more. Because I went to Haiti the first time [in late 2017], and then I started playing well, I think, because I started appreciating everything . . . Literally, they have to walk miles for water and it's just like, 'Why are you complaining about your life?'"

When her annual income stretched into tens of millions about a year after her first trip to her fatherland, Naomi made Haiti the focus of her charity work, particularly the school Leonard founded in his hometown of Jacmel. Though she has spent relatively little time in the country—less than a month cumulatively through her twenty-fifth birthday—Naomi frequently foregrounds her Haitian heritage when talking about her identity. "Representing Haiti is very important: those are my people," she said in 2022. "I always consider Haiti to be like half of me; that's my bloodline. So I think it's very important to own your culture and your heritage."

When Naomi went to Haiti again months after her 2018 U.S. Open win, she was treated both as a local hero and foreign dignitary. She was welcomed by President Jovenel Moïse in a ceremony at the National Palace in Port-au-Prince, where Moïse named her a goodwill ambassador for Haiti. "She is young, she is a woman, a symbol of renewal," Haitian minister of tourism Marie-Christine Stephenson told *L'Équipe*. "A symbol of what our country could be."

· · · · · · ·

When she moved from Florida to California in early 2019, Naomi bemoaned the lack of Haitian cuisine in her new locale. But while her stomach was missing out, Naomi's connection to Haiti grew stronger in heart and mind in 2020. Cordae, a voracious reader, passed Naomi books to deepen her understanding of Black world history, including Frantz Fanon's canonical *The Wretched of the Earth*; Naomi tweeted a picture of her copy on Juneteenth.

Instead of being inspired by Haitians because of what they lacked, Naomi began feeling empowered by what they had: a unique, revolutionary history as the only country where slaves had overthrown their colonizing captors to form a nation. "I always tell myself: you're Haitian, you're not supposed to have any fear," Naomi later said. "And it's because my dad's always shouting '1804,' which is the Haitian Revolution."

After Naomi stopped play for the day during the Cincinnati tournament, she attributed her willingness to take a stand to her Haitianness. "My dad's Haitian; we do this," Naomi told ESPN's Chris McKendry. "So yeah, it's in my blood."

"What do you mean, 'We do this'?" McKendry asked.

"I mean, the history of Haiti," Naomi replied.

When she won the U.S. Open two weeks later, Naomi again credited her roots. "I would like to thank my ancestors," she wrote, "because everytime I remember their blood runs through my veins I am reminded that I cannot lose."

Naomi was, indeed, incapable of losing when the tour resumed in 2020. And when she returned to the courts in 2021, she had a lot more winning left in her.

THIRTY

Imperial Phase

Pop music historians often use the term "imperial phase," as coined by Neil Tennant of the Pet Shop Boys, to describe a superstar musical artist's peak. The imperial phase is a period of seeming invincibility, lasting months or years, in which the code has been cracked. Everything clicks. Every single is a surefire hit, perfectly meeting and dictating the cultural moment, its power multiplied by the strength of the artist's recent output. Tom Ewing wrote in *Pitchfork* in 2010 that imperial phases are "accelerated moments in a career, times where intense scrutiny meets intense opportunity." Ewing outlined three ingredients for an imperial phase: command ("the happy sensation of working hard and well and having the things you try resonate with your desired public"); permission ("a level of public interest, excitement, and goodwill towards your work"); and self-definition ("it defines an act, setting the tone for the rest of a career").

Naomi Osaka's imperial phase began at some point during the 2020 pandemic. Perhaps it was when *Forbes* named her the highest-paid female athlete ever for her previous year's earnings. Perhaps it was when she started speaking up on social causes. Perhaps it was when the tour resumed in August 2020—and perhaps, more specifically, when she stopped play on the day of the Cincinnati semifinals. Wherever you backdated the starting line, there was no doubt that Naomi was at the top of her game on the court and resonating off of it, in full command of her talent and the spotlight, as the 2020 season ended. Because of her lingering hamstring injury and lack of time to prepare for clay courts—and overwhelming exhaustion from what she had achieved competitively and symbolically in New York—Naomi had pulled out of the French Open days after winning the U.S. Open, which meant she ended her 2020 season on a major winning streak.

Naomi remained the player to beat when the tour resumed in 2021, as much for her cultural preeminence as for her tennis. She hadn't won the vote for the 2020 WTA Player of the Year—Sofia Kenin, who both won the Australian Open and made the final of the French Open, took that honor—but Naomi had an imperiousness that her team could sense as she trained in the offseason. "By the time she was about to leave, I remember, I was telling people: she's winning the Australian Open," her hitting partner Karue Sell told me. "She left so dialed in. I found it hard to believe that someone's going to beat her."

· · · · · · · ·

The 2021 Australian Open, delayed from January to February, was a restless resumption of the tour. The pandemic was still an issue—vaccines were not yet widely available—and Australia's quarantine laws were some of the world's strictest. In order to compete in the Australian Open, players were forced to quarantine in Melbourne hotels, only allotted about five hours for training. The Australian Open, which paid for charter flights, food, and accommodations for more than twelve hundred players, coaches, and officials in order to pull off the event, lost roughly $80 million staging the 2021 tournament, in large part because international fans couldn't attend and many locals were still skittish about attending large public gatherings. Many of the players quarantined in Melbourne complained about the strict rules and things like hotel room windows that couldn't be opened to let in fresh air. Players who were unlucky enough to be on the same charter flight as someone who tested positive were not allowed to leave their rooms at all for a full fourteen days after their arrival.

Naomi, however, was one of the chosen few who benefited from considerably consequential star treatment. Along with Serena Williams, Simona Halep, Novak Djoković, Rafael Nadal, and recent U.S. Open champion Dominic Thiem, Naomi was selected to do her quarantine in Adelaide, not

Melbourne. The stars in Adelaide had earlier and greater access to practice courts and training equipment, had balconies in their rental apartments where they could get fresh air, and would each be allowed to bring another player there as a practice partner. Serena brought Venus; Halep brought Irina-Camelia Begu; Naomi, who didn't like practicing with other players, invited no player to join her in Adelaide; instead, Fissette brought Seppe Cuypers, a Belgian hitting partner (Sell was unable to leave the United States while awaiting his green card). "We can definitely say it was an advantage, yes, especially mentally," Fissette said of the Adelaide accommodations.

At the end of their stay in the South Australia capital, the Adelaide stars played an exhibition event in front of a full stadium, the first time any of them would have played in front of such a crowd in nearly a year—Australia had handled the pandemic so well that there were few pandemic restrictions still in place for nontraveling citizens. In a lighthearted, low-stakes, casually dressed match, Serena beat Naomi 6–2, 2–6, 10–7. "I think both of them didn't really want to show where they were at and were just kind of playing around a little bit," Fissette said. "Naomi tested herself for like two games, saw and felt it was good, and then, yeah, just had a little bit of fun on the court."

. . . .

Instead of spreading around Australia and New Zealand as usual, all the warm-up events for the 2021 Australian Open were consolidated in Melbourne, similar to the Cincinnati–U.S. Open combination months earlier in New York. Naomi played three matches at an event called the Gippsland Trophy, winning all three and withdrawing before the semifinals to rest for the major. She was on a fourteen-match win streak as the Australian Open began and showed no signs of trouble, even when dealt one of the toughest first-week paths possible.

In the first round Naomi played Anastasia Pavlyuchenkova, a Russian veteran who had reached the quarterfinals in three of the four previous years in Melbourne and who would make the final of the French Open

three months later. Naomi was completely undaunted by the task, rolling
to a 6–1, 6–2 victory for her fifteenth straight win. In the next round
Naomi faced Caroline Garcia, who was a past and future Top 5 player.
Garcia fared little better than Pavlyuchenkova, winning just five games as
Naomi secured her sixteenth straight win with a 6–2, 6–3 victory. Next up
was Ons Jabeur, a fast-rising Tunisian known for her flair and court craft.
Again Naomi dropped just five games, smoothly rolling 6–3, 6–2 past Ja-
beur to win her seventeenth straight.

In the fourth round, Naomi ran into her toughest challenge yet. Garbiñe Muguruza was a former No. 1 and a two-time major champion, having
won titles at the 2016 French Open (over Serena) and 2017 Wimbledon
(over Venus). Muguruza took a strong start against Naomi in their first
meeting, racing out to a 6–4, 2–0 lead. Naomi came back to take the second set 6–4, but Muguruza again pulled ahead in the third set. When
Naomi double-faulted on break point to trail 3–2 in the third set, she was
mad. She had thrown her racquet, she had whined to her box. She put a
towel over her head. She shuffled through her racquets noisily, as if franti-
cally paging through a book looking for a solution. But Muguruza, who
was taller than Naomi and used her wingspan to cover the net to great effect, was simply outplaying her. Muguruza took a 5–3 lead in the third set
with a crisp backhand winner down the line, leaving Naomi looking at her
team in disbelief. Muguruza was a great player—she had made the Australian Open final the year before—but Naomi wasn't supposed to lose this
match. But in the next game she hit an error, double-faulted, and then hit
a backhand into the net—her fortieth unforced error of the match—to put
herself down 15-40, giving Muguruza two match points.

· · · · · · ·

As Naomi and Fissette had gotten to know each other over the past years,
one of the things he quickly learned about Naomi was how much she relied
on instinct on the court, which she said was a relic of how she had been
coached as a child. "'My father always sent me out to play matches with no
plan at all—I was supposed to figure out the plan by myself,'" Fissette

recalled Naomi telling him in an interview with Dutch journalist David Avakian. Fissette was the opposite as a coach, relying heavily on statistics and analytics to prepare for each opponent his player would face.

With her back to the wall, Naomi found a new clarity, able to process the notes he had given her, merging them with her own intuition. "I feel like I released a lot of the thoughts that I had," Naomi said. "It just made me go more into, like, instinct-based tennis."

Naomi hit an ace to save Muguruza's first match point. On the second match point she had to hit a second serve—and could only hit it 84 mph. Muguruza pounded a hard return back down the middle, which Naomi was able to wrangle back across the net. On the seventh shot of the rally, Muguruza's forehand sprayed long, unable to keep up with Naomi's pace. Naomi had suddenly found the sweet spot in her game between aggression and caution, hitting the ball powerfully but with clear margins. After having hit her fortieth unforced error to go down match point, Naomi didn't hit another unforced error for the remaining twenty-two points of the match. When Naomi won the match 4–6, 6–4, 7–5, she smiled up to Fissette with a mix of pride and relief. "In the stressful points, I feel like I just had to go within myself," Naomi said in her on-court interview.

Fissette had repeatedly seen Naomi flip into an extra gear in big moments. Such a transcendent flow state is often called "the Zone"; Fissette called it Naomi's "Supermode," a gear of unstoppability he said he never quite discovered how to initiate from the sidelines. "A mystery, definitely," Fissette said. "It's actually a topic we discussed a lot because Naomi, she has this Supermode, but only she knows how to switch it on . . . When it goes on, like, it's scary."

· · · · · · ·

Naomi's quarterfinal match was against Hsieh Su-wei, the tricky Taiwanese veteran who had tormented her repeatedly in 2019. Naomi won with the ease of her first three rounds, dismissing Hsieh 6–2, 6–2 to make it to a blockbuster semifinal: her first meeting at a major against Serena Williams since their unforgettable 2018 U.S. Open final.

Naomi's attitude toward Serena had both evolved and remained the same in the years since their last big match. In press conferences and in her posts on social media, she consistently went out of her way to lavish admiration and affection on Serena. When she was asked in her first press conference in Australia how she felt about "being seen as the face of women's tennis these days," Naomi replied that she didn't feel that way. "As long as Serena's here, I think she's the face of women's tennis," Naomi said. After the two had played their Adelaide exhibition, Naomi posted a photo the next day with the caption "Yesterday with the queen [crown emoji]," also uploading her 2014 selfie with Serena in Stanford for good measure. "I could not stop smiling that day."

It was the second time Naomi had played a pre–Australian Open exhibition with Serena in as many years; the previous time, Naomi had posted a photo of the two of them sitting together on a bench with the caption "me and my mom lol." When a commenter said it was a "bit improper" to call Serena that, Naomi responded. "I literally would not be here without her. If that's not some definition of mom idk what is. But sure, get offended by my internet slang I guess." Serena, also, seemed to take the remark in stride. "I have always had some sort of admiration for her, because I met her when she was super, super young," Serena said when asked about the comment. "It was really cool to see her grow from that age to No. 1 and multi–Grand Slam champion. I thought the picture was cute, so I felt like I should like it and comment on it. Definitely not the mom, though. Definitely more or less . . . cousin?

"I don't know how Olympia would feel about that," Serena added, laughing. "She would love to have her as a sister, though. That would be really cool. She could be Olympia's sister."

Though she had come within one match four times, Serena hadn't won a major since giving birth to Olympia nearly three and a half years earlier. Serena was thirty-eight years old, and time was undoubtedly running out, but she had looked better than she had in years heading into her match against Naomi in the semifinals. Serena looked fitter at the 2021 Australian Open than she had since going on maternity leave, both with how she filled out her Flo-Jo–inspired Nike catsuit and how she had been able to run down balls in her 6–3, 6–3 demolition of second-ranked Simona Halep in the quarterfinals. After winning several long rallies against Halep, Serena was asked when the last time was that she had felt she could win those sorts of long rallies. "It's definitely been a minute, it's been a long minute," Serena said, smiling. "I think 19 . . . 1926, the summer of 1926, I think, was the last time I felt that."

But as good as Serena had felt, Naomi felt better, and confidence in her camp was high. "We all felt that Naomi was the better player at that time," Fissette told me. "We all felt like the match was in Naomi's hands; it was not in Serena's hands."

More than his major wins, Fissette's calling card as a coach was his success against Serena. Since he had first coached Kim Clijsters to a win over Serena at the 2009 U.S. Open, Fissette had coached four more different players—Sabine Lisicki, Simona Halep, Victoria Azarenka, Angelique Kerber—to victories over Serena, giving Fissette more wins than any individual on-court opponent had earned against Serena in that time frame. Fissette's tactics for how to beat Serena, especially in this late stage of her career, were clear. "Going to the forehand much more, especially on bigger moments," he said. "Pretty simple: on defense, go long in the middle so she has to create a little bit more distance where she's not that light-footed anymore; on offense, you try to push her more in the forehand, but then make her make a run to the other side."

But more than the Xs and Os, the biggest factor in this match between Naomi and Serena seemed to be in the players' mindsets: from early on in the match, Serena didn't look like she believed she could win. "It was not the Serena that came on the court like 'I'm the best player and over my dead body you're going to win and I have zero doubt I'm going to win this match,'" Fissette said. "It was Serena realizing like, 'Okay, I'm not unbeatable anymore. If someone like Naomi plays her best level, she's better than me.'"

Serena got off to a 2–0 lead in the first set and had a break point for 3–0, only for Naomi to reel off five straight games to take a 5–2 lead.

Serena grew louder, grunting and shouting, but Naomi took the first set 6–3. The two were playing similar styles, but Naomi was simply doing it better. It was a scratchy set, statistically—both women hit more unforced errors than winners—but Naomi had played her best on the most important points. As Naomi broke in the opening game to take an early lead in the second set, Serena grew more emotive and expressive during and after points. There were only a few thousand fans in attendance in Rod Laver Arena—Melbourne had just finished a short lockdown after a spate of positive cases—but the small number was resoundingly urging Serena to get back in the match. It seemed to work briefly—Naomi played a poor game, double-faulting three times, and Serena broke back to level the second set at 4–4. But just as quickly as Serena had leveled the set, Naomi tilted it steeply back in her direction, breaking at love with three backhand winners.

Naomi served for the match up 6–3, 5–4 and started with an ace. Two more unreturned serves put her up 40–0. On Naomi's first match point, Serena netted a backhand, and the match was over, 6–3, 6–4. Naomi, the winner, came to the net and Serena, the loser, reached out to give her a one-armed embrace—as much contact as ever happened in the pandemic era, where racquet taps were the standard net greeting. Naomi bowed her head repeatedly as she encountered Serena at the net. "It's always an honor to play her," Naomi said in her on-court interview. "Just to be on the court playing against her, for me, is a dream."

No one, in dreams or reality, had been so successful against Serena. The semifinal win improved Naomi's record against Serena to 2–0 at majors and 3–1 overall. Naomi was one of only two players who had faced Serena at least three times and had a winning head-to-head record against her; the other was Arantxa Sánchez-Vicario, who had scored three of her four wins against Serena before she turned seventeen (and then Serena won their last three matches in straight sets before Sánchez-Vicario retired). "It took two decades, but in Osaka, women's tennis may finally feature a star who is legitimately better than Serena—albeit a Serena who is far past her prime," wrote tennis analyst Jeff Sackmann.

· · · · · · · ·

As decisive as the match had been, the knockout seemed most apparent as Serena walked off the court. Serena normally exited posthaste after losses, but on this day she stopped as she was walking off the court. She waved to the cheering crowd, put her hand over her heart, and then waved again.

Serena came to her press conference more quickly than usual, still visibly processing the defeat. When asked to explain the result, Serena reverted to the excuses she had used often early in her career to minimize losses, focusing on her own mistakes rather than her opponent's success. "The difference today was errors," she said. "I made so many errors today . . . Big error day for me today."

Karen Crouse of *The New York Times* asked Serena the pressing question: What had her poignant, hand-on-heart exit from the court meant? "Um, I don't know," Serena said. "The Aussie crowd is so amazing, so it was nice to see."

"Some people wondered if you were almost saying farewell," Crouse followed up.

Serena smiled and looked down. "Um, I don't know," she said. "If I ever say farewell, I wouldn't tell anyone." Serena laughed again, but as the next question was asked, her eyes began to well up, and she took a sip of water. "I don't know," she said to a question about her errors, shaking her head as the tears slipped from her eyes. "I'm done," she said, standing up and walking off the podium.

When Crouse asked Naomi in her later press conference how much it meant to have gotten to play Serena because "there's no telling how much longer Serena will play," Naomi seemed taken aback by the obvious insinuation.

"It's kind of sad when you say it like that," Naomi said. "Because, for me, I want her to play forever—that's the little kid in me. But, yeah . . ."

It would be another two and a half years before her retirement was official, but her loss to Naomi in the 2021 Australian Open semifinals had effectively ended Serena Williams's decades-long run as a contender for major titles.

Serena wouldn't ever return to the Australian Open.

Serena wouldn't ever return to a Slam semifinal.

Serena wouldn't ever play Naomi Osaka again.

. . . .

One of the toughest things for Serena in the late stages of her career had been closing out big tournaments. Until the 2015 U.S. Open, Serena had made it to the semifinals of a major twenty-eight times and had won the title on twenty-one of those occasions, a staggeringly good 75 percent conversion rate. But starting with her shocking loss to Roberta Vinci in the 2015 U.S. Open semifinals, Serena made it to twelve major semifinals and only left with the trophy twice, her conversion rate plummeting to 16.7 percent.

Naomi, in her first years on tour, had trended in the complete opposite direction. In the four times she had made the quarterfinals of a major, she had never lost a match for the rest of the tournament. "She would say, 'Oh, I'm in the quarters now, so it's definitely worth it to deliver more effort today,'" Fissette told me. "That's something she would say before a match."

Naomi's focus peaked at the final. "I have this mentality that people don't remember the runners-up," she said after winning her semifinal. "You might, but the winner's name is the one that's engraved. I think I fight the hardest in the finals. I think that's where you sort of set yourself apart."

After beating Serena in a blockbuster semifinal, the final matchup was something of an anticlimax. For the first time in her four major finals, Naomi was the more accomplished player as she faced Jennifer Brady, the powerful American who had been one of the best players on tour since the sport had resumed from the pandemic stoppage, including a run to the semifinals of the U.S. Open, where she had given Naomi all she could handle in a three-set tussle.

But when they met again five months later, the drama was never nearly as high. Naomi's hold on the match seemed secure throughout, though the score remained close through the opening games. Brady had a chance to take control of the first set with Naomi serving at 4–4 and earning a break point with a flick lob over Naomi's head. But Naomi saved it with a forehand crosscourt that she yanked into the far corner, past an outstretched Brady, staving off the challenge. In the next game, Brady had a 40-15 lead but made a string of four costly errors to hand Naomi the set. Naomi kept rolling from there, reeling off six straight games in total to extend her lead to 6–4, 4–0. Brady began swinging more freely, taking risks that landed inside the lines, but her comeback fell far short: Naomi maintained her lead and closed out the match for a 6–4, 6–3 win, clinching her fourth major title. When Brady's return sailed long on the first championship point after an hour and seventeen minutes, Naomi smiled and bounced up and down as the ball landed long, then waved to the thousands in attendance after meeting Brady at the net.

When it came time to accept the Daphne Akhurst Memorial Cup for a second time, Naomi was far more comfortable at the microphone than two years before, speaking fluently for nearly three minutes, congratulating Brady and thanking her team, fans in attendance, and the tournament staff. Naomi also deftly acknowledged the unique mid-pandemic circumstances of the embattled tournament, the holding of which had been controversial amid Melbourne's lockdowns. "Thank you for opening your hearts and your arms towards us," Naomi said. "For sure I feel like playing a Grand Slam right now is a super privilege, and it's something that I won't take for granted, so thank you for this opportunity." As Naomi spoke, Tennis Australia's chairman Jayne Hrdlicka nodded appreciatively behind her, clearly thrilled that her champion was hitting all the right marks during the ceremony, too.[*]

---

[*] Naomi's only verbal misstep came right at the very beginning of her remarks, when she turned to Brady with a sudden query.

"Do you like to be called Jenny or Jennifer?" Naomi asked.

"Jenny," Brady replied with a smile.

"Okay. Firstly I want to congrat Jennifer," Naomi continued.

· · · · · · ·

Naomi was one of only three men and women to win their first four major finals in the Open Era, joining Roger Federer and Monica Seles. Further, what she had done going undefeated once reaching major quarterfinals and beyond in her career—a 12–0 record—was completely unprecedented.

On his analytics website Tennis Abstract, Jeff Sackmann deemed Naomi's overall record of 16–2 from the fourth round and beyond in majors mind-bogglingly remarkable. "Had Osaka performed at her expected level for each of her eighteen second-week matches, we'd expect her to have won 10.7 of them," Sackmann wrote. "Instead, she won 16. The probability that she would have won 16 or more of the 18 matches is approximately 1 in 200. Either the model is selling her short, or she's playing in a way that breaks the model." Part of the reason why Naomi was breaking Sackmann's model, of course, was that she had been far more beatable when playing somewhere that wasn't the business end of a major, bringing down her predictive ratings. But when the stakes were highest, Naomi's ability to elevate was otherworldly and unprecedented. Even comparing her to legends of the game whose games also peaked in the biggest moments, including Serena and Monica Seles, "the difference between Osaka's levels is on another planet," Sackmann wrote.

· · · · · · ·

That Naomi's fourth major final wasn't particularly memorable or a classic almost seemed to count in her favor among pundits: Naomi was winning majors so regularly now, adding to her haul was more routine—daresay mundane—than extraordinary by this point.

The fourth major title Naomi tallied in her column put her behind only Serena and Venus among active players in women's tennis, and ahead of all active men's players besides Roger Federer, Rafael Nadal, and Novak Djoković. Talk now shifted to how many Naomi could end up with by the end of her career. Mats Wilander, himself a seven-time major winner in the 1980s, declared that Naomi would soar past his haul. "I think she has ten in her, minimum, I really do," Wilander said on Eurosport. He acknowledged that Naomi hadn't yet shown her comfort on clay or grass but said he considered her unflappability to be her greatest asset. "There's no way you can disturb her," Wilander said. "You just see the calm victory celebrations. That tells me something: she was expecting to win and she is going to win a lot more."

* * * * * * *

"There's something double-edged about the concept," Tom Ewing wrote of imperial phases in *Pitchfork*. "It holds a mix of world-conquering swagger and inevitable obsolescence. What do we know about emperors? That they end up naked: The phase always ends."

In a 2023 interview, Naomi listed the aftermath of the 2021 Australian Open as her third and most difficult moment of post-success depression. "It got to a point after I won the Australian Open for the second time," Naomi said. "I'm like, I need to do something about it because I don't want to keep living this way."

But before Naomi's hold on the crown would tremble, another era would come to an end: for the first time in Naomi's life, she would become the only Osaka sister playing tennis.

THIRTY-ONE

A Journey Which She Didn't Enjoy Ultimately

While Naomi was in Australia, Mari had been in a small town near the Alabama-Georgia border for a tournament on the minor league ITF Pro Circuit.

While tournaments with lucrative television contracts had resumed months earlier, lower-level events had been scarce since the pandemic began, and players ranked outside the Top 200 had few opportunities to compete. Mari hadn't played a tournament in ten months since the pandemic began; with rankings largely frozen due to the pandemic, she was ranked 333rd, right about where she had been before. Mari's goals, she told me, had become more modest over time. "I always told myself I would be No. 1 or win a Grand Slam," she said of her original career goals. "For me, that was success. Probably not the healthiest way to push yourself . . . I started setting my goals lower and lower progressively as the years went on. At a certain point my goal was just to get in the qualifying of a Grand Slam [about 230th]. I didn't have the ranking for it, and I wasn't going to be satisfied with just qualifying, so that thought was definitely a little depressing at the time."

Mari told me that Naomi's success didn't increase the pressure she felt. "I only felt proud of her," Mari said. "I never felt any pressure from her success, honestly. I only felt pressure from myself after years of trying to do something and constantly failing. I think she could be No. 1,000 in the world and I would still have felt this way. I played for my family to be in a better situation, not myself. That was the biggest obstacle I didn't overcome . . . Especially during the Covid quarantine moments, I thought that any other field I go into would help my family more than tennis does."

Mari missed the main draw in Georgia by several spots, so her run at the tournament began in the qualifying draw. Her first qualifying match was on the afternoon of Monday, January 25, 2021, on indoor court 5 at the Berry College indoor tennis center. Her opponent was Sarah Hamner, an unranked eighteen-year-old who had been recruited to play at the University of South Carolina. Hamner, who hadn't played a professional match in more than a year, beat Mari in straight sets, 7–6(3), 6–4. When Mari picked up her first prize money check in ten months, it was for just $142.

• • • • • • • •

Unlike a team sport, where an athlete's career can effectively end when no team signs them to a contract, a tennis player can keep entering tournaments as long as their body, mind, heart, and wallet are able. After losing in her long-awaited return to competition, Mari took stock of her tennis career.

"My whole life, when I played, I was always thinking, 'Am I enjoying this? Am I not?'" Mari said in *Racquet* months later. "Because I never really had the choice to actually choose to play . . . After Covid, I thought that I was going to finally enjoy my next match. I had some excitement for playing the tournament. But then when I played, I thought, 'I don't want to be here.' Even though I hadn't played for all that time. And then from that match, I knew there's no way in the future . . . I probably would never be able to enjoy playing competitively."

Mari decided to retire from tennis. She was twenty-four years old.

The "hardest part," Mari said, was telling her parents of her decision; she said they were "understanding," but urged her to take time to consider before making it official. "That's what my dad told me to do," Mari said. "He was like, 'Well, you should let it settle. And in your mind, have peace with it first. And then tell everybody.'"

In her interview with *Racquet* conducted by the artist Honor Titus, Mari was asked what had been her "proudest accomplishment in tennis"; she paused for a long time before answering. "Maybe this is part of why I quit, because I don't really feel like I accomplished anything, to be honest," she said. "I can't even think of one thing that I'm proud of that I did . . . It was never good enough, really. I'm sorry . . . I'm being a Debbie Downer right now."

· · · · · · · ·

Naomi said that Mari's decision was "a sad moment for our entire family," but one that she saw coming. Tamaki later wrote that she "couldn't help but feel sorry for" Mari, a feeling that was mixed with a relief that Mari had retired before suffering a serious injury. Still, Tamaki wrote, she sensed guilt in her elder daughter. "Mari must have thought, 'If I stop playing tennis, it will be bad for my father and mother,'" Tamaki wrote in *Through the Tunnel.* "'Even though my parents risked their lives, pouring money, time, and passion into their tennis, and even though I had been playing tennis since I was little, I quit before I could even make it to the Grand Slams.' It seems that she was tormented by the thought." Tamaki said that she worked to assure Mari that there was more to look forward to, that tennis had merely been the "first chapter" of her life.

Mari talked about her tennis career as if it had been an abject failure—and, harshly, it could be considered so: she had failed to earn a viable income by playing tennis despite dedicating her entire childhood to it; if it hadn't been for her sister's successes, the family's sacrifices would have been in vain. Others were more generous. Darren Cahill, the coach who had been won over by Mari's work ethic and attitude during Naomi's Adidas audition seven years earlier, emphasized the positives of the heights she did reach in career. "There are millions of people who would love to be the 280th best tennis player in the world," Cahill said, mentioning Mari's career-high ranking. "She accomplished what most people haven't been able to accomplish. But, you know, Naomi's always been that level above."

. . . .

On March 9, 2021, six weeks after her last match and about a month after talking to her parents, Mari Osaka posted a photo of a blue sky above a calm blue sea on her Instagram. "I am retired from playing tennis," Mari announced in the caption. "It was a journey which I didn't enjoy ultimately but I'm grateful for all the memories and support I've gained and received over the years from the sport. I'm moving on now so you can look forward to new fun projects upcoming in the future."

The retirement of a player who had never broken into the world's Top 250 would rarely gain much notice outside of their family and friends. But because of Mari's proximity to Naomi, her decision was widely covered across mainstream media, with outlets from *Sports Illustrated* to *People* to *TMZ* all writing news articles about her announcement.

While *Yahoo! News* called Mari's post a "heartbreaking announcement," others savored the unusual bluntness with which Mari had assessed her career. *The Body Serve Podcast*'s hosts, Jonathan Newman and James Rogers, titled their next episode "A Journey Which I Didn't Enjoy Ultimately," quoting what Newman called "one of the best phrasings that I've heard in forever" from Mari's statement.

"It's unusual to see that type of candor in a retirement statement," Rogers concurred. "It's a good lesson to learn how to make clean breaks with things—with parts of your life or jobs you've had—that you ultimately didn't enjoy. Luckily for Mari, she discovered this at age twenty-four. She's super young . . . She has her whole life ahead of her. Go do something you do enjoy!"

. . . .

Mari moved from Florida to Los Angeles soon after she retired, though not into her sister's mansion; she got an apartment of her own downtown, which she soon began turning into the studio for her increasingly busy art career. Mari, who had been a Venus fan just as Naomi had been a Serena fan, had thought she could follow in Venus's footsteps and become a designer while playing tennis. Even before Mari retired, Naomi had begun looping her into projects as a designer and illustrator; now that she had officially hung up her racquet, Mari would be getting a lot more work.

"I always told myself if I was able to give back to my family in the way that they've given so many things up for me, that's something that I think is the most important part," Naomi said "So for me, I clearly wouldn't be here without my sister. She's the person that pushed me when we were little. I had no drive at all . . . That's why I go to her for most of my projects. She helps me out a lot. That's the least that I can do to repay her."

Often, the images Mari was commissioned to draw were of her sister. She drew pictures of Naomi to accompany profiles in *GQ Japan* and *Esquire*. She also consulted on a manga series, *Naomi Unrivaled*, that took pains to depict Naomi with a more accurate skin tone than the Nissin ad from nearly two years earlier.

In April 2021, one of the first collections Mari released after her retirement was a set of NFTs (non-fungible tokens): six works titled "The Colors of Naomi Osaka." According to the auction website, the collection reportedly sold for a total of nearly $600,000, all to anonymous bidders.

Mari's most prominent work was far more tangible: she painted the original watercolor designs for the dress Naomi wore on the 2021 Met Gala red carpet, drawing on both Haitian and Japanese traditions to fit the prompt of "American," which was the theme for that year's gala. "It's a celebration of cultures, like America itself, a melting pot of so many special and unique elements," Mari told *Vogue*. The finished product was a collaboration between Mari and Nicolas Ghesquière, the women's creative director for Louis Vuitton. It centered on a corseted dress made from a blue and purple jacquard. The look was completed with a red belt like the obi worn around kimonos, and a ruffled black cape made of nearly 70 meters of silk and leather satin meant to evoke the ruffles of a Haitian *quadrille* dress.

Mari also borrowed from Japanese and Haitian culture to create virtual fashions, too: she designed two *Fortnite* skins* released in early 2022 based on her sister and their shared heritages: one a pink-haired Harajuku-style princess and the other a voodoo-inspired "Dark Priestess," both of whom wield racquet-shaped weapons and wear necklaces made of tennis balls. She designed real racquets soon after: in the summer of 2022, Mari's gold and purple dragons were used on a new signature racquet by Yonex, the OSAKA EZONE 98. Days after that launch, Mari teamed with the brand Market and Naomi's agents to sell a collection at a pop-up shop in Lower Manhattan, coinciding with the 2022 U.S. Open.

· · · · · · ·

The connections she had through Naomi opened numerous doors that other upstart artists would dream of unlocking so early in their careers, but Mari also wanted to prove to herself that she could earn her own success. So, unsolicited, she entered the Geisai competition organized by acclaimed Japanese artist Takashi Murakami in the summer of 2022. To her immense gratification, she was invited to show her art at the exhibition hall in Tokyo. "Geisai was something that I decided to do and chase on my own," Mari told me. "So it felt like it was my personal accomplishment." She sold her first painting there and met Murakami.

Mari didn't win in the competition but said Murakami gave her "very important advice" when they met that she considered a prize in itself. "He told me that, even now, he's still learning," Mari recounted weeks later. "Like even now, he's still practicing every day. And that to me was kind of insane. Like, he doesn't need to practice, he makes millions and millions! But just the mindset of learning, I think, is just so extremely important, so that you never really think that you're done, you know?" Mari has continued learning and experimenting with her art, exploring mediums from glass etching to tattooing.

One day in the summer of 2022, Mari posted a picture of artwork in

---

* The *Fortnite* characters were officially licensed Naomi Osaka avatars, unlike the knockoff character "Niki Kyoto," which appeared in Miniclip's mobile tennis game in 2023.

progress on her Instastory, as she often did. This one, however, was accompanied by a long, reflective comment. "Because of the years I spent doing something I didn't really like, now that work is stuff I actually like doing, I like to spend my relaxing moments working," Mari wrote. "It actually stresses me out when I'm not working when it was the complete opposite before. I just think that was a super weird realization I had at the moment and wanted to share for the people who are currently procrastinating from their jobs, or dreading the thought of having to work. Maybe you aren't lazy or unmotivated, you just don't like what you're doing . . . and there is always something else for you out there."

Mari finished her thought on a second Instastory slide; this time the background was completely black and the message was equally stark. "Because I didn't like tennis and it was such an important, all-encompassing part of my life, it ended up with me really hating my life in general," Mari wrote. "Don't get to the point that I got to."

THIRTY-TWO

Sliding

To try to understand everything that happened with Naomi Osaka during the clay court season of May 2021, it could help to first briefly glance back two years earlier.

Naomi, winner of the two previous majors and ranked No. 1, was having a promising clay court season in the spring of 2019. She had compiled a 7–1 record on the red European clay, reaching the semifinals in Stuttgart (withdrawing before her semifinal with an abdominal injury), the quarterfinals in Madrid (losing to frequent nemesis Belinda Bencic), and winning two matches in Rome to reach the quarterfinals of the Italian Open, showing that her immense talent could indeed shine through on the dusty, slower surface.

Minutes before she was set to walk onto a practice court in Rome to warm up for her quarterfinal, Naomi looked at her physiotherapist Natsuko "Nana" Mogi and started laughing. "When I'm nervous, I start laughing," Naomi said after. What Naomi was nervous to tell Mogi and the rest of her team was that her right hand had become swollen and stiff overnight. "'I can't move my thumb and I'm not sure if I can grip my racquet, so I'm not sure if I can play my match'—I'm laughing while I'm saying this," Naomi recounted. "So I think I kind of, like, completely sabotaged Nana just now, because I'm supposed to tell her even if I feel a little pain in any way, like early in the morning or whatever. I tried to sweep it under the rug every hour. I was thinking it was going to get better; then, it didn't."

Without adequate time for possible treatment to her injury, Naomi withdrew from the match. She took full responsibility for how her tournament had ended. "I mean, I'm going to be honest: this was completely my fault," she said. "Because I'm the type of person that sort of sweeps something under the rug until it gets extremely bad."

• • • • • • • •

Naomi Osaka was doing very, very well in early 2021, at least on paper. She hadn't lost a single match since the onset of the pandemic more than a year earlier, racking up a streak of wins that had included her third and fourth major titles at the U.S. Open and Australian Open. When Naomi won her fourth-round match at the 2021 Miami Open, it was her twenty-third match win in a row.

Naomi was racking up wins off the court, too, in the form of unprecedented commercial earnings. A *New York Times* article titled "How Naomi Osaka Became Everyone's Favorite Spokesmodel"—published not in the Sports section but in the front of Thursday Styles—did not exaggerate: when Sportico would publish its next ranking of the world's highest-paid female athletes, Naomi's endorsement income would be a record-shattering $50 million—breaking the record she had previously held herself—by far the most ever for any female athlete. Cindy Gallop, a brand consultant quoted in the *Times* piece, called Naomi "the perfect storm" of factors brands wanted in 2021. "She's a spectacular athlete; she has a strong sense of social justice, she's prepared to speak her mind," Gallop said. "Thirdly, she's female, and fourthly, she's not White. I hate, loathe, and detest terms like this, but she is, in quotes, 'diverse.' She ticks every box. You can practically hear the brand managers thinking: 'She is absolutely the right person to sponsor, right now.'"

A brand partnering with Naomi could not only sell products; it could signal virtues (which would then sell products, they hoped). As brands faced scrutiny for their disproportionately old, White, and male boards, Naomi was the perfect antidote, with social justice bona fides to boot. Embattled brands like lingerie maker Victoria's Secret, which signed Naomi in

2021, were especially eager to harness symbolic power to salvage their brands, particularly with Gen-Z consumers.

Now that Naomi was the answer to more and more brands' calculations, the equations in her portfolio were all addition and multiplication. In addition to the Japanese sponsors Naomi had acquired when she started winning major titles, Naomi was now wanted worldwide. She could be covered head to toe by American and global brands that sponsored her: on her ears there were Beats by Dre headphones; on her wrist was a TAG Heuer watch; on her legs were Levi's jeans; over her shoulder was the strap of a Louis Vuitton purse that carried her Mastercard; covering her swimsuit areas there were Frankies Bikinis. When she came off court in her sweaty Nike clothes with the logo patch from HR software company Workday, she could use Hyperice recovery equipment and refuel by washing down her Sweetgreen salad with a Bodyarmor drink. Even when undressed, Naomi could still be wearing Kinlò, the skincare product line she co-created that emphasized sun protection for "melanin-rich" skin. Her business footprint in sports extended beyond tennis: she took a small ownership stake in the North Carolina Courage, a National Women's Soccer League team from Cordae's birth state. Steve Malik, the team's primary owner, told me Naomi fit into the ownership group because she "aligned on core values" with the two-time league champions. "Women's soccer and the Courage are all about gender equity and a number of other social missions," he said. "And then, for us as a franchise, winning."*

Naomi was being showered not only with cash and prizes, but with adulation and celebration. In March, Naomi first heard—though it was a closely kept secret until the moment it happened—that she would be given the honor of lighting the cauldron at the opening ceremony of the rescheduled Tokyo Olympics in August, a prestigious role previously given to the likes of national heroes such as Muhammad Ali in Atlanta and Wayne Gretzky in Vancouver.

---

* Unusually, Naomi did not attend a Courage game during her first three seasons as a team owner, but she has worn their jersey at tournaments sometimes.

It wasn't only sporting events clamoring for Naomi: in early May, Naomi was announced as one of the hosts of that year's Met Gala, one of a quartet of young luminaries chosen for the honor. Naomi would be one of the faces of the star-studded September soiree alongside the singer Billie Eilish, the actor Timothée Chalamet, and the poet Amanda Gorman. Also in early May, Naomi was named the Laureus World Sports Award's Sportswoman of the Year for 2020, having won the similar honors awarded by the Associated Press and *Sports Illustrated* months earlier. The Netflix documentary *Naomi Osaka*, directed by Oscar nominee Garrett Bradley, was slated for a July release.

. . . .

But between the shiny new honors—far clearer with the benefit of hindsight—there were also visible signs of brewing trouble. After Naomi's twenty-third consecutive win, a routine 6–3, 6–3 victory over Elise Mertens, a reporter in Naomi's post-match press conference asked Naomi about closing in on retaking the No. 1 ranking from Ash Barty, who had been holding on to the top spot despite Naomi's recent dominance because of adjustments made to the rankings calculations during the pandemic. Naomi said she hadn't been focused on the rankings or tracking what she would need to do to regain the top spot.* "Like, I understand how important it is and what an honor it would be to be No. 1, but for me, I realize that my mind doesn't function well if I keep thinking about all the things that could be," Naomi said. "So right now I'm just thinking that I'm playing this tournament. Every round that I play is against a really tough opponent."

When Naomi took the court again two days later for her quarterfinal in Miami, she got drubbed: 25th-ranked Maria Sakkari blanked her in the first set, then hung on for a 6–0, 6–4 win, dealing Naomi her first defeat in more than a year. As she tried to explain the loss, Naomi revealed that

---

* Naomi would have regained the No. 1 ranking in Miami if she had won the tournament and Barty didn't reach the final. Barty would, in fact, go on to win the tournament.

the pressure she felt on court had been planted in her by the seemingly innocuous question about the rankings she had been asked two days earlier.

"The last time I was in this seat I wasn't really thinking at all about rankings, but someone asked me that question, so then I did start to ponder about it a lot," Naomi said. "So maybe, unwillingly, that put pressure on myself. But I feel like even if it did, I should be able to rise above that, you know? I'm going to be asked various questions in the future, anyway, so this is definitely something that shouldn't bother me as much as it did."

Naomi's team had also noticed a shift in her that week, though they read it foremost as a drop-off in motivation. "Miami was a bit like she wasn't really there," Fissette told me. But he and the rest of her team thought there was no major cause for concern. "I mean, we were all hoping that was, like, just a onetime motivation problem," he said.

When Naomi described the loss later, however, she described it less of a shortage and more of an overload. "I don't know how to describe it," she said, "but I felt like everything was sort of loud in my head."

· · · · · · ·

A lot of the noise in Naomi's head was the echoing of Japanese cheers that had rung out at the Buenos Aires Hilton eight years earlier, when the International Olympic Committee chose Tokyo to host the 2020 Summer Olympics over competing bids from Istanbul and Madrid. Only two years earlier, Japan had been rocked seismologically and psychologically by an earthquake and tsunami that killed nearly 20,000 people and caused a nuclear accident at the Fukushima Daiichi nuclear power plant. Japan jubilated over its winning bid, a triumph that restored stability and confidence in the country both domestically and abroad.

Sponsors and media alike had seen Naomi as a potential Olympian from the moment she came on the scene; Naomi was asked about playing the Tokyo Olympics during her very first major main draw appearance, the 2016 Australian Open, when she was still an eighteen-year-old ranked outside the Top 100.

The concurrence of Naomi's career with an Olympics in Japan—the country's first Summer Olympics since 1964—was a coincidence that proved a massive boon to Naomi's earnings. As corporations sought to align themselves with the surest bets on that ultimate sporting stage, Japanese sponsors lined up to sign her—first in a trickle in 2016, then in a deluge once she started winning majors. Naomi was frequently dubbed the unofficial "face of the Tokyo Olympics" for both her visibility in media and her viability as a medalist. Major Olympic sponsors, from Airbnb to Panasonic, signed Naomi as the face they wanted next to their logos, both for her winning and her activist spirit. The corporations spoke in far vaguer terms than she did, of course, not explicitly endorsing her causes like defunding the police. "We hold a strong common belief with Naomi's attitude toward society and her value system," Panasonic executive Yoshihiro Mori said in a presentation announcing their partnership that focused on corporate social responsibility. "Panasonic also has an ardent wish to achieve an ideal world."

The world in 2020, however, was far from the ideal, which Japan had hoped to showcase when it won the right to host the Games of the XXXII Olympiad and spent more than $20 billion to stage them. Originally scheduled to be held in the summer of 2020, the games were postponed by a year due to the Covid-19 pandemic, adding another full year for pressure to build on would-be Tokyo Olympic stars like Naomi and Simone Biles. These would be the oddest Olympics: literally the only ones ever held in an odd-numbered year, though the incongruous "Tokyo 2020" branding remained in 2021.

Because of circumstances both within and beyond the control of organizers, the Tokyo Olympics became perhaps the least popular edition of the games before they even began. The Olympics felt increasingly discordant with the priorities of the people as residents of Tokyo, Osaka, and other major metropolitan areas in Japan were under lockdowns. While winning the Olympics had been a triumph for the Japanese government, keeping them was a liability: a May 2021 poll by *The Asahi Shimbun* showed that a staggering 83 percent of respondents said that the Olympics should be postponed or scrapped. In May 2021, a group of six thousand primary-care doctors in Tokyo wrote to Japanese prime minister Yoshihide Suga urging that the Olympics be canceled.

That same month, Japanese media asked Naomi if she thought the Olympics should be canceled. "Of course I would say I want the Olympics to happen, because I'm an athlete and that's sort of what I have been waiting for my entire life," she said. "But I think that there is so much important stuff going on . . . I feel like if it's putting people at risk and if it's making people very uncomfortable, then it definitely should be a discussion."

Tricky questions like that had become common for Naomi in the Olympic buildup: as public support eroded, being the "face" of these Olympics had become a perilous perch for Naomi, worsened by unforced errors within Olympic leadership. Yoshiro Mori, the eighty-three-year-old chairman of the Tokyo 2020 organizing committee and a former prime minister of Japan, ignited furor in February 2021 by saying that women talked too much at board meetings. In Japan, where women are underrepresented in leadership roles in both business and government, the remarks drew outrage.

Naomi was asked her thoughts on Mori's remarks on the eve of the Australian Open. Did she think he should resign? Naomi seemed taken aback to be asked to render such a verdict. "I'm a tennis player," she responded. "For me, I feel like—hmm, wow, what an interesting subject matter to be thrown. Do I think he should resign? I think that someone that makes comments like that, they need to have more knowledge on the thing that they're talking about. I feel like that was a really ignorant statement to make." Sure enough, after the superstar had weighed in, coverage of the growing controversy put Naomi's assessment of "really ignorant" near the top. Mori resigned days later and was replaced by Seiko Hashimoto, a female cabinet minister.

The Olympics, and everything around them, wouldn't be incidental to Naomi's anxiety peaking during the clay court season. "This year it seems a bit chaotic, especially with the Olympics coming for me," she said in May

2021. "I feel like it's a really important time; I would have loved to be at home for more."

. . . .

To quiet the noise, Naomi kept her tournament schedule increasingly minimal for a young, uninjured player. Instead of playing either of the midsize clay court events in Charleston and Stuttgart in 2021—which might've been an obvious choice to improve her readiness for the French Open, considering she had missed the entire 2020 clay swing—Naomi took nearly a month off the tour, returning for the mandatory tournament in Madrid. When she explained her scheduling decision in Madrid, Naomi focused on a need to quell her racing thoughts. "Actually after Miami I took, like, a bit of a break because I felt like—I don't know—I needed to slow my mind down a little bit," she said.

Fissette had been frustrated by their preparations for the clay court season, which Naomi had decided to hold at home in Los Angeles, where there was no red clay comparable to the conditions in Europe. Naomi came to Madrid, as Fissette described it, "definitely not ready to perform her best." After winning her first round against 79th-ranked Misaki Doi, the second-best Japanese player, Naomi lost 6–4, 3–6, 6–1 in the second round to 20th-ranked Karolína Muchová.

A loss to Muchová, a crafty Czech with much more experience on European clay who would reach the 2023 French Open final, was hardly disastrous. What was of concern to Fissette, however, was that he sensed a lack of commitment from Naomi as the team began their preparations in Rome. "I had some discussions with her, because I was feeling that she was doing what we asked her to do but not really with her heart on the court," he said. The talk got through to Naomi, it seemed: "So then suddenly, like two days before her first match, it was much better," he said.

After receiving a first-round bye, Naomi's first match in Rome was a second-round match against 31st-ranked Jessica Pegula, an American whose results had been consistently improving that season. The atmosphere was eerily quiet: for the first time in months, due to pandemic restrictions in Rome, Naomi was playing a match without fans in attendance. It was a particularly surreal venue for an empty match: the second-round match was being played on the court of Stadio Pietrangeli, the sunken marble stadium that had been built in grand Roman style by Benito Mussolini's Fascist regime. Pietrangeli is usually known for having one of the liveliest atmospheres on tour, but on this day the humans in attendance—the players, officials, ball kids, and respective coaching teams—were roughly equal in number to the eighteen towering marble statues of nude athletes that circled the perimeter of the court.

Naomi had played well without fans before, of course, particularly during her success in New York the year before, and she began this match in strong form. "Osaka has started like a train out here," commentator Anna Smith said as Naomi raced out to a 3–0 lead in just eight minutes. "You can already tell how confident she is and how well she's timing the ball . . . She just makes it look so effortless, doesn't she?" But Pegula steadied, leveling the first set 3–3, and the match changed tracks. "The No. 2 seed Naomi Osaka started like a train," echoed broadcaster Tim White, "but she may be in danger of being derailed a little here by Jessica Pegula." Naomi earned a set point on Pegula's serve at 4–5, but missed a forehand into the open court. After a strange moment of confusion in the next game—Naomi thought that a tiebreak had begun at 5–5 instead of 6–6—Naomi earned two more set points at 5–6. But Pegula's strong shots saved both of those as well, and the first set went into a tiebreak. Naomi had been the better player in the match to that point, winning forty-three points to Pegula's thirty-seven, but the quirks of the tennis scoring system left it all level.

When Pegula pulled ahead in the tiebreak, taking a 5-2 lead on Naomi's backhand into the net, Naomi suddenly snapped, angrily whacking her racquet into the red clay three times. "You can see those set points that she didn't take are playing on her mind," Smith said. "It's not too often that we see Osaka let fly with the racquet, but the frustration is just boiling over." After replacing her racquet, Naomi lost the tiebreak 7-2, then sat on her chair between sets with a towel draped over her head, occasionally wiping her eyes.

When I asked her about the match nearly a year later, Naomi's first response was succinct: "Yikes," she said. "So, I got really emotional for some reason. I think I just had a lot of pressure on me because I wanted to do well on the clay. So, yeah, I was stressing myself out. I knew that I had a chance in the first set, but for some reason I did something wrong, and then it just went superfast from there. I know I lost the second set quite easily."

Indeed, after the fifty-eight-minute first set, the second set took less than half as long: Pegula won it 6–2 in twenty-nine minutes. But rather than any exceptional play by the underdog, the story of the match was Naomi's poor play—"Oh dear, oh dear, oh dear," White said after Naomi's overhead missed wildly. "It sums it up for Naomi Osaka, who is facing a real mountain now. She literally throws away her serve. Scarcely can you have seen that in the Japanese player's career." More than the errant shot, the concern centered on Naomi's uncharacteristically defeatist attitude. "Body language is poor now," White said. "She started this match so well. We were talking about her positive attitude . . . Osaka looks like she just wants to get into the locker room right now." When Naomi readied to serve down 2–5 in the second, White dramatically ramped up his scrutiny of her mentality. "How's your state of mind, Naomi Osaka?" he asked aloud for the viewers. "Do you have the mental resolve to dig your way out of this one in the sunken arena that is the Stadio Pietrangeli at the Foro Italico? Her Italian Open life is hanging by a thread."

Pegula remembered the match, the biggest win of her career by ranking to that point, for what she saw across the net. "I end up playing really well in the second set, but at the same time, I could tell that she was really not handling the situation that well," Pegula recalled. "She was very frustrated—and I can relate to that; I think we all can. We've all had those matches where you just kind of want to hit the ball into the fence and get off the court as fast as possible."

Fissette, sitting courtside, had been disappointed by Naomi's attitude

as well. What Naomi most needed to improve her results on clay, he believed, was "hours and hours on the court," battling through her discomfort on the surface. "I had doubts how much she was mentally ready to
really go through, like, difficult times," Fissette said. "She got broken, and,
like, she was giving up."

Despite having only three matches—one win, two losses—on clay
under her belt heading into the French Open, Naomi still had time on her
side: due to pandemic-related lockdowns and restrictions in France, the
French Open had been postponed by a week from its normal dates, giving
players more time to prepare on European clay. "I feel like I need the extra
time on clay, especially with my past results," Naomi had said when asked
about the schedule change before her match in Rome. "Hopefully I do better here, but I'm not really mad at, I guess, grinding on clay and practicing
here for a couple more weeks."

But in her same answer, Naomi also sounded a negative note about the
change. "I was a bit sad because it definitely means more time away from
home," she said.

That desire to retreat home when things felt "chaotic" in her life ultimately won out: after her loss to Pegula, rather than stay in Europe to train
further on the clay until the French Open began, Naomi decided to fly all
the way from Rome to home in Los Angeles.

Fissette said he was discouraged after the loss when he found out Naomi
was leaving Europe. "Going home after that, of course, wasn't the right
signal to be at your best in Paris," he lamented. "Because we needed time
on the court."

But though he was skeptical, Fissette also felt as though he had to believe that, ultimately, Naomi knew herself best; despite her short-term
struggles, she had still won the last two majors she had played, after all.
"Give her the trust that, okay, she won the last two Slams," he said. "If she
thinks that is exactly what she needs to be the best at the French? That she
needs to be home for a week? Okay. Trust her. At that moment, if we hadn't
been successful for months, I would say, 'Hey, let's do it different.' But she
was successful, so I was just giving her all the trust."

. . . .

Like stars Serena Williams and Maria Sharapova before her, once she became a major champion Naomi Osaka isolated her training regimen from the rest of the tour, almost exclusively using male practice partners for her training sessions rather than hitting with other WTA players.

When Fissette first accompanied Naomi to a tournament, the WTA event in Brisbane in the first week of the 2020 season, he asked Naomi if he could set up some practice sets against other players for her before the tournament began to help her tune up after several months without competition. "She's like, 'No, I don't like that,'" he recalled. Fissette was surprised but receptive. "Okay, again, give her the confidence; you won two Grand Slams, you definitely know what you need, right?" Fissette was convinced by what he saw: Naomi showed no competitive rust in Brisbane, reeling off three three-set wins over Top 25 opponents to reach the semifinals. "I mean, if it works, it works," he said. But having used them with other players throughout his coaching career, Fissette still believed that practice sets were a useful developmental tool. "I'm definitely pro–practice sets, because as a coach, I want to develop. And I think, like, when you play a practice set and you can really see that it's not about winning or losing... It seems ideal.

"If a player is not comfortable with that, if the player can lose confidence doing that, that's, of course, something we don't want," he added. "And actually, the first time when I kind of pushed her, it went the wrong way."

Fissette decided to insist on practice sets at a vulnerable time. When Naomi returned to Europe days before the 2021 French Open began, having not practiced while home in Los Angeles, Fissette believed practice sets against other top players were the best way to jump-start her preparations for the upcoming Grand Slam, since she had only played three matches on clay in the past two years. "We all agree that you need matches to find that ideal game plan on clay that works for you, so let's plan a few matches," Fissette recalled telling Naomi. When she seemed convinced by his logic,

Fissette contacted other players' teams and set up practice sets with the best he could find: top-ranked Ash Barty.

Once they began, Fissette saw Naomi's discomfort in the unfamiliar practice set situations, "overthinking" about trying to make sure her training session was also beneficial for her partner. "It was just obvious that Naomi was not able just to feel free and just play her normal tennis," he said. "She couldn't do that. Again, she's the opposite of being selfish, so she always thinks about the other one." The score doesn't really matter in unofficial practice sets, but it was a rout: No. 1–ranked Barty, who had lengthened the gap between herself and Naomi in the rankings with strong results on clay, beat Naomi 6–1 in their practice session on Court Philippe-Chatrier, the main stadium of Roland Garros. "I had felt at that point that was exactly what she needed," Fissette said of the practice competitions. "But it took her confidence away."

· · · · · · ·

Naomi Osaka wasn't going to be the most talked about player at the 2021 French Open, really. Despite her having won the previous two Grand Slam events she had played, pundits understood her struggles on clay and saw her recent losses and weren't spotlighting her much in pretournament coverage. Naomi still had an outside chance of reclaiming the No. 1 ranking at the French Open—if she made the final and Barty lost before the semifinals— but that was an improbability few discussed given her recent form. Oddsmakers, similarly, only had Naomi as roughly the fifth-favorite to win the title behind other clear contenders: No. 1 Barty was returning to Roland Garros for the first time since her 2019 title there, and defending champion Iga Świątek had just ferociously won the Italian Open final 6–0, 6–0 over Karolína Plíšková; there was also Serena Williams, who, while also a realistic long shot, remained a source of intrigue in any tournament she entered.

In the days before the tournament, Naomi's social media posts— including showing off the sparkly crystals on her purple French Open kicks (the NikeCourt Air Zoom GP Turbo Naomi Osaka), and giggling as she jumped for the camera on the court of Chatrier—were standard fare. As much as she could be as the world's highest-paid female athlete—a new Sportico report that came out on Tuesday, May 25, announced that Naomi had earned an estimated $50 million in endorsements over the previous twelve months, the most of any female athlete, and behind only Roger Federer, LeBron James, and Tiger Woods among all athletes—Naomi Osaka was under the radar as the sun set over Paris on the evening of Wednesday, May 26.

That changed quickly: on the night of Wednesday, May 26, at 11:24 p.m. in Paris, Naomi did something she had done several times before as a big tournament approached: write and share her thoughts via the modern medium of a screenshot of the Notes app. But whereas her previous Notes posts had been affirmational, this one was confrontational:

> Hey everyone-
>
> Hope you're all doing well, I'm writing this to say I'm not going to do any press during Roland Garros. I've often felt that people have no regard for athletes' mental health and this rings very true whenever I see a press conference or partake in one. We're often sat there and asked questions that we've been asked multiple times before or asked questions that bring doubt into our minds and I'm just not going to subject myself to people that doubt me. I've watched many clips of athletes breaking down after a loss in the pressroom and I know you have as well. I believe that whole situation is kicking a person while they're down and I don't understand the reasoning behind it. Me not doing press is nothing personal to the tournament and a couple journalists have interviewed me since I was young so I have a friendly relationship with most of them. However, if the organizations think that they can just keep saying, "do press or you're gonna be fined," and continue to ignore the mental

health of the athletes that are the centerpiece of their
cooperation then I just gotta laugh. Anyways, I hope the
considerable amount that I get fined for this will go towards
a mental health charity.

xoxo [peace sign emoji][heart emoji]

On Instagram, Naomi added two archival video clips to the Notes image to illustrate her point: a 1994 clip of Richard Williams interrupting an interview of his then fourteen-year-old daughter Venus when he didn't like ABC News reporter John McKenzie's repeated questions challenging her self-confidence, and a 2015 clip of Seattle Seahawks running back Marshawn Lynch answering every question at his pre–Super Bowl XLIX press conference with the repeated phrase "I'm here so I won't get fined."

THIRTY-THREE

Read All About It

Naomi's statement landed late at night in Paris, but the splash it made quickly rippled around the restless internet, making waves across the broad cross section of media and pop culture that Naomi occupied. Naomi had framed her new protest compellingly to meet the cultural moment: she was an individual—a young woman of color—standing up to what she described as a cruel and unjust system—that was seen as predominantly old, male, and White—putting her own well-being and peace of mind ahead of being part of a capitalist profit machine. Many of the celebrities who followed and supported Naomi, including pop stars Nicki Minaj and Janelle Monáe, quickly cheered her on in the replies to her post.

While Naomi had broad, vocal support from beyond the sport, within tennis there was considerable confusion. Among tour administrators, reporters, and other players, the overriding reactions to Naomi's announcement were frustration and bewilderment. People took issue with both the medium and the message. Unlike her statement that she wouldn't play her match in New York the year before, the tournaments had received no forewarning this time. Naomi had thrown down a gauntlet in a surprise social media post that was received as strident and accusatory. If Naomi had had an issue with press conferences, why didn't she raise it with someone on the tour—who could have helped her find a quiet solution to ameliorate the things that made her uncomfortable—before putting the sport on blast publicly? Why was she turning the public against journalists who believed they had treated her with respect for years, particularly the Japanese ones who had accommodated her answering their questions in a language foreign to them? There was also considerable confusion over why Naomi felt this way at all: no one could point to a clear moment in Naomi's recent press conferences that would have led her to the critical conclusions she had drawn about the format. Naomi hadn't been requested to do a press conference after her loss to Pegula in Rome; her most recent media appearance before that, a pretournament press conference in Rome, was scrutinized for clues after her pronouncement, but it was highlighted by questions like if she hoped to meet Rihanna at the Met Gala. In the eyes of reporters, Naomi's press conferences had been uniquely quirky, refreshing, and charming for years. What had changed?

Players and agents discussing Naomi's stance often remarked on the timing: in their uncharitable framing, how can you be reported to be earning $50 million in sponsorships one day and say you don't want media attention the next? Many of the players who were earning a fraction of the attention and cash Naomi was raking in—and that was pretty much all of them—struggled to be sympathetic.

Suddenly, with one post, the tenor of the tennis establishment's relationship with Naomi had shifted dramatically. They didn't see her message as a cry for help; they saw it as a challenge and even an existential threat, rattling a foundational part of the business of sport that had existed since its beginnings.

. . . .

As the newspaper industry boomed around the turn of the twentieth century, sports coverage was seen as key to attracting lower- and middle-class readership, particularly in the United States. In his 1933 book *The Rise of the City,* the historian Arthur M. Schlesinger Sr. estimated that the percentage of newspaper space devoted to sports coverage septupled from 0.6 percent in 1878 to 4.2 percent by 1898; by 1920, other estimates said sports coverage was taking up to a whopping 20 percent of newspaper space. The sports' owners and organizers, naturally, welcomed this attention on their businesses and the accomplishments of their athletes. Interviews and press conferences became standard practice.

The more a sport needed publicity, the more willing they were to do whatever they could to facilitate media outlets who would give them exposure. As an underdog sport often overlooked by the male-centric sports media establishment, women's tennis players worked particularly hard for media attention in the fledgling days of the pro tour in the early 1970s, when women's professional sports were still an unproven concept. After the nonet known as the Original 9 signed contracts to become the first touring professionals in 1970, one of their main obligations was making sure there was an audience who cared enough to come watch them play, and they knew that that audience could be best reached by earning ink and airtime on newspapers, television, and radio that was more valuable than any advertisements they could afford.

"Crazy things would happen on the new circuit," Julie Heldman, one of the Original 9 players, recalled. "A newspaper would send out the fashion reporter instead of the sports reporter. We had to explain to them how the scoring worked, what a backhand was. But I didn't see the off-court stuff as a distraction. It was simply putting in our time for something we were all working for. We needed to do it. We all had to go to cocktail parties and do clinics and go on TV and talk to journalists, because that was the way we were going to get the tour started."

None of the Original 9 worked harder to promote the new tour than their best player, Billie Jean King. During the prime of her career, King spent roughly as much time seeking out media coverage for the product as she did on court, knowing that women's tennis needed every ounce of publicity she could earn in order to survive in the market. "Everybody pitched in enormously," King wrote in her 2021 autobiography, *All In*. "As our top-ranked player, I was most often cast as the main spokeswoman . . . The demands were constant. I would wake up before dawn to be interviewed on the morning TV and radio shows, and I'd sometimes lie on my hotel bed and dial up reporters until midnight or later to promote the next stop on our schedule . . . The players did everything we could to help. If the print reporters or TV stations wouldn't send someone to us, we'd often get in a car and drive to them." King's hustle, media savvy, and star power helped build women's tennis into the enduring juggernaut it became, helping her and the legions that would follow her become the highest-paid female athletes in the world.

When *Los Angeles Times* columnist Helene Elliott had interviewed King for an article on the Original 9 on the group's fiftieth anniversary in 2020, King again spoke of how crucial spending time promoting the nascent tour to the press had been. "If the traditional media didn't tell our story, we were nothing," King said then.

. . . .

A year later, when Elliott was writing a column about Naomi's anti–press conference stance and how the player-media dynamics had shifted in the sport, she reached back out to King, whom she described as "ever an avid promoter of the sport at 77," for her perspective on the shifting landscape and its new star's stance. King replied with an emailed statement:

> I fully admire and respect what Naomi is doing with her platform, so I am a little torn as I try to learn from both sides of this situation. While it's important that everyone has the right to speak their truth, I have always believed that as professional athletes we have a responsibility to make ourselves available to the media. In our day, without the press, nobody would have known who we are or what we thought. There is no question they helped build and grow our sport to what it is today. I acknowledge things are very different now with social media and everyone having an immediate ability to speak their truth. The media still play an important role in telling our story. There is no question that the media needs to respect certain boundaries. But at the end of the day it is important we respect each other and we are in this together.

King's words in Elliott's column did not draw outsized notice behind the *Los Angeles Times'* paywall. But when King, who has maintained a robust social media presence with comments on social issues and current events, decided to upload her statement onto Twitter, her seemingly unsolicited thoughts landed in the fray with an unexpected thud. Instead of being valued as the feminist pioneer with experience dealing with the tennis media whose expertise had been sought out, King was overwhelmingly and harshly criticized by thousands—a pile-on known in Twitter parlance as getting "ratioed"—who didn't appreciate reading her two cents. Their displeasure, in a nutshell, stemmed from the notion that King was an older White woman offering unsolicited opinions that weren't entirely supportive toward the issues raised by a young woman of color, when she could have simply minded her own damn business.*

"NOTHING irks White women more than a Black woman prioritizing herself," Rebecca Carroll, the author of *Surviving the White Gaze,* replied to King.

The playwright Claire Willett framed her disappointment at King's words more generationally: "Always deeply, deeply sad when older and more professionally established women look down at younger, emergent women in their fields and basically say, 'if I had to suffer, you have to suffer.'"

After what Naomi had done in New York the year before, many had been quick to celebrate the similarities between Naomi and King as outspoken pioneers who were part of a shared legacy. Less than a year later, they were on opposite sides of a cultural divide.

· · · · · · · ·

As it happened, Naomi's first extended public comments about what had happened at the French Open came in a conversation with King during a panel discussion hosted by *Racquet* magazine three months later in New York. Generation divides were starkly on display.

As a discussion prompt for the panel, Naomi was asked to respond to a

---

* Several tweeters replied to King with the meme of R&B star Jill Scott singing the line "Or maybe we could just be silent?" from her music video for "A Long Walk."

tweet the swimmer Simone Manuel, the first Black American woman to win an individual gold medal in swimming, had made earlier that month during the Tokyo Olympics: "Please stop interviewing athletes right after a disappointing performance before they have any time to process anything. Trust me. They gave it their all. Nothing else people need to know at that time."

"I would be the first person to agree with her," Naomi said of Manuel. "It's really tough to answer repetitive questions from people that don't train as hard as us, that don't experience the life that we've experienced."

King, sitting across from Naomi, visibly winced at Naomi's umbrage at something King saw to be as benign as repetitive questions. "In our generation, we played for $14 a day—and we played for more than ourselves," King began. "We only had the traditional media, so if we didn't get them to tell our story, we wouldn't have what we have today."

Later in the conversation, Naomi said that she had felt obligated to speak to the media because she was "conditioned" to do so from a young age. "Like, I've been doing that since I was fifteen," she said. "In my mind I'm starting to question: 'Why?' Like, I know it's to grow the sport, all these amazing things, but I also feel like at some point talking to us is a privilege and some people abuse that privilege."

"You guys make a lot of money because of the media, whether you realize it or not," King later said. "That's why people know you."

"Do you feel like we should be obligated to talk to them—because of earnings?" Naomi asked in reply.

"To a point, yes," King answered. "We're all winning from this experience. We all have a job. We all are getting paid because of it."

• • • • • • •

The tennis press corps had already been jittery for years before Naomi threw down her gauntlet. As newspapers struggled to find a profitable business model in a digital age around the turn of the millennium, tennis travel budgets were frequently an early casualty of budget cuts. The number of full-time tennis reporters covering the tour had dwindled; the majority of remaining writers worked as freelancers, often subsidizing their reporting income with work outside of journalism.

It wasn't just the consumer-side changes to the newspaper industry, where the shift to digital and the loss of classified ads destabilized profits, that had made sustaining the job of tennis reporting difficult. When Grand Slam tournaments started building out their own websites in the late 1990s, they quickly realized that the transcripts of the post-match press conferences they organized could be ready-made, popular content for tennis fans surfing the World Wide Web. Now in the digital age, tennis fans could see the raw press conferences and read the full questions and answers directly from the players rather than only the select bits distilled by the writers in newspaper articles. By the 2010s, tournaments were also uploading full videos of the press conferences onto their websites and YouTube. Reporters frequently pleaded with tournaments to embargo the content—and quibbled with one another over things like whether or not it was proper to tweet quotes from press conferences before they could be published in articles—but to little avail: the tides had shifted toward information being instantaneously online. The sped-up landscape often halted travel: for many reporters and editors, it was difficult to justify an expensive trip—to, say, Australia—if the same quotes could be retrieved by sitting in the office and refreshing a website. The pandemic, which introduced remote access to press conferences using teleconferencing software, further hastened the slashing of travel budgets.

Though their potency was diluted, press conferences remained the reservoir from which tennis reporters watered their stories with the quotes and insights from the sport's stars (tennis, unlike the major North American team sports, does not offer reporters locker room access to approach players). Except for a small handful of well-connected reporters from prominent publications who could obtain one-on-one interviews or arrange special access—Andy Murray, for example, held an additional, separate, exclusive media availability for reporters from British daily newspapers after his press conferences—press conferences were the only access most media ever got to the game's biggest stars.

So when Naomi made her stand, and seemed to be rallying more players behind her, the stakes were stark. As one reporter warned others: "If we give in, even by an inch, we are dead."

• • • • • • • •

While the media had taken the brunt of Naomi's criticisms, their recourse was limited pretty much just to complaining. But they weren't her ultimate target: that was "the organizations" who made the rules requiring players to hold press conferences. Those organizations had considerably greater leverage over Naomi and her career, and the ball was in their court, so to speak. But as it sat on their side of the metaphorical net, there were four racquets—each gripped by many hands fighting for control—trying to figure out how best to take their next swing in this unprecedented rally, with the whole world watching.

Whereas most superstar athletes only compete under one governing body for most of their professional careers—e.g., LeBron James in the NBA—tennis players navigate a far more divided terrain. At its top level, professional tennis is currently balkanized into what I often call "the Seven Kingdoms": the Australian Open, the French Open, Wimbledon, the U.S. Open, the women's tour (WTA), the men's tour (ATP), and the International Tennis Federation, which governs realms including Olympic tennis and national team competitions. Though they share the players who rotate through their respective realms, each of the Seven Kingdoms has its own executives, its own corporate culture, its own geographic footprint, and its own wedge of the tennis calendar to fiercely defend against encroachment from the others. Mergers and unifications have often been floated as an obvious path to harmony that would improve the sport, but there is little willingness on any wedge of the seven-slice pie to concede any territory or autonomy.

Within the Seven Kingdoms, the four Grand Slam tournaments—the Australian Open, the French Open, Wimbledon, and the U.S. Open—often act in concert. Though each tournament has its own director and its own referee, the Grand Slam events share the *Grand Slam Rule Book*. And when Naomi Osaka announced her intention to break Rule III.H in that rule book—

> Unless injured and physically unable to appear, a player or team must attend the post-match media conference(s) organised immediately or within thirty (30) minutes after the conclusion of each match, including walkovers, whether the player or team was the winner or loser, unless such time is extended or otherwise modified by the Referee for good cause . . . All media obligations include, but are not limited to, interviews with the host and player's national broadcaster. Violation of this Section shall subject a player to a fine up to $20,000

—the other three Grand Slam events sprang into action to support the French Open with NATO-esque solidarity.

. . . .

When tennis authorities responded the next day, it was readily clear that they were not going to back down. At his press conference the day after Naomi's statement, French Tennis Federation president Gilles Moretton called her stance "a phenomenal mistake," adding that her pledge to break a rule showed the need for "strong governance" and a commitment to the "laws and rules" of the sport and its penalties and fines. Moretton did not underplay the threat Naomi's challenge posed. "This is a general problem that we must solve, or at least worry about," Moretton said. "It's very detrimental to the sport, to tennis—to herself, probably. She hurts the game. She hurts tennis. It's a real problem."

. . . .

While the public pronouncements were happening, tennis authorities were desperate to have a dialogue with Naomi behind the scenes to quell the brewing storm.

On the twenty-seventh, French Open tournament director Guy Forget and FFT president Gilles Moretton had received an email from Naomi Osaka. The subject line was left blank, but the topic was obvious.

> Dear Guy and Gilles,
>
> I hope you are both doing well. Thank you for your efforts in working so hard to put on the French Open this year.
>
> In reference to my stance on press during RG, I wanted to explain the following:
>
> This is 100% nothing against the French Open or even the press members themselves. The stance is against the system requiring athletes to be forced to do press on occasions when they are suffering from mental health [sic]. I believe it is archaic and in need of reform. After this tournament I want to work with the Tours and the governing bodies to figure out how we best compromise to change the system.
>
> Unfortunately for Roland Garros this has happened during your tournament, which is just pure coincidence and nothing personal. I have nothing but respect for your event.
>
> I am going to focus on tennis now but should you have any future questions please direct all communication to Stuart, cc'd here.
>
> Thanks,
> Naomi

The email, while far more conciliatory in tone than her social media statement a day before, only made the outlook more bleak. Naomi's stated desire for "compromise" was to come only "after this tournament," meaning she planned to maintain her standoff into the event. And more crucially—though they didn't know it yet—when they read Naomi say that

she was "going to focus on tennis now," it meant none of the various officials who tried to reach out to her over the next several days would have any
success making contact. This was the last they would hear from Naomi
Osaka for the next three days.

· · · · · · · ·

Because of how she initially framed the issue, Naomi's stance was seen as a
broadside against the media; months and years later, she would speak about
the moment with considerably more nuance. Her anxiety had been ramping up, and she had identified press conferences as a stressor she thought she
could mitigate. Her issues with press conferences, she later articulated,
stemmed in large part from changes that had occurred during the pandemic. Relatedly for millions of others working remotely during the
pandemic, Naomi struggled to feel connected to people who were only oc-
cupying a square on a screen, instead of sitting in the room with her. "The
human interaction is taken out," she said of virtual press conferences.

The switch to Zoom also greatly expanded the pool of people who now
had access to Naomi. Because anyone could now virtually pop into the
interview room from around the globe, outlets which would have never
previously spent their travel budgets on tennis tournaments could now have
a reporter in front of Naomi with a few clicks, in the hopes of her words
generating many clicks. "Recently it's gotten very strange because there's
new people that I've never talked to—I feel they're trying to get like a one-
liner to print that's really negative about me," she said. "So I feel like I have
to have a guard up."

The shift had happened around the time Naomi stopped play in New
York nine months earlier; from then on, she was seen as a magnet for controversy and a reliable driver of traffic. "There just started to be new reporters joining the press conferences that I don't know; I didn't grow up with
them," she said. "So the energy started to be off . . . So I started feeling like
I needed to protect myself more. And what I did, I wasn't trying to dig at
the reporters I know. Because for me, I feel a very strong bond with some
press people, like Japanese press and some tennis journalists. So I'm sorry if

I unintentionally hurt them—that wasn't really my thing that I was going for."

Talking about the standoff years later, Naomi acknowledged how much she had enjoyed many of the press conferences that allowed her to find her voice in raw, unfiltered ways she rarely could elsewhere. "In the interview room I have a very open character," she said. "Sometimes I say stuff that I probably shouldn't say in the pressroom, and it often gets me in trouble. But it's because I like journalists. I don't think they know this, but I like talking to them and I like hearing their questions. And for me, it's cool that someone cares enough about me to ask me questions."

Only when that previously safe space felt violated by new faces and dehumanizing technology, Naomi said, did she start to feel vulnerable and want to shut down. "Then I felt myself becoming a bit closed off and I felt my character changing," she said. "And I didn't really like that."

Had Naomi been able to explain her thoughts with that perspective back in May 2021, the entire episode likely would have been avoided. But after everything she had been through in the previous months and years, Naomi didn't have anywhere near the wherewithal to articulate her feelings that way. "I've never felt, like, mentally drained like that before," she later said.

As the tennis writer Hannah Wilks wrote: "Fun fact about depression and anxiety for those who've never suffered: The times when it's most urgently necessary to ask for help, support, respite—the times when you need it the most—are the times when you're least capable of communicating what you need."

. . . .

Though he spent every day on tour with her, Naomi's coach Wim Fissette had also been caught off guard by her sudden hard-line stance against press conferences. Like Sascha Bajin before him, Fissette said he often watched Naomi's press conferences to gain insights into his player that he couldn't glean from his own conversations with her, "because sometimes she was more open to the press than to the team." Naomi had never discussed any reticence regarding press with him, he said, and he had seen "no negativity towards Naomi" in the many press conferences he'd watched. "I think that was always a good relationship," Fissette said of Naomi's interactions with the media. "She was always correct [with the press], and the press was always correct to her."

Fissette also agreed with those who said that Naomi's fame was due to media coverage of her. "I mean, everyone knows that Naomi also became big because of the press," he said. "As an athlete, you need the press to become big and to become famous and to get a lot of sponsor deals."

When he read Naomi's statement, Fissette quickly thought that something else was at hand rather than what she had written. "I was very surprised, but on the other hand, mentally, she wasn't great at that time," he said. "She wasn't really herself."

Though Fissette had his opinions on the situation, and was spending more time with Naomi in Paris than anyone else, he did not feel it was his place to step into the fray. He said he felt as though he and the rest of the team with Naomi in Paris—Yutaka Nakamura and Natsuko Mogi—were "completely outside" the brewing controversy. "It was something between the Grand Slams, Naomi, and Stuart," Fissette said.

Others were trying to rope him into the mix, however: as various tennis officials struck out on their attempts to reach Naomi, several tried to contact her via her coach. Fissette said he received messages from figures like Australian Open tournament director Craig Tiley and U.S. Open tournament director Stacey Allaster, hoping he could be the connection to the star who remained out of reach.

"'Can we speak to her?'

"'How can we help?'

"'Naomi should know we all love her, we want the best for her.'

"'Can we speak to her?'"

Fissette, wanting to keep his focus on the tennis side, didn't feel it was his place to get involved. "A lot of support, I feel," he said of the messages he received. "But it was really something between them."

Amid the growing storm, Fissette continued onward with his job of preparing for Naomi to play the tournament. The draw had come out, and it offered Naomi a comfortable path to ease her way into competition. In the first round, Naomi was set to play 63rd-ranked Patricia Maria Țig, who had never before played against a Top 10 player. The second round looked comfortable, too: Naomi would play either 102nd-ranked Ana Bogdan or 113th-ranked Elisabetta Cocciaretto.

But with so little confidence on clay, Fissette still thought Naomi needed more competitive play before her first match. So while many of her peers were talking about her in the pressroom on the Friday before the French Open began, Naomi stood across the net from one of them, Angelique Kerber, and played her second practice set of the week.

Naomi was again out of her element and lost to Kerber in a rout, just as she had to Barty. After she and Kerber shook hands, Naomi went to her chair at the side of Court Simonne-Mathieu, where Fissette knelt by her side. Though she had covered her face with a towel, photographers courtside still snapped pictures of Naomi wiping away her tears.

· · · · · · ·

The images of Naomi on the practice courts were accompanied by quotes from other players. Except for a supportive Instagram comment from Venus Williams, no top players had commented publicly about Naomi's stance in its first thirty-six hours, leaving their own discussions of her stance confined to the locker rooms, lounges, and group texts. That would change on Friday, two days before main draw play began, when the French Open held its pretournament media day for the tournament's top stars. Naomi was not on the day's lineup, as expected, but most of the game's biggest names had agreed to take to the podium.

Top-ranked Ash Barty, with whom Naomi had practiced hours before posting her statement, was up first. Barty answered with her typical folksiness. "Oh, I think in my opinion, press is kind of part of the job," she said. Barty downplayed the perils of a press conference, saying it was "not something that's ever fazed me too much" during her career. "I can't comment on her personally for what she's going through," Barty added of Naomi, "so I suppose you'll have to ask her that next time you chat to her."

Defending champion Iga Świątek, who had been one of the players whom Naomi had hosted during her quarantine Instagram Live interviews, echoed Barty's "part of the job" phrasing. "I feel that media is really important as well, because you are giving us a platform to talk about our lives and our perspective," she said.

Rafael Nadal, the thirteen-time champion at Roland Garros, was the first male player to weigh in. "I respect her decision," Nadal began, before he echoed the earlier sentiments. "We as sportspeople, we need to be ready to accept the questions and to try to produce an answer, no?" Nadal went further, saying that athletes owed their standing in the world to the media who traveled to cover them and write about their achievements. Without them, Nadal said, "probably we will not be the athletes that we are today. We [wouldn't] have the recognition that we have around the world, and we will not be that popular, no?"

Petra Kvitová, who had lost to Naomi in the 2019 Australian Open final, said she had "faced many tough questions" in her career. Kvitová revealed she had once taken a shot of the Czech spirit slivovica for courage before the first press conference where she was going to discuss the knife attack that had kept her off tour for months. "It was very difficult, to be honest," Kvitová said. "On the other hand, I was kind of proud afterwards that I had done it."*

With plenty of quotes from big names to fill the day's articles about Naomi, and a seemingly clear verdict from the sampling of top players, the questions about Naomi subsided at Roland Garros, but the rest of the world wouldn't shut up about her.

* * * * * * *

Once she made her stand at the French Open, Naomi Osaka wasn't just a tennis player; she was a tennis ball, being blasted back and forth across the

---

* In a bizarre, ironic twist, Kvitová actually sustained an injury while doing the media rounds after her first-round win at the French Open—turning her ankle on a ramp down from the Tennis Channel set—that forced her to withdraw from the tournament.

net of the culture wars. While she had received support from the left before, Naomi's controversial stance made her a target for voices on the right like never before. For the first time in her life as a public figure, Naomi was acquiring caustic critics, including some of the most obvious suspects in the world's media.

Piers Morgan found a handy new target for grievances in Naomi. "Get over yourself, @naomiosaka—playing the mental health card to avoid legitimate media scrutiny is pathetic," Morgan tweeted. He then teased his upcoming *Daily Mail* column about "world sport's most petulant little madam." He added some of his favorite targets to the headline for good measure, knowing the clickability of both names at that moment for the tabloid's readers: "Narcissistic Naomi's cynical exploitation of mental health to silence the media is right from the Meghan and Harry playbook of wanting their press cake and eating it."

Morgan, like others, would use Naomi as a reflection of everything he thought was wrong with the world. "This Osaka nonsense sadly epitomises the state of the woke-ravaged world today," he wrote, before confidently rendering his diagnosis: "One thing's very clear: this has got nothing to do with mental health."

Antipodally, columnist Will Swanton of the right-wing newspaper *The Australian* also chimed in by writing that the "immaturity, preciousness, and hypocrisy of Naomi Osaka leaves me speechless. Having told everyone to speak out against the injustices of this world, she's decided to clam up, refusing to do press conferences at the French Open . . . while being happy enough to pocket the millions of dollars in prize money being offered by the very tournament and government body she's flipping the bird to. Trailblazer? Come off it. Try princess." For good measure, Swanton called Naomi "so uppity" for putting herself above others in the locker room. "Is she in there with the rest of them? Or does the diva have her own trailer?"

Naomi was drawing plenty of right-wing attention stateside, too. American conservative commentator Candace Owens tweeted at Naomi that she was "a special snowflake" who had "become insufferable." On a subsequent

Instagram Live she held to further discuss how much she didn't care about Naomi's feelings, Owens used the timing of Memorial Day weekend to unfavorably compare Naomi's actions in France with those taken eight decades earlier. "She's in the age group—I think she's twenty-three years old—of those soldiers that died: three thousand soldiers didn't make it past D-Day, [dying] on the beaches of Omaha in France," Owens said. "This generation just can't deal with it."

· · · · · · · ·

As the din echoed across media, quieter conversations of increasing desperation were continuing in the back channels of the sport. Officials from the tour and majors had been unsuccessful getting through to Naomi. What they had been able to gather from limited conversations with those around her was a sense not that she was unwell but that she foremost wanted to bolster her reputation as a crusader, to make a stand for the sake of making a stand.

Naomi had threatened to break a rule that hadn't been seen as the most sacrosanct. In practice, fines for not attending a press conference had never approached the maximum $20,000 allotted in the rule book: Venus Williams had been fined between $3,000 and $5,000 for skipping early-round press conferences after losses; Novak Djoković was fined $7,500 for bailing on press after he was defaulted from the 2020 U.S. Open for hitting a lineswoman in the throat with a ball.

Venus's and Djoković's decisions, however, had been mitigated as crimes of passion, committed in the heat of defeat. The Grand Slams saw what Naomi was plotting differently: her rule-breaking, in their eyes, had escalated from something like a misdemeanor to a felony: premeditated, aggravated, and designed to incite a wider uprising and unrest.

After executives from all four Grand Slams weighed in, a response was crafted. As the tournament approached, a showdown between player and person was set for the earliest possible date: Naomi was scheduled for the opening match of the opening day of the tournament on the biggest court. The day before she played, the Grand Slams emailed Duguid a draft of what their response would be if Naomi made good on her threat and didn't attend her post-match press conference.

· · · · · · ·

Despite the media interest in Naomi's off-court standoff, her first-round encounter against 63rd-ranked Patricia Maria Țig didn't have much pull for fans at Roland Garros—first in the morning, mismatch on paper. Due to pandemic restrictions, the crowd was sparse inside Court Philippe-Chatrier: a maximum of a thousand masked guests were allowed in to take a fraction of the 14,962 seats, and it seemed like perhaps fewer than that had shown up.

On the court, Țig was solid, but Naomi was better. Naomi finished the 6–4, 7–6(4) win in an hour and forty-seven minutes, knocking a backhand down the line on match point to seal the victory. As she walked to the net, Naomi smiled broadly and pulled her visor brim down over her eyes, the sort of reaction she'd often had after winning the most high-stakes matches in her career—which perhaps this felt like in the moment. "Look at that smile, look at that relief from Naomi Osaka," commentator Tatiana Golovin said.

Naomi had won the match, but now it was time for the questions. The first: Would she do the standard on-court interview?

She would. In a warm but strange gesture, on-court interviewer Fabrice Santoro brought Naomi a large bouquet of flowers for Mother's Day; they were perhaps intended for Țig, who'd given birth to a daughter in 2018. Santoro told Naomi they were for "her mom," who was not in France; Naomi said her mom was watching and would "accept these flowers, virtually."

Santoro's final question was standard: "How can you adapt your game and your movement on clay?" Naomi wore a mask over the lower half of her face, but there was no mistaking her annoyance at being asked about clay courts. "I would say it's a work in progress," she said. "Hopefully the more I'll play, the better I'll get." She then shrugged and gave a double thumbs-up.

"And the good news for Naomi Osaka is she *will* play more matches this year," commentator Pete Odgers said as Naomi walked off the court, "because she won today."

It was an understandable presumption by Odgers, that a player who won her first round would play in the second round. But Naomi's tournament was going to end before her next match was played, without her setting foot on court again.

· · · · · · ·

After speaking to Santoro, Naomi also stopped for a brief interview with Wowow, the Japanese broadcaster. But after that, she made good on her days-old promise not to attend a post-match press conference. Once her decision was clear, the Slams published the letter they had shown Duguid the day before, titled "STATEMENT FROM GRAND SLAM TOURNAMENTS REGARDING NAOMI OSAKA."

The four biggest tournaments' chefs had created a strong, acerbic broth, with a large fine—a $15,000 fine—and threats of further, far more severe punishments. "We have advised Naomi Osaka that should she continue to ignore her media obligations during the tournament, she would be exposing herself to possible further Code of Conduct infringement consequences," the Slams wrote. "As might be expected, repeat violations attract tougher sanctions including default from the tournament (Code of Conduct article III T.) and the trigger of a major offence investigation that could lead to more substantial fines and future Grand Slam suspensions (Code of Conduct article IV A.3.)."

Loathe to be seen by the rest of the player field as giving any degree of star treatment, the Slams also emphasized that the issue was one of competitive fairness. "We want to underline that rules are in place to ensure all players are treated exactly the same, no matter their stature, beliefs or achievement," they wrote. "As a sport there is nothing more important than ensuring no player has an unfair advantage over another, which unfortunately is the case in this situation if one player refuses to dedicate time to participate in media commitments while the others all honour their commitments."

The Slams repeatedly reiterated in their statement that they had tried and failed to communicate with Naomi directly, that they "asked her to reconsider her position and tried unsuccessfully to speak with her to check on her well-being, understand the specifics of her issue and what might be done to address it on site." The blame for that communication breakdown, they said, rested solely on the "lack of engagement by Naomi Osaka."

Amid the harsh rhetoric, there was also an acknowledgment of "mental health," the phrase that Naomi had invoked three times in her statement. "The mental health of players competing in our tournaments and on the Tours is of the utmost importance to the Grand Slams," they wrote.

The Slams' statement was immediately and roundly received as being shockingly harsh; ESPN's Howard Bryant said it was "using a machine gun to kill a fly."

Pam Shriver, who had previously been a USTA board member, wrote the organization's current leadership to express her dismay at the statement they had cosigned. "I sent an email, just saying they misread this badly," Shriver said, saying she hadn't been as mad at the tennis authorities since the Australian Open had undone equal prize money in the 1990s. "They were not understanding, or not stepping back and saying: Maybe there is something really going on there."

Naomi, whose second-round match was three days away, didn't respond to the statement from the Slams that day. But, unexpectedly, someone else close to her did.

· · · · · · ·

The year before, Mari Osaka had been interviewed as part of a profile in *Highsnobiety* where she discussed both her closeness with her sister and the boundaries they still had. For the most part, Naomi did not "talk about her feelings, or her problems, or if she's hurt, or anything like that," Mari said. "She keeps it inside."

So while Mari didn't have a full understanding of what was happening inside Naomi's head, she couldn't bear to stay silent as the pile-on continued against her sister. To get her thoughts heard, Mari logged on to Reddit and wrote a post on the r/tennis page—where she'd often been a lurker—to try to defend and explain her sister in a post she titled "Hi I'm Mari Osaka."

"So it's a little hard for me to see all these different opinions from everyone and not being able to share Naomi's side even just a little bit," Mari began. "She sucks at explaining her actions most of the time and she's playing a grand slam so there's even less of a chance that she will take her time to dwell and explain something that she doesn't want to even think about. Right now she wants to focus solely on her matches and the tournament."

Mari had her own theory about what was going on with Naomi, elaborating on the part of her statement where Naomi had cited "people that doubt me" as her main trouble. "Naomi mentioned to me before the tournament that a family member had come up to her and remarked that she's bad at clay," Mari wrote. "At every press conference she's told she has a bad record on clay . . . in order to do well and have a shot at winning Roland Garros she will have to believe that she can. That's the first step any athlete needs to do, believe in themselves. So her solution was to block everything out."

Mari said Naomi was not suffering from any particular condition but rather shielding herself. "So many people are picky on this term thinking you need to have depression or have some sort of disorder to be able to use the term mental health," Mari wrote.

Mari said she fully supported Naomi's stance and hoped that her taking a stand would help players who couldn't afford to be fined. Mari then mentioned her own experience in Miami two years earlier. "When I lost my one WTA match where I had to do a press conference afterwards, I broke down in the room unfortunately and then saw headlines after of me, crying," Mari wrote. "It was embarrassing and it's forced on players. Some can take it and some struggle with it."

Within a couple hours, Mari had taken down her message and replaced it with a short paragraph saying she had "fucked up" by writing a post that had led people to think Naomi's "taking care of mental health is strategic" rather than genuine.

"I'm sorry Naomi," Mari wrote. "I probably made the situation worse."

· · · · · · ·

Naomi made her decision to withdraw from the French Open the next day. She spoke with her agent, and together they wrote a statement that would again change the terms of the dispute, this time by revealing more than she ever had before. It was published through the pseudo-casual method of a screenshot of her Notes app, but it had been carefully prepared by a team, with Naomi herself getting the final edit:

> Hey everyone, this isn't a situation I ever imagined or intended when I posted a few days ago. I think now the best thing for the tournament, the other players and my well-being is that I withdraw so that everyone can get back to focusing on the tennis going on in Paris. I never wanted to be a distraction and I accept that my timing was not ideal and my message could have been clearer. More importantly I would never trivialize mental health or use the term lightly. The truth is that I have suffered long bouts of depression since the US Open in 2018 and I have had a really hard time coping with that. Anyone that knows me knows I'm introverted, and anyone that has seen me at the tournaments will notice that I'm often wearing headphones as that helps dull my social anxiety. Though the tennis press has always been kind to me (and I wanna apologize especially to all the cool journalists who I may have hurt), I am not a natural public speaker and get huge waves of anxiety before I speak to the world's media. I get really nervous and find it stressful to always try to engage and give you the best answers I can. So here in Paris I was already feeling vulnerable and anxious so I thought it was better to exercise self-care and skip the press conferences. I announced it preemptively because I do feel like the rules are quite outdated in parts and I wanted to highlight that. I wrote

privately to the tournament apologizing and saying that I
would be more than happy to speak with them after the
tournament as the Slams are intense. I'm gonna take some
time away from the court now, but when the time is right I
really want to work with the Tour to discuss ways we can
make things better for the players, press and fans. Anyways
hope you are all doing well and staying safe, love you guys I'll
see you when I see you [heart emoji]

· · · · · · ·

Shortly after Naomi's withdrawal, French Tennis Federation president
Gilles Moretton came to the interview room to read a written statement.
"First and foremost, we are sorry and sad for Naomi Osaka," Moretton
began. "The outcome of Naomi withdrawing from Roland Garros is unfortunate. We wish her the best and the quickest possible recovery. We look
forward to having Naomi in our tournament next year. As all the Grand
Slams, the WTA, the ATP, and the ITF, we remain very committed to all
athletes' well-being and to continually improving every aspect of players'
experience in our tournament, including with the media, like we have always tried to do. Thank you."

With no sense of the immense irony, Moretton left the podium without
taking questions.

THIRTY-FOUR

Torchbearer

As her long-planned moment in the spotlight approached, the "face" of the Olympics wanted no one looking at her. In what was set to be the most climactic period of her career, all Naomi wanted was to become invisible.

After she flew home from Paris, she went into near-total seclusion in Los Angeles, withdrawing from Wimbledon and the rest of the grass court season. "I holed up in my house for a couple of weeks," she later said. "I was a little bit embarrassed to go out because I didn't know if people were looking at me in a different way than they usually did before." Naomi's biggest fear, she said later, was that people would think less of her for admitting her vulnerability. "Sometimes, in that moment, I wished I didn't say anything," Naomi said. "I'm not really sure why, but I felt embarrassed about it, and I felt like people were going to call me 'weak,' and that I should be tougher than this and stuff like that. Those were the thoughts that were resonating in my head."

Naomi struggled to process the "unconventional" way her French Open had ended and the enormous scrutiny she received. "I felt judged by a lot of people," Naomi said months later. "And it was a bit weird because I'm used to people judging me for losing, but I feel like in the situation that I withdrew, I didn't win or lose, but it was still that feeling of judgment. I felt like it got a lot of media attention; I wasn't quite used to that to that scale, so it was a little bit scary."

The magnitude of attention Naomi received after her withdrawal and revelation of struggles with depression had been massive in public—figures ranging from Steph Curry to Alexandria Ocasio-Cortez had sent her messages of support on social media—but there had also been quieter A-list contacts through private channels, including from Michelle Obama, Meghan Markle, and Michael Phelps. Among tennis players, Novak Djoković's private messages of support stood out. And across other social media, rafts of regular folks were sending Naomi messages, too, expressing their admiration and gratitude for her example as someone who spoke out and sacrificed a major tournament to put her own well-being first. "In that moment, I wasn't thinking about how my decision could affect other people as well," Naomi later said. "But I'm really glad that it had a positive reach."

The reach was remarkably wide across the culture. In his Netflix special *Shame the Devil*, comedian Michael Che riffed that Naomi's ability to admit sadness was a sign of historic progress. "There was a tennis player, Naomi Osaka, right?" he began, drawing applause for the mere mention of her name. "She took a mental health break from the French Open. That was fucking crazy. I never heard of that . . . I know you're clapping, but do you realize how progressive that shit actually is? . . . That's not something Black people could claim for many years! I don't know if you guys are history buffs—imagine two slaves in a cotton field and one is like, 'Hey, man, what's wrong? You seem down.'"

Naomi's withdrawal even inspired a ripped-from-the-headlines *Law & Order* plot. The episode, "Fault Lines," centered on a Black female tennis player—played by Naomi's look-alike, actress Christen Sharice—described as "a global icon" who had publicly struggled with her mental health. "Isn't she the one that had that breakdown a while back and had to pull out of that big tournament?" asks Detective Cosgrove (Jeffrey Donovan), upon the character's introduction. "Yeah, the French Open," responds Detective Kevin Bernard (Anthony Anderson), indubitably identifying Naomi and her struggles in Paris the year before as the character's inspiration.

Naomi also inspired many quieter conversations and reflections by those who admired her ability to prioritize her own well-being. Her quitting the French Open was often linked to the "Great Resignation," a trend in which employees unhappy with their work-life balance left their jobs in noteworthy numbers. Naomi's supporters similarly also often praised her for heeding a three-word refrain that had gained resonance among Black Americans: "Protect your peace."

Psychotherapist Robin D. Stone defined the phrase as Black women "unapologetically prioritizing their mental health" instead of silently suffering. "Toughing out situations that aren't beneficial to our mental health used to be seen as a measure of strength," wrote Stone. "But these days, many of us recognize the changes we need to make in how we respond to life's curveballs." Stone cited Naomi's withdrawal from the French Open as her first example of a breakthrough act of self-preservation that defied generations of subjugation. "We're finally putting those days behind us," she wrote.

ESPN columnist Clinton Yates also repeatedly used "protect your peace" to articulate his support for Naomi. "'For the past year-plus, this mantra has become not only a way of life for happiness, but survival as well—especially for Black folks," Yates said on *Outside the Lines*. "And Naomi Osaka is no exception."

· · · · · · · ·

Naomi's peace needed the most protection on social media. The betting website Pickswise calculated that Naomi received 32,415 "mentions that had a negative sentiment" on Twitter in 2021, nearly double Serena Williams, who at 18,118 had the second-most of any tennis player. "I think online abuse—just in general, not even for athletes—is very intensified towards people of color and women," Sloane Stephens, who was invited to the White House to discuss her experiences with social media abuse, told me. "Whether an athlete or not, like if you check any of those boxes, then know you're probably not in a safe place." Naomi deleted the Instagram and Twitter apps, which had once been her lifelines to self-expression from her phone, but found herself unable to look away completely.

Though there had been a respite on direct attacks in the immediate aftermath of Naomi's admission of mental health struggles and withdrawal, many right-wing voices eagerly ended that grace period weeks later, when a slew of the media engagements Naomi had booked earlier were rolling out. There was a whole lot coming out of the spigot in anticipation of the fast-approaching Olympics: magazine covers—*Vogue Japan*, *Vogue Hong Kong*, the *Sports Illustrated* swimsuit issue—and a Netflix documentary, and the second Barbie doll based on her likeness (the first one mass produced and sold to the public). Naomi's management team had done what they could to slow the deluge—the planned launch of a Naomi Osaka collection by Nike was delayed—but much of the media rollout was beyond her team's control by the time she wanted to retreat.

For those disinclined to sympathy, there was ample ammunition. "Since saying she's too introverted to talk to the media after tennis matches, Naomi Osaka has launched a reality show, a Barbie, and now is on the cover of the SI swimsuit issue," tweeted conservative commentator Clay Travis.

"Let's not forget the cover of (& interview in) Vogue Japan and Time Mag!" former Fox News pundit Megyn Kelly chimed in.

Naomi, who had almost entirely stayed out of the discourse about her, logged back on to reply to Kelly. "Seeing as you're a journalist I would've assumed you would take the time to research what the lead times are for magazines," Naomi tweeted in reply. "If you did that you would've found out I shot all of my covers last year. Instead your first reaction is to hop on here and spew negativity, do better Megan [*sic*]."

Kelly then showed that Naomi had blocked her on Twitter, displaying a screenshot like a trophy. "Poor @naomiosaka blocked me while taking a shot at me (guess she's only tough on the courts)," Kelly wrote.

Naomi later said the bad-faith bashing around her magazine covers gave her a new resolve. "It made me not care anymore about what people have to say," she said. "I was like, You know what? These aren't real people. Like they know me, but I don't know them. So honestly, the opinion, it's on there, but it's not affecting me anymore."

Naomi said part of what made it tough for her to block out noise from strangers was that she'd had so little practice meeting new people during her isolated youth. "I knew five people in my whole life, you know what I mean?" she explained. "Suddenly there's all these new people and I'm just like, Damn, what they say really matters, you know? Because I grew up [with] like my parents, my sister; family members, their words hold a lot of weight. So all of these other people, their words must hold a lot of weight as well? It took me a really long time to realize, like, I can put power [or not] in what people are saying. Like if it doesn't mean anything to me, then what they're saying immediately becomes irrelevant."

· · · · · · · ·

Those sorts of affirmations and acts of self-care were, to the frustration of some around her, the primary methods Naomi had used to cope with her mental health in the weeks after the French Open. To cheer herself up, Naomi got a French bulldog, named Butta, and downloaded an app on her phone that would play calming music and relaxing nature sounds. What she did not do, despite being the focus of a worldwide conversation around mental health and depression, was seek or accept meaningful professional help from mental health professionals, which many outside her circle assumed was happening given the public spotlight on her mental health.

"As much as we all speak about mental awareness, it's still a topic which is not that simple," Naomi's coach Wim Fissette later told me. "It's still easier to say 'Hey, we need a physical trainer' than 'We need a mental coach.' We gave her the advice, of course, to speak to someone. But at the end, it's her decision, right? It's not that I could—or as a team, that we could—push that. It was her decision, her responsibility. I always feel like the players are in charge of their own career."

There was a clear template that Naomi didn't follow: her buddy Iga Świątek, one of the best players in women's tennis, had been traveling the tour with the sports psychologist Daria Abramowicz for years. Abramowicz, who often sits in on Świątek's press conferences, told me she grew frustrated at how Naomi's struggles in Paris became a referendum of press conferences instead of an exploration of how athletes can learn to navigate challenges. "I particularly didn't like how the center of attention, [drifted] towards media," she said. "We went very far from discussion about mental health and personal well-being in terms of functioning in high-performance sports."

Abramowicz was also wary of how Naomi became the face of a worldwide conversation around mental health without any qualifications on the topic. "If an athlete has such a big platform as Naomi Osaka, Novak Djoković, there is this sense of responsibility that I think should be around that," Abramowicz said. "So that's why I'm very hesitant about this idea of athletes speaking so bravely and freely about mental health when they are not experts in this area." There is a thin line, Abramowicz said, between an athlete discussing her own experiences and using mental health terminologies without a proper grasp of them in an attempt to "educate" the public. "It is irresponsible," Abramowicz said of the latter.

· · · · · · · ·

Soon, it was time for Naomi to return to the stage. Naomi made her first public appearance about five weeks after her French Open withdrawal, while many of her peers were battling in the second week of Wimbledon, when she attended the ESPYs in New York. Naomi accepted the award for Best Athlete, Women's Sports, receiving warm applause from a wide array of stars from across the sports spectrum. "I just really want to not say a long speech because I'm a bit nervous," Naomi began, facing a microphone for the first time since her withdrawal. "But I just want to say thank you . . . I know this year, it hasn't even finished, but it's been really tough for a lot of us. And for me, I just want to say I really love you guys."

Naomi's next role onstage would be the biggest in sports, albeit a wordless one: as she had been told months earlier, the organizers of the Tokyo Olympics had picked her for their ultimate honor: being the last of the 10,515 people who carried the Olympic torch around Greece and Japan in the prelude to the Olympics.

At the end of the four-hour opening ceremony, which was attended only by a small percentage of the athletes due to pandemic protocols and precautions, the Olympic flame entered the Olympic stadium carried by a judoka and a wrestler. They passed it to a trio of baseball players, including former Yankees star Hideki Matsui, who passed it to a doctor and a nurse, who passed it to a Paralympian, who passed it to a group of six students. All had been wearing masks. When the lead student rounded a corner, she turned and saw the open face of Naomi Osaka, who was ready to run the anchor leg of the two-thousand-kilometer relay. Naomi bowed, touched her torch to the student's torch with her own, carried the flame up a staircase, and jogged across a stage to the base of a structure built to resemble Japan's iconic Mount Fuji. As the stadium darkened and a spotlight lit Naomi alone, the mountainside parted to reveal a glowing stairway, and a cauldron designed by Japanese architect Oki Sato opened like a flower, its petals covered with mirrors to reflect the light shining from within. Naomi slowly and purposefully mounted the stairs, brushed one of her red braids away from her face, and turned to face each side of the stadium before turning and igniting the hydrogen-powered cauldron. Once the flame caught, Naomi turned, smiled, and raised her own torch high as crescendoing orchestral music reached its peak.

Naomi's flame mostly glowed only for those who saw it through screens: the eighty thousand seats in the newly renovated stadium were normally for what would be the exultant moment of the Olympics. She was alone next to the torch, but there was support for her in the building: while the cameras had focused on Emperor Naruhito and the smattering of Olympic athletes in attendance, Naomi's family had also made it inside. "I wanted to see my daughter with my own eyes, not through someone's camera on the screen," Tamaki wrote in *Through the Tuinnel*. When she saw her daughter lighting the cauldron, Tamaki later wrote, she burst into tears.

"Undoubtedly the greatest athletic achievement and honor I will ever have in my life," Naomi wrote that night.

Naomi wasn't the only multiethnic athlete the Japanese Olympic Committee had chosen to spotlight that night: NBA player Rui Hachimura, whose father is Beninese, was one of the two flagbearers for the Japanese team. That two mixed-race athletes were chosen from the otherwise largely homogenous Japanese team caused debate within the country, seen both as a breakthrough for inclusion and a disinformative distortion of the diversity issues the country still needed to address.

Megumi Nishikura, who directed the 2013 documentary *Hafu: The*

Mixed-Race Experience in Japan, told me she had initially found the Tokyo Olympics using the motto "Unity in Diversity" laughable, given her knowledge of how marginalized and ostracized racial minorities often were in Japan. "I was just like, What is this crap?" Nishikura recalled, laughing. But when she saw how Naomi and Hachimura were foregrounded, she said, she gave the organizers credit for following through, even as others suggested the gesture was so at odds with cultural reality as to be hollow propaganda. "They stuck to their slogan by choosing those representatives; they didn't cop out," Nishikura said. "I can definitely understand the criticism people had that it was just for show, and it isn't really what the reality is on the ground. But I think these kinds of celebratory moments are in some ways always projections of what the ideal Japan is, and what the future can hold."

· · · · · · ·

Olympic organizers, Naomi, and her sponsors had planned for her to be the face of the Tokyo Olympics for years; what no one could have anticipated was how Naomi would become the voice of the Olympics, too. After her withdrawal from the French Open, Naomi had unwittingly become the poster child for mental health advocacy, particularly among athletes. Her public struggles had resonated with athletes and audiences alike, and became one of the most common framings to discuss the upcoming Olympics. When Naomi appeared on the cover of *Time* magazine in the lead-up to Tokyo, it wasn't with the sort of superhero pose that Olympians—their very title invoking Greek gods—had often struck on the covers of Olympic-focused magazines. Rather, Naomi appeared in a close-up, black-and-white photo with the headline "It's O.K. to Not Be O.K."

Naomi's initial ambivalence and embarrassment about her French exit abated when she was around the world's best athletes in Tokyo. Naomi was staying in an off-site apartment, but when she was around other athletes in the Olympic Village or at the Tokyo airport, many approached her and thanked her for her openness and vulnerability. "The biggest eye-opener was going to the Olympics and having other athletes come up to me and say that they were really glad that I did what I did," Naomi later said. "So after all that, yeah, I'm proud of what I did, and I think it was something that needed to be done."

The scale of Naomi's reach became clearest several days into the Tokyo Olympics, when the biggest star on Team USA flew off a vault and realized, horrifyingly in midair, that she had lost control. Simone Biles was such a dominant gymnast that four maneuvers she had invented to challenge herself were named after her (A *Biles* on the vault, for example, is a "roundoff, back handspring with half-turn entry; front-stretched somersault with two twists"). For constantly raising the bar and topping the podium, Biles had earned G.O.A.T. acclaim, which she embraced by rhinestoning an outline of the animal on her leotard. But midway through the women's gymnastics team finals, all the attention and expectation came crashing down on Biles and she fell out of the air from her vault, miraculously without injuring herself. Realizing she was at risk of catastrophic injury if she kept going while having lost her self-awareness in the air—a yips-like phenomenon gymnasts call "the twisties"—Biles pulled herself out of the team finals mid-competition. The risks for Biles were much different than what Naomi had faced in Paris—one catastrophic landing from one of Biles's flips could render her a paraplegic, after all—but Biles said it was to focus on her mental health first, just as Naomi had.

Biles said what Naomi had done in Paris two months earlier had given her a sense of permission to put her own well-being over the expectations and demands of others. "We also have to focus on ourselves because at the end of the day, we're human too," Biles told reporters in Tokyo. "We have to protect our mind and our body rather than just go out there and do what the world wants us to do."

Though the two had never met—Naomi sent Biles a text message when she withdrew—they were frequently paired in discussions of mental health for the rest of 2021. In a year-end column, *Washington Post* columnist Kevin Blackistone said the two women were unparalleled for what they meant to sports, and not for their winning. "At a time when so many among us are struggling with darkness, loneliness, and sorrow in this public health catastrophe, Osaka and Biles—no matter how vulnerable on a world stage—showed us we shouldn't feel ashamed if we don't feel okay, that it is okay to take time off, if you can, and seek help from those trained to provide it," Blackistone wrote. "Osaka and Biles are my 2021 sportspersons of the year."

Biles withdrew from the individual all-around event and almost all of the apparatus finals. She ultimately recovered enough to perform a pared-down routine on the balance beam, the apparatus that required the least aerial work. Biles, who had been projected before the Olympics began to win four individual golds, did well enough on the beam to earn a bronze medal.

· · · · · · · ·

Naomi's own quest for a medal started more smoothly. Playing in the main stadium in front of empty stands, Naomi—who was only entered in singles, unlike many Olympic tennis players who try to maximize their medal haul by also entering doubles and mixed doubles—won her first two matches in routine fashion, beating Zheng Saisai and Viktorija Golubic in straight sets. Naomi's coach Wim Fissette told me that they had started practicing again three weeks before the Olympics. "And practices were really good," he said. "She was super motivated to do well in Tokyo. And honestly, I think she played a pretty good tournament under that pressure as well."

Naomi's third-round opponent at the Olympics was Markéta Vondroušová, a player some thought shouldn't have been in Tokyo at all. Olympic tennis limits singles participation to four players from each country, and Vondroušová hadn't been among the top-four Czechs when the rankings cut-off was made. But because she had been out injured for much of the 2019 season, Vondroušová was eligible to enter on a "protected" ranking that would qualify her ahead of the fourth-best Czech, Karolína Muchová. When they realized Vondroušová would leapfrog ahead of Muchová on the technicality, many tennis fans voiced their displeasure. "In Eastbourne I was crying so much because I heard all the people talking," Vondroušová told me. "Like, 'She doesn't belong there!' I was so nervous, because I wanted to win, with this pressure and everything."

Vondroušová's career swung sinusoidally between peaks and valleys, giving her an ironic reliability for success out of nowhere. Two years earlier, an unseeded Vondroušová had emerged from a broken draw to reach the final of the 2019 French Open. Two years later, Vondroušová would make history by becoming the 2023 Wimbledon champion, the first unseeded women's singles champion in tournament history.

At the Olympics that was roughly equidistant between those two breakthrough runs at majors, Vondroušová was again peaking. Vondroušová had beaten 16th-seeded Kiki Bertens in the first round—abruptly ending what Bertens had said would be the last singles competition of her career— and then easily winning her second round over Mihaela Buzărnescu 6–1, 6–2. Unexpectedly, her third-round match against 2nd-seeded Naomi got off to a similarly swift start: Naomi, spraying errors, trailed 4–0 after just thirteen minutes. Naomi found her range in the fifth game and staved off break points to get on the board, but Vondroušová broke for a third time to take the first set 6–1.

The court was playing especially slow at night, and Vondroušová felt comfortable and at no disadvantage from Naomi's status as a local hero, because the stands were empty. "Maybe if the stadium was full of Japanese people and everything?" she told me. "That also helped me, I think, in that match."

The second set was on more level terms and was on serve into the tenth game with Naomi serving down 4–5. Vondroušová earned a match point, and Naomi hit the ball blisteringly from corner to corner. But Vondroušová hung tough, scrambling to get each additional ball back. When one of Vondroušová's shots hit the net tape and bounced high and slow back into the court, it gave Naomi more time for a putaway. But with the extra second to think, Naomi flinched, and sent a backhand wide of the court. After just sixty-eight minutes on court, Vondroušová's hands flew up in the air as a 6–1, 6–4 victor, and Naomi Osaka's Olympics were over.

Vondroušová would consolidate the upset victory, winning two more rounds to earn a silver medal before falling to Belinda Bencic in the gold medal match. "But I think this match with Naomi was the biggest one," Vondroušová told me. "Everybody wrote to me; everywhere, they wrote so much about it. I beat Elina [Svitolina in the semifinals], and I think it wasn't that big . . . If you lose in the third round—it's nothing in the Olympics."

Naomi, left with nothing for her third-round defeat, was taken aback by falling short: previously, she felt whenever she had set her mind on winning a tournament, she had manifested it. The Tokyo Olympics were the first time her eyes had been dead-set on a prize and she had blinked.

Naomi articulated her thoughts on her Olympic failure months later. "It's a bit hard to describe it, but I guess I just thought I could do everything, if that makes sense?" she said. "It wasn't really rational, but just to play my first Olympics and win it in Tokyo, I just thought that that would be something that I could achieve. I'm not saying it would have been easy, but I just think, after winning the Grand Slams and stuff, I thought it was kind of an automatic thing. Losing there kind of reminded me that I was human—not saying that I didn't think I was human, but, like, it was on hard court."

As she watched the 2022 Winter Olympics in Beijing six months later, Naomi posted on Instagram about her mixed emotions on Tokyo. "I realized that I had regrets about the whole experience (not the torch lighting though that was [fire emoji] literally), there was a deep sense of sadness for not having more fun for the time I was there," Naomi wrote. "Can't believe I was at the Olympics in Tokyo and I failed to consistently find the immense joy in that."

THIRTY-FIVE

The Brakes

The best and worst thing about the tennis calendar is that it never stops, with tournaments held week after week from January to November. A rough loss can be healed by a great win when a new tournament begins days later; so, too, can a soaring champion be shot down to earth by a defeat days later. There's no time to mope and wallow, but also little time to process and recover.

After one of the tough losses of her career at an event that she had been building up to for at least five years, Naomi was back on the tour in Cincinnati, where she hoped to prepare for her fast-approaching title defense at the U.S. Open.

Naomi's return to a WTA Tour event also meant her return to press conferences, which weren't required by the Olympics. In an encouraging sign, Naomi agreed to do a pretournament press conference for the Cincinnati tournament, held over Zoom, as all press conferences were in those days. It started very well: Naomi readily answered about her reluctance as a mental health advocate, her brief contact with Simone Biles, and her disappointment in her Olympic result. In the third question of the press conference, American tennis writer Chris Oddo asked Naomi if she could "give some advice to people on this side of the Zoom how we can help make it a better experience for athletes who are going through difficult losses and difficult moments as we ask them questions in pressers."

Naomi was ready to engage with the topic. "This is just me as a person: I'm pretty open when it comes to press conferences, I feel like I have been that way my whole life," Naomi began. "There are times where I would say there's people that I don't know that well that ask me really, really sensitive questions, and then especially after a loss that kind of amplifies a bit." Naomi then suggested that reporters could check previous transcripts to make sure their questions weren't overly repetitive for players. "I'm not a professional in press conferences or anything," she added as a caveat. "But yeah, just to make it a bit more of a friendlier experience, I would say." She also suggested players who weren't feeling up to the task could perhaps get a "sick day" or answer questions by email.

With many reporters on eggshells and tour officials holding their breath in the wings, the first five minutes of Naomi's return to the press conference format had been hugely successful, with both sides showing some deference given the delicate nature of the occasion of Naomi's return. The fourth reporter called upon, however, changed the tenor.

Paul Daugherty of the *Cincinnati Enquirer* was a prototypical local sports columnist, primarily covering local Cincinnati sports teams with takes that were designed to draw reactions from readers. "I provoke honestly [*sic*] and always have the back of the fans," read Daugherty's Twitter bio. He and Naomi had never before spoken, and his camera was turned off during the Zoom call. Daugherty began in a familiar, jocular manner, challenging Naomi about her relationship to media and publicity. "You're not crazy about dealing with us, especially in this format, yet you have a lot of outside interests that are served by having a media platform," Daugherty said. "I guess my question is, How do you balance the two? And also, do you have anything you'd like to share with us about what you did say to Simone Biles?"

With no face to look at on the screen in front of her, Naomi's eyes flitted around as he spoke. "Um, when you say I'm 'not crazy about dealing with' you guys, what does that refer to?" Naomi asked when he finished, taken aback by Daugherty's initial framing.

"Well, you have said you don't especially like the press conference format," Daugherty said.

"Mmmmmm," Naomi said, showing disagreement.

"Yet that seems to be obviously the most widely used means of communicating to the media and through the media to the public," Daugherty finished.

"Hmm, that's interesting," Naomi said. "Um, I would say the occasion like when to do the press conference is what I feel is the most difficult, but . . . hmm."

Naomi then looked up toward the ceiling in silence as tears began to well in her eyes.

"Sorry. I'm thinking. Um . . ."

"I think we can move on to the next question, Naomi?" WTA moderator Catherine Sneddon asked, breaking the silence. "Do you want to move on to the next question?"

But Naomi, who had been treated very gently by those around her for months, didn't want to back down from a sudden challenge. Daugherty's framing was not unlike what people like Megyn Kelly had raised online for the previous month, that Naomi was criticizing a media ecosystem that also paid her handsomely; now, she had a chance to tackle that critique head-on.

"Um, no, I'm actually very interested in that, like, point of view," Naomi said. "So if you could repeat that, that would be awesome."

After Daugherty restated his question, Naomi answered. "Um, I mean, for me . . . I can't really speak for everybody—I can only speak for myself—but ever since I was younger, I have had a lot of media interest on me, and I think it's because of my background as well as how I play," Naomi said. "Because in the first place, I'm a tennis player; that's why a lot of people are interested in me. So I would say in that regard I'm quite different to a lot of people, and I can't really help that there are some things that I tweet or some things that I say that kind of create a lot of news articles or things like that, and I know it's because I have won a couple of Grand Slams and I have gotten to do a lot of press conferences that these things happen."

Naomi then acknowledged she didn't have a satisfactory answer to the discrepancy Daugherty had poked at. "I would also say, like, I . . . I'm not really sure how to balance the two," she said. "Like, I'm figuring it out at the same time as you are, I would say."

Sneddon then said there would be time for four more questions, and Naomi again looked toward the ceiling. Naomi dabbed at her eyes with the cuffs of her hoodie and pulled the brim of her hat low over her face as one of the reporters she knew best, *WTA Insider*'s Courtney Nguyen, asked her the next question, which was about her recent pledge to donate her prize money from the tournament to earthquake relief in Haiti.

"I think we're just going to take a quick break," Sneddon said as it became clear Naomi wasn't ready to speak. "We will be back in one moment."

Naomi got up and walked to the side of the room, and Sneddon asked her what had been upsetting—had it been the Haiti question?

"No, it was just the guy from before," Naomi said.

"I could sense you really wanted to answer it," Sneddon said. "We can stop right now—we've already done seven or eight minutes, we don't have to do any more."

"No, it's okay," Naomi said.

Duguid had been on the Zoom call and was already on the phone to Sneddon. He was put on speakerphone to talk to Naomi.

"Hey, yeah I'm good," Naomi assured him. "I don't really know why I started crying . . . It was the guy, he was—I don't know why, it just felt like he . . . he was just so aggressive."

Sneddon again offered Naomi the chance to end the press conference; Naomi was determined, however, that she wasn't going to give up. "I'm good though. I'm going to answer Courtney's question, I haven't seen her in a while," she said. After confirming with Sneddon that there were Japanese reporters on the Zoom as well, she said she'd answer their questions, too, and returned to the podium.

"Sorry for walking out," Naomi told Nguyen as she returned.

"All good," Nguyen replied.

"It's nice to see you," Naomi said, then began answering her question.

· · · · · · ·

Daugherty's query wasn't cruel or mean-spirited in isolation, but he had badly misread Naomi's readiness to handle a pointed question from an unfamiliar voice. In the four minutes in which Naomi was away from the podium, panic had set in among reporters who feared she might never return to a press conference. "That was a disaster . . . nightmare," another veteran tennis reporter on the call texted me as it unfolded.

Duguid, ever protective of Naomi, was also furious, and asked to be quoted with his thoughts on what had just happened: "The bully at the *Cincinnati Enquirer* is the epitome of why player/media relations are so fraught right now," Duguid wrote to me. "Everyone on that Zoom will agree that his tone was all wrong and his sole purpose was to intimidate. Really appalling behavior. And this insinuation that Naomi owes her off-court success to the media is a myth—don't be so self-indulgent."

The video of Naomi's tears at the podium—the first visual proof of the sort of hardship she had been describing for months—made her emotional state major news again. The moment was perhaps not as bad as it had seemed: the clips showed her sadness and her fragility but downplayed the strength she had also shown by returning, and the readiness the WTA had to protect her and give her as much control over the proceedings as they could. In many ways, the system had worked: Naomi was offered the chance to skip the question, offered the chance to leave, but showed resilience and returned. She did her post-match press conferences for the rest of her season, including after winning her first match in Cincinnati over Coco Gauff, and then losing her second match against eventual finalist Jil Teichmann, a Swiss lefty.

. . . .

Naomi went into the U.S. Open with some reasons for optimism. She was defending champion. She had won the last two majors played on hard courts; because she hadn't technically lost at the French Open, she had an active fifteen-match win streak at majors. In her first match of the 2021 U.S. Open, a night session against Marie Bouzková, Naomi won in just over an hour and a half, 6–4, 6–1, to extend her major winning streak to sixteen.

Things were looking up, including on Naomi's Notes app, where the most recent post was much more positive. "I'm gonna try to celebrate my-self and my accomplishments more, I think we all should," Naomi wrote. "Seeing everything that's going on in the world I feel like if I wake up in the morning that's a win. That's how I'm coming."

After Naomi's second-round opponent Olga Danilović withdrew and gave her a walkover, Naomi's third-round opponent was 73rd-ranked Ley-lah Annie Fernandez. From the beginning, Naomi seemed uncomfortable. She took the court wearing a Nike skirt and halter top that left her mid-riff bare but pulled a yellow dress over the outfit midway through the first set to cover herself more. Though she struggled with reading the eighteen-year-old Canadian's lefty serve, Naomi got the lone break of the opening set in the eleventh game to take a 6–5 lead, and served out the set 7–5.

The second set seemed like it would be more of the same. Again Naomi broke in the eleventh game, and again she served for the match at 6–5. But where Naomi had been composed and lethal in the first set, this time, with a seventeenth straight major win on her racquet, she sputtered. Having not faced a break point in the entire match, Naomi began to spray forehands wildly, badly missing four, and gifting Fernandez a lifeline. The second set went into a tiebreak. As Fernandez grew more vocal and motivated—encouraged both by herself and the crowd inside Ashe, which was excited to see the match extending—Naomi's frustration was unmissa-ble. She swiped angrily with her racquet, screamed in frustration, and pulled her visor low over her face. When she missed yet another fore-hand to go down 0-4 in the tiebreak, she tossed her racquet to the ground, drawing scattered boos from the normally supportive New York crowd. On the next point Naomi missed still another forehand to go down 0-5 and spiked her racquet again. Naomi got on the board but hit two last forehand errors to lose the tiebreak 7-2, sending the match to a third set to the de-light of a crowd, which was suddenly firmly behind the little-known Fer-nandez.

Fernandez broke Naomi in the opening game of the final set, and though Naomi kept it close, that would be enough: Naomi didn't earn a single break point in the final set, and lost 5–7, 7–6(2), 6–4, finishing on one last missed forehand. Naomi didn't know that this was the beginning of a magical run for Fernandez, who would go on to reach the U.S. Open final, where she lost to another teen surprise, qualifier Emma Raducanu. But she did know her season was over.

. . . .

As she had after many of her toughest losses at majors, Naomi came to her press conference still wearing her sweaty match outfit, a sign of how dazed and disconsolate she was in defeat.

Asked about her racquet tossing and other moodiness on court, Naomi said she was "really sorry" to have lost control of her emotional thermostat. "I was telling myself to be calm, but I feel like maybe there was a boiling point," Naomi said. "Normally I feel like I like challenges, but recently I feel very anxious when things don't go my way, and I feel like you can feel that. I'm not really sure why it happens the way it happens now." On her struggles to return Fernandez's serve, Naomi discounted the difficulty of the shot and the stage. "I don't think it was her serve, because I've been able to return pretty well against people that served better," she said. "I don't think it's the occasion, because I've been in this situation before. So, I know that . . ."

Naomi then paused, unable to land on an explanation. "I guess we're all dealing with some stuff, but I know that I'm dealing with some stuff, so . . . ," she said.

Gary Sussman, the U.S. Open's interview moderator, then switched proceedings into the Japanese section of Naomi's press conference. The first Japanese question asked Naomi about the upbeat, affirmational note she had posted before the tournament: Was that an attitude she would be able to use to process this defeat?

"Yeah, I mean, definitely, I would love to carry on that mindset," Naomi began. She then paused, breathed deeply, and paused again. She then looked to Duguid, who was standing on the side of the room, as if to warn him of what was about to come. "I'm going to say what we said, I think," she said.

"Okay, how do I go around saying this?" Naomi continued. "I feel like for me, recently, like, when I win I don't feel happy. I feel more like a relief. And then when I lose, I feel very sad. And I don't think that's normal? And I didn't really want to cry, but basically I feel like, um . . ."

As Naomi paused again and began to rub her eyes, Sussman interjected, eager to stop the press conference before Naomi began openly crying for the second straight tournament. "Gentlemen, I'm done, okay?" Sussman declared. "Thank you."

But Naomi didn't want to be done. "No, I kind of want to finish this, though. I'm sorry," she told him.

"It's up to you," Sussman conceded.

"Yeah, so basically I feel like— Okay, so . . . hmm, this is very hard to articulate," Naomi resumed. "Well, basically I feel like I'm kind of at this point where I'm trying to figure out what I want to do. And I honestly don't know when I'm going to play my next tennis match."

As her voice cracked, Naomi held her hand to her eyes again, then pulled her visor down low. "I'm sorry, but . . ."

After another pause, the tears began to flow in earnest. "Sorry," Naomi said, apologizing for her emotions for the fourth time in the press conference.

"Thank you, everyone," Sussman interjected once more, eager to drop the curtain on the distraught display unfolding on his stage.

Naomi patted her cheeks with her hands to try to calm her emotions. "Okay, yeah," she said. "But I think I'm going to take a break from playing for a while."

Naomi gave a thumbs-up to show that she had thus completed what she wanted to say. She put her mask back on, picked up her phone and water bottle, and walked off the podium and into an uncertain future.

. . . .

Naomi's tears and emotions—pictures and video of which were once more beamed around the world—were again saddening and distressing for the sport, but there was also a sense of relief among many that she had at last chosen to take a break from a tour that was so clearly causing her so much turmoil.

Stepping away from tennis had been commonly suggested as a remedy for Naomi in the previous weeks and months as her unhappiness remained clear. But getting off the tennis tour, a carousel on which powerful centripetal forces of money, ranking points, and hope keep players hanging on, isn't easy, even if the break is only meant to be temporary.

The week before the U.S. Open, Naomi had taped a panel discussion with other figures in the sport, including Billie Jean King, who urged her to recognize her own agency over her career. "First and foremost, I want you to be happy and healthy," King told Naomi. "That's always. So whatever that takes for you, you need to do for yourself . . . You don't ever have to hit another ball the rest of your life. You can stop right now, right?"

Naomi didn't seem to process or react to King's statement in the moment. But a former pro sitting between them on that panel, Mardy Fish, knew what a revolutionary suggestion that could be for a tennis player to hear.

Fish had been a thirty-year-old veteran with ample experience on the sport's biggest stages during the 2012 U.S. Open, but he didn't know how to handle what was happening to him. As Fish and his wife, Stacey, rode in a tournament car to Ashe for his fourth-round match against Roger Federer—a showcase match to be aired CBS on Labor Day afternoon—Fish was overwhelmed by an all-consuming anxiety that had been mounting since his ATP ranking first climbed into the Top 10. In his previous match in New York that year, he'd suffered an on-court anxiety attack but managed to win in a trance. As tears streamed down his face and a maelstrom of doubts and dread stormed inside his head as his car lurched toward the Open once more, his wife told him something that hadn't occurred to him as an option: "You don't have to play."

Fish told me hearing the perspective of someone who had grown up outside the tennis bubble—his wife was a lawyer who had also been a briefcase model on *Deal or No Deal*—pierced through the tunnel vision that had narrowed around him after a lifetime inside tennis, including an up-rooted adolescence spent training at Florida academies. "We're just not trained like that," Fish said of relenting. "At such a young age, we're trained to never show weakness, never show fear, never show a negative emotion . . . so it was eye-opening to hear—it was like a weight lifted off my shoulders when my wife told me that. Because I was like, 'Oh wow, you're right. I *don't* have to play' . . . I'm a male tennis player that played in an era where it was 'Show no weakness, be strong, and don't tell me that you're injured, go do more, do another sprint,' that sort of thing. And that's a fine way to train, but that's not a fine way to live your life."

After leaving New York, Fish stayed in his house for months without leaving. He was ultimately diagnosed with severe anxiety disorder and given therapy and medication to help him manage his symptoms. "Ironically, showing weakness and showing fear and letting people in was a huge part of my comeback," he said in *Untold: Breaking Point*, a 2021 Netflix documentary on his journey. Fish came back to the tour after several years of recovery and treatment and retired at the U.S. Open three years later. But even without tennis as a stressor, Fish said, his anxiety would be a life-long opponent. "It still is a daily battle," he said. "But I win, every day."

Fish was hardly short on toughness, he was quick to point out: he took up mixed martial arts training after his tennis retirement, and eagerly sparred with all-comers in Muay Thai. But tennis, he said, dealt tougher blows: players isolated on court for hours on end in one-on-one combat, unable to talk to anyone during stoppages in play, with nearly every week ultimately ending in a crushing knockout. Further dizzying, he told me, were the lack of geographic stability on tour and the lack of grounding and perspective ambitious young players received in their youth as they spent hours just staring at the lines of a tennis court. "Add on the travel, add on the fact that none of us went to school . . . Is this just our world?" he said. "It's brutal, man . . . I know tennis is not a contact sport where you just get punched in the face, but it's brutal on your body and brutal on your mind."

Fish and I spoke days after Naomi said she didn't know when she would play her next match, which he recognized as her pushing against the same ingrained tennis coding that he had struggled to reprogram inside himself. Fish said Naomi's battle might be tougher than his own. "She's got so many blue-chip sponsors," he said. "She probably feels like she's obligated to play."

THIRTY-SIX

Game Over?

I 've never been more excited for a year to be over," Naomi tweeted on December 31, 2021.

That was not an unexpected sentiment; what was surprising, after everything that had happened in her 2021 season and the tearful note on which she had ended her season in New York, was that Naomi was already back on tour for the start of the 2022 season in Melbourne.

Naomi said she had been able to process her 2021 as the culmination of a life that had overwhelmed her. "It was just like an extreme buildup, and you just happened to see it all release last year," she said. "I don't really feel the same way. I feel like everyone has their moments, of course, and that's what makes you human, but I'm going into this year a bit more optimistic."

Naomi had spent her months away from tennis with family and friends, catching up on things she never got to do in her childhood like staying over with friends who were studying in Northern California. "I haven't been able to have sleepovers and stuff like that," Naomi, now twenty-four, said. "It was cool to be able to do that."

She said she felt ready to resume tennis again, having rediscovered her love for the sport. "It got overshadowed by a lot of emotions that I was feeling just by constantly playing year after year since I started tennis when I was three years old, and I never really took a break," she said.

Naomi was uncertain how her team, from whom she had gone incommunicado after the U.S. Open, might feel about reuniting with her. "I probably traumatized them last year," she said. "Honestly there's a lot of things that were happening that I wasn't talking to them about, so it was kind of unfair to them, and I really appreciate them for sticking with me because *I* wouldn't want to be in my team last year."

By mid-November, Wim Fissette and strength coach Yutaka Naka-mura had received a text message from Naomi asking them if they could come back and start working again. "Something like, 'I'm sorry for my communication after the U.S. Open, but I really felt like I needed a break, but honestly, I'm missing it right now, and I'm really ready to train again. Is it okay for you guys if we start?'" Fissette recalled.

They didn't hesitate. "We were, of course, ready to go," he said. "We were excited to start again."

After winning her first match of the year, Naomi admitted that she hadn't expected herself to be back on tour so soon. "I actually really thought I wasn't going to play for most of this year," she said. "I think that I'm actu-ally really—I don't think 'proud' is the right word—but I'm really happy with myself that I love the sport that much, because I literally said that I was unsure when I was going to play after the U.S. Open, and I'm here right now."

Naomi said her angst had been both existential and unremarkable. "In the break I was feeling kind of like I didn't know what my future was going to be; I'm pretty sure a lot of people can relate to that," she said. "Of course you never know what the future holds, but it was definitely a kind of inde-cisive time. But I'm really happy to be sitting here right now."

Naomi's sponsors were happy, too. Mastercard bought billboards in Melbourne with her face on them that went up after her first match back. "Priceless: it's not just being back on court . . .'"

· · · · · · · ·

So much had happened in the intervening twelve months that it was hard to remember that Naomi was still the reigning champion at the Australian Open. After Naomi won her first two rounds in convincing straight sets, hype grew around a tantalizing match looming in the fourth round be-tween herself and top-seeded Ash Barty. The blockbuster match was one point away from being booked, but Naomi couldn't close out her third-round opponent Amanda Anisimova. The American's excellent returns neutralized Naomi's serves, and Anisimova saved two match points to end Naomi's title defense in the third round. Barty, avoiding Naomi, went on to win the title.

It was the first time Naomi had lost since her tearful description of how losses made her feel four months earlier, and she had come incredibly close to winning. But from the moment she came off court, Naomi was able to put the result in perspective. "I thought she played really well," Naomi said of Anisimova as she opened her press conference. "For me, I thought it was a pretty high-level match. I think the pace of her ball surprised me, but other than that, it was fun to play."

Fissette, too, was heartened by Naomi's performance and attitude. "You had some good matches, but you're just missing that last five percent, and now we continue for the rest of the season—good things will happen," Fissette said. "That was the vibe in the team, for sure, and she was the same."

· · · · · · ·

Naomi hadn't been the main story at the 2022 Australian Open; that was Novak Djoković, whose deportation saga made international headlines. Naomi was repeatedly asked about Djoković during her press conferences in Melbourne; she expressed empathy for his position in the cross fire. "I know what it's like to be in his situation . . . getting asked about," Naomi said. "[As] that person, to just see comments from other players, it's not the greatest thing." Around the fifth question Naomi got about Djoković, she'd had enough. "Is my opinion going to help anything?" she asked. "Yeah, I'll kind of pass on that. Thanks, though."

Then Indian Wells, where the heckler made her cry, happened, and Naomi was again the player in the spotlight. But after Naomi began speaking to a therapist over the phone—"It only took, like, a year after French Open," she said self-deprecatingly—her results rebounded: she won six matches at the Miami Open to reach the final.

Naomi lost the final 6–4, 6–0 to Iga Świątek, the dominant new WTA No. 1 who was in the midst of what would become a thirty-seven-match win streak, but she felt like a winner, too. James Blake, the Miami Open tournament director, singled Naomi out for praise during the trophy ceremony. "You've inspired so many throughout your career, and it makes me feel so good, it makes so many feel so good, to see you happy on the court again," Blake told Naomi. She then received a long ovation, which left her on the verge of tears. "It kind of almost made me cry, but I don't want to cry in public anymore," she later said of the warm reaction. "I appreciated the fact that people were happy to see me playing again, or happy to see me happy. I appreciated it, like, on a human-being basis."

Though she had lost the second set of the final in lopsided fashion, Naomi's spirits and targets were high that afternoon. Asked about her ranking—which she had rapidly improved from 77th to 35th by reaching the Miami final—Naomi said she hoped to be seeded for the French Open. That was a modest goal, given that she would only need to improve her ranking from 35th to inside the Top 32 over the next two months, but Naomi didn't stop there.

"By the end of this year I would love to be Top 10," she said. "By next year I would love to be the No. 1."

Naomi seemed to have startled herself by having spoken such an ambition aloud. "Oh, that's a big statement," she said as she heard herself declare her intention to get back on top. She began to hedge. "Close to . . . Top 5," she said, walking back her bravado. "Erase that. Top 5."

She then paused, also not content to be shrinking away from a challenge.

"You know what? I'm going to set that goal," she resolved. "Top 1. Yeah. No. 1."

· · · · · · ·

As it happened, Naomi didn't reach her ranking goals, not even the most modest one about being seeded for the French Open. Like she had the year before, Naomi entered a minimal schedule of clay court tournaments, just the 1000-level WTA events in Madrid and Rome. Unlike the year before, Naomi traveled to Mallorca a week before her first tournament to acclimate herself to the European clay, albeit only for about a week. "I wanted to have it a little longer," Fissette said. "It was like six days but still, it was positive, really good." Naomi admitted, though, that her start in Mallorca had been shaky because she had taken about three weeks off. "The first couple of days were pretty rough just because I actually hadn't hit or exercised since Miami," she said.

A relative lack of preparation hardly showed in her first clay court match of the season in the first round of Madrid. As she rolled to an emphatic 6–3, 6–1 victory over Anastasia Potapova, a young Russian who had been on a nine-match winning streak, Naomi had chances to try out a new trick she had borrowed from Rafael Nadal, stepping to her left to blast forehands from the backhand corner, like Nadal* had done with such devastating effect on clay for nearly two decades. When Naomi won match point after starting far to the left side of the court to return Potapova's serve, she turned to her team and smiled broadly. "I think a lot of really good clay court players do that," Naomi said afterward. "So I'm trying to learn how to do that, as well."

The auspicious start to her clay season quickly ended. Naomi didn't practice the next day and had her ankle taped for her second-round match against Sara Sorribes Tormo, the first sign of an Achilles injury that would linger for months. The loss was as emphatic as the win had been: Sorribes Tormo won 6–3, 6–1 to the delight of the Spanish crowd. "I'm sure it will be fine," Naomi said of her left heel.

It wasn't. Naomi traveled to Rome but withdrew before her first match. The focus, as always, was on being ready to play at a major, or as close to ready as she could be. "For me, there is no way I'm not going to play this tournament," Naomi said in her pretournament press conference at Roland

---

* Nadal is a lefty, so his steps are mirrored when he does this.

Garros. "Of course you kind of have to manage things, but at the same time, like, I'm going to pop a few painkillers—it is what it is."

·······

Yes, Naomi did press conferences in Paris this time. Returning to the scene of the previous year's debacle wasn't easy. "I'm not gonna lie, when I first came here, I was very worried," Naomi said of returning to Roland Garros. "Of course I also didn't like how I handled the situation, but I was worried that there were people that I offended in some way and I would bump into them."

Those fears had not been realized on the grounds; in fact, the newly appointed French Open tournament director Amélie Mauresmo, who herself had often struggled in the media spotlight during her career as a major champion, had gone out of her way to greet Naomi and try to make her as comfortable as possible. "It was important for me—I think it was also important for her—to show her that it's different, and we all have learned in one year," Mauresmo told me later in the tournament. Mauresmo took pride in taking measures to give the players more tranquility at Roland Garros, including restricting access to certain corridors of the stadiums that the media had previously been able to enter.

Naomi had learned a lot in a year, too, especially in the months since she had been talking to a therapist after her breakdown at Indian Wells. She was quick to admit that what had happened a year ago had been concerning her. "It hasn't left my mind; of course I'm still thinking about it," Naomi said as she first addressed the media at Roland Garros. "I'm also prepping just in case I go on the court and a fan says something like in Indian Wells. Yeah, for the most part, I think I'm okay."

·······

Naomi's mental readiness couldn't fix her left leg, however. Unseeded at the French Open—the first time in more than four years that she had been unseeded at a major—Naomi drew a daunting first-round test: 27th-seeded Amanda Anisimova, who had beaten her in Melbourne. Given the uncomfortable opponent, surface, and body she was dealing with, Naomi acquitted herself well, and the crowd on Court Suzanne Lenglen was warm, but she struggled to make first serves and lost in straight sets 7–5, 6–4.

It was uneventful, but still notable, that a year after a standoff over the issue, Naomi was attending a post-loss press conference at the French Open. The reporter who asked the last English-language question went out of his way to address the occasion. "Let me say we are thanking you for being so nice," he said. "To come to this press conference and you answer all the questions we asked, it was nice of you, especially after a loss."

• • • • • • •

While playing a scant schedule of matches, Naomi took big swings off court throughout the season. Naomi and Duguid left IMG to start their own sports management agency, Evolve. Male superstar athletes like Roger Federer, Tom Brady, and LeBron James had done similarly before, but Naomi was the first female sports star to branch out on her own. Their new agency added two clients in 2022: Nick Kyrgios, whom Duguid had already represented at IMG, and Ons Jabeur.

Naomi and Duguid also created their own media production company in conjunction with LeBron's SpringHill Company: Hana Kuma, named for the "flower bear" that had been Naomi's personal logo. "The symbol—a strong and fearless bear paired with a large, soft flower—represents Naomi's double-sided nature," Naomi's brand book explained. "She's both a fierce and powerful player and a kind and nurturing figure." Hana Kuma's first two projects were short documentaries: one on Patsy Mink, the first Asian-American woman elected to Congress; one on girls' soccer programs in Haiti.

Following the footsteps of other sports stars' business ventures also backfired for Naomi in 2022, however, when she joined the parade of celebrities promoting the cryptocurrency platform FTX. An all-the-cool-kids-are-doing-it message was crucial to convince consumers to buy into FTX's amorphous assets, and Naomi made clear in her announcement that she was joining a bandwagon. "If @StephenCurry30 @TomBrady and

@giseleofficial are in then you know I am too!" she tweeted. "Excited for the journey ahead with @FTX_Official and SBF_FTX [rocket ship emoji]." Duguid said that the constellation of other sports stars on FTX's roster represented "the kind of company we want to keep." Naomi, who signed an equity deal with FTX in lieu of a normal compensation agreement, updated her profile photo on the WTA website to make sure her new FTX logo patch was visible. When FTX entered the Japanese market in August 2022, Naomi and baseball star Shohei Ohtani featured on the large electronic billboards FTX Japan bought at Tokyo's iconic Shibuya Crossing, the busiest pedestrian crossing in the world.

The "SBF_FTX" whom Naomi mentioned in her announcement was Sam Bankman-Fried, the thirty-year-old founder of FTX. "Our partnership with Naomi Osaka will further our goal of getting more diverse voices involved in the future of digital currency and Web3," Bankman-Fried said as he announced Naomi as the first woman of color on FTX's celebrity roster. Naomi's quote in the statement said she hoped her presence at FTX could help "further democratize the space."

Before it could democratize, the space disintegrated: in November 2022 Bankman-Fried was arrested in the Bahamas, where FTX had been based for regulatory reasons, accused by U.S. authorities with "orchestrating a massive, years-long fraud." Within another week, debris from FTX's rapid collapse reached Naomi's doorstep: a class-action lawsuit filed in Florida named Bankman-Fried, Naomi, and ten other FTX spokespeople as defendants, claiming damages from being "exposed to some or all of Defendants' misrepresentations and omissions regarding the Deceptive FTX Platform."

· · · · · · ·

Wimbledon was five weeks away after Naomi's French Open loss, and she began training as she continued to rehab her Achilles tendon. After two weeks of training in Los Angeles—including on a rare grass court in the area—Naomi decided to withdraw from the grass court tune-up in Berlin she had entered. A week later, she also pulled out of Wimbledon for a second year in a row, still not confident in her footing on the surface after her injury.

Missing Wimbledon once more increased Fissette's frustration with what he saw as Naomi's growing aversion to playing outside of hard courts; she hadn't played a grass tournament since 2019. "I was super disappointed that we were going to skip Wimbledon again," he said. "If you see the last four years, she almost didn't play on the grass or the clay courts; it was only going to get more difficult in the future."

Fissette was growing more concerned about Naomi's approach to her career. "I wanted to have some clarity over a few things: I think that's a conversation you do once every six to twelve months, just to speak a bit about everyone's goals and motivation," Fissette said. "I had a conversation with her where she couldn't really give me a lot of answers."

After she returned from a vacation to Japan, Naomi officially split with Wim Fissette, ending their partnership after two and a half years and two major wins together.

When she returned to the tour at a hard-court tournament in San Jose, she was quick to praise Fissette and "confirm that there's no bad things happening" to cause the end of their partnership. "It was really good times with Wim, and he's a really amazing coach and we didn't part on bad terms," she said. "I just felt like I needed . . . different energy? And also at the same time, he's a very ambitious guy. Like, I was getting injured, and I'm sure he would have wanted to go to Wimbledon and stuff. So it was kind of like two different mindsets, I would say."

· · · · · · ·

After seemingly having everything figured out when she'd made her resurgent run to the Miami final, Naomi's mindset was less clear when the tour returned to hard courts. She was in good spirits in San Jose, and won a round before losing a hard-fought second-round match against Coco Gauff. She'd lost, but Naomi had boldly staved off seven match points in the second set before succumbing. Invigorated, she sounded a defiant, triumphant note in her press conference. "When I was playing the match just now, I realized that I've been letting people call me mentally weak for so long that I forgot who I was," she said. "... So yeah, I lost the match today, but I really feel confident with who I am. And I feel like the pressure, it doesn't beat me. Like, I am the pressure. So I'm really happy with that."

But in ensuing tournaments, Naomi seemed increasingly directionless, in large part because she didn't have a professional coach. Instead of hiring a replacement for Fissette, Naomi had her father return to a more prominent role as a de facto coach for her tournaments. But Leonard's coaching, Naomi was rediscovering, had little actual coaching involved. After winning a round in San Jose, Naomi said she felt like she could communicate well with her father but also that she had to "try to relearn his coaching style, which is: he did not tell me anything before this match."

As the summer hard-court season continued, the quirky setup just seemed quizzical. Without Fissette there to guide the sessions, Naomi's practices seemed increasingly disorganized and aimless; no one stepped up to give the sessions structure, including Naomi herself, despite being the true head of the team.

The disarray showed on court. Having picked up a back injury, Naomi lost to unseeded opponents in the first round of her next two tournaments, Toronto and Cincinnati; it was the first time she had lost consecutive opening-round matches in four years. When she went to the U.S. Open, she was ranked 44th, still not good enough to earn a seeding in the draw.

In the first round, she drew 19th-seeded Danielle Collins, a hot-and-cold player whose peak earlier in the year had been reaching the Australian Open final but who hadn't entered any of the U.S. Open warm-up events. Despite the uncertain form of both, it was a marquee match; the tournament scheduled it for a Tuesday night session in Ashe. Naomi was ready for the stage as the match began racing out to a 3–0 lead in just nine minutes. But Collins roared back to level the first set at 3–3, and the two ultimately needed to settle the first set in a tiebreak. The quality from both was high, and the margins were small: when Naomi was flummoxed by a few Collins mishits, she lost the opening set 7–6(5). Naomi had many chances to pull ahead in the second set but went only one for six on break points. Collins, who went two for three, won the match 7–6(5), 6–3. It was Naomi's third consecutive first-round loss, the most she had suffered in five years, before she had ever won a tournament.

"She's in her flop era," a reporter lamented to me as we walked out of the stadium.

This first-round loss, on the court where she had become a global superstar four years earlier, felt different. Naomi had never lost a first-round match at the U.S. Open before.

Before leaving the court, Naomi did something she'd never done: after shaking Collins's hand, she sat down on her chair, took out her phone, and took a picture of the court. In her post-match press conference, I asked her why she'd done that.

"Just to, like, remember it," she said.

. . . .

The tennis that most interested Naomi in the summer of 2022 was being played by forty-year-old Serena, who announced that the U.S. Open would be her last tournament. Naomi sat inside the stadiums to watch Serena's matches in person during her summer farewell tour, seeking every last drop of her idol's career. "I just think she's the biggest thing that will ever be in the sport," Naomi said.

Serena, ever competitive, said she felt like she had nothing to lose on court for the first time in decades, finally allowing herself some grace with the finish line in sight. "I have had a big red X on my back since I won the U.S. Open in '99; it's been there my entire career, because I won my first Grand Slam early in my career," she said. "But here, it's different. I feel like I've already won, figuratively, mentally. It's just pretty awesome, the things that I've done."

Serena's career ended with a loss in the U.S. Open's third round.

. . . .

The next tournament on Naomi's schedule was Tokyo. Naomi brought two friends—the children of her strength coach Abdul Sillah—with her on the trip, but still no tennis coach. She hadn't hired any replacement for Fissette, who had been gone from her team for nearly three months; Leonard, who had nominally been her coach for the previous few months, had gone to Haiti while his daughter went to Japan.

"Of course, the year has been . . . not the best year for me," Naomi said in a pretournament press conference in Tokyo before her opening-round match against Daria Saville. "But I think overall I've learned a lot about myself . . . I think life is kind of ups and downs and this one was kind of more down than up."

. . . .

Uniquely on tour, the Seiko digital match clock on court at Tokyo's Ariake Coliseum shows not just hours and minutes but seconds ticking by.

Two minutes and fifty-four seconds into her first-round match, Naomi won her opening service game with a backhand down-the-line winner.

Seven minutes and ten seconds into the match, which was still in just its second game, Naomi hit a forehand that clipped the net cord and popped up in the air, landing short on Saville's side of the court.

Seven minutes and thirteen seconds into the match, Saville ran up to the short ball and smacked an easy forehand winner into the open court.

Seven minutes and fourteen seconds into the match, Saville collapsed to the ground screaming, having landed awkwardly on her left leg after hitting the forehand. "Ow, my knee," she moaned, covering her face and rolling onto her side. "Oh my God."

Seven minutes and thirty-six seconds into the match, Naomi ran to the other side of the court and knelt by Saville's side, having brought her two towels. There wasn't much Naomi could do to help as Saville laid on the court in agony, but she asked Saville if she wanted ice or water.

Eight minutes and seven seconds into the match, the WTA physiotherapist arrived at the court to evaluate Saville, eventually helping her to the side of the court.

Fourteen minutes and thirteen seconds into the match, Saville, who had injured her ACL before, told the physiotherapist she was going to retire from the match, then looked at Naomi and said: "I can't." Naomi and the crowd applauded softly as Saville walked off the court on her own, declining the wheelchair that had been brought out for her.

Addressing a Japanese crowd for the first time in three years in her post-match interview, Naomi spoke in English. "First of all, I want to say 'Hi, everyone,'" she said. "It's good to be back. I'm very sad how the match ended, but yeah, just thank you all for being here, and I hope that you're here tomorrow—if I play tomorrow." A man translated Naomi's answer into Japanese, and the crowd applauded once they had heard it. The interviewer then encouraged the crowd to give Naomi a round of applause to welcome her back to Japan, which they obliged. In turn, she had a suggestion for Naomi, too.

"Can you say *okaerinasai* to your fans?" the translator rephrased for Naomi, suggesting the Japanese phrase for warmly welcoming someone who is returning home. Naomi giggled nervously and stuck to her English, and to the topic of the scene she had just witnessed. "Yeah, I mean, for me I feel really bad right now, because obviously how it ended," she said of Saville.

In her post-match press conference, Naomi said it was "really scary" to see Saville's sudden injury and hear her screams. "I also felt sad for her because she was kind of going through it in front of a lot of people," Naomi said. "That was my immediate thought."

. . . .

Given how the match had abruptly ended with a major, acute injury, it was reasonable to wonder if the brief match might've been career-ending for Saville. But as time passed, the scope of whose career might have ended that day unexpectedly expanded; in fact, Saville, who had torn her ACL as she feared, would return to the tour in June 2023, before Naomi set foot on a match court again.

Naomi withdrew from the Tokyo tournament before her second-round match, citing abdominal pain. There were more tournaments left on the WTA calendar for the 2022 season—including two big North American hard-court events, her bailiwick, in San Diego and Guadalajara—but

Naomi didn't enter any. Instead, after spending several days in Japan to fulfill sponsor obligations, Naomi flew to Europe to join Cordae on the European leg of his concert tour. Soon after that trip ended, Naomi went on vacation to Hawaii with friends and her mom.

Naomi wasn't entering tournaments. Naomi wasn't training. Naomi had no coach. Naomi's motivation was unclear. Naomi was receding from the sport. Was she still a professional tennis player? It was an open question, even among those who knew her.

When I spoke to Wim Fissette in late September 2022 about what he thought the future held for the player he had coached to two major titles, he was blunt.

"I don't know," Fissette said. "I have no idea."

. . . .

Naomi didn't have much more certainty in her own statements, including a message she posted on her twenty-fifth birthday in October 2022. "Honestly with each passing year I always expect myself to be more put together or to magically be more of an adult," she wrote. "I've realized though that a lot of things you can't rush and it will all come eventually through the experience of living life. Thank you, thank you, thank you for watching me go on this journey and I'm so grateful for all the love and messages, I really don't know what I did to deserve it all. Love you and I'm sure I'll see you around [heart emoji]."

Where that would be was anyone's guess.

In early December, Naomi did a small round of network television appearances in New York to promote a picture book she had published, *The Way Champs Play*. After getting through all the various things Naomi had done and was promoting, *Good Morning America* host Robin Roberts turned to the uncertainty of her very near future. "Okay, let me get this right: you're an author, you started a production company, you've got the book coming out—people want to know: Will you be returning to the court in 2023? What can we expect from you on the court."

Naomi giggled. "Um, I don't know," she told Roberts. "For me, I feel like I'm a very curious person, so I've really been grateful to be given all these avenues to explore. So I'm definitely looking forward to doing a lot of stuff.

"But, I am a tennis player," Naomi then acknowledged. "So, you know, if I don't play tennis for too long, I get an itch."

"Ah," Roberts said. "Well, we get an itch when we don't see you on the court. We love seeing you out there."

* * * * * * *

When Naomi didn't enter any of the tournaments scheduled for the beginning of the 2023 season, the private whispers amplified into public conversations. When she withdrew from the 2023 Australian Open, many saw it as a signal that she was unofficially done with tennis.

Jonathan Liew, a columnist for *The Guardian,* suggested that Naomi's public behavior toward her tennis career "bears all the hallmarks of 'quiet quitting.'" A term that came into vogue during the pandemic, "quiet quitting" describes when an employee gradually disengages from their work until they are spending the minimal required amount of time, effort, and emotion—rather than formally declaring that they are leaving the job. In other words, checking out while still cashing checks. Liew conceded that he had little idea of what Naomi had been up to, her physical or emotional condition, or what she desired out of this stage of her life. "We don't really know what she wants, and we don't even know if she does," he wrote. "All we can really do is wish Osaka well; perhaps even admire her small, quiet act of rebellion."

* * * * * * *

Liew's diagnoses hadn't been entirely wrong when it came to Naomi's frame of mind and her commitment toward the end of the 2022 season, which had been more about ambivalence than ambition.

But in the months since her last match, unbeknownst to Liew and everyone except a close circle around Naomi, there was also something entirely new happening within her.

Reset

■

On January 11, 2023, several days after her withdrawal from the 2023 Australian Open, Naomi posted a screenshot from her Notes app, as she had many times before at inflection points in her career.

This time, however, Naomi accompanied the screenshot with something entirely different: a photograph of an ultrasound from a month earlier, showing the early stages of a baby growing inside her.

And just like that, Naomi Osaka gave an answer to her short-term future, and opened many more questions about what the long-term could hold for her as a person and player.

. . . .

A flagging, ambivalent player could see a pregnancy as an obvious exit ramp to pull off the road she no longer wanted to go down. But Naomi took the news she was pregnant as a "magical moment" and did the opposite: used it as a boost of nitrous, turbo-charging a tennis career that had been low on fuel. As she watched the 2023 Australian Open from her couch, Naomi's mind raced with ideas about where she could next take her own game, and which coach might be best to lead her back to the top of the sport.

Naomi wasn't just watching; she got back on the court herself while in the early months of her pregnancy, holding high-quality hitting sessions as well as off-court fitness sessions. She was working more than she had been in the months just before she found out she was pregnant.

· · · · · · ·

Women returning from maternity leave in recent years of women's tennis have found mixed fortunes. In one of the most iconic images in twenty-first-century women's tennis, Kim Clijsters posed with her eighteen-month-old daughter in one hand and the 2009 U.S. Open trophy in the other after winning what was just her third tournament back from maternity leave. Clijsters, who had only won one major singles title before her maternity leave, then won two more major titles and regained the No. 1 ranking, making her chapter as a mother on tour more successful than the ones before.

But there are no guarantees: the most prominent returning mothers in the last decade have been less successful. Victoria Azarenka and Serena Williams both had even better careers than prematernity-leave Kim Clijsters had, and both had been winning big tournaments immediately before they went on pregnancy leave: Azarenka won Indian Wells and Miami back-to-back during the early stages of her 2016 pregnancy with her son, Leo, vaulting herself back into the Top 5; Serena won the 2017 Australian Open while she was about two months pregnant with her daughter Olympia, to regain the No. 1 ranking. But in the years since they returned, neither Azarenka nor Serena has been able to regain those ranking heights or win another major title, hitting unforeseen complications. Azarenka had a disruptive custody dispute with her son's father; Serena struggled to regain her pre-maternity fitness after her birth complications. Both mothers also had to face another obstacle they could not overcome: an in-form and inspired Naomi Osaka across the net in a U.S. Open final.

For Serena, who had come back in the hopes of equaling Margaret Court's asterisk-spangled record of twenty-four major singles titles, reaching four major finals while carrying a banner for working moms but falling well short in all four matches was painful. "I had my chances after coming back from giving birth," Serena wrote in her 2022 retirement essay in *Vogue*. "I went from a C-section to a second pulmonary embolism to a grand slam final. I played while breastfeeding. I played through postpartum depression. But I didn't get there. Shoulda, woulda, coulda. I didn't show up the way I should have or could have. But I showed up twenty-three times, and that's fine. Actually it's extraordinary."

Some of Serena's most extraordinary tennis achievements as a mother, ultimately, were written not in the record book but in the rule book. Because of the attention she brought to maternity issues, and the outcry when she was unseeded at tournaments after having been ranked No. 1 before she left the tour, the WTA changed its rules for returning mothers in late 2018, allowing them more time to come back and greater protections for entries and seedings once they return. Women throughout the WTA rankings and pay scale have benefited from these new changes, giving them greater flexibility and ability to have children without derailing their careers. Once again, because of Serena's pioneering, things will be easier for Naomi.

There are also protections in place for Naomi's off-court income because of the experiences of other female athletes. After an outcry in 2019 over a lack of protections or provisions for maternity in Nike's contracts for track stars like nine-time Olympic medalist Allyson Felix, Naomi's most recent Nike contract already included language securing her income in the event of pregnancy. "That all came on the back of your experience with them," Duguid told Felix when he was a guest on her podcast in 2023. "I think they learned so many lessons."

• • • • • • •

While the frustrations of forebears like Serena and Felix paved a path that Naomi can comfortably use when returning to competition, it also became clear during her absence from the tour in 2023 just how much of a path Naomi herself has already paved for others.

On the same day Naomi revealed in social media posts that she was expecting a girl, a familiar scene was unfolding without her on the tour: a reigning Australian Open champion seeded No. 2 at Roland Garros was again making headlines for opting out of a French Open press conference, citing her mental health as the reason.

After her second-round win, a Ukrainian reporter grilled second-ranked Aryna Sabalenka of Belarus about her country's role in the Russian invasion of Ukraine, asking specific, pointed questions that did not allow for the vague platitudes on which Russian and Belarusian players had relied to deflect questions about the war.

Sabalenka, who said "no comments" to each successive query, was upset by the extended exchange, and spoke afterward with tournament and tour communications officials. Instead of threats or penalties, accommodations were made and a plan was devised: after her third-round win two days later, Sabalenka spoke only to a tour staffer who conducted a post-match interview one-on-one, beginning by addressing its unusual circumstances. "I should be able to feel safe when I do interviews with the journalists after my matches," before echoing Naomi's language: "For my own mental health and well-being, I have decided to take myself out of this situation today, and the tournament has supported me in this decision. It hasn't been an easy few days, and now my focus is to continue to play well here in Paris."

Unlike two years earlier, a solution had been reached that would allow the No. 2 player in the world to continue competing at the French Open despite her apprehensions about press conferences. Sabalenka played on and reached the semifinals, a career-best result for her at Roland Garros. Avoiding anything like Naomi's fiasco two years earlier was undoubtedly a successful result for both the player and the tournament. But many reporters covering the tournament had concerns: Why was the Sabalenka transcript labeled a "press conference" when it had been something closer to an in-house PR release? Why could Sabalenka, one of the world's most prominent Belarusians, duck questions about her country's role in an ongoing war? Under what criteria could a player now opt out of their press conferences citing "mental health"? After his first-round win at the same tournament, the Brazilian player Thiago Seyboth Wild looked angry to be asked about pending domestic violence accusations against him by an ex-girlfriend; should he, too, have been able to avoid that topic by citing his mental health?

The newfound flexibility in French Open press conference requirements wasn't the only example of how Naomi had changed the landscape of tennis;

several other players were also following her lead in openly discussing their mental health troubles. Amanda Anisimova, who had beaten Naomi twice at majors in 2022, announced in May 2023 that she had "really been struggling with my mental health and burnout since the summer of 2022" and was taking a break from the tour. "It's become unbearable being at tennis tournaments," Anisimova wrote.

There was also positive mental health news while Naomi was out from another sport: Simone Biles, often paired with Naomi in conversations in 2021, returned to competition two years after stepping back from nearly all Olympic competition. After less than four months of full-time training, Biles won her first event back, the August 2023 U.S. Classic, in dominant fashion, retaking her rightful spot atop the podium. When talk turned to the next year's Paris Olympics, where Biles could reclaim what she had lost in Tokyo, she brushed it back. "When you get married, they ask you when you're having a baby," said Biles. "You come to Classics, they're asking you about the Olympics. I think we're just trying to take it one step at a time." Biles wasn't missing any of those steps as the year progressed. By the World Championships in October, she was back to her world-beating best, winning four gold medals and one silver.

· · · · · · ·

Naomi was far bolder than Biles in her remarks about returning. Despite Duguid's advice not to give a planned date for her return that might cause undue pressure, Naomi declared in her pregnancy announcement post that she intended to return to the tour in Australia in January 2024, just under six months after giving birth.

Her drive and determination were not limited just to the timetable of her return. On a trip to Japan in April 2023, around the start of her third trimester, Naomi sat for an interview with Shuzo Matsuoka, the former pro who had been Japan's best ever ATP player before Kei Nishikori, to discuss her goals. Matsuoka has become a popular TV personality since his retirement; it was easy to see why as he sat across from Naomi, with exaggerated shock on his face underscoring her audacious answers.

Matsuoka was most expressive after asking Naomi about her hopes for the remainder of her career, which he playfully called her "second set."

"You won four Grand Slams in the first set of Naomi life," Matsuoka began. "Second set of Naomi life, what are you aiming for?"

Naomi glanced downward briefly and then looked back at Matsuoka. "Eight," she said flatly.

"Huh?" said Matsuoka, his eyes widened.

"Eight," Naomi repeated.

"Eight," Matsuoka echoed again after picking up his dropped jaw. "Eight Grand Slams?"

"Mmmhmm!" Naomi confirmed with a close-lipped smile.

"Eight more Grand Slams?" he asked to clarify that she intended to extend her total to twelve.

Naomi nodded.

"Wimbledon . . ." Matsuoka began.

"French," Naomi said, continuing the wish list. "Olympic gold. I want to try to win the Olympics next year. I don't know. It makes me very excited to return to the sport and—I don't know—it's something that's going to make me very happy."

* * * * * * *

That Naomi would state such a hugely lofty goal aloud seems unfair to herself; given the hardships she has faced in recent years, and the challenges of returning to the sport after an extended layoff, winning just one more major title would be a phenomenal accomplishment. But even before she began hitting balls again, Naomi had already scored a major win: the renewed belief of her former coach.

Wim Fissette admitted that, after his partnership with Naomi ended in summer 2022, it hadn't been easy moving on. "Naomi was definitely the highlight of my career," he told me. "Working with the greatest female athlete of that time—of the last five years, at least—it's a huge honor. It's not easy: What happens after that?"

Though not sure what his follow-up act should be, as 2023 began

Fissette's coaching prowess was in demand. In February, he was appointed captain for the Billie Jean King Cup team of his native Belgium; in June, he accepted a job coaching Zheng Qinwen, the promising twenty-year-old who is China's brightest prospect in women's tennis. Zheng had several strong results in her first months with Fissette—including winning her first WTA title and reaching her first major quarterfinal at the U.S. Open—but Fissette told me he didn't feel his coaching style was registering or resonating with her how he hoped it could. "I don't feel like I had the impact on her that I want to have on a player," he said of Zheng.

Fissette had gotten a call from Duguid in summer 2023, asking him if he had any coaches he'd recommend for Naomi, whom Duguid said was "more motivated than ever" about her tennis. "I gave them a few names," Fissette recalled. "He was telling me all about her motivation, and I was, like, Wow, that's great news for tennis. Great news for Naomi."

After Fissette returned home to Belgium following Zheng's quarterfinal run in New York, he got a call from Duguid again. This time, Naomi called, too, to tell Fissette that she wanted him to be her coach again. After talking to Naomi, he was convinced to end his work with Zheng and reunite with Naomi, rejoining forces fourteen months after their separation.

Naomi's apparent directionless ambivalence about her tennis career had troubled Fissette in the time leading up to their breakup a year earlier. "She knows I'm not interested in just hanging around," Fissette said. But the Naomi he spoke to in September 2023, he told me, was "like it's a different person now." Not only did Naomi tell Fissette about her desire to have a long career, she told him she wanted to play a full schedule of tournaments in 2024. "Yeah, I really felt that she has more motivation and ambition than maybe ever before," he said.

Though it hadn't been a consideration when Naomi first hired him in 2019, Fissette has extensive experience coaching mothers rejoining the tour. His first coaching job on the WTA Tour was with Kim Clijsters during her fairytale comeback; he also worked with Victoria Azarenka during her turbulent return. "Especially if you're at the top and you have the financial possibilities, you can travel the world in a very comfortable way, with your child," he said. He also acknowledged that stability would dictate the range of possible outcomes for a new mother. "The ideal family situation, it's great," he said. "If the situation is not ideal, of course it's difficult."

Fissette told me he spoke with Naomi during their initial call about the importance of staying buoyant if success was not immediate, but he shared her goal to ultimately return her to the pinnacles of the sport. "With Naomi, the opportunity is there," he said. "The energy and vibe I'm getting from her is super positive. I mean, she won four Grand Slams, played amazing tennis, but I always felt there's a lot more in her, and that she really can develop a lot more. And that is my desire: to help her really go to a next level. And I do think that is possible. I just can't wait to get started. I still kind of see her as this raw diamond, and I just want to get everything out of her in the next years, in the way that I always imagined how I would try to develop her as an even more complete player."

Completing her as a player would mean achieving success in Europe, on clay and grass, which has eluded Naomi. "If you just think about all the top one hundred players, I don't think there are many players that have spent less time or played fewer matches than Naomi has on clay and grass," he said. "The sky's the limit. It will depend on her. It will depend on how much she wants to keep developing her game. She needs to be patient, but also at the same time very proactive."

In addition to adjusting her strokes and her footwork on uncomfortable surfaces, Fissette also wants to prioritize making sure the team Naomi assembles has the right people to take care of both her body and her mind this time around. "Definitely something I want to speak to her over the next two weeks: in modern sports, a sports psychologist should be part of the team," Fissette told me days before rejoining Naomi. "I feel it will definitely help. I'm never going to push that, but of course we will, for sure, speak about that."

Fissette traveled to Los Angeles to begin working with Naomi anew in mid-October. He was impressed by her focus from their first practice together on October 9. "Being away from tennis and having a child definitely gives you a different perspective," Fissette said. "I guess everyone wants to have their children be proud of their parents. And if you have the chance to do the greatest things in front of your children, that's the next level [beyond] doing it for yourself. She knows she has the opportunity and the skills to do something exceptional."

· · · · · · ·

Can Naomi Osaka return to the top of tennis? There are, of course, reasons for optimism. Though she has not advanced past even the third round at either the French Open or Wimbledon, Naomi has summoned world-beating tennis on hard courts on many distinct occasions in the past. She will remember how to hit a ball and how to win matches. If she remains fit and motivated, there is space for her at the top. Coming shortly on the heels of Serena's retirement, women's tennis during Naomi's pregnancy and maternity leave was more devoid of household names than it had been in decades, a drought somewhat quenched by nineteen-year-old Coco Gauff winning her first major title at the 2023 U.S. Open. Though only a small percentage of Serena's haul, Naomi's four Grand Slam titles have not yet been surpassed by any player in her generation.

But there is also reason to temper expectations. After her resurgence in Miami, Naomi only won three of the nine matches she played in the remainder of the 2022 season (generously counting the seven-minute-long match against Saville in Tokyo as a win) and finished the year ranked 42nd. Perhaps more worryingly, a longer glance back to her withdrawal from the 2021 French Open shows her overall record since at a middling 18–12. When it came to her ability to win matches, Naomi just hadn't been the same player since admitting to the world how much she had been struggling.

But Naomi will also not be the same person she was when she stepped away. "Honestly, I think this year, this break that I'm taking, has been really important to me, because it sort of made me remember who I am," Naomi said in 2023. "There's a lot of things that happened over the past three years, since the French Open. It just kind of made me a little angry inside. I felt like I was changing a lot, like the energy that I exude. So it's been nice to kind of just center myself and remember all the things that are important to me."

Naomi has been able to use the year off to catch up to her racing mind.

"I'm just trying to take this year to, like, relax," she said. "Since I won my first Slam, everything's been happening really, really fast for me, and I've never really had time to process it as much as I wanted to. Even when I look back on now: I was talking with my mom and she was like, Oh, that was just five years ago. And when I think about it, five years is a very short time, but it feels like such a long time ago in my brain."

Being away from tennis, Naomi said, had shifted the balance of her inner monologue. "I kind of feel like I have two inner voices, and usually I try to listen to the one that's very nice," Naomi explained. "I would describe her as a 'she,' and she's very soft-spoken and positive. But then sometimes when I'm on the tennis court, it's like a different voice that's a little bit more stern. I hear from the gentle one now more . . . I haven't heard the harsh voice in a while."

. . . .

How Naomi will respond to future successes and future struggles is yet unknown. She could double down and keep fighting, or she could walk away. Her legacy as a legend of the sport and surefire Hall of Fame inductee is already secure in the eyes of the public no matter what comes next; seeing herself as worthy can be trickier. Being gentle and generous to herself has not been a strong suit of Naomi's. The most striking scene in the 2021 Netflix documentary *Naomi Osaka* is a scene from a family dinner celebrating Naomi's twenty-second birthday in October 2019 at a hibachi restaurant in Japan. Naomi has already won two major titles, reached No. 1 in the world, and earned tens of millions of dollars. But still, she doesn't seem satisfied. "Did you think, by the time I was twenty-two, I would have done more?" Naomi asks her mother. "Or do you think this is, like, acceptable?"

Tamaki shakes her head. "More than acceptable," she tells her daughter.

Naomi isn't convinced. "This bothers me sometimes," she says. "I don't know. I just think about it sometimes. Sometimes when I think, that's just what I think about. I know there's not supposed to be a timeline on stuff, but I wonder if I'm late."

Even years later, having won two more major titles and earned hundreds of millions dollars more, that lingering sense of dissatisfaction has been difficult for Naomi to shake. Because of how stark the stakes had been at the beginning of her career, when her parents sacrificed security and stability for the perilous pursuit of a tennis dream, Naomi developed a desperate hunger. The drive that resulted from that hunger not only lifted her family out of poverty but made her the highest-earning female athlete ever, to the point where her goals have shifted to becoming the first billionaire female athlete.

But despite her undeniable wealth and the luxury in which she and her family now lived, the starving sensation she developed in her youth remained switched on. No matter what her ranking on a *Forbes* list or the numbers on her account balances told her, Naomi still could not shake the feeling that she needed to be doing more. "Sometimes I wish my parents were rich so I don't have to feel like I need to work for everyone's survival," Naomi tweeted in August 2022. She then allowed that there could be a silver lining. "I don't think I would be where I am if my parents were rich cause I would have no motivation," she added. "So I guess everything happens for a reason." With time, Naomi is also learning to draw comfort from how her parents shaped her childhood around a high-risk, high-reward dream of tennis glory.

. . . .

"I think it comes from being a kid," Naomi said in 2022. "My parents believed in me so much to the point where sometimes I was like, Man, I wish I could believe in myself as much as they did. And now I'm getting to the point where I'm like, Yeah, I see what they saw. So I think that that's a really strong thing. I guess I would say the younger me looking at me now would be very proud and happy."

. . . .

Naomi gave birth to her daughter, Shai, in early July 2023. She was back on the track for her first fitness workout just ten days later.

"Well that was a cool little intermission," Naomi tweeted with a photo showing Shai on her lap in a tennis-themed onesie. "Now back to your regularly scheduled program [tennis ball emoji][peace sign][hearts emoji]."

ACKNOWLEDGMENTS

I had already wanted to write a book about women's tennis for years when, on August 19, 2020, Naomi Osaka's protest stopped play in New York. Naomi, I realized within minutes, would be a fascinating subject. I had known her since she was a wry but shy teenager; watching her find her voice and understand her power had been one of the most remarkable transformations in the decade or so I had covered the tours. The next weeks and months only deepened my conviction: Naomi wore seven names on her masks, won two more major titles, and sparked global conversations about mental health and what it means to be a champion. I wanted to learn as much as I could and share it with the world.

Her story proved irresistible but also elusive: the period in which I began writing this book and traveling the tour with the express focus of shadowing Naomi was one of the most unpredictable chapters in her life. As she evolved and drifted in and out of the sport, trying to put a subject that wouldn't hold still into focus was one of the most challenging undertakings of my career.

But with help, I think we got there. I am deeply grateful to my editor, Jill Schwartzman, and the rest of her team at Dutton (particularly Charlotte Peters, who helped land this plane in the end) for their patience and guidance as we adjusted time and again to adapt this book to our evolving subject and her ever-changing story. And to my agent, Doug Stewart of Sterling Lord Literistic, who steadily nurtured this seed—through some rather biblical weather events—into the rather large tree it became.

I also, of course, could not have told this story without Naomi herself. I have been staggered by her remarkable candor and vulnerability since first meeting her; she's the type of honest that makes you realize how much everyone else is holding back. Her openness over many years—to me, to others, and to herself—is what made telling this story possible. I also thank Naomi and her agent, Stuart Duguid, for being cooperative and engaged during this project specifically, from first idea to final fact-checking. I also am indebted to everyone I interviewed for this book, including the dozens of interviewees who didn't make it into this final version but whose invaluable insights informed my writing.

Finishing this book feels like a bookend to the dozen years I've spent covering tennis, the beautiful and maddening sport that has bounced me around the world. I, too, got hooked into tennis by watching the Williams sisters on TV in the 1990s, and went to New York to watch them at the U.S. Open for many years with my dad. I never could have imagined where those trips would ultimately take me—or that Venus, who first hooked me during the 1997 U.S. Open, would still be playing as I finished this book!

Combining my loves for tennis and writing into a viable career was something I never would have dreamed possible as my dad and I sat in the upper decks of Ashe. But that became possible in 2011 thanks to Karen Crouse, who was amused and bemused during press conferences in Cincinnati by my asking Serena questions about Britney Spears lyrics and generously introduced me to her editors at *The New York Times*, where I wrote about tennis for the next ten years or so. With the brilliant editors Naila-Jean Meyers and Jason Stallman at the helm—who believed in telling the little-known stories I'd pitch (like the one about a Haitian-Japanese-American teenager outside the Top 100)—and consummate colleagues like Karen, Chris Clarey, David Waldstein, John Branch, Harvey Araton, Kurt Streeter, and Greg Bishop at my side, I got to learn from the best every day.

The hours were long—fourteen straight days of staying in a Melbourne pressroom until long after midnight can wear on a guy—but it was never a burden because I found my tribe. Friends in the trenches like Courtney Nguyen, Reem Abulleil, Tumaini Carayol, René Denfeld, Carole Bouchard, Ricky Dimon, David Avakian, Nick McCarvel, Matt Trollope, and Robert "Jimmie" Prange made the work fun, and their tireless day-in, day-out coverage also built the reporting foundation of this book (and pretty much everything else that's ever been written about modern tennis stars like Naomi). I also owe a special shout-out for a book on this subject to Aki Uchida, the grande dame of Japanese tennis reporting, whose generosity in interpreting Japan both culturally and linguistically has been revelatory. I also want to thank David Shaftel and Caitlin Thompson of *Racquet*, who have given so many of my biggest and strangest ideas a home; Josh Levin of *Slate*, whose brains and bravery have helped me achieve some of my proudest work; and the listeners of my podcast *No Challenges Remaining*, who have so generously supported me with their ears (and their crowdfunding) since 2012.

I also want to thank so many of the people who were already a part of the tennis fabric for welcoming me in, from the U.S. beat writers like Doug Robson, Tom Perrotta, and Matt Cronin to the WTA communications staff who facilitated so many of the interviews quoted in these pages. Becoming friends with so many of the tennis media stars whose coverage I had obsessed over as a fan since my youth—people like Mary Carillo, Pam Shriver, and Jon Wertheim—makes me think everyone should get to meet their heroes.

Traveling the tennis tour made me a tumbleweed in many ways, but being able to stay still to grow this book over the past year has been a blessing. Thank you to my Wednesdays boys for giving me a semblance of a social life during this solitary work; their unceasing brilliance is inspiring and humbling in equal measure. And thank you to my beloved dog, Betty, for being endlessly affectionate and adorable (and completely unfazed by my unknowable sleep schedule).

Lastly, a thank-you to my sister, Maria, and my mom, Margaretta. I tell everyone that I am the worst writer in my family because of those two, and I mean it. Thank you for your love and support here, there, and everywhere.

SOURCE NOTES

INTRODUCTION: LIKE NO ONE EVER WAS

Interview with Naomi Osaka by author.

Press conference with Naomi Osaka at 2016 Australian Open.

Aurélien Delfosse, "L'énigme multiculturelle Naomi Osaka, nouvelle star du tennis." *L'Équipe,* January 26, 2019.

CHAPTER 1: PARADISE

Interviews with Sergey Demekhin, Wim Fissette, Tommy Haas, Yutaka Nakamura, Chanda Rubin, Daria Saville, fan at Indian Wells by author.

Press conferences with Naomi Osaka at 2022 Indian Wells, 2022 Miami, 2022 Madrid, 2021 Cincinnati.

Press conference with Rafael Nadal at 2022 Indian Wells.

Broadcast of Naomi Osaka vs. Veronika Kudermetova. Tennis Channel, March 12, 2022.

Broadcast of Naomi Osaka vs. Daria Kasatkina. Tennis Channel, March 18, 2018.

Broadcast of Serena Williams vs. Kim Clijsters. Eurosport, March 17, 2001.

Kurt Badenhausen, "Naomi Osaka Is the Highest-Paid Female Athlete Ever, Topping Serena Williams." *Forbes,* May 22, 2020.

Gregg Doyel, "Doyel: Naomi Osaka Heckler Shows What Courage Looks Like, and What It Doesn't." *The Indianapolis Star,* March 13, 2022.

Soraya Nadia McDonald, "The One and Only Naomi Osaka." *The Undefeated,* March 8, 2019.

Serena Williams and Daniel Paisner, *On the Line.* Grand Central Publishing, 2009.

Fearless with Jason Whitlock, March 15, 2022.

Late Night with Seth Meyers, March 16, 2022.

Alyson Watson and Naomi Osaka, "Elevate 2022 Opening Keynote." *Modern Health,* September 7, 2022.

BNP Paribas Open website, https://bnpparibasopen.com/.

CHAPTER 2: THE MOTHERLAND

Interviews with Pedro Herivaux by author.

Brook Larmer, "Naomi Osaka's Breakthrough Game." *The New York Times Magazine,* August 23, 2018.

Yomiuri Shimbun, "Raising Naomi, as Told by Her Mother / Naomi Osaka's Mother Dreamed of Tennis-Playing Sisters." *The Japan News*, August 10, 2023.

Naomi Yamaguchi, "Osaka Tamaki: Mom of Tennis Star Osaka Naomi on Life and Her Daughter's Determination." *Nippon.com*, July 12, 2022.

Tamaki Osaka, *Through the Tunnel: Just One More Day, My Days of Chasing a Reckless Dream.* Shueisha, 2022.

Venus Williams Instagram post, March 4, 2021.

Tamaki Osaka Instagram story, May 20, 2023.

CHAPTER 3: WHERE DREAMS ARE MADE OF

Interviews with Mari Osaka, Sulaah Bien-Aime, Katrine Steffensen by author.

Press conferences with Naomi Osaka at 2020 U.S. Open, 2022 Miami.

Sean Gregory, "Tennis Star Naomi Osaka Doesn't Like Attention. She's About to Get a Ton of It." *Time,* January 10, 2019.

Brennan Kilbane, "Naomi Osaka Wants to Win More than Anyone Else." *Allure*, July 16, 2019.

Elisa Lipsky-Karasz, "Naomi Osaka on Fighting for No. 1 at the U.S. Open and Why She's Speaking Out." *Wall Street Journal*, August 25, 2020.

Ben Machell, "Tennis Star Naomi Osaka: The One to Beat at Wimbledon." *The Times (UK)*, June 22, 2019.

Tamaki Osaka, *Through the Tunnel: Just One More Day, My Days of Chasing a Reckless Dream.* Shueisha, 2022.

Selfish Love, directed by Leonard Maxime François, 2007.

The Late Show with Stephen Colbert. CBS, December 6, 2022.

"MINK! Naomi Osaka and Ben Proudfoot in Conversation." *Breakwater Studios* (YouTube), December 14, 2022.

TennisRecruiting.net results for Naomi Osaka and Mari Osaka.

CHAPTER 4: CHASING SUNSHINE

Interviews with Naomi Osaka, Bill Adams, Tom Downs, Christophe Jean, Andrei Kozlov, Stefan Kozlov, Rick Macci, Johnnise Renaud, Eliseo Serrano, Harold Solomon, Eddie Sposa, Patrick Tauma, Neha Uberoi by author.

Naomi Osaka at Hana Kuma/Hypebeast event, August 24, 2022.

Dave Hyde, "An Uncommon Dream Came True on South Florida Courts for Naomi Osaka." *South Florida Sun Sentinel,* March 16, 2019.

Elisa Lipsky-Karasz, "Naomi Osaka on Fighting for No. 1 at the U.S. Open and Why She's Speaking Out." *Wall Street Journal*, August 25, 2020.

Christophe Jean Plaintiff vs. Leonard Francois, et al Defendant. Broward County Clerk of Courts, February 7, 2019.

CHAPTER 5: EARLY START

Interviews with Naomi Osaka, Anamika Bhargava, Richard Russell by author.

Akatsuki Uchida, "大坂なおみが18年間を振り返る「お姉ちゃんこそ最大のライバル」." Sportiva, October 5, 2016.

"Naomi Osaka Shares Her First Time Meeting Serena Williams & More." *Teen Vogue* (YouTube), May 5, 2020.

WTA, *2023 WTA Official Rule Book.* 2023.

CHAPTER 6: SISTER ACT 2

Interviews with Naomi Osaka, Mari Osaka, Bill Adams, Darren Cahill, Christophe Jean, Rick Macci, Johnnise Renaud, Harold Solomon, Patrick Tauma by author.

Press conferences with Naomi Osaka at 2014 Stanford, 2016 French Open, 2017 Wimbledon, 2021 Miami.

Press conference with Mari Osaka at 2019 Miami.

Naomi Osaka interview. *Wide World of Sports,* January 26, 2019.

Naomi Osaka interview. Tennis Channel, March 22, 2019.

The Last Dance, episode 2, April 19, 2020.

Naomi Osaka at Hana Kuma/Hypebeast event, August 24, 2022.

Elena Bergeron, "How Putting on a Mask Raised Naomi Osaka's Voice." *The New York Times,* December 16, 2020.

Rob Hodgetts and Christina Macfarlane, "Naomi Osaka on Setbacks, Role Models and Inspiring Others." CNN, July 3, 2019.

Dave Hyde, "An Uncommon Dream Came True on South Florida Courts for Naomi Osaka." *South Florida Sun Sentinel,* March 16, 2019.

Brook Larmer, "Naomi Osaka's Breakthrough Game." *The New York Times Magazine,* August 23, 2018.

Mari Osaka, "To My Sister Naomi Osaka, a Love Letter." *Glamour,* June 29, 2020.

S. L. Price, "Who's Your Daddy?" *Sports Illustrated,* May 31, 1999.

Tim Wigmore, "Why Are Great Athletes More Likely to Be Younger Siblings?" FiveThirtyEight, December 1, 2020.

Tamaki Osaka, *Through the Tunnel: Just One More Day, My Days of Chasing a Reckless Dream.* Shueisha, 2022.

Amanda de Cadenet, "VS x Naomi Osaka." *VS Voices*, December 17, 2021.

"Mari & Naomi 1st Golf Day "初ゴルフの日(打ちっぱなし)'08." *Liberty NY* (YouTube), July 25, 2008.

TennisRecruiting.net results for Naomi Osaka and Mari Osaka.

CHAPTER 7: THE DOTTED LINE

Interviews with Daniel Balog, Belinda Bencic, Ivan Bencic, Darren Cahill, Nori Shimojo by author.

Press conferences with Naomi Osaka at 2022 Miami.

Michael Mewshaw, *Ladies of the Court*. Crown, 1993.

Tamaki Osaka, *Through the Tunnel: Just One More Day, My Days of Chasing a Reckless Dream*. Shueisha, 2022.

CHAPTER 8: MAKING MOVES

Interviews with Daniel Balog, Darren Cahill, Kevin Fischer, Petra Martić, Simon Rea, Samantha Stosur by author.

Press conferences with Naomi Osaka, Andrea Petkovic at 2014 Stanford.

Press conference with Serena Williams at 2016 Australian Open.

Broadcast of Naomi Osaka vs. Andrea Petkovic. Tennis Channel, July 30, 2014.

Brennan Kilbane, "Naomi Osaka Wants to Win More Than Anyone Else." *Allure*, July 16, 2019.

Susana Castelo, et al Plaintiff vs. Tamaki Osaka, et al Defendant. Broward County Clerk of Courts, July 8, 2014.

Tamaki Osaka, *Through the Tunnel: Just One More Day, My Days of Chasing a Reckless Dream*. Shueisha, 2022.

CHAPTER 9: RISING SUN

Interviews with Naomi Osaka, Leonard François, Katrina Adams, Daniel Balog, Florent Dabadie, Mary Joe Fernández, Treat Huey, Jason Jung, Patrick McEnroe, Johnnise Renaud, Ena Shibahara, Harold Solomon, unnamed tennis parent by author.

Ben Rothenberg, "Bogomolov Switches Flags in a Boost for Russia." *The New York Times* (Straight Sets), January 19, 2012.

Ben Rothenberg, "A Best-Ranked Player for One Country Has Decided to Represent Another." *The New York Times,* August 27, 2013.

Ben Rothenberg, "Questioned About Body, Townsend Rises and Inspires." *The New York Times,* May 27, 2014.

James Buddell, "Kei Nishikori: Project 45 No Longer a Secret." ATP Tour, November 7, 2008.

Jenny Cosgrave, "Maria Sharapova: I Won't Trade Russian Citizenship." CNBC, March 23, 2015.

Aurélien Delfosse, "L'énigme multiculturelle Naomi Osaka, nouvelle star du tennis." *L'Équipe,* January 26, 2019.

Miguel Morales, "How Rising Tennis Star Kei Nishikori Made $10 Million This Year." *Forbes,* August 26, 2013.

Nick Pachelli, "Defying Tennis Tradition, a Product of Public Courts Is on the Rise." *The New York Times,* March 5, 2017.

Tom Perrotta, "Why the USTA Benched America's Best Junior." *The Wall Street Journal,* September 7, 2012.

———, "Tennis Legends 'Livid' About USTA Decision." *The Wall Street Journal,* September 7, 2012.

———, "Naomi Osaka: The Tennis Star Who Was Overlooked by Everyone." *The Wall Street Journal,* September 12, 2018.

Mike Cation and Noah Rubin, "Behind the Racquet with Ernesto Escobedo: Why He's Now Playing for Mexico." *Behind the Racquet,* February 1, 2023.

Draw of 2008 USTA National Clay Court Championships.

CHAPTER 10: RISING STAR

Interviews with Naomi Osaka, Caroline Garcia, Ons Jabeur by author.

Press conferences with Naomi Osaka at 2015 Singapore, 2021 Australian Open.

Reem Abulleil, "Reem's Diary: New Star Is Born at WTA Rising Stars in Osaka." Sport360, October 25, 2015.

"Vote for Naomi Osaka." *ioaproductions* (YouTube), September 28, 2014.

Twitter post of Andy Murray, May 26, 2011.

CHAPTER 11: TRANSLATING

Interviews with Naomi Osaka, Florent Dabadie, Wim Fissette, Elina Svitolina, Aki Uchida by author.

Press conferences with Naomi Osaka at 2016 Australian Open, 2016 French Open, 2016 U.S. Open.

Ben Rothenberg, "Another Win for a Player Getting in Touch with Her Japanese Roots." *The New York Times,* January 21, 2016.

Aurélien Delfosse, "L'énigme multiculturelle Naomi Osaka, nouvelle star du tennis." *L'Équipe,* January 26, 2019.

Rakuten Research, Inc., "Rakuten Research Announces Results of Survey on Attitudes Towards English." August 26, 2016.

Ben Rothenberg and Courtney Nguyen, "Episode 141d: Australian Open Day 4: Hooroo, Hewitt! Yokoso, Osaka!" *No Challenges Remaining,* January 21, 2016.

Courtney Nguyen, "New Year, New Me: Naomi Osaka Bringing Positive Vibes into 2019." *WTA Insider Podcast,* December 30, 2018.

Tamaki Osaka, *Through the Tunnel: Just One More Day, My Days of Chasing a Reckless Dream*. Shueisha, 2022.

CHAPTER 12: CLOSE

Interviews with Daniel Balog, Christine Keys by author.
Press conferences with Naomi Osaka, CoCo Vandeweghe, Madison Keys at 2016 U.S. Open.
Broadcast of Naomi Osaka vs. CoCo Vandeweghe. USTA, August 29, 2016.
Broadcast of Naomi Osaka vs. Madison Keys. USTA, September 2, 2016.
News Watch 9. NHK, September 27, 2016.
Reem Abulleil, "Rising Teens Naomi Osaka and Ana Konjuh Discuss Challenges of Life on Tour." Sport360, March 7, 2017.
Harvey Araton, "As Williamses Age, Here Comes Youth." *The New York Times,* August 31, 2011.
Marc Berman, "Coco Vandeweghe Blasts Ump over Disputed Bathroom Break." *New York Post,* August 29, 2016.
Christopher Clarey, "Long Anticipated, Madison Keys's Big Moment Is Here." *The New York Times,* January 28, 2015.
Craig DeVrieze, "Former Q-C Girl Has Potential to Win Grand Slams." *Quad-City Times,* June 13, 2009.
Noah Rubin, "Madison Keys." *Behind the Racquet*, February 18, 2019.

CHAPTER 13: THE SOCIAL GAME

Interviews with Taro Daniel, Ana Konjuh by author.
Press conferences with Naomi Osaka at 2017 U.S. Open, 2019 Australian Open, 2020 Brisbane, 2022 Miami.
Press conference with Madison Keys at 2017 Indian Wells.
Reem Abulleil, "Rising Teens Naomi Osaka and Ana Konjuh Discuss Challenges of Life on Tour." Sport360, March 7, 2017.
Levi Baker and Debra Oswald, "Shyness and Online Social Networking Services." *Journal of Social and Personal Relationships,* November 2010.
Courtney Nguyen, "Daily Dispatch: Naomi Osaka's Worst Day Ever." *WTA Insider Podcast,* February 19, 2017.
Instagram Live with Naomi Osaka and Iga Świątek.
Twitter accounts of Naomi Osaka, Taro Daniel, Ana Konjuh, Madison Keys.

CHAPTER 14: INTO VENUS'S ORBIT

Interview with David Taylor by author.
Press conferences with Naomi Osaka at 2017 Wimbledon, 2017 U.S. Open.
Press conferences with Venus Williams at 2017 Wimbledon.

Broadcast of Naomi Osaka vs. Karolína Plíšková. WTA, August 10, 2017.

Broadcast of Naomi Osaka vs. Angelique Kerber. USTA, August 29, 2017.

René Denfeld, "WTA Stuttgart—Getting to Know: Naomi Osaka." *Inside Out* magazine, April 25, 2017.

CHAPTER 15: FOOTSTEPS

Interviews with Sascha Bajin, Sven Groeneveld, Daria Kasatkina by author.

Press conferences with Naomi Osaka at 2018 Australian Open, 2018 Indian Wells, 2018 Miami, 2022 Miami.

Naomi Osaka interview. Tennis Channel, May 28, 2018.

Naomi Osaka at Hana Kuma/Hypebeast event. August 24, 2022.

Broadcast of Naomi Osaka vs. Sachia Vickery. Tennis Channel, March 12, 2018.

Broadcast of Naomi Osaka vs. Daria Kasatkina. Tennis Channel, March 18, 2018.

Sascha Bajin, *Strengthen Your Mind: 50 Habits for Mental Change*. Asuka Shinsha, 2019.

Jonathan Newman and James Rogers, "Rogers Cup Wrap, Sascha Bajin Chat." *The Body Serve Podcast,* August 12, 2018.

Craig Shapiro, "Big Sascha Talks with Craig Shapiro." *The Craig Shapiro Tennis Podcast,* July 22, 2022.

Leslie Koroma Sr., "A Conversation with Abdul Sillah, a Trainer of World Champions." *African Sports Monthly* (YouTube), September 13, 2021.

Vera Papisova. "Naomi Osaka on Her US Open Victory and Serena Williams." *Teen Vogue* (YouTube), September 11, 2018.

CHAPTER 16: WELCOME TO SERENA

Press conference with Naomi Osaka at 2018 Miami.

Broadcast of Naomi Osaka vs. Serena Williams. WTA, March 21, 2018.

"Chapter 1, Fear," May 2, 2018; "Chapter 4, Change," May 23, 2018; "Chapter 5, Resolve," May 30, 2018. *Being Serena*. HBO, 2018.

Twitter account of Ivanka Trump.

CHAPTER 17: CHARLESTON

Press conference with Naomi Osaka at 2018 Charleston.

Broadcast of Naomi Osaka vs. Laura Siegemund. WTA, April 4, 2018.

Broadcast of Naomi Osaka vs. Julia Görges, WTA, April 5, 2018.

Kevin Nguyen, "Naomi Osaka Is the Coolest Thing in Tennis." *GQ,* May 24, 2018.

Amanda de Cadenet, "VS x Naomi Osaka." *VS Voices*, December 17, 2021.

Allyson Felix and Wes Felix, "Naomi Osaka: Motherhood, Grand Slams, and Nike (Feat: Stu Duguid)." *Mountaintop Conversations by Saysh*, August 1, 2023.

CHAPTER 18: COLLISION COURSE

Press conferences with Naomi Osaka, Serena Williams at 2018 U.S. Open.

Press conference with Madison Keys at 2018 Wuhan.

Broadcast of Naomi Osaka vs. Aryna Sabalenka. ESPN, September 3, 2018.

Broadcast of Naomi Osaka vs. Madison Keys. ESPN, September 6, 2018.

Brook Larmer, "Naomi Osaka's Breakthrough Game." *The New York Times Magazine,* August 23, 2018.

Sascha Bajin, *Strengthen Your Mind: 50 Habits for Mental Change.* Asuka Shinsha, 2019.

Craig Shapiro, "Big Sascha Talks with Craig Shapiro." *The Craig Shapiro Tennis Podcast,* July 22, 2022.

"US Open Interview: Naomi Osaka." *US Open* (YouTube), September 7, 2018.

Twitter account of Naomi Osaka.

CHAPTER 19: BOILING POINT

Champion's roundtable for Naomi Osaka at 2018 U.S. Open.

Press conference with Serena Williams at 2018 U.S. Open.

Drew Nantais, "2018 U.S. Open Odds: Serena, Djokovic Open as Betting Favorites." *The Sporting News,* August 27, 2018.

Nerisha Penrose, "Virgil Abloh Creates Ballerina-Inspired Collection for Serena Williams' U.S. Open Return." *Elle,* August 13, 2018.

J.S., "An Overzealous Chair Umpire Overshadows Naomi Osaka's Impressive Victory." *The Economist*, September 9, 2018.

Steff Yotka, "Serena Williams Will Return to the U.S. Open in Virgil Abloh x Nike." *Vogue,* August 13, 2018.

Broadcast of Serena Williams vs. Jennifer Capriati. USA Network, September 7, 2004.

Broadcast of Serena Williams vs. Kim Clijsters. CBS, September 12, 2009.

Broadcast of Serena Williams vs. Samantha Stosur. CBS, September 11, 2011.

Broadcast of Naomi Osaka vs. Serena Williams. ESPN, September 8, 2018.

Dave Meyers (director), "Queen of Queens" commercial. *Beats by Dre,* August 2018.

Grand Slam Board, *Official 2018 Grand Slam Rule Book,* 2018.

CHAPTER 20: FROM ASHE TO WILDFIRE

Champion's roundtable for Naomi Osaka at 2018 U.S. Open.

Press conferences with Naomi Osaka at 2018 U.S. Open, 2018 Beijing.

Press conference with Serena Williams at 2018 U.S. Open.

Naomi Osaka interview. ESPN, September 8, 2018.

Today. NBC, September 10, 2018.

The View. ABC, September 10, 2018.

America's Newsroom. Fox News, September 10, 2018.

Saturday Night Live. NBC, September 29, 2018.

The Project. Channel 10, September 17, 2018.

MSNBC Reports (with Stephanie Ruhle). MSNBC, September 10, 2018.

Don Van Natta Jr., "Backstory: Serena vs. the Umpire." ESPN, August 19, 2019.

Reem Abulleil, "Naomi Osaka on Her 'Bittersweet' US Open Win, the Difficulty of Opening Up, and Her Belief in Future Grand Slam Success." Sport360, October 1, 2018.

———, "Naomi Osaka's Coach Sascha Bajin Discusses Her 'Sad' Reaction to US Open Win, Her Mental Strength and WTA Finals Campaign." Sport360, October 25, 2018.

Breanna Edwards, "So . . . About Mark Knight's Racist Serena Williams Cartoon." *Essence,* September 10, 2018.

Mark Anthony Green, "Love All, with Naomi Osaka and Cordae." *GQ,* February 10, 2021.

Sean Gregory, "Tennis Star Naomi Osaka Doesn't Like Attention. She's About to Get a Ton of It." *Time,* January 10, 2019.

Sally Jenkins, "At U.S. Open, Power of Serena Williams and Naomi Osaka Is Overshadowed by an Umpire's Power Play." *The Washington Post*, September 8, 2018.

Soraya Nadia McDonald, "The One and Only Naomi Osaka." *The Undefeated,* March 8, 2019.

Louisa Thomas, "Full Swing." *Vogue,* March 21, 2019.

Serena Williams, "Serena Williams Poses Unretouched for Harper's BAZAAR." *Harper's Bazaar,* July 9, 2019.

Naomi Osaka interview. Tennis Channel, March 22, 2019.

Sascha Bajin, *Strengthen Your Mind: 50 Habits for Mental Change.* Asuka Shinsha, 2019.

Billie Jean King, Mardy Fish, Naomi Osaka, Nick Kyrgios, and Stuart Duguid, "The Players' Lounge." *Racquet,* August 2021.

Josh Levin, Vann Newkirk, and Louisa Thomas, "The Let's Talk About Serena Edition." *Hang Up and Listen Podcast,* September 10, 2018.

Ira Madison III, Kara Brown, and Louis Virtel, "A Binderella Story." *Keep It,* September 11, 2018.

Courtney Nguyen, "Champions Corner: Naomi Osaka Wins the US Open." *WTA Insider,* September 10, 2018.

Taylor Swift, "The Man" (official video). Directed by Taylor Swift, February 27, 2020.

CHAPTER 21: THE TALK OF TOKYO

Interviews of Florent Dabadie and Baye McNeil by author.

Press conferences with Naomi Osaka by Nissin, September 13, 2018, and 2019 Australian Open.

Press conferences with Petra Kvitová and Madison Keys, 2018 Wuhan.

Akihide Anzai and Daisuke Uozumi, "Naomi Osaka Serves Japanese Brands a Golden Olympic Opportunity." *Financial Times* (*Nikkei Asian Review*), September 25, 2018.

Mike Dickson, "Naomi Osaka Is Set to Become One of Sport's Highest Earners After Winning the Women's US Open Aged Just 20." *Daily Mail,* September 9, 2018.

Sean Gregory, "Tennis Star Naomi Osaka Doesn't Like Attention. She's About to Get a Ton of It." *Time,* January 10, 2019.

Motoko Rich, "In U.S. Open Victory, Naomi Osaka Pushes Japan to Redefine Japanese." *The New York Times*, September 9, 2018.

Stephen Wade and Mari Yamaguchi, "Osaka Charms Japan with Her Manners—and Broken Japanese." Associated Press, September 10, 2018.

"Japanese React to Naomi Osaka Winning US Open." *Asian Boss* (YouTube), September 15, 2019.

"Should Naomi Osaka Be a Japanese or US Citizen? [Street Interview]." *Asian Boss* (YouTube), February 20, 2019.

"Are Half Japanese HAFU Athletes Like Naomi Osaka Changing Japan? | Biculturalism ft. Joe Oliver." Max D. Capo (YouTube), December 12, 2018.

Allyson Felix and Wes Felix, "Naomi Osaka: Motherhood, Grand Slams, and Nike (Feat: Stu Duguid)." *Mountaintop Conversations by Saysh*, August 1, 2023.

Quarterly Publication of Individuals, Who Have Chosen to Expatriate. Internal Revenue Service, 2015–2023.

Twitter account of Naomi Osaka.

CHAPTER 22: DOWN UNDER TO THE TOP

Champion's roundtable for Naomi Osaka at 2019 Australian Open.

Press conferences with Naomi Osaka at 2019 Brisbane, 2019 Australian Open.

Press conference with Serena Williams at 2018 U.S. Open.

Broadcast of Naomi Osaka vs. Lesia Tsurenko. WTA, January 4, 2019.

Broadcast of Naomi Osaka vs. Karolína Plíšková. Tennis Australia, January 23, 2019.

Broadcast of Naomi Osaka vs. Petra Kvitová. Tennis Australia, January 25, 2019.

Broadcast of Naomi Osaka vs. Petra Kvitová. ESPN, January 25, 2019

Naomi Osaka interview. *Wide World of Sports,* January 26, 2019.

Sascha Bajin, *Strengthen Your Mind: 50 Habits for Mental Change.* Asuka Shinsha, 2019.

Courtney Nguyen, "New Year, New Me: Naomi Osaka Bringing Positive Vibes into 2019." *WTA Insider Podcast,* December 30, 2018.

Courtney Nguyen, "Champions Corner: Naomi Osaka Ascends to No.1 After Australian Open Triumph." *WTA Insider Podcast,* January 27, 2019.

Craig Shapiro, "Big Sascha Talks with Craig Shapiro." *The Craig Shapiro Tennis Podcast,* July 22, 2022.

CHAPTER 23: HEAVY IS THE HEAD

Interviews with Christophe Jean, Cyril Saulnier, Eddie Sposa by author.

Press conferences with Naomi Osaka at 2019 Dubai, 2019 Indian Wells, 2019 Cincinnati.

"Tennis Channel Live." Tennis Channel, February 11, 2019.

Mark Anthony Green, "Love All, with Naomi Osaka and Cordae." *GQ,* February 10, 2021.

Dave Hyde, "An Uncommon Dream Came True on South Florida Courts for Naomi Osaka." *South Florida Sun Sentinel,* March 16, 2019.

Courtney Nguyen, "Naomi Osaka Finds Peace and Happiness After Coaching Split." *WTA Insider,* February 17, 2019.

Christophe Jean Plaintiff vs. Leonard Francois, et al Defendant. Broward County Clerk of Courts, February 7, 2019.

Tamaki Osaka, *Through the Tunnel: Just One More Day, My Days of Chasing a Reckless Dream.* Shueisha, 2022.

Allyson Felix and Wes Felix, "Naomi Osaka: Motherhood, Grand Slams, and Nike (Feat: Stu Duguid)." *Mountaintop Conversations by Saysh,* August 1, 2023.

"Naomi Osaka Shares Her First Time Meeting Serena Williams & More." *Teen Vogue* (YouTube), May 5, 2020.

"Mari Osaka—Porto Open 2019." *Bola Amarela* (YouTube), July 30, 2019.

WTA, *2023 WTA Official Rule Book.* 2023.

Twitter accounts of Naomi Osaka, Sascha Bajin.

CHAPTER 24: MARI'S SHOT

Interviews with Mari Osaka, James Blake, Krasimir by author.

Press conferences with Naomi Osaka, Mari Osaka, Novak Djoković at 2019 Miami.

Broadcast of Mari Osaka vs. Whitney Osuigwe. WTA, March 21, 2019.

David Gertler, "Mari Osaka Wild Card an Embarrassment." *Last Word on Sports,* March 17, 2019.

CHAPTER 25: SHOOTING STARS

Interview with Yulia Putintseva by author.

Press conferences with Naomi Osaka at 2019 Stuttgart, 2019 French Open, 2019 Birmingham, 2019 Wimbledon, 2019 Toronto, 2019 Cincinnati, 2019 U.S. Open.

Press conference with Serena Williams at 2019 Toronto.

Press conferences with Coco Gauff at 2019 U.S. Open, 2022 Berlin.

Naomi Osaka. Directed by Garrett Bradley. Netflix, July 16, 2021.

Broadcast of Naomi Osaka vs. Serena Williams. WTA, August 9, 2019.

Broadcast of Naomi Osaka vs. Aliaksandra Sasnovich. WTA, August 14, 2019.

Broadcast of Naomi Osaka vs. Coco Gauff. ESPN, August 31, 2019.

Interview of Kobe Bryant. Tennis Channel, August 30, 2019.

Tennis Channel at U.S. Open. Tennis Channel, August 31, 2019.

Simon Briggs, "Exclusive Naomi Osaka Interview: Quirky, Quizzical and Brilliant—Meet a Different Kind of Tennis Superstar." *The Sunday Telegraph,* June 23, 2019.

Susan Cheng, "Naomi Osaka Is Ready to Go Supernova." *Highsnobiety,* August 26, 2020.

Helene Elliott, "Column: Kobe Bryant Has Nothing but Adulation for Coco Gauff and Naomi Osaka." *Los Angeles Times,* August 29, 2019.

Josh Smith, "GLAMOUR Women of the Year Sports Gamechanger: Naomi Osaka on Activism, Racism and Speaking Out—'I Want to Be a Voice for Change.'" *Glamour UK,* March 8, 2021.

Steff Yotka, "US Open Champion Naomi Osaka Returns to Queens in a Custom Sacai x Nike Outfit." *Vogue,* August 23, 2019.

"Why Naomi Osaka Is 'Nervous' to Talk to Serena Williams." *CBS This Morning* (YouTube), August 23, 2019.

"Naomi Osaka | 2019 Birmingham Pre-Tournament Interview." WTA (YouTube*),* June 17, 2019.

"Kobe Bryant | US Open Now Interview." US Open Tennis Championships (YouTube), August 30, 2019.

Twitter account of Naomi Osaka.

CHAPTER 26: STAYING IN, SPEAKING OUT

The Ingraham Report. Fox News, February 15, 2018.

Caitlin Brody, "An Easy Risotto Recipe Care of Tennis Champ Naomi Osaka." *Glamour,* May 11, 2020.

Susan Cheng, "Naomi Osaka Is Ready to Go Supernova." *Highsnobiety,* August 26, 2020.

Evan Hill, Ainara Tiefenthäler, Christiaan Triebert, Drew Jordan, Haley Willis, and Robin Stein, "How George Floyd Was Killed in Police Custody." *The New York Times,* May 31, 2020.

Elisa Lipsky-Karasz, "Naomi Osaka on Fighting for No. 1 at the U.S. Open and Why She's Speaking Out." *Wall Street Journal,* August 25, 2020.

Naomi Osaka, "I Never Would've Imagined Writing This Two Years Ago." *Esquire,* July 1, 2020.

Instagram Live of Venus Williams with Naomi Osaka.

Instagram Live of Naomi Osaka with Iga Świątek.

TikTok account of Naomi Osaka.

Twitter account of Naomi Osaka.

CHAPTER 27: STOP AND START

Interviews with Roberto Bautista Agut, Wim Fissette, Elise Mertens, Yutaka Nakamura, Karue Sell by author.

Press conference with Naomi Osaka at 2019 Cincinnati.

Press conference with Milos Raonic at 2019 Cincinnati.

Press conference with Victoria Azarenka at 2019 Cincinnati.

Interview of Chris Paul. TNT, August 24, 2020.

Interview of Naomi Osaka. ESPN, August 28, 2020.

David Avakian, "Osaka Door de Ogen van Fissette." *Tennis* magazine (Netherlands), December 2020.

Twitter account of Naomi Osaka.

CHAPTER 28: THE NAMES ON HER LIPS

Interviews with Wim Fissette, Baye McNeil, Chanda Rubin, Rennae Stubbs by author.

Press conferences with Naomi Osaka at 2020 U.S. Open.

Press conference with Victoria Azarenka at 2020 U.S. Open.

Broadcast of Naomi Osaka vs. Misaki Doi. USTA, August 31, 2020.

Interview of Naomi Osaka. ESPN, September 8, 2020.

Broadcast of Naomi Osaka vs. Shelby Rogers. ESPN, September 8, 2020.

Broadcast of Naomi Osaka vs. Jennifer Brady. ESPN, September 10, 2020.

Broadcast of Naomi Osaka vs. Victoria Azarenka. USTA, September 12, 2020.

Jerry Bembry, Bill Connelly, and D'Arcy Maine, "How Naomi Osaka Carved Her Own Path onto World's Biggest Stage." ESPN, July 22, 2021.

Allyson Felix and Wes Felix, "Naomi Osaka: Motherhood, Grand Slams, and Nike (Feat: Stu Duguid)." *Mountaintop Conversations by Saysh*, August 1, 2023.

"Naomi Osaka and Billie Jean King in Conversation." Mastercard (YouTube), October 9, 2020.

Twitter account of Naomi Osaka.

CHAPTER 29: ANCESTORS

Press conferences with Naomi Osaka at 2019 Australian Open, 2022 San Jose.

Aurélien Delfosse, "L'énigme multiculturelle Naomi Osaka, nouvelle star du tennis." *L'Équipe,* January 26, 2019.

Allyson Felix and Wes Felix, "Naomi Osaka: Motherhood, Grand Slams, and Nike (Feat: Stu Duguid)." *Mountaintop Conversations by Saysh*, August 1, 2023.

Interview of Naomi Osaka. ESPN, August 28, 2020.

Twitter accounts of Naomi Osaka, Michelle Obama, Shizzy Shane.

CHAPTER 30: IMPERIAL PHASE

Interviews with Wim Fissette, Karue Sell by author.

Press conferences with Naomi Osaka at 2021 Australian Open.

Press conferences with Serena Williams at 2021 Australian Open.

Broadcast of Naomi Osaka vs. Garbiñe Muguruza. Tennis Australia, February 13, 2021.

Broadcast of Naomi Osaka vs. Jennifer Brady. Tennis Australia, February 20, 2021.

David Avakian, "Osaka Door de Ogen van Fissette." *Tennis* magazine (Netherlands), December 2020.

Kurt Badenhausen, "Naomi Osaka Is the Highest-Paid Female Athlete Ever, Topping Serena Williams." *Forbes,* May 22, 2020.

Tom Ewing, "Imperial." *Pitchfork,* May 28, 2010.

Dan Quarrell, "Australian Open 2021—'Naomi Osaka Can Win at Least 10 Grand Slams'— Mats Wilander." Eurosport, February 20, 2021.

Jeff Sackmann, "Expected Points, Feb. 18: Naomi Osaka Makes the Hardest Things Look Easy." *Tennis Abstract,* February 18, 2021.

———, "How Much Does Naomi Osaka Raise Her Game?" *Tennis Abstract,* February 21, 2021.

Instagram account of Naomi Osaka.

CHAPTER 31: A JOURNEY WHICH SHE DIDN'T ENJOY ULTIMATELY

Interviews with Mari Osaka, Darren Cahill by author.

Press conferences with Naomi Osaka at 2021 Australian Open, 2021 Miami.

Mari Osaka at Racquet House at Rockefeller Center. August 2022.

Liam Hess, "Naomi Osaka's Met Gala Look Is a Powerful Celebration of Her Heritage." *Vogue,* September 13, 2021.

Honor Titus, "Honor Titus vs. Mari Osaka." *Racquet,* summer 2021.

Tamaki Osaka, *Through the Tunnel: Just One More Day, My Days of Chasing a Reckless Dream.* Shueisha, 2022.

Jonathan Newman and James Rogers, "A Journey Which I Didn't Enjoy Ultimately." *The Body Serve Podcast,* March 16, 2018.

Instagram account of Mari Osaka.

CHAPTER 32: SLIDING

Interviews with Wim Fissette, Steve Malik, Jessica Pegula by author.

Press conferences with Naomi Osaka at 2019 Rome, 2021 Australian Open, 2021 Miami, 2021 Madrid, 2021 Rome, 2022 Miami.

Broadcast of Naomi Osaka vs. Jessica Pegula. WTA, May 12, 2021.

Kurt Badenhausen, "Naomi Osaka's Historic Year Includes Record $55 Million Payday." Sportico, May 25, 2021.

Sheila Marikar, "How Naomi Osaka Became Everyone's Favorite Spokesmodel." *The New York Times,* May 19, 2021.

"Why Panasonic Appointed Naomi Osaka." *Panasonic* (Facebook), July 18, 2021.

Twitter account of Naomi Osaka.

Instagram account of Naomi Osaka.

CHAPTER 33: READ ALL ABOUT IT

Interviews with Wim Fissette, Pam Shriver by author.

Press conferences with Ash Barty, Petra Kvitová, Daniil Medvedev, Gilles Moretton, Rafael Nadal, Iga Świątek at 2021 French Open.

Broadcast of Naomi Osaka vs. Patricia Maria Tig. Tennis Channel, May 30, 2021.

Michael Beattie, "The Women Who Changed the Sport of Tennis Forever." ITF, September 23, 2020.

Oliver Brown, "Naomi Osaka's Press Omerta at French Open Is Diva Behaviour at Its Worst." *The Daily Telegraph,* May 27, 2021.

Susan Cheng, "Naomi Osaka Is Ready to Go Supernova." *Highsnobiety,* August 26, 2020.

Helene Elliott, "The 'Original Nine' of Women's Tennis Made History—and a Dollar Each—50 Years Ago." *Los Angeles Times,* September 24, 2020.

———, "Column: Why Naomi Osaka's News Conference Boycott Is a Major Tennis Talking Point." *Los Angeles Times,* May 29, 2021.

Piers Morgan, "Narcissistic Naomi's Cynical Exploitation of Mental Health to Silence the Media Is Right from the Meghan and Harry Playbook of Wanting Their Press Cake and Eating It." *Daily Mail,* May 31, 2021.

Quentin Moynet, "Gilles Moretton: Naomi Osaka « fait du mal au tennis » avec son boycott des conférences de presse." *L'Équipe,* May 27, 2021.

Will Swanton, "Princess Naomi's Comical Media Ban." *The Australian,* May 30, 2021.

Jayne Hrdlicka, Gilles Moretton, Ian Hewitt, and Mike McNulty, "STATEMENT FROM GRAND SLAM TOURNAMENTS REGARDING NAOMI OSAKA." Roland Garros, May 30, 2021.

Arthur M. Schlesinger Sr., *The Rise of the City.* The Macmillan Company, 1933.

Grand Slam Board, *Official 2021 Grand Slam Rule Book.* 2021.

Billie Jean King, Mardy Fish, Naomi Osaka, Nick Kyrgios, and Stuart Duguid, "The Players' Lounge." *Racquet,* August 2021.

Allyson Felix and Wes Felix, "Naomi Osaka: Motherhood, Grand Slams, and Nike (Feat: Stu Duguid)." *Mountaintop Conversations by Saysh,* August 1, 2023.

Luvvie Ajayi Jones, "Naomi Osaka on Gratitude and Greatness." *Can't Wait to Hear from You.* Hana Kuma, June 29, 2023.

Email sent by Naomi Osaka to FFT.

Twitter accounts of Naomi Osaka, Piers Morgan, Hannah Wilks.

Reddit post of Mari Osaka.

Instagram account of Venus Williams.

CHAPTER 34: TORCHBEARER

Interviews with Daria Abramowicz, Wim Fissette, Megumi Nishikura, Sloane Stephens, Markéta Vondroušová by author.

Press conferences with Naomi Osaka at 2021 Cincinnati, 2022 Indian Wells.

Kevin B. Blackistone, "Naomi Osaka, Simone Biles and the Enduring Sports Message of 2021." *The Washington Post,* December 26, 2021.

Naomi Osaka, "It's O.K. Not to Be O.K." *Time,* July 8, 2021.

Robin D. Stone, "Protect Your Peace." *Psychology Today,* July 15, 2021.

Tamaki Osaka, *Through the Tunnel: Just One More Day, My Days of Chasing a Reckless Dream.* Shueisha, 2022.

"Social Media Abuse of Tennis Stars." *Pickswise,* February 2022.

Amanda de Cadenet, "VS x Naomi Osaka." *VS Voices*, December 17, 2021.
Michael Che, *Shame the Devil*. Netflix, November 16, 2021.
"Fault Lines," *Law & Order*. NBC, March 17, 2021.
Outside the Lines. ESPN, June 2021.
The 2021 ESPY Awards. ESPN, July 10, 2021.
Twitter accounts of Megyn Kelly, Clay Travis.
Instagram account of Naomi Osaka.

CHAPTER 35: THE BRAKES

Interview with Mardy Fish by author.
Press conferences with Naomi Osaka at 2021 Cincinnati, 2021 U.S. Open.
Billie Jean King, Mardy Fish, Naomi Osaka, Nick Kyrgios, and Stuart Duguid, "The Players' Lounge." *Racquet,* August 2021.
Untold: Breaking Point. Directed by Chapman Way, Maclain Way. Netflix, September 7, 2021.

CHAPTER 36: GAME OVER?

Interviews with Wim Fissette by author.
Press conferences with Naomi Osaka at 2022 Melbourne, 2022 Australian Open, 2022 Miami, 2022 Madrid, 2022 French Open, 2022 San Jose, 2022 U.S. Open, 2022 Tokyo.
Press conference with Amélie Mauresmo at 2022 French Open.
Press conference with Serena Williams at 2022 U.S. Open.
Broadcast of Naomi Osaka vs. Iga Świątek. WTA, April 2, 2022.
Broadcast of Naomi Osaka vs. Daria Saville. WTA, September 20, 2022.
Good Morning America. ABC, December 6, 2022.
Jonathan Liew, "Quietly Quitting: Osaka's Unapologetic Hiatus Is a Small Act of Rebellion." *The Guardian,* January 10, 2023.
"Naomi Osaka Brand Book." Red Antler, 2020.
Craig Shapiro, "Superstar Tennis Agent Stuart Duguid." *The Craig Shapiro Tennis Podcast,* June 21, 2022.
Twitter account of Naomi Osaka.

EPILOGUE: RESET

Interviews with Wim Fissette by author.
Press conferences with Aryna Sabalenka at 2023 French Open.
Naomi Osaka at Hana Kuma/Hypebeast event. August 24, 2022.
Shuzo Matsuoka interviews Naomi Osaka. *Hōdō Station*. TV Asahi, April 2023.
Emily Giambalvo, "With 'Obvious' Motivation, Simone Biles Sets Sights on a Third Olympics." *The Washington Post*, August 6, 2023.

Serena Williams and Rob Haskell, "Serena Williams Says Farewell to Tennis On Her Own Terms—And In Her Own Words." *Vogue*, August 9, 2022.

Naomi Osaka (2021). Directed by Garrett Bradley. Netflix, July 16, 2021.

Allyson Felix and Wes Felix, "Naomi Osaka: Motherhood, Grand Slams, and Nike (Feat: Stu Duguid)." *Mountaintop Conversations by Saysh*, August 1, 2023.

Luvvie Ajayi Jones, "Naomi Osaka on Gratitude and Greatness." *Can't Wait to Hear from You*. Hana Kuma, June 29, 2023.

Instagram account of Amanda Anisimova.

Twitter account of Naomi Osaka.

INDEX

BEN ROTHENBERG is a sportswriter from Washington, D.C. He has covered Naomi Osaka around the world since she emerged onto the WTA Tour in 2014, both in print for *The New York Times* and on his podcast, *No Challenges Remaining*. His work has focused on the intersections of social and cultural issues in tennis. He is a senior editor for *Racquet* magazine and has appeared frequently as a tennis expert on international networks such as CNN, the BBC, and the Australian Broadcasting Corporation. With an eye for finding stories and dogged determination as a reporter, Rothenberg has become by many metrics the world's leading tennis journalist, including on Twitter, where he has more than 130,000 followers.